The Distant Magnet

Italian family seeking luggage, Ellis Island 1905. Photograph by Lewis Hine, George Eastman House Collection.

PHILIP TAYLOR

The Distant Magnet

EUROPEAN EMIGRATION TO THE U.S.A.

A TORCHBOOK LIBRARY EDITION

Harper & Row, Publishers

New York, Evanston, San Francisco, London

Contents

Illustrations

MAPS

DIAGRAMS

CARTOONS

To the memory of

GABRIEL NAHMANI
1915–1968

Son of Emigrants
Citizen of Israel
Scientist
Friend

Preface

To say that this is the story of thirty-five million Europeans during the years 1830 to 1930 is to admit that the historian's task is almost impossible. The century is already remote: my own memory extends no further than the late 1920s, and impressions treasured within my family go back no more than another thirty years. An urban Englishman can scarcely hope, in any intimate sense, to understand peasant Europe; nor can a low-church Anglican grasp Catholic or Jewish tradition with complete success. Most emigrants unfortunately wrote nothing that can be traced.

I made my choice early. Since I could do little fundamental research on the entire subject, and since I did not wish to specialize in one people or one place, I would attempt to sum up other men's factual research, supplementing this with investigations of my own, and imposing upon the whole what had become, after many years of thought and study, my own judgements. In addition to many monographs, therefore, I read great numbers of books by travellers, whose eyes could see much that has long been hidden from the late twentieth-century view. Similarly, I have used the work of officials, social workers, early sociologists, investigating problems in Europe and America. A few discoveries of my own, for example steamship plans, gave additional solidity to eye-witness accounts.

All the time, however, I was aware of how much more could be done, of how, if I waited, another dissertation, another autobiography, another collection of letters, might shed light on one corner or another of my field. Instead, therefore, of direct vision and academic completeness, I have sought balance. I have looked seriously at Europe, at the United States, and at the world economy in which they played a part; and I have not neglected the ocean that linked them all. I have tried to do justice to early and to later emigrants, to those who settled on American land as well as in American cities, to Catholics and Jews as well as to Protestants. I have shown them as workers in a dynamic economy, and not merely as foreigners trying to build protective institutions while accepting a few American ways. I have looked with sympathy at the problems of three generations. Above all, I have made an effort to reveal both the broad trends of my century – the forces to which emigrants consciously or unconsciously responded – and the multiplicity of individual experience.

Department of American Studies   Philip Taylor
University of Hull   *May 1971*

Acknowledgements

Although, as always, I have worked alone, engaging in few discussions about research, constructing my own index, and reading my own proofs, I am deeply grateful for several people's aid. I received valuable advice in the State Paper Room of the British Museum, and admirable cooperation in Liverpool City Libraries. Mr E. W. Paget-Tomlinson, when Keeper of Shipping in the City of Liverpool Museum; Mr B. W. Bathe of the Science Museum, South Kensington; Mr G. A. Osbon and Mr D. J. Lyon of the National Maritime Museum, Greenwich; Mr A. Hedgley, of Harland and Wolff, Belfast; Mr W. B. Brown of the Cunard Steamship Company; the staff of the Ulster Museum, Belfast, and of the research library at George Eastman House, Rochester, N.Y. – all helped me find pictures and plans. Many years ago, the Editor of the *Western Gazette*, Yeovil, Somerset, permitted me to work in his offices on old copies of the *Sherborne, Dorchester and Taunton Journal*. Elderly citizens of Grimsby – Messrs. Ayscough, Hudson and Westland – allowed me to exploit their memory of events before 1914. Dr Charlotte Erickson of the London School of Economics showed me several unpublished papers. Mrs Margrit Healey and Mr G. K. Orton made translations for me. Not only have I received much help from the staff of the Brynmor Jones Library at my own university, and especially from the late A. C. Wood: the Library Committee has begun subsidizing the collection of research material for American Immigration, and this helped me in the final stages of my work. Professor Geoffrey Moore advanced departmental funds to finance some of my journeys. Much typing was done by Miss A. Barrick and Miss Jeanne Fletcher. Under my direction, maps and diagrams were prepared by Neil Hyslop.

The words of my title are Lord Acton's. When, in January 1866, he addressed the Literary and Scientific Institution of Bridgnorth, not far from his Shropshire estate, he was particularly concerned to stress the influence of the United States on those Europeans who stayed at home. I, on the contrary, have studied the millions whom the magnet drew away.

Thanks are due to the following for permission to reproduce photographs and other illustrations: George Eastman House, Rochester, N.Y. (Back jacket, Frontispiece, and Nos. 16b. to 32 inclusive); National Maritime Museum (Nos. 3a. and b., 4a. and b., 13a. and b., 14a. and b., 15a. and b. and Diagram 5); Liverpool City Libraries, Record Office and Local History Department (Nos. 10b., 11a. and b.); City of Liverpool Museum (No. 12); *Illustrated London News* (Nos. 1, 2a. and b., 5a. and b.); Radio Times Hulton Picture Library (Nos. 6 and 16a., and the cartoons); Harvard University Press (Nos. 7 and 8); Fleming H. Revell Company, Old Tappan, N.J. (Nos. 9a., 10a.); Mansell Collection (No. 9b.); and the Ulster Museum, Belfast (Front jacket).

CHAPTER ONE

North-West Europe and the Nineteenth-Century World

There are, indeed, marvellous riches, mineral, vegetable and animal, in these more distant provinces, which only require the whistle of the steam-engine to give them vent and hand them over to the capitalist and to industry. And this is at hand . . . and in the wake of the steamer and the locomotive follow enterprise and industry, capital and civilization, peace and prosperity.

Wilfrid Latham, *The States of the River Plate: their industries and commerce*, 200.

A French traveller, visiting Sofia in the first years of the twentieth century, saw new streets being driven through old Turkish slums, new shops and offices going up, a new post office, a new opera house, a new cathedral, a new parliament building, a new royal palace. It was a city, he said, '*aussi neuve qu'une Johannesburg ou une Kalgoorlie.*'[1] He was right. During the nineteenth century and the early twentieth, the empty regions overseas were transformed. What is less commonly understood, the more backward areas of Europe underwent changes little less remarkable; and the transforming agency, acting upon both zones, was the influence of Britain and France, which, combined, made up the power-house of the world.

I

Britain continued to build her colonies of white settlement, her empire in India, her scattered coaling-stations and naval bases, and founded an almost new empire in Africa. After surrendering Napoleon's conquests, France laid new imperial foundations in Africa and south-east Asia. But, great as were the opportunities empire held out to soldiers and administrators, to merchants and missionaries, north-west Europe's influence affected far more than

[1] Louis de Launay, *La Bulgarie d'hier et de demain*, 268–9. Most books cited are listed again in the Bibliography, with their essential publication details. A few used infrequently or for not very important facts are mentioned in footnotes only. General readers will not be interested in publication details of such sources: professional students will have at their disposal all the bibliographical aids that large libraries contain.

the areas under political control. Political ideas probably, religious ideas certainly, went into foreign lands too. The Church of England and the Free Churches gave as much attention to China as to Nyasaland or Uganda, while the Church of Rome built itself in the United States with even more energy and success than in French colonies. The generalization is even truer of economic life. Britain invested more money in foreign lands than in all her colonies and dominions: as much in the United States as in South Africa and India combined, more in Latin America than in Australasia. France had ten times as much capital invested in foreign countries, in 1914, as in her colonies: three times as much in Russia alone.[1]

Because Britain had equipment and skill beyond anything to be found in other countries in the late eighteenth and the early nineteenth centuries, she took a lead in economic development more direct than the word 'investment' suggests. Workers went to France, Belgium, the German states and beyond, installing textile machinery and steam engines, and teaching local men how to use and build them. Wilkinson, Manby, and Cunliffe-Lister in France, the Cockerills in Belgium, Mulvaney in the Ruhr, contributed managerial as well as technical skill. Brassey helped build railways in northern France. British engineers bridged the Danube at Budapest – it was cheaper to bring English ironwork via the Adriatic than to procure local material – and the Dnieper at Kiev. Travelling on an early Danube steamboat, Michael Quin found both captain and engineer British. At the same time, Europeans visited Britain, in search of the most advanced methods of making iron and steel.[2] Then, as the century advanced, British enterprise moved more and more overseas. Investors developed interests in American ranches and Brazilian rubber. The greatest of British contractors, Weetman Pearson, simultaneously built water-works and drainage systems in Britain, railways in China, and harbours from Dover to Vera Cruz. British travellers were now able to see, not steamboat engineers on the Danube but British engine-drivers in the Argentine.[3] Meanwhile, in Europe, British influence was first supplemented, then almost supplanted, by that of France. French scientific and technical publications diffused knowledge. Foreigners were

[1] Herbert Feis, *Europe the World's Banker 1870–1914*, 23, 27, 51. All subsequent investment figures are taken from this source. For some other influences, see Stephen Neill, *A History of Christian Missions*.

[2] Johann G. Kohl, *Austria* 220–4; John Paget, *Hungary and Transylvania*, II 607; Michael J. Quin, *A Steam Voyage down the Danube*, I 11, 26; John A. Hammerton, *Countries of the World*, I 1014, V 3456; William O. Henderson, *Great Britain and the Industrial Revolution in Europe*.

[3] Desmond Young, *Member for Mexico: a Biography of Weetman Pearson, First Viscount Cowdray*; John A. Hammerton, *The Real Argentina*, 282–3; and see the list of projects – railways, gasworks, bridges, drainage systems, tramways, sugar refineries – between the 1860s and the 1890s, in Alan K. Manchester, *British Preeminence in Brazil: its Rise and Decline*, 322–7.

attracted by the courses offered at the *Polytechnique* and the *Ecole des Ponts et Chaussées*. Frenchmen trained in these institutions took appointments all over Europe. Engineers were active in Spanish mining, machinery-building, and gasworks; in docks and harbours from Antwerp to Varna; in improving the river Main and running zinc smelters in the Rhineland. French capital went into railways, from Spain to Russia, into Italian and Swiss textiles, into Austrian mining, into London omnibuses and Roumanian bridges. Not only did the French invest heavily in industry, transport, and government securities: they provided models, in the shape of the *Crédit Mobilier* and similar institutions, for other countries wishing to finance industrial growth.[1] Later, though on a smaller scale, certain other countries pioneered in economic improvement. In the 1890s, Belgians installed a water system at Philippopolis and a tramway at Salonika. In 1905 a British officer, travelling through one of the more prosperous parts of European Turkey, saw a Belgian driver in charge of a new steam-plough, made in Britain. During the Second World War, I myself saw Cairo trams bearing brass plates inscribed 'Charleroi 1893'.[2]

In the nineteenth-century world's economic growth and unification, transport and communications were central, and because they were the most costly of enterprises, north-west Europe's contribution was particularly significant. In 1914, Britain alone had more than £1,500 million invested in railways – £616 million in the United States, £467 million in Latin America and other foreign parts, £140 million in India, £306 million in other parts of the Empire. If the nearly £78 million in tramways are added, and the £7 million in canals and docks, transport made up more than forty per cent of her entire investment overseas.

What might be expected from this was eloquently expressed by a British traveller, C. B. Elliott, in 1838, who consoled himself for the discomforts of Danube navigation by musing upon the revolutionary effects the steamboat might bring:

> Instead of complaining, a traveller of enlarged and philanthropic mind will turn with admiration to the enterprise and patriotism which have set on foot so grand an undertaking, and to the important moral consequences likely to result, remembering with satisfaction that steam is calculated to prove the precursor of civilization. . . . The effect of the perfect organization of the existing arrangements will be to bring all the provinces on the banks of the Danube, with those

[1] Thomas C. Banfield, *Industry of the Rhine*, II 197, 243; and especially Rondo E. Cameron, *France and the Economic Development of Europe 1800–1914*.
[2] Henry C. Woods, *Washed by Four Seas*, 88; Edward Dicey, *The Peasant State*, 306–7; William Miller, *Travels and Politics in the Near East*, 365. On the entire subject, see Eric J. Hobsbawm, *The Age of Revolution*, Part II, and Charles Morazé, *Les bourgeois conquérants*. Woods, *op. cit.*, 129–30, also found Italian engineers building military roads for the Turks.

Map 1 EUROPE 1914: COUNTRIES
The ethnic map is highly simplified. In particula

GIONS AND ETHNIC DIVISIONS

ermans and Jews were scattered throughout eastern Europe.

bordering them, into contact with the arts and sciences, the civil institutions and the moral, commercial and religious resources of western Europe. . . . Nor will these countries be a limit to the bound of the operations of the mighty moral engine. The steam communication now arranged between England, Spain, Malta, Marseilles, Italy, Greece, Egypt, Syria, Constantinople, Crim Tartary, and Odessa, completes the line which may encircle Europe with a zone of blessings, and unite it to Asia and Africa by the golden tie of gratitude for benefits conferred; it promises to enlarge the empire of science, religion, and happiness; to wave the sceptre of liberty over Africa's injured soil; and, by facilitating the dissemination of the truths of the Gospel, to prostrate the crescent at the foot of the cross.[1]

Steamboats did, indeed, play a part in the world's development. In 1830, Cobbett crossed the Humber, a year later Tocqueville travelled the length of Lake Champlain, before the end of the decade Samuel Laing reached the northernmost part of Sweden's Baltic coast; and in the same years other steamboats were to be found on the Irish Sea, the English Channel, the North Sea, on Thames, Seine, Moselle and Rhine. They carried passengers and goods along the coasts of Australia and the United States. Later in the century, they could be found on the rivers of Russia, India, China and Africa. So valuable were they that very often they were built in Britain, dismantled, transported in sections, and rebuilt at their place of work.[2] The effects Elliott hoped for, however – and they were far more complete than he could have guessed – were achieved much more by the combined operation of railway, ocean steamship and telegraph.

Wilfrid Latham wrote his prediction, used as this chapter's epigraph, when Argentina was still a land of cattle and sheep, and when Buenos Aires, with its 200,000 inhabitants, lacked waterworks or tramway. Forty-five years later, in a series entitled 'The Conquests of Science', Frederick Talbot published *The Railway Conquest of the World*.[3] The link between Adelaide and Perth had even then not been made, and some lines in China were still to come; but he was able to celebrate the railway's triumph from Alaska to Borneo, from Rhodesia to the Andes, from Norway to the Hejaz. The rock-drills which bored the St Gotthard and Loetschberg tunnels, the

[1] C. B. Elliott, *Travels in the Three Great Empires*, I 192–3.
[2] William Cobbett, *Rural Rides* (ed. G. D. H. and M. I. Cole), II 645, 650; George W. Pierson, *Tocqueville and Beaumont in America*, 345; Samuel Laing, *A Tour of Sweden in 1838*, 155; Michael J. Quin, *Steam Voyages on the Seine, the Moselle, and the Rhine*; Henry Mayhew, *London Labour and the London Poor*, III 334–6; R. Carlyle Buley, *The Old Northwest*, I 432–7 (early services on the Great Lakes); Charles Griffith, *Present State and Prospects of the Port Phillip District*, 6; Basil Greenhill, 'The Steamers of the Brahmaputra and Ganges', *Mariner's Mirror*, LII (1966), 53–60.
[3] London, 1911. On 206–7 he describes the Lake Baikal train ferries, an essential link in the Trans-Siberian, and also assembled on the site after construction in Britain.

'travellers' which laid girders on steel bridges, the mighty steam-shovels which removed tons of earth and rock, aroused in him the same enthusiasm as would be shown, in our own day, by popular writers describing polar submarine voyages, transplants of human organs, or a rendezvous in outer space.

The speed of the railway's growth was extraordinary. Between 1840 and 1860, mileage in Britain increased from one thousand to ten thousand. In the latter year, France had about six thousand miles of track, Germany about a thousand more. Twenty years later again, Germany had 20,000 miles, France and Britain very little less. Austria-Hungary had 12,000, Italy more than 5,000, the Russian Empire 15,000, and the Trans-Siberian lay not far ahead.[1] At the same time, the railway spread beyond the seas. By 1880, India had 10,000 miles, Canada more than 7,000. The next quarter-century saw Canada's trans-continental lines and much development in Australia. When Latham wrote, Argentina had only three very short lines: by 1892 a network was outlined on the Pampa, and the foothills of the Andes had been reached; and by 1908 the country had 14,000 miles.[2] Largest of all was the system which grew in the United States. There were 3,000 miles of railway in 1840, more than 30,000 in 1860, more than 100,000 in 1880, and a quarter of a million by the end of the Great War. Even as early as the 1850s, the Middle West was linked to the Atlantic coast; and in the years after the Civil War, in addition to large-scale new laying of track, bridges were built over the Ohio, Mississippi and Missouri, and the gauge was standardized.[3]

On the oceans, steam triumphed more slowly. By the 1840s, a few services existed on the North Atlantic, the Mediterranean and the Indian Ocean, and between Britain, the West Indies and South America. Only in the 1860s, however, did Britain begin to build more steamship than sailing-ship tonnage; and it was in that decade that steam replaced sail in the North Atlantic passenger trade. Elsewhere, and for bulk cargoes, the years from the 1850s to the 1870s gave the sailing ship many of its greatest successes, for clippers were independent of coaling-stations, and were more reliable, even faster, than most steamers of their day. Only in the 1880s did steel hulls, the triple-expansion engine, and improved boilers enable the steamship to capture the long-distance bulk trades. At the beginning of that decade, Britain still had rather more sailing-ship than steamship tonnage; the United States had

---

[1] It is sufficient to refer to Michael Robbins, *The Railway Age*. The effectiveness of railways was all the time being increased by double-tracking, standardized gauges, longer trains, and more powerful locomotives.

[2] Mark Jefferson, *Peopling the Argentine Pampa*, esp. the railway maps at the end.

[3] John F. Stover, *American Railroads*; George R. Taylor and Irene D. Neu, *The American Railroad Network 1861–1890*.

three times as much; most other countries' merchant fleets were still under sail. Thirty years later, sailing-ships had almost vanished from the seas.[1]

The telegraph was the last component of the new communications system. In 1861, the United States had 50,000 miles of line, and had just spanned the continent. Twenty years later, even the Ottoman Empire had 15,000 miles. Under the oceans, technical problems were more severe. The narrow seas between Britain and Europe were spanned by cables in the 1850s. In 1866 the North Atlantic was at last spanned. In the decade that followed, Britain was linked with India, Singapore, Shanghai and Australia; Australia was crossed from Darwin to Adelaide; a telegraph line across Siberia was extended by cable to China and Japan; North and South America were connected; and Portugal was linked with Brazil. Only the Pacific had to wait for its cables until the twentieth century.[2]

These innovations, organized by men in London, Paris, Liverpool and a handful of other cities, did more than open up new countries. They brought distant regions into relationship one with another, and linked areas of primary production with the industrial lands that needed their raw materials and food. It was the railway that made practicable the cattle-ranching of Texas and the Pampa, the wheat-growing of the Ukraine, Hungary, Argentina and Australia, the Dakotas and Saskatchewan. The steamship brought the product to a hungry Britain. In the 1830s, Britain's import of wheat was often less than a million quarters a year. From 1869, it fell only once below ten millions, and from 1891 to the Great War never below twenty millions. In 1914, the United States contributed one-third; Canada, after a four-fold increase in fifteen years, nearly as much; and large cargoes came also from Australia, India, Russia and Latin America. Cotton imports, largely from the United States, nearly trebled in the half-century before the Great War; wool imports quadrupled, three-fifths in 1914 coming from Australia and New Zealand, the remainder from South Africa, Latin America and India.[3] The Suez Canal, which in its first year (1869) had been used by no more than half a million tons of shipping, now carried twenty million tons. It was the Great Lakes steamship, similarly, aided by short-distance railways, which brought iron ore from Michigan and Minnesota to become steel at

[1] Gerald S. Graham, 'The Ascendancy of the Sailing Ship 1850–1885', *Economic History Review*, Second Series, IX (1956), 74–88. Britain built steamships not only for herself but for other countries, even advanced ones. Noel R. P. Bonsor, *North Atlantic Seaway*, 131–3, 303–4, shows Harland and Wolff, and Palmers, building for the Holland-America and Hamburg-America lines down to the eve of the Great War.

[2] Stover, *op. cit.*, 144–6, 174. Useful figures are in Michael G. Mulhall, *Dictionary of Statistics*, 441–2. In 1913 Britain had nearly £44 million invested in telegraph and telephone systems throughout the world.

[3] William Page, *Commerce and Industry*, II 140–9.

Pittsburgh and Gary. It was the railway that brought South Wales coal to the sea, and the steamship which took it away in holds and bunkers. With food and raw materials coming into a single and competitive world market, industrial regions could specialize more freely, confident that factories and workers would be fed. In such a unified world, cities could grow in many parts of the world – Buenos Aires, Sydney and Montreal joining Birmingham and Hamburg. While expanding trade and industry could take root there, new forms of transport enabled their inhabitants, in far greater numbers, to lead convenient lives.[1]

North-west Europe's economic leadership, however, did not proceed at a steadily increasing rate through the nineteenth century, nor was its balance always the same. Large investment in railways and other enterprises brought about a burst of economic growth overseas; then activity died away, and investment became more prominent in industry, building, or other sectors at home, after which another boom in overseas investment was likely to develop. Nor did British investment overseas move steadily in a single direction. Although there were periods of activity in Canada, Australia and Latin America, until late in the nineteenth century the United States tended to be the main recipient. Then, however, that country became independent of foreign funds, and British capital moved far more into South Africa, Canada, and then again Australia.[2] Such waves of investment, and the associated changes in speed of economic growth, helped shape the attractiveness of one area after another for emigrants from Europe.

II

Change was rapid in all the overseas lands receiving Europeans in the nineteenth century. It did not, however, take the same form everywhere; nor did it start at exactly the same time.

In the 1830s, the British colonies of New South Wales, South Australia and Western Australia had fewer than a quarter of a million people, most of them living within a hundred miles of the scattered coastal settlements. The interior beyond the eastern mountains was only beginning to be known, for Sturt's was the only one of the famous journeys of exploration yet completed. Port Phillip (later Melbourne) had perhaps ten thousand people by the end of the decade. There were a few prosperous farms nearby, but most of the region was occupied by sheep-stations, at the centre of each a bungalow and a

---

[1] In a sense, all this is common knowledge; yet probably it was Lee Benson's discussion in *Turner and Beard*, 42–52, that crystallized my views.

[2] A very lucid account of these phenomena may be found in Brinley Thomas, *Migration and Economic Growth*.

cluster of huts, the owner and his family subsisting mainly on mutton and 'damper', as the local unleavened bread was called. Sydney was dominated by the barracks which housed convicts and their guards; and such farming as New South Wales possessed depended on convict labour.[1]

Brazil was older-established, with a population of some seven millions, great natural fertility, and considerable mineral wealth. Travellers, however, were impressed by the obsolete methods employed and by the indolence of the inhabitants, which they ascribed to the institution of slavery that gave all heavy manual work, and many duties elsewhere performed by draft-animals, to Negroes. In Rio de Janeiro, slaves carried close-stools through the streets at night, to be emptied in the bay; for although the city had water brought from the hills by a magnificent eighteenth-century aqueduct, it had no sewers and no privies until the 1850s. Yet free Negroes could become shopkeepers and even priests; and 'if wearing shoes and a neckcloth', they could ride in omnibuses and enter restaurants on the same footing as whites.[2]

Argentina was no more than a bundle of loosely-federated states, with perhaps half a million people. Agriculture was confined to the environs of towns, while the interior was given over to the gauchos and their open-range cattle. Buenos Aires was still primitive. The rich depended for water on cisterns in their houses: the poor bought theirs from men who filled huge barrels from the river, and mounted them in ox-carts. Ocean-going ships had to anchor miles from shore, passengers completing their journey first in small boats, then in big carts dragged into the water to meet them.[3]

Upper and Lower Canada, Prince Edward Island, New Brunswick and Nova Scotia, collectively termed British North America, had a million and a half inhabitants, few of them further west than the St Lawrence valley. Although exploration had reached the Arctic and the Pacific before the end of the eighteenth century, the barren plateau between Lake Superior and Hudson's Bay denied settlers access to the fertile prairies: they could not, like fur-traders, depend for their living on the birch-bark canoe. Although there were steamboats on the St Lawrence and the bigger lakes, and coach services of a sort, Adam Fergusson noted, in 1831, the poor state of the roads, the wretched bridges, and the absence of settlement more than a few miles from water. Montreal had 20,000 people, at a time when New York City had ten times as many. As for York (Toronto), 'It was interesting to observe the sudden transition from the streets . . . to the solemn stillness of the forest, as, I think, we could not have proceeded above two or three

[1] Griffith, *op. cit.*; P. Cunningham, *Two Years in New South Wales.*
[2] Thomas Walsh, *Notices of Brazil in 1828 and 1829,* esp. I 134–41. See also a description a quarter of a century later, in the American Thomas Ewbank's *Life in Brazil.*
[3] Woodbine Parish, *Buenos Ayres and the Provinces of the Rio de la Plata.*

miles, ere we were immersed in all the wild magnificence of a cedar swamp, and hemmed in by towering pines and hemlocks on every side.' A few years later, James Silk Buckingham found a larger Montreal, its shops, though not yet its streets, lit by gas, with water piped to those houses whose owners could afford to pay for the service, and with a recently-founded police force. Neither Toronto nor Quebec, however, had a single daily newspaper.[1]

Of the world's underdeveloped countries, the United States was much the most advanced. In the 1830s, it is true, it took a fortnight to travel from the Atlantic to the Mississippi, which was roughly the western limit of settlement. Northward, the inhabited area stopped short near the southern end of Lake Michigan. Between Detroit and Saginaw, Tocqueville was able to write a vivid description of the wilderness; and a few years later Harriet Martineau observed Chicago's first boom.[2] Beyond the Mississippi stretched the region of Indians, U.S. Army outposts, and trappers; and the nature of the Great Basin was still imperfectly understood. Anywhere west of the Appalachians, some features of life still looked crude. Population was sparse, log cabins were numerous, many people's clothing and furniture were homemade. Yet in other directions, there were signs of skill and sophistication. Americans were immensely ingenious in their use of wood, whether for utensils, water-pipes, waggons, covered bridges, or water-wheels.[3] Steamboats were well developed. Railways were just beginning. The whole country, moreover, though vast in extent and composed of twenty-six states in 1837, formed a single economic unit. Goods transported at that time through the Italian states might pay a fresh toll every twenty miles or so, and the German states were only beginning to organize the Zollverein: but the United States made up one market which, super-imposed on the map of Europe, would have stretched from Bordeaux to Bucharest, from Hamburg to Naples.[4]

---

[1] Adam Fergusson, *Practical Notes made during a Tour of Canada and a Portion of the United States in MDCCCXXXI*; the quotation is on 276. James Silk Buckingham, *Canada, Nova Scotia, New Brunswick* . . . esp. 135, 149–50, 242–5. See also Charles Lucas, *Lord Durham's Report*, II 212.

[2] Pierson, *op. cit.*, 231–82, Tocqueville's narrative '*Quinze jours au désert*'; Harriet Martineau, *Society in America*, I 350.

[3] The best guide is Jared Van Wagenen, *The Golden Age of Homespun*, though a visit to the Farmer's Museum at Cooperstown, N.Y., brings the subject even more to life. Karl J. R. Arndt, *George Rapp's Harmony Society*, 311, mentions a water-pipe at New Harmony, Ind., made from hollowed tree-trunks bound together, which was half a mile in length.

[4] I refer only to the settled area, not the much larger United States recognized by treaty. On road travel, see Buley, *op. cit.*, I 444–81. On steamboats, see Patrick Shirreff, *A Tour through North America*, 93 (the Hudson), 267–71 (the Ohio); James Silk Buckingham, *Eastern and Western States of America*, II 378 (the Ohio), III 77–90, 170–3 (the Mississippi) and chapters xv to xvii (the Great Lakes); as well as that great monograph, Louis C. Hunter, *Steamboats on the Western Rivers*.

Map 2   THE UNIT

ESOTA

WISCONSIN

IOWA

MISSOURI

nsas City

Jefferson
City

ARKANSAS

LOUISIANA

New Orleans

Milwaukee

Chicago

St. Louis

MICHIGAN

Detroit

ILLINOIS

INDIANA

Ohio

OHIO

Louisville

Cleveland

Pittsburgh

Johnstown

Cincinnati

Portsmouth

KENTUCKY

WEST
VIRGINIA

TENNESSEE

MISSISSIPPI

ALABAMA

GEORGIA

Toronto

Buffalo

Rochester

NEW YORK

Quebec

Montreal

Burlington

VERMONT

NEW
HAMP-
SHIRE

MAINE

Albany

MASSA-
CHUSSETS

Lawrence
Lowell
Boston

Fall River

New Haven

RHODE ISLAND

CONNECTICUT

New York

NEW JERSEY

PENNSYLVANIA

Philadelphia

MARYLAND

Baltimore

DELAWARE

VIRGINIA

Appalachian Mountains

NORTH CAROLINA

SOUTH
CAROLINA

FLORIDA

Kilometres
0 100 200 300 400 500

0   100   200   300   400
Miles

NSH

TES OF AMERICA

There were flourishing cities, though New York and others looked much more like English towns than they would at the end of the century.[1] Even in the backwoods, however, travellers detected signs of civilization. Again and again Tocqueville insisted that men inhabiting the crudest dwellings were likely to be literate, and interested in public affairs. Equipped, as he put it, 'with the Bible, an axe, and some newspapers', they were subduing the wilderness, not merely responding to its influence.[2] The description was truer in the zone of New England migration than further south; but the whole West had a growth of governmental institutions, democratic politics and, if only in log buildings, churches and schools. Citizens of the United States were proud – too proud, many travellers thought – to inhabit a country built upon principles: absence of hereditary privilege and religious discrimination, guarantee of rights under the law, dispersal of political power. They claimed that the Union's continued existence proved men capable of self-government, and they hoped that all men everywhere would come to imitate their achievement. Such feelings, already voiced by the Founders in the eighteenth century, were strongly alive in the early nineteenth. When Tocqueville attended a Fourth of July ceremony at Albany, he and his friend Beaumont were surprised at the absence of military pomp, and were likewise impressed by the reception given to the reading of the Declaration, and by the respect paid to the handful of survivors of the Revolution.[3] Neither reports the oration, though its theme was 'Liberty', but it was on such occasions that Americans were most accustomed to dwell upon their country's virtues. Editors followed suit:

> We live under republican institutions, where the sole power of the government is in the hands of the people, and where every act of sovereignty is but an emanation of the public will. No mighty monarch graciously assumes the burden of conducting our affairs; no hereditary parliament kindly relieves us from the difficult task of enacting our own laws; no established church, in charitable consideration of our weakness, deigns to accept the tithe of the produce of our labours, in return for the amiable office of directing our consciences in the world, and selling us the right of admission to a better existence. In government, in religion, in social life, we think our own thoughts, and act at our own pleasure.[4]

[1] See the illustrations in James Truslow Adams, ed., *Album of American History*, II 214, 216, 257–8; *The Diary of George Templeton Strong* (ed. Allan Nevins), I; and, on Western cities, Richard C. Wade, *The Urban Frontier . . . 1790–1830*. Nor was American culture negligible. Kent and Story were leading lawyers; Bancroft and Prescott were starting their careers as historians; Irving and Fenimore Cooper were still productive; and Emerson and Poe were beginning to write.
[2] Alexis de Tocqueville, *Democracy in America* (ed. Phillips Bradley), I 317. For earlier versions, see Pierson, *op. cit.*, 190, 237–8, 242–4.
[3] Pierson, *op. cit.*, 179–84.
[4] Buley, *op. cit.*, I 315, quoting James Hall in the *Western Monthly Magazine* of Cincinnati. See also James K. Polk's Message to Congress, 7 December 1847, quoted in Leonard D. White, *The*

However exuberant his language, such a writer was not straying too far from the truth. In one community after another, in churches, counting-houses, factories, law-offices, court-houses and legislatures, men of ability and enterprise were able to rise to leadership or wealth. The United States was at least half a century ahead of Britain as a political democracy. Local government and voluntary associations engaged the attention of large numbers of citizens.[1] In free competition one with another, brands of religious faith existed in great variety, from the most refined Unitarianism to the crudest frontier camp-meeting. The scene was offensive to some Europeans. An English gentleman, lying ill at Terre Haute, Indiana, rebuffed an Irish labourer who claimed acquaintance. The doctor was shocked. 'In vain I tried to make him understand that such a one, in England, if he had come to any gentleman's house, would not have presumed to enter even the servants' hall, but would have waited in the courtyard while his message was being delivered. The American shook his head disapprovingly.'[2] Other travellers welcomed the contrast with more caste-ridden lands, and sympathized with Americans' hopes for the future. Attending church at Toronto in 1839, James Silk Buckingham found several grades of pew, saw troops come on parade, and observed the lieutenant-governor, in full-dress uniform, enter with a staff. He recalled that, a short time before in Washington, he had seen Martin Van Buren, eighth president of the United States, walk unattended to an Episcopalian church and take his place in a pew with other gentlemen who happened to be already there. More elo-quently, the same writer reflected, on board a Mississippi steamboat:

> On the Nile, the Euphrates, the Tigris, and the Ganges, it is the wreck of former grandeur that most engages the attention and affects the feelings. On this great river of America, it is the anticipations of the future that fill the mind and expand the heart.[3]

Jacksonians, 17. Compare, too, expressions from the late eighteenth century: Thomas Pownall's 'totally and entirely a New System of Things and Men' (Frank Thistlethwaite, *The Great Experiment*, 38); Washington's reference to the hopes of America entertained by 'all the philosophers, patriots and virtuous men in all nations' (Douglas S. Freeman, *George Washington*, VI 134-5); and the rhyme in the *Massachusetts Centinel*, 21 September 1785 (Merrill Jensen, *The New Nation*, 90),
Where happy millions their own fields possess
No tyrant awes them, and no lords oppress.

[1] Tocqueville, *op. cit.*, I 68-82, 392-4, II chapter xvi. See also Chilton Williamson, *American Suffrage from Property to Democracy* and Stanley Elkins and Eric McKitrick, 'A Meaning for Turner's Frontier', *Political Science Quarterly*, LXIX (1954), esp. 140-43.
[2] John R. Beste, *The Wabash*, II 15-17. Basil Hall, Mrs. Trollope and Charles Dickens all have un-favourable comments. Such travellers were failing to see the essentials, insisted William G. Ouseley, *Remarks on the Statistics and Political Institutions of the United States*. Certainly he, Tocqueville, Michel Chevallier, and Harriet Martineau seem to the modern reader much more fair-minded.
[3] Buckingham, *Canada, Nova Scotia, New Brunswick*, 18-19; *Eastern and Western States of America*, III 179.

III

From their primitive situation of the 1830s, America's overseas rivals underwent striking, if uneven, development.

The transportation of convicts to the Australian colonies was soon brought to an end. Gold rushes in the 1850s brought in large numbers of free settlers. The 1870s and 1880s brought the exploitation of non-precious metals, further expansion of sheep- and cattle-rearing, a great increase in the area under wheat, and considerable railway-building, all stimulated by British investment; and in the latter decade, refrigeration made possible the export of meat as well as wool. Yet in 1890, soon after the long boom had collapsed, Australian population reached a total no higher than that of white people counted at the very first census of the United States, exactly a century before. Twenty years later, after prolonged depression and just before a new wave of immigration, there were still no more than 4½ million inhabitants. Yet Sydney and Melbourne were great cities, their public buildings, Melbourne's especially, looking very like those of Manchester or Leeds.[1]

The second half of the nineteenth century saw five major changes in Brazil. The province of Sao Paulo experienced a boom in coffee-growing. A little later, a boom in rubber caused a large internal migration towards the Amazon region. Slaves were emancipated. The monarchy gave way to a republic. Economic growth and the change in the labour system brought about a need for immigration, and this was vigorously promoted by provincial and federal governments. Although one recent authority has claimed that the country's per capita income increased nearly as fast as that of the United States, it remains true that, after decades of stagnation, Brazil's modern development started from a much lower point.[2]

Argentina's growth started later, but was even more rapid. In the quarter-century before 1914, population doubled, largely because of massive immigration. The value of exports grew sevenfold. After years of producing only hides, tallow and jerked beef, the country became a source of wool and beef, then of wheat. By 1906, agricultural products exceeded livestock in value of export trade. Argentina stood next to the United States and Russia in the number of its cattle, second only to Australia in sheep; and, after a

[1] Edward Shann, *An Economic History of Australia*; Asa Briggs, *Victorian Cities*, chapter vii; Hammerton, *Countries of the World*, IV 2706–14.
[2] Celso Furtado, *The Economic Growth of Brazil*, Pierre Denis. *Le Brésil au xxme siècle*; Robert F. Foerster, *The Italian Emigration of our Time*, chapters xv and xvi. In 1907, Brazil's estimated population approached 20 millions. It is interesting to observe that, unlike Argentina and the United States, Brazil was taking in huge numbers of immigrants in the 1890s, then rather fewer in the early twentieth century, when those two rivals were enjoying booms. All, however, as well as Australia, saw a high peak of immigration just before the Great War.

fivefold increase in acreage since 1888, it ranked after the United States, Russia, France and Austria-Hungary in the production of wheat. Buenos Aires, once so backward in the mode of disembarking passengers and goods, now had six miles of modern quays, and in 1908 ranked as the twelfth seaport of the world. Travellers commented on the city's noise, on the rapidity of its expansion and the ostentation of its buildings, on its cruelty to animals, on the dangers of the streets at night. It was a booming city, raw as a mining-camp in some aspects, in others glittering like Paris.[1]

By the 1870s and 1880s, with its greatest boom still far ahead, Canada's eastern cities were no longer mere outposts. They displayed all the solidity of Victorian England or Second Empire France. But although cities contributed greatly to the rise of population from about $3\frac{1}{2}$ millions in 1871 to $4\frac{3}{4}$ millions in 1891 and to over 7 millions in 1911, the most remarkable growth occurred in the West, where railways at last permitted settlement to spread. In round figures, Quebec province grew between 1891 and 1911 from $1\frac{1}{2}$ to 2 millions, and Ontario from 2 to $2\frac{1}{2}$ millions. In the same twenty years, Manitoba grew from 152,000 to 461,000, Saskatchewan from nothing to 492,000, Alberta from nothing to 374,000, and British Columbia from 98,000 to 392,000, a total growth in the West of more than $1\frac{1}{4}$ million people. One district will serve as example. Travelling in 1875 from Toronto, an Anglican missionary, using carts and boats, took five months to reach Edmonton, then a Hudson's Bay Company fort. For a long time he lived on little but pemmican and soup; on his journeys he had to take a cart loaded with equipment; and on one such trip, soon after his arrival, a Methodist colleague froze to death. He had to build his own log cabin, where his evenings were often spent in darkness because tallow was costly and there was no oil. It took him two years to find money, material and labour for a church, which was so small and simple that, later on, it was sold as a stable for fifty dollars. Most of the people around him were half-breeds and Indians, the latter, he reports, only recently beginning to use iron for arrow-heads instead of flint. By 1890, the Canadian Pacific railway, its transcontinental line complete, was advertising large tracts of prairie as 'the richest soil in the world'. In several cities, company and government agents were stationed to advise prospective settlers, tours of inspection were arranged, and a man's fare was refunded if he bought a 160-acre farm. By about 1907, with the arrival of the Canadian Northern and the Grand

[1] Latham, op. cit., and Michael G. and E. T. Mulhall, Handbook of the River Plate deal with conditions in the 1860s. For more recent developments, see Albert Martinez and Maurice Lewandowski, The Argentine in the Twentieth Century; Hammerton, The Real Argentine; Pierre Denis, La république Argentine: la mise en valeur du pays; and Aldo Ferrer, The Argentine Economy, trans. Marjory M. Urquidi, esp. Part III.

3

Trunk Pacific, Edmonton and its region experienced a rush of settlers, including many Americans. In 1901, the town had fewer than 5,000 people: in 1911 it had more than 31,000. In addition to a government immigration office, it had a hall where land-seekers could be housed, together with the workers who flocked to earn, if skilled, half a dollar an hour, or, if labourers, two dollars a day. Women could make twenty dollars a month as children's nurses or housemaids.[1] Such phenomena were widespread, for immigration, outstripping the boom of the 1880s, topped 100,000 a year between 1902 and 1914, and five times exceeded a quarter of a million.

Although the exploration of the United States was still going on in 1870, and some of the country remained unused long after that, one area after another was opened to settlement. In the 1820s and 1830s, the booming areas were western New York and Pennsylvania, and Ohio. In the 1840s, they were southern Wisconsin, Illinois, Missouri, and the Gulf states. In the 1850s, they were eastern Iowa, southern Minnesota, and the Californian goldfields. After the Civil War, they were Kansas and Nebraska, the Dakotas, the Pacific Northwest, then Oklahoma. In quick succession, gold was found in California and Colorado, silver in Nevada, copper in Michigan, iron in Michigan and Minnesota, oil in Pennsylvania; while by 1890 three million farms had been added to the million and a half that had existed at mid-century. Americans themselves possessed much of the technical skill needed to subdue their continent – the 1830s alone saw the McCormick reaper, Colt's revolver and Morse's telegraph – and they could call skilled foreigners to their aid. Rugged individuals could rely on much governmental coopera-tion, whether in removing Indians, subsidizing a railroad, or setting up a tariff to frustrate the competition of British manufactures. They were helped by foreign investments too.

Towards the end of the century, the balance shifted towards industry, though agriculture kept on growing. The value of farm products rose from $1,600 million in 1850 to $2,460 million in 1889 and $8,498 million in 1909, but the value of manufactures rose in the same years from $,1000 million to over $9,000 million and then to more than $20,000 millions. As late as 1890, less than eighteen per cent of American exports, by value, consisted of manufactures and semi-manufactures: in 1910 the percentage was almost forty-five. Wage-earners in manufactures numbered about 2 millions in 1869, $4\frac{1}{2}$ millions in 1889, more than $8\frac{1}{4}$ millions in 1909. The

[1] W. T. Easterbrook and H. G. J. Aitken, *Canadian Economic History*; J. Russell Harper and Stanley Triggs, *Portrait of a Period: a Collection of Notman Photographs 1856 to 1915*; William Newton, *Twenty Years on the Saskatchewan*; Canadian Pacific Railway, *Free Farms*; *The Canadian Settler's Handbook*; Marcus L. Hansen, *The Mingling of the Canadian and American Peoples*, esp. 227–8. Many immigrants, and especially Americans, did not stay long.

proportion of Americans classified as urban rose from one-fifth in 1860 to one-quarter in 1870, then to one-third in 1890 and nearly half in 1910. By the beginning of the twentieth century, the country was largely self-sufficient as to capital and skill, and was beginning to export both.[1]

Growth, of course, was not uninterrupted. Just as the boom in canals and land-sales had collapsed in 1837, to be followed by a long depression, so there were slumps in the more industrialized United States of the mid seventies, the mid nineties, 1907–8, and 1913–15, when people were put on short time, had their wages cut, or lost their jobs. In the 1890s especially, the country was profoundly disturbed, with waves of labour unrest and agitation for political reforms and for economic regulation and control. Yet expansion was the dominant fact of the century. As population rose from 13 millions in 1830 to 31 millions in 1860, opportunities multiplied, for farmers and businessmen, for labourers on canal, railroad and dock. As it rose to 63 millions in 1890 and 92 millions in 1910, opportunities became yet more varied, though now, in an industrial and urban age, the demand, and especially the demand for foreigners, was for semi-skilled or unskilled workers in factories and mines. Where Harriet Martineau had noticed Irish labourers' shanties by a railroad in the Mohawk valley, and James Silk Buckingham had seen them beside a canal at Peru, Illinois, by the end of the century a traveller would see Italians on a railroad or digging city subways, Poles and Slovaks in coal and steel, Russian Jews in garment work in New York City. The environment was now not the backwoods or the steamboat, but the skyscraper, the elevated railway, and the streetcar.[2] At each stage, growth piled up. Workers in basic industries needed supplies of materials, food, housing, and a variety of services. As immigrants arrived, settled, and raised families, their labour, and their demand for the product of others' labour, became in turn a major factor in national growth. At each stage, finally, the United States was clearly more complex, more dynamic, than any of its overseas rivals, and as a field for Europe's emigrants it could be expected to keep its lead.

[1] For these developments, it is sufficient to refer to Thistlethwaite, *op. cit.*, chapter iv; Douglass C. North, *The Economic Growth of the United States 1790–1860*; and to the following volumes in the Holt-Rinehart-Winston series on economic history: Paul W. Gates, *The Farmer's Age*, George R. Taylor, *The Transportation Revolution*, Fred A. Shannon, *The Farmers' Last Frontier*, and Edward C. Kirkland, *Industry Comes of Age*. American progress may be judged by three simple comparisons. In 1870 the country produced one-third as much coal as Great Britain and about one-quarter as much steel. In 1890, it produced slightly more steel and nearly as much coal. In 1910, it produced nearly twice as much coal and more than four times as much steel; and by that date American steel production exceeded that of Britain and Germany combined, with coal production not far behind them.

[2] Martineau, *op. cit.*, II 189; Buckingham, *Eastern and Western States of America*, III 222–3; Blake McKelvey, *The Urbanization of America*; Sam B. Warner, *Streetcar Suburbs: the Process of Growth in Boston 1870–1900*.

IV

The attracting force of America's economic opportunities, and of its free institutions, was exerted upon a Europe which was itself rapidly changing, which was experiencing, at one and the same time, dislocation and growth.

In the 1830s, even Britain's economy was in some respects primitive. A high proportion of her workers were still blacksmiths, carpenters, shoe-makers and tailors, producing for their customers direct. The stage-coach was still the fastest means of travelling long distances, and the canal-barge the most efficient carrier of heavy goods.[1] Yet by the end of the decade Britain was producing thirty million tons of coal a year, and a million tons of iron – respectively eight times and three times as much as any other country of Europe. At that time, too, she had more steam-engines than the rest of Europe combined.

It is not surprising, then, that travellers contrasted the efficiency, the prosperity, the freedom of their own country with the poverty and oppression they increasingly found as they moved across Europe southward and east-ward from the Channel. 'From the time I left the Netherlands,' wrote one, 'through Saxony, Prussia, Poland, Austria, Bavaria, and Württemberg, till I entered France, I never saw, either in the bakers' shops, in the hotels, or in private houses, a loaf of wheaten bread.' In southern Italy, in addition to poverty, governmental oppression was obvious, with swarms of tax-collectors roaming the region, intent on collecting even the most trivial sums. On the Vistula, barges could be seen, hastily built on the river bank, carrying wheat on a floor of straw, and uncovered, floating with the current down to the Baltic, steered by half a dozen men. The city of Buda had unpaved streets, and was connected with Pest (across the Danube) only by a bridge of boats, which was removed before each winter to escape the ice. Even where there was prosperity in Europe, it was likely to be of an almost medieval kind, peasants going out each morning with the crudest implements to till their scattered strips of land.[2] Such travellers were likely to argue that only in Britain did energy, skill and ambition earn their reward, in the shape of public esteem and an opportunity to take a dignified part in public life.[3]

At the end of the century, contrasts between north-west and south-east Europe could still be seen, but the latter region was no longer backward in

[1] John H. Clapham, *Economic History of Modern Britain*, I chapter v, is a masterly survey.
[2] William Jacob, *Report on the Trade in Foreign Corn and on the Agriculture of the North of Europe*, 17–18, 36 (the quotation); Crauford T. Ramage, *The Nooks and Byways of Italy*, 28, 43–4, 184–5; Elliott, *op. cit.*, I 64; Banfield, *op. cit.*, I 165.
[3] Samuel Laing, *Observations on the Social and Political State of the European People in 1848 and 1849*, 307–9.

the same absolute sense. Budapest, for example, now had six great bridges, telegraph and telephone linked it with other cities, and two hundred steam-boats were in service on the Danube.[1] Roads and railways were beginning to open up much more backward districts, and changes in government also played their part. In Bosnia and Herzegovina, the Turkish past was clearly to be seen in the minarets in every town, in the water-carriers on station platforms, and in the rolls of carpet which travellers carried to add comfort to the hard wooden seats of fourth-class railway carriages. But government offices no longer kept records in a leather bag, shaken on to the floor when-ever a document was required: Austrian civil servants received orders by telegraph and kept organized files.[2]

Beneath the surface impressions of travellers, several great changes can be singled out, though their causes, and the relations between them, cannot always be identified exactly. In very broad terms, they shared one charac-teristic, that they tended to spread across the continent from north-west to south-east.

From starting-points which cannot be dated with precision, but which were certainly later in eastern Europe than in the British Isles, the rate of population growth sharply increased.[3] With disastrous epidemics and crop-failures less common, fewer people died and fewer people felt it necessary to postpone marriage. Death-rates began to fall earlier than birth-rates. With the notable exception of France, more young people came forward to seek work and food, and to found families of their own. Britain and Scandinavia were affected very early in the nineteenth century: by its end, annual rates of natural increase of more than 10/1,000 were common in the extreme east and south of Europe, and in some districts were much higher than that. Such increase could sometimes be met by taking more land into cultivation, by changing the use of what was already cultivated, by developing alternative occupations, or by a movement of people over short distances in search of more lucrative work. Sooner or later, however, a threat to traditional standards of living was likely to emerge. Men would then be faced with a choice between resigning themselves to great hardship, working against heavy odds towards social change, and uprooting themselves to seek improve-ment overseas. The decision depended on many factors: a region's resources, its economic and political leadership, its access to news of the outside world,

[1] Guillaume Vautier, *La Hongrie économique*, esp. 93–5; Hammerton, *Countries of the World*, II 1014–36; W. B. F. Bovill, *Hungary and the Hungarians*, 30–2, who underlines the change from waggon travel, and town pumps in the squares from which women fetched water in tubs, to piped water and electric trams, all within fifty years.
[2] Miller, *op. cit.*, 116, 133.
[3] This topic, and the topics which follow, will be dealt with more fully in my next two chapters, where references will be given.

and the state of transport. It depended also on the calculations, and on the temperament, of individual men.

Some European countries – Norway and Sweden for example, and Serbia – had not known a full feudal order. In the remainder of Europe, the formal emancipation of the rural population occurred in the nineteenth century. German states which had known Napoleonic influence changed first, then Austria-Hungary, then Russia and Roumania. Legal improvement, however, did not guarantee advance in all spheres of life. Lords commonly took a large proportion of land for their own use. They had to be paid compensation for the rights they had surrendered. Many people who had ranked as less than full peasants received little or no land. With freedom, too, there appeared a growing inequality, as energy, initiative, lack of scruple, or luck enabled some men to forge ahead of their neighbours. If the social order did not necessarily change to everyone's advantage, neither did emancipation automatically bring about technical progress. In Bohemia, traces of the three-field system could be seen after 1900, and the same was true of other parts of Austria-Hungary.[1] Consolidation of land into individually operated farms, the prerequisite of technical advance, occurred in Sweden in the context of a quite different social order; in the German states it usually followed emancipation, but slowly and under separate procedures; in Russia it occurred very late and only under intense governmental pressure. On the other hand, there were regions of Europe – the eastern parts of Prussia for example, and central Hungary – where very modern practices were to be found by the end of the century, including considerable mechanization. These were regions of extreme social inequality, where masses of mainly landless people depended for employment on highly privileged gentry or nobles, who were specializing in capitalist production for a market.

The spread of modern transport was revolutionary. In the 1850s, a rail network linked the chief towns of England; extended from the Channel ports through Paris to the Spanish border and Marseilles; joined Paris with Switzerland and Bavaria; spread out from Vienna to Trieste, to Cracow and Warsaw, to Budapest and Temesvar; while there were many lines in northern Germany not yet effectively linked with a European system. Before the end of the nineteenth century, branch lines had made the network much more complete; Alpine tunnels, and bridges over great rivers, had made continuous

---

[1] Emily G. Balch, *Our Slavic Fellow Citizens*, 40–1; Geoffrey Drage, *Austria-Hungary*, 76, 306, 321. Doreen Warriner, *Contrasts in Emerging Societies*, 307–8, records the primitive system of shifting cultivation long surviving in Serbia. Woods, *op. cit.*, 190–91, found three-cornered wooden ploughs, and carts with solid wooden wheels, in European Turkey. An able modern treatment of the whole subject, though regrettably condensed, is Werner Conze, 'The Effects of Nineteenth-Century Liberal Agrarian Reforms on Social Structure in Central Europe', in F. Crouzet, W. H. Chaloner and W. M. Stern, eds., *Essays in European Economic History 1789–1914*, 53–81.

travel possible; and Italy, the Iberian peninsula, Russia, and the Balkans had received all the railways they were ever to have.

Changes such as these made possible both the export of food from country to country and the development of industrial cities and zones. In Germany, where at the beginning of the century craftsmen had journeyed from town to town, early in their careers, in medieval fashion, and which in the 1830s had seen the first coalmine sunk in the Ruhr and the first steam-engine installed by Krupp, there grew up the continent's greatest and the world's second greatest industrial system. There were smaller industrial regions in France, northern Italy, and Russia. Even Budapest became an industrial centre of some note. At the middle of the century, when many towns retained the fortifications of the Middle Ages or of Vauban's time, Samuel Laing could remark: 'The city on the Continent stands like a guard-ship riding at anchor on the plain, keeping up a kind of social existence of its own, shutting her gates at sundown, and having privileges and exactions which separate her from the main body of the population.' Cities had a tangle of narrow streets, even if some were in process of installing gaslighting. In Cracow, there were several quarters, each with its own customs, some with their own boundary walls.[1] Fifty years were enough to sweep away walls, slums, and the isolation of cities. London, for example, saw the development of the Embankment, such improvements as Charing Cross Road and Kingsway, the building of great railway stations, bridges across the Thames, railways on the surface and below, electric trams in the streets.[2] On their smaller scale, Paris and Vienna shared similar improvements, while many of the more purely industrial small towns of England, Germany or Poland were almost wholly new creations. The question remained, whether towns and industries could generate enough opportunities to absorb the pressure of surplus population on the land.

Along with economic change, stimulated by it no doubt, but also in some degree facilitating it, went changes in institutions. In the first instance, much of the stimulus came from France. Although Napoleon had been defeated and the old dynasties restored, his reforms of codes of law, administration, land-tenure, weights and measures, largely survived the withdrawal of his armies. When France overthrew the Bourbons in 1830, she held up a new model of government for the imitation of European liberals; and her

[1] Laing, *Observations*, 274; Kohl, *op. cit.*, 499–500. See also the pre-Haussman map in Galignani's *New Paris Guide* of 1837; but the best illustration I know is the relief model of Strasbourg in that city's *Musée historique*.
[2] Theodore C. Barker and Michael Robbins, *History of London Transport*, I, esp. maps of transport and expansion on xxviii–xxix, 47, 136–7, 185, 212–13, 258–9. For city-planning, the name of Bazalgette should be ranked with Haussman, though the effect achieved was less theatrically symmetrical.

influence continued at least as late as 1848. The revolutions of that year spread to Austria-Hungary the rural reforms which elsewhere had closely followed Bonaparte's rule. At the middle of the century, of course, the contrast was enormous between the England of Peel and the Austria of Metternich, the Naples of Ferdinand II, or the Russia of Nicholas I. Where Britain and France had genuine, if narrowly-based, parliaments, Sweden, Prussia and the Austrian provinces had legislatures which gave the propertied classes far heavier representation than peasants or townspeople, and gave those legislatures little, or only precarious power. The nobility and gentry still dominated much of Europe. A British traveller compared society in the German states with the typical theatre there: princes and nobles in the boxes, middle class in the stalls, the masses nowhere to be seen. In Hungary it was enough to look like a gentleman to enjoy substantial advantages: 'a good coat frees its wearer from toll'.[1] It would be foolish to suggest that Europe had become democratic by 1914. Russia had only just begun experimenting with central representative institutions. Hungary was essentially a one-party state dominated by the gentry. Austrian provinces and some German states retained class privilege in their local assemblies. The German Empire, which had what seemed a democratic parliament, reserved important classes of business to the executive, or voted vital measures for terms of years, or wrote important policies into the constitution. Austria showed some of the same characteristics. Yet, apart from women's political rights, democracy was a fair description of the institutions of Britain, France, the Low Countries, Scandinavia and Italy.[2]

A further development in nineteenth-century Europe was national self-consciousness. Nationalism in Italy and Germany, leading to political unification, is familiar enough; but the same tendency can be found among one after another of the Slav peoples of eastern Europe, while Zionism is only a special version. Although mainly unsuccessful in Austria-Hungary down to 1914, nationalism achieved the setting up of some Balkan states; and everywhere it set men questioning established ways.

New technology, new institutions, and new ideas wrought damage as well as improvement. In Brinley Thomas' phrase, 'an innovation necessarily leaves a trail of victims in its wake'.[3] Agricultural regions throughout the world were brought into competition. The English landlord lost rent; the

[1] Laing, *Notes of a Traveller on the Social and Political State of France, Prussia. . . .* 270–71; Paget, *op. cit.*, I 244; and see the early sections of David Thomson's *Europe since Napoleon*.
[2] The most convenient authority, and interesting because contemporary with the systems described, is Abbott L. Lowell, *Governments and Politics of Continental Europe*. On Turkey, with its endless stamping of passports and the police escort for travellers, see Woods, *op. cit.*, 69–70, 73–5, 123–4.
[3] Thomas, *op. cit.*, 24.

labourer in eastern Europe found less work; the Kansas wheat farmer saw his prices fall. Junkers could protect themselves, and Populists could at least agitate: many European peasants lacked power, felt the state alien, and could not therefore turn readily towards planning reform. Those who went into industry were subjected to unfamiliar discipline in factories, and had severe strains put upon their family life.[1] Railways, too, for all their obvious advantages, dealt a blow at some men's interests. The coachman at the beginning of *Felix Holt* was no doubt foolish to think so much of accidents. Given his trade, he was not being wholly fanciful when he exclaimed, 'Why, every inn on the road would be shut up,' and when he 'looked before him with the blank gaze of one who had driven his coach to the outermost edge of the universe, and saw the leaders plunging into the abyss.'

V

The very same forces, originating so largely in north-west Europe, that were disturbing, or liberating, the old world and opening up new lands to human exploitation, were simultaneously creating transport links between them. The frustrated or oppressed could now seek new opportunities with growing ease, instead of facing their continent's changes with resignation or reacting against them in blind revolt.[2] They could move from country to town, from one town to another, from province to province, but also over-seas; and they could hope to return if they became disillusioned. Information flowed more regularly. People responded more quickly. Journeys became habitual for thousands and millions, which at the beginning of the century would have been unimaginable to any but the boldest of men.

In the 1830s, a year of exceptionally heavy emigration saw fifty thousand people from the British Isles go to the Canadian colonies, a few thousand more to the Australian, seventy thousand Irish, British and Germans to the United States – movement to Latin America still being negligible. Such figures would soon look insignificant. A peak year in the early 1850s would find more than 400,000 Europeans entering the United States, one in the 1880s nearly 650,000, and several early in the twentieth century more than a million. By that time, Canada was sometimes receiving a quarter of a million in a year, and Argentina not many less.

Districts of Europe would continue to differ widely one from another in their response to change, and millions of men would take their separate decisions, whose inner character we shall never know. What would remain

---

[1] See, on England as the pioneer, Sidney Pollard, *The Genesis of Modern Management*, chapter v.
[2] Eric J. Hobsbawm, *Primitive Rebels*, has examples of revolts from Spain to Russia.

true was that most districts would continue sending more people to the United States than anywhere else. Because of its early start, the variety of its economic growth, the freedom built into its institutions, and the abundance of its commercial and intellectual links with Europe, that country continued to possess advantages that no other overseas land could rival.

CHAPTER TWO

The First Fifty Years

I had heard about America. Its rich soil and industrial advancement right now offered a home, a means of livelihood, and an independent life to thousands of Europeans who in one way or another had found their hopes dashed in their own homelands. Labour, no matter in what sphere, if only honest, was no disgrace. There, every faithful worker had in his civic reputation his certificate of nobility. Conventional prejudices, class interests, petty public opinion, and the harlequin-wraiths of changing fashions did not cling to one's coat tails or dog one's heels.

> *A Pioneer in Northwest America 1841–58: The Memoirs of Gustaf Unonius* (translated by Jonas Oscar Backlund and edited by Nils William Olsson), I 5–6.

It is never enough to think of migration continent by continent, or nation by nation. Emigrants were not Europeans or even Germans and Swedes: they were dwellers in a Norwegian valley, or in the Black Forest district of Württemberg; they were Slovaks from the northern hills of the Kingdom of Hungary, Bulgarians from Macedonia, or Ashkenazite Jews from the western provinces of Czarist Russia. No scholar, of course, will ever be able to comprehend all this local detail. The countries of nineteenth-century Europe were not all equally thorough in keeping statistics. Not all that were kept can be believed. All people were not equally literate, equally capable of leaving their own evidence of what they did and why. The nearer, however, we approach districts and individuals, the nearer our study will be to the truth.

I

Because their statistics were the most useful in Europe from the earliest date, the logical starting-point is Norway and Sweden. Their emigration experience, moreover, has such striking features, which can more or less be explained, that the region may serve as a model, so to speak, against which to test what was going on elsewhere.

The central phenomenon to be explained is the sudden upsurge of emigration, almost all of it to the United States, in the late 1860s, after much smaller emigration for the previous twenty years from Sweden and forty from Norway. In 1867, Swedish emigration numbered 9,000; in 1868 it was 27,000, and in 1869, 39,000. In no year before 1860 had there been as many as 5,000 emigrants: in no year from 1868 to 1914 were there as few as 10,000, in only fourteen were there fewer than 20,000, and in eight years there were more than 40,000. The decade of highest emigration was the 1880s.

Both Norway and Sweden experienced a rapid growth in population. In Norway where, from the late eighteenth century to the end of the nineteenth, the birth-rate was around 30/1,000, the death-rate fell, from about 1815, to a level usually somewhat below 20/1,000, and below 15/1,000 after 1900. In the 1860s, the annual natural increase was about 13/1,000, and in some later decades it was 15/1,000. Birth- and death-rates in Sweden were both somewhat higher, and the rate of increase was a little lower; but the figure of 11/1,000 for the 1860s was higher than in most of Europe, and it rose a little further in the 1880s. This pressure of population, as all observers of Norwegian figures have noted, did not move in perfectly uniform fashion. Rather it advanced in waves, as one high proportion of young people came forward, reproduced themselves, and put their children into the labour-market twenty years later. The crests of these waves came in the 1820s, the 1850s, and the late 1870s and 1880s.[1]

Even after rapid growth, towns accounted for little more than one-seventh of Norway's population at the middle of the century, and in Sweden for not much more than one-tenth. Scattered rural manufactures in Sweden, fisheries in Norway, lumber-camps in both countries, could do something to absorb surplus population. Agriculture, however, had to play the major part. Totally new land was taken into cultivation, and in Sweden, where opportunities were better, this process was especially marked in the 1840s. Improved methods of farming or of rural organization helped to feed more people; and this meant in particular the enclosure movement and the introduction of the potato. Although in both countries there was a strong tradition against breaking up freehold farms, it was found possible to arrange for small holdings, or for gardens attached to cottages, for a rapidly growing class of dependent persons whose labour could be used by farmers. In Sweden, where more than a million additional people were absorbed into farming between the middle of the eighteenth century and the middle of the nineteenth, the number of freeholders increased very little, that of farm-

[1] *Cambridge Economic History of Europe*, VI Part I, esp. tables on 61, 69; Dorothy S. Thomas, *Social and Economic Aspects of Swedish Population Movements, 1750–1933*; Michael Drake, *Population and Society in Norway, 1735–1865*. Brinley Thomas, *Migration and Economic Growth*, 310–11, shows the high intensity of Swedish emigration relative to population: in 1881, 1882, 1887 and 1888 it exceeded one per cent, came close to that in 1869 and 1892, and rose above 0·7 per cent in 1902 and 1903. In the early 1880s and the early 1900s, Norway showed an intensity of emigration slightly higher still.

servants living-in grew fast, and that of crofters and cotters increased most of all, nearly quadrupling in the same period.[1]

Inheritance practices, it is true, varied from place to place. In some parts of Norway a farmer handed over his land at his eldest son's marriage, in others when he became too old to work, taking an allotment or a pension paid in kind. In 1845 there were 46,000 such pensioners. Elsewhere, a son might buy or rent land of his own, returning to the original farm on his father's death. Everywhere, if the eldest son were disabled, or if he chose not to accept his inheritance, another child could take the farm. The heir, whoever it was, compensated his brothers and sisters in cash or in kind. A single purpose lay behind all these arrangements: to keep holdings intact, for Norway's free-holders were so full of pride as the leading social class that at funerals long genealogies might be recited.[2]

The difference between the standard of living of these classes was great. Samuel Laing describes the farms of Norway in the 1830s, with their clusters of solid buildings and abundance of food. Hans Mattson describes the dignified routine of a similar class: tailors and shoemakers calling near Christmas for the year's order, presents for the village schoolmaster, baskets of food sent to the poor. A crofter who emigrated from Varmland, however, and who wrote his reminiscences in 1881, lamented his poor soil, meagre crops, high taxes, and the need to travel long distances to winter work in lumber camps in order to make ends meet. The poorest rural classes in Sweden, down to early in the present century, were living in wretched shacks, sometimes even lacking a privy.[3] Pressure of population made it harder for the dependent classes to improve their lot. Freeholders thought themselves in danger of sinking to a lower class. Increasingly, younger children found their compensation inadequate, when farms of their own, or alternative jobs carrying a satisfactory status, were harder to find. An heir who had worked for his father without wages, and who took over a farm

[1] Drake, *op. cit.*, esp. chapter 3; Dorothy Thomas, *op. cit.*; John S. Lindberg, *The Background of Swedish Emigration to the United States*; Florence E. Janson, *The Background of Swedish Immigration*, esp. chapter iv, 'The Landless Agrarians'.

[2] Rigmor Frimmenshend, 'Farm Community and Neighbourhood Community', *Scandinavian Economic History Review*, IV (1956), esp. 65–8; Karen Larson, *A History of Norway*, 335, mentions a genealogy of sixteen generations. At mid century, as Janson, *op. cit.*, and Theodore C. Blegen, *Norwegian Migration to America*, 8, show, Sweden had, in very round figures, 100,000 freeholders, 100,000 crofters, 45,000 cotters, 70,000 married and 600,000 unmarried farm workers, the last-named usually sons and daughters of the other classes; while Norway had 78,000 freeholders, 58,000 crofters, 25,000 tenants, and 200,000 labourers mostly living-in, as well as the pensioners referred to.

[3] Samuel Laing, *Journal of a Residence in Norway*, 29–31, 44–51, 96–8, 300, 309; Hans Mattson, *Reminiscences*, 5–8 (referring to the 1840s); Janson, *op. cit.*, 307; Vilhelm Moberg, *When I Was a Child*, 14–15, 144–5; and the illustrations in Gustav Sundbarg, *Sweden, Its People and Its Industry*, many of prosperous farms, one of a shack on 611.

already in debt, could not easily grant his father the accustomed pension, compensate his brothers and sisters, and still save the estate from the moneylenders.[1] Although it is harder to prove, it is at least possible that the economic changes of the nineteenth century raised people's estimate of a proper standard of living: if so, the strain was all the greater.

It needed only a temporary worsening of agricultural conditions to produce a breaking-point. This occurred in very striking form in Sweden, a monetary crisis quickly followed by crop failure and by local famine in the winter of 1867-8. It was at that stage that large numbers of people were willing to seek improvement abroad: the dependent and labouring classes especially, but many farmers and farmers' sons too. Workers in decayed handicrafts joined the movement, as did townspeople, many of whom may have been recent arrivals from the land, disappointed in their expectations. Over long periods of time, however, large towns in Sweden offered self-improvement to inhabitants of neighbouring rural counties, which showed a lower rate of overseas emigration than might otherwise have been expected.[2]

Later in the century, the pressure began to ease. As methods changed, and especially as transport improved, rural industries and towns both grew. In Sweden, in 1930, one-third of the people lived in towns, and the number of industrial wage-earners had increased sixfold since 1870. By the twentieth century, after migration had almost removed crofters and cotters, and farming had been reorganized with a work-force of landless labourers, the rural population itself began to show a lower rate of increase. But until such forces could come into operation, the emigration movement went on. Even when the birth-rate began to fall, the death-rate continued to do so; and in the 1880s Sweden's natural increase was of the order of 50,000 a year. Emigration removed a large number of those who had been the excess births of the former generation; but the surplus of the 1880s could not all be absorbed at home in the early 1900s.[3]

---

[1] Emigrants' reminiscences quoted in Blegen, *op. cit.*, 115-16.

[2] On the famine, see Janson, *op. cit.*, 223. Adolph B. Benson, in his little autobiography *Farm, Forge and Philosophy*, 3-4, records that hardship was so severe that his grandfather had to move to another part of his province to seek work, while his grandmother took a load of baskets to sell in Germany, leaving the younger children in the care of a ten-year-old daughter. On the social composition of the emigration, and background factors, see Dorothy Thomas, *op. cit.*; and two articles by Ingrid Semmingsen, both in *Scandinavian Economic History Review*, 'The Dissolution of Estate Society in Norway', II (1954), 166-203, and 'Norwegian Emigration in the Nineteenth Century', VIII (1960), 150-60.

[3] Dorothy Thomas, *op. cit.* In the 1880s, emigration was three-fifths of Sweden's natural increase and two-thirds of Norway's: a misleading expression, of course, since it was the surplus of an earlier generation that was being removed. My discussion, naturally, masks many fluctuations which Thomas records: low emigration when Sweden was prosperous and America depressed, high when America was prosperous and Sweden depressed. Even more important, my arguments do not explain innumerable local phenomena. Investigations of these, especially by researchers

The reason for the mass emigration of the late 1860s is clear enough. It remains to account for the decades of preparation, before economic difficulties had become acute. There is much evidence to suggest that the first people to uproot themselves were those who felt some powerful ideological discontent towards their country's society. Resentment at the concentration of power in the hands of officials, at imperfect representation in the legislature, at high taxes, and at military service, played some part.[1] Even more important was hostility to the organization, practices and beliefs of the established Lutheran church. Deeply devout people, in both countries, disliked the domination of the church by the university-educated clergy, many of whom were trying to make their religious teaching more rational in the eighteenth-century style. Such people desired a return to the classic theological position of the Reformation, and more freedom for the laity to read the Bible together, hold prayer-meetings, and if they felt inspired, to preach. In Norway, such attitudes were especially associated with the followers of Hans Nielsen Hauge. In Sweden, people with such views were commonly called 'Readers', who stayed within the church's framework; but there were also small sects, like that of Eric Janson, Some were influenced by Baptist and Methodist ideas from abroad; and the earliest Norwegian emigrants were somewhat influenced by Quakerism. Long afterwards, similar people, in the Mission Friends movement, helped to swell Swedish emigration.[2] Once dissenters had begun to leave, their personal example, and the news they sent back from America, began to influence the ideas of those at home. Norway shows clearly how this worked before the 1860s: beginning immediately around Stavanger, emigration spread eastward to the counties round Oslo Fjord, then northwards, though the northernmost counties were still only slightly affected.[3]

Such pioneers were not necessarily indifferent to economic changes; but their other discontents were crucial.[4] Articulate about their motives, taking very seriously the social and political attractions of the United States,

---

based on the University of Uppsala, are reported in *Nordic Emigration: Research Conference in Uppsala, September 1969*, my copy of which I owe to the kindness of Dr Sune Ackerman.
[1] Blegen, *op. cit.*, 164–5, 324–30; Larson, *op. cit.*, 433–6; Sundbarg, *op. cit.*, 175–83; John A. Hawgood, *Modern Constitutions*, 53–8.
[2] Lindberg, *op. cit.*, 1–43; George M. Stephenson, *Religious Aspects of Swedish Immigration*, esp. chapters 2, 3, 4 and 7; Vilhelm Moberg, *The Emigrants* (on the atmosphere of religious revival); Einar Molland, *Church Life in Norway, 1800–1950*, esp. 3–20, 36–57.
[3] Blegen, *op. cit.*, 357–61.
[4] Janson, *op. cit.*, 151–2, notes that in the 1850s prosperity seems to have outweighed dissent, and emigration fell. A very clear picture of the relationship appears in the history of Dutch emigration. Neglect by the clergy of Calvinist dogma, the merely ethical view of Christ they commonly

emigrating usually in families, and emigrating never to return, they were models of that 'Old Immigration' about which American writers were to become so enthusiastic later in the century. Scandinavia produced a 'New Immigration' too: masses of young single people – by 1900 two-thirds were single in both countries' emigration, and most were between fifteen and thirty years of age – following a simple economic routine or even a family fashion, much less likely to settle on American land, and considerably more likely to return home.

II

In Scandinavia, population pressure acted upon a relatively prosperous rural economy. A severe but temporary shock displaced large numbers of farmers and labourers. The continent-wide agrarian difficulties of the 1880s, and continuing population pressure, together with forces of persuasion from America, kept the emigration movement going during the decades before alternative opportunities at home could come into existence on a sufficient scale. In Ireland, on the other hand, similar pressures acted on a poorer economy and a very different social order. The result was an emigration so heavy as to reduce population, not merely slow its growth; but by the end of the century, relative to population, the intensity of Irish emigration fell below the Scandinavian level.

Between the mid-eighteenth and the mid-nineteenth century, Irish population grew no faster than did that of England or of Norway; and, considering the supply of fertile soil, rural opportunities could hardly be judged as poorer than in the latter country. Ireland's problem was especially one of social organization. Eastern districts were more prosperous than the coast of Connaught, but poverty and underemployment were very wide-spread and there was little incentive to improve the land. Very commonly, absentee owners operated their estates through professional agents, and these either leased to farmers in the English sense, or leased the entire estate to a middleman who in turn sub-let to very small tenants at the highest rent he could exact. Such people were too poor to undertake im-

---

preached, their abandoning of the catechism, and their re-writing of the hymn-book to emphasize their rationalist beliefs aroused much discontent, just as did similar tendencies in Scandinavian Lutheranism. Secession was widespread in the 1830s. Emigration, however, started only in the next decade, when the countryside suffered an economic crisis, though Seceders were then very prominent in the movement. Religious discontent may have weakened the ties binding them to their country, but it needed a further blow, and a material one, to push them to their final decision to leave. See Henry S. Lucas, *Netherlanders in America*, esp. chapter ii; and, for an individual experience, James Moerdyke's account in Lucas' *Dutch Immigrant Memoirs and Related Writings*, II 408–16.

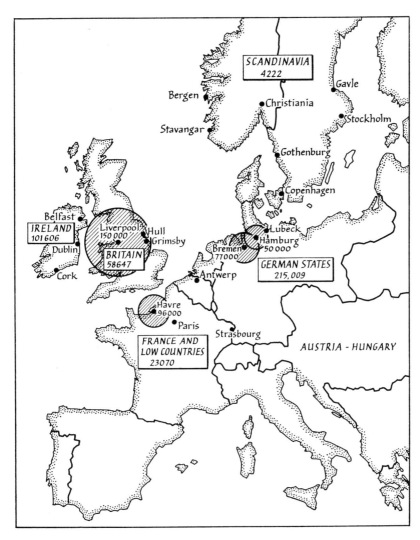

Map 3   EUROPEAN EMIGRATION
TO THE U.S.A., 1854

4

provements, too poor to be assessed for rates, so poor, very often, that they had to spend part of their time working for others, if work could be had. Some men needed to take, by the year, a tiny potato patch at a competitive rent, a system called *conacre*. In western districts, yet another system was widespread: landlord or middleman leased land to a group of people, who then made their own detailed arrangements for scattered plots of arable, sometimes reallocated periodically, and for grazing rights on rough pasture. Only in the north did tenants have any right to reward for improvement, when their leases fell in. The problem that dominated much of Irish rural life was this: the only way to manage an estate more efficiently was to displace large numbers of people. When one middleman's lease expired, the 240 acres were found to have upon them 39 cabins and 176 tiny fields. The landlord's decision to rationalize involved making five farms, ejecting thirty families, and keeping only a small minority of the people as labourers. Evictions were likely to lead either to pauperism or to agrarian outrage.[1]

Apart from certain eastern districts of Ulster, no industrial zone offered opportunities away from the land. Although Irish towns had flour mills and sawmills, breweries and distilleries, ropewalks and tanneries, and small factories for candles and soap, textiles were in decay; and the number of people employed, in relation to population growth, could not be large.[2] There were few mines and almost no railways. For many Irishmen, a better supplement to local resources was seasonal migration to the richer farming districts of their own country or to England and Scotland, where they could hope to save £5 with which to pay their rent, yet still return home in time to dig their potatoes.[3] Even with this outlet, the situation of the poorer classes was dangerous, particularly so in the degree of their dependence on a single crop. As Aubrey de Vere testified in the 1840s, 'the circulating medium of Ireland for agricultural purposes is to a great extent the potato; that is to say, the labourers are paid in conacre, which means in potato. They are paid by the farmers, who would be utterly unable to pay them in any other manner.'[4]

[1] *Parl. Papers 1845*, XIX, Royal Commission on Law and Practice . . . Occupation of Land in Ireland, Q. 28, 29 – though there are other examples. On land-tenure in general, see E. R. R. Green's chapter in R. Dudley Edwards and T. D. Williams, *The Great Famine*; and on the poverty of western districts, T. W. Freeman, *Pre-Famine Ireland*.
[2] Anthony Marmion, *The Ancient and Modern History of the Maritime Ports of Ireland*, esp. 425-33 (Sligo) and 450-67 (Galway).
[3] *Parl. Papers 1847*, VI, Select Committee of the House of Lords on Colonization from Ireland, Q. 2312-16; Johann G. Kohl, *Ireland*, 14-15; James E. Handley, *The Irish in Britain 1798-1845*; Barbara M. Kerr, 'Irish Seasonal Migration to Great Britain 1800-1838', *Irish Historical Studies*, III (1942-3), 365-80. In 1841, the flow was said to exceed 57,000.
[4] *Parl. Papers 1847*, VI, Q. 4705, while the following sixty questions and answers give further information.

Travellers in the 1830s and early 1840s were unanimous about the widespread wretchedness of the people, though of course they found a few well-kept towns, some fine country houses, some well-fed farmers. In county Wicklow, a cabin was seen in 1834 with no bedstead, no equipment at all except stool and cooking pot, lacking even the embers of a fire. The occupier worked for sixpence a day; he had a wife and five children; and his pig had just been taken for arrears of rent. At Waterford, the same traveller found pigs' backbones being sold for 1½d or 2d a pound, all the animals' better parts having been exported. At Limerick, he found slums as bad as the worst rural cabins. At Galway market, many women lacked shoes or stockings. To Newport market girls came many miles to sell five eggs, and hundreds of women stood about trying to sell no more than an apron-full of wool. As his coach left Ballina for Castlebar, he counted twenty-seven beggars around it.[1]

Irishmen in large numbers found it necessary to cross the Atlantic, probably 850,000 of them between 1815 and 1845, most of them from the northern counties or the south-east.[2] Then came failures of the potato, starvation and disease, a disaster so complete that, even had the British government been less bound by Poor-Law dogma, the system of distribution would have been so primitive as to doom any relief measures to failure. An enormous emigration was the result. It took only eight years, after 1846, for nearly a million and a quarter Irish to rush to America; and in 1854, when the first flood was already over, the Irish contributed one-quarter of all European emigrants to the United States.[3] Yet extreme hardship did not automatically bring about flight; nor did the western districts, notorious for the smallest farms, the poorest housing, and the lowest literacy, contribute the major share. Ulster, indeed, contributed few emigrants during the Famine, for there was little destitution in the east and in the west there was strenuous philanthropy. The west of Catholic Ireland saw emigration only when landlords gave help, and in Mayo where a few tenants were able to sell their crops and leave before their possessions could be seized for rent. Elsewhere, immediately after the potato failure, emigrants were chiefly very small tenants in districts where landlords were evicting, or rather more substantial men where pauperism was so high that the poor-rate threatened

---

[1] Henry D. Inglis, *A Journey through Ireland during . . . 1834*, I 30–2, 64, 302–4, II 22–34, 99–100, 119.
[2] S. H. Cousens, 'The Regional Variations in Emigration from Ireland between 1821 and 1841', *Transactions of the Institute of British Geographers*, XXXVII (1965), 15–29, confirms William F. Adams, *Ireland and the Irish Emigration to the New World from 1815 to the Famine*, esp. 413–14.
[3] On the Famine, see James Hack Tuke, *A Visit to Connaught in the Autumn of 1847*; Edwards and Williams, *op. cit.*, which has a long chapter on emigration by Oliver MacDonagh; and Cecil Woodham-Smith, *The Great Hunger*.

them with ruin. Much of this continued after 1850; but some labourers also found resources to go. The western counties remained quiet, for the land was so poor that few landlords bothered to evict, and so many people had died that marginal land was fairly easy for even poor men to obtain.[1]

During the decades that followed, emigration rates showed little difference from one province to another, though there was considerable variation between single counties. In the relatively prosperous east, eviction continued in the interests of consolidating farms; and no town, not even Dublin, could absorb the displaced people. The local response, over a long period, was delayed marriage among those who remained, and therefore a low birth-rate. In the west, on the contrary, land remained available until the 1860s, and the number of very small holdings did not fall. This made possible a continuation of fairly early marriage, a high birth-rate, and a rate of natural increase of 12/1,000 in large areas, and over 15/1,000 in a few districts. Emigration on a large scale occurred only at times of crop failure, when families moved out, including many of the more prosperous who sold their land and escaped the poor-rate. By 1881, however, western small holdings were in decay, the rate of natural increase was considerably nearer that of the east, and, in time, western population declined. In the last decades of the century, the proportion of population emigrating from Connaught was only very slightly higher than from Munster and Leinster. By that time, Irish emigration was overwhelmingly one of young single people, especially between the ages of fifteen and twenty-four; and in some years girls were in the majority, bound, presumably, for domestic service in American cities.[2]

Although the ingenuity of modern scholars can discover much about the economic and social causes of Irish emigration, one factor existed which for some people must have overridden the influence of such material hardships or frustrations. In the second half of the nineteenth century, remittances flowed into the country from early emigrants, and this on such a scale that the entire movement of people could easily have been paid for from that source alone. Not all the money, of course, was used for that

[1] S. H. Cousens, 'The Regional Pattern of Emigration during the Great Famine, 1846–51', *Transactions of the Institute of British Geographers*, XXVIII (1960), 119–34; and 'Emigration and Demographic Change in Ireland, 1851–1861', *Economic History Review*, Second Series, XIV (1961), 275–88. Such people looked destitute on arrival in America: that does not prove that they were Ireland's poorest.

[2] S. H. Cousens, 'The Regional Variations in Population Change in Ireland, 1861–1881', *Economic History Review*, Second Series, XVII (1964), 301–21. Annual figures appeared in *Parliamentary Papers*; summaries from 1851 are in the 1911 *Census of Ireland*; valuable figures appear conveniently in Walter F. Willcox and Imre Ferenczi, *International Migrations*, I 730–3, II 276–9, and in Brinley Thomas, *Migration and Economic Growth*, 270, 278–81. Even Leinster and Ulster were losing nearly one per cent of population each year about 1880. Apart from the young people mentioned, most emigrants were aged 25–34.

purpose, for large sums were absorbed in the maintenance of old people or in the improvement of farms. Remittances, however, must have made many young people independent of the poverty of their immediate families, and must have given them a more genuine choice of going to America or staying at home.[1]

III

Irish emigration reverted to small proportions towards the end of the nineteenth century. Population had been greatly reduced, changing patterns of marriage guaranteed an absence of population pressure in the future, and even mainly rural opportunities were now roughly sufficient. The German states, and the Empire founded in 1871, saw a very different development, one that demonstrated what could happen to emigration when very big and very sudden industrialization took place.

In the 1840s, the German rate of natural increase was very slightly lower than in Scandinavia, though in some states it exceeded 10/1,000. With the death-rate falling and the birth-rate staying high (over 35/1,000 until 1900), the increase was greater in the 1890s and early 1900s than ever before. Rates which in the Rhineland and the Polish districts approached 20/1,000, and were high everywhere, brought about an annual surplus of births, before the Great War, of 800,000. Emigration, however, did not follow the expected pattern. Eighteen times between 1852 and 1892, it exceeded 100,000 persons a year, almost all going to the United States. Three times (1854, 1881, and 1882) it exceeded 200,000; and in 1854 it was half of all European emigration to America. From 1893, however, it dropped to a much lower level, and never recovered, only twice rising above 50,000 in the years down to 1930. Although the immediate fall in 1893 can be explained by American economic depression, the movement's course thereafter can only have reflected conditions at home.[2]

Statistics compiled at the time, and American census figures a little later, show that most German emigration, in the 1840s, 1850s and 1860s, went from western and south-western districts. The American census of 1870 showed more surviving immigrants from Bavaria, Baden, Württemberg and Hesse than from the whole of Prussia, though that state itself had large western districts.[3] Several economic and social causes may be suggested, but

[1] Arnold Schrier, *Ireland and the American Emigration, 1850–1900*. More detailed treatment will be given to remittances in my chapter 5.
[2] Willcox and Ferenczi, *op. cit.*, II 315–16, 333–8, deal with population growth, rates of emigration, and problems of handling German and American statistics.
[3] A. Legoyt, *L'émigration européenne, son importance, ses causes, ses effets*, 15–34 (on p. 28 he shows that, for the period 1844–58, more than one-third of Prussia's emigrants went from the Rhine province, and more than half from Rhine and Westphalia, though Saxony and Pomerania, and even Silesia, were already contributing). See also *U.S. Ninth Census*, I 338–9.

the sheer fact of easy access to the Atlantic, the stimulus of a higher degree of modernization, even perhaps some memory of the emigration of the previous century, may all have contributed to a movement of people so much greater than from the eastern provinces.

In some western districts, certainly, pressure of population caused subdivision of land beyond anything that could provide a tolerable living. One village near the junction of the Neckar and the Rhine, described by a traveller in the 1840s, had common pasture and 1,400 acres of arable. Of the latter, one-third was in twelve plots each of more than 20 acres; about one-fifth was in twenty plots of between 10 and 20 acres; another fifth consisted of 41 parcels of 5 to 10 acres; there were 142 plots of 1 to 5 acres and 163 of less than 1 acre each. With such holdings, and paying heavy taxes, many people were forced to work at some domestic trade, or serve as labourers on other men's land. Such a village was not necessarily typical of a whole region. Peasants in the German states, as elsewhere, made strenuous efforts to keep workable farms intact. Most of them avoided intestacy, which would have led automatically to division among children. Where the law required portions to be left to children, by will, a peasant might arrange for his heir to compensate his brothers and sisters rather than divide the land, even, on occasion, going through a fictitious sale, at a sacrifice price.[1] If however, children without land also found their employment opportunities threatened, if farmers with secondary occupations found these undermined, and if expectations about standards of living rose, many Germans would look for opportunities beyond their own borders. Very briefly, Russia was considered as a possible emigration field.[2] Usually, the abundant land of America seemed more promising.

In the 1830s, an English traveller, in the mountainous region between Saxony and Bohemia, found workers incensed at the influx of British cottons and linens, which they alleged were being sold at local fairs as German products. True or false, there was soon abundant evidence that local industries were in danger. Although Germans had won back some of the export trade lost during the Revolutionary and Napoleonic Wars, smaller spinning establishments began to give way to larger factories using modern machinery. In weaving, into which, as in Britain, unskilled workers continued to pour, standards deteriorated and goods became harder to sell. British linens,

---

[1] Thomas C. Banfield, *Industry of the Rhine*, I 206–9; *Parl. Papers 1870*, LXVII, Report of H.M. Representatives ... Tenure of Land ... Europe, esp. Part I, 78–90 (Württemberg), 307–87 (Prussia), II 188–221 (Grand Duchy of Hesse). The reports make clear how much of the open-field system had survived, and how many people needed a secondary occupation even when they held a plot of land.
[2] Mack Walker, *Germany and the Emigration, 1816–1885*, chapter 1.

produced at a higher level of efficiency, drove down prices; then linens were threatened by cotton goods whether German or British. Wages were steadily forced down. Weavers suffered in diet and health. In 1844 the crisis in Silesia was severe enough to bring about revolt.[1] This was an extreme case, and there were places where handicrafts flourished as late as the 1860s, especially when low-quality goods were in local demand. Nevertheless, 1848 not only saw mobs plundering castles and destroying records, but brought about events that proved discontent among several kinds of worker. Conventions of individual trades were held, then general congresses of master craftsmen and journeymen, all protesting against the economic liberalism of the Frankfurt Parliament. They demanded restriction of machinery and factories, guild control over the admission of workers, bank credit for small craftsmen; and the journeymen pressed in addition for workers' representation in the running of guilds. More violent action occurred. Waggoners tore up lengths of railway track. Rhine steamboats were fired on by men whose older carrying trades were being superseded. Much machinery was wrecked. All these events showed fear of the sweeping away of traditional safeguards and routines in their own trades, and of the impact of competition from new and more advanced technology.[2] The danger may have been felt first by the more specialized workers. It could not pass by people whose lives were part agricultural, part industrial, people whose standards of living were already under threat. It is worth noting, too, how many craftsmen there were whose fortunes depended upon the prosperity of farming. Even if competition from factory-made implements and carts came later, blacksmiths, carpenters, wheelwrights and many others would suffer whenever agriculture became depressed. At that point, however, their skills, and the cash resources they were likely to possess, might make them more mobile than peasants.

In the 1840s Thomas Banfield noticed that, in Rhineland village inns, conversation seldom turned to politics. Probably he was right, for although peasants played a part in purely local affairs, in no German state, then or much later, did they have a voice at higher levels of government. Such constitutions as the states possessed were regarded as the gift of princes. Ministers were responsible to monarchs, not to legislatures. Narrow franchises, indirect elections, open voting, were all characteristic.[3] Peasants and

[1] G. R. Gleig, *Germany, Bohemia and Hungary in 1837*, II 108; Gustav Schmoller, *Zur Geschichte des deutschen Kleingewerbe in 19en Jahrhundert*, esp. chapters 4 to 9: I acknowledge help from Mrs Margrit Healey in using this work.
[2] Theodore C. Hamerow, *Restoration, Revolution, Reaction*, esp. 107–9, 164–5; Edwin Clapp, *The Navigable Rhine*, chapter 3.
[3] Banfield, *op. cit.*, I 85–6; Abbott L. Lowell, *Governments and Politics of Continental Europe*, I 334–77.

craftsmen may have been not at all resentful over such matters, but the same was unlikely to be true of the policies which resulted, whether high taxes, military service, or restrictions on the marriage of people who could not prove economic independence.

Underlying conditions of these kinds made it certain that, sooner or later, a large emigration would take place. The exact timing, however, depended on some special event which would jolt men from their routines, would cause them suddenly to decide that their future at home could not be believed in. The commonest of such events, in the middle decades of the nineteenth century, was a crop failure, with high food prices. In 1846 the potato failed in the south-western states. There were poor harvests in the early 1850s. In some places the result was an increase in fore-closures of farms, in others, hunger riots. In either case, emigration was stimulated.[1]

There was no economic unit called 'Germany', any more than there was a political unit until 1871. In the years around 1850, the imperfect figures of those days showed that for a short time Württemberg was losing one per cent of its population each year, and the Rhenish Palatinate even more. Baden and Hesse both lost heavily. Even as early as the 1850s, however, states further east were affected – the Mecklenburgs, for example, and the eastern districts of Prussia – and this was a very different social world. Here, commercial farming was the preoccupation of the estate owners: in other words, the prime concern was to cut costs rather than maintain people at an accustomed standard of living. Often, former serfs worked in person on an estate, or sent their women into domestic service, in return for a cottage, a garden, and the right to collect firewood. As crops became more specialized and techniques more efficient, even this impressed the lords as involving too much social responsibility. More and more they relied on day-labour, employed seasonally. As population grew, so the lords, fearing an excess of poor people, limited house-building in order to restrict marriage.[2] Protest was useless, for the same men controlled government and land. Many of Prussia's communes were organized as manors, with the lords appointing mayors. The Mecklenburg duchies, with separate Grand Dukes but a common Landtag, were particularly indifferent to popular rights. Town

---

[1] Walker, *op. cit.*, esp. chapters ii and vi.

[2] *Parl. Papers 1870*, LXVII, Reports of H.M. Representatives ... Tenure of Land ... Europe, Part I 313–14, 354–61, Part II 177, 184–5. Walker, *op. cit.*, 162–7. A table in Witt Bowden, Michael Karpovich and Abbott P. Usher, *An Economic History of Europe since 1750*, 280–1, shows how different were patterns of landholding. In Posen, Brandenburg and Pomerania, farms of less than nineteen acres made up no more than five or six per cent of the land area: in the Rhine and West-phalia provinces, the proportions were 36·8 and 18·8 per cent.

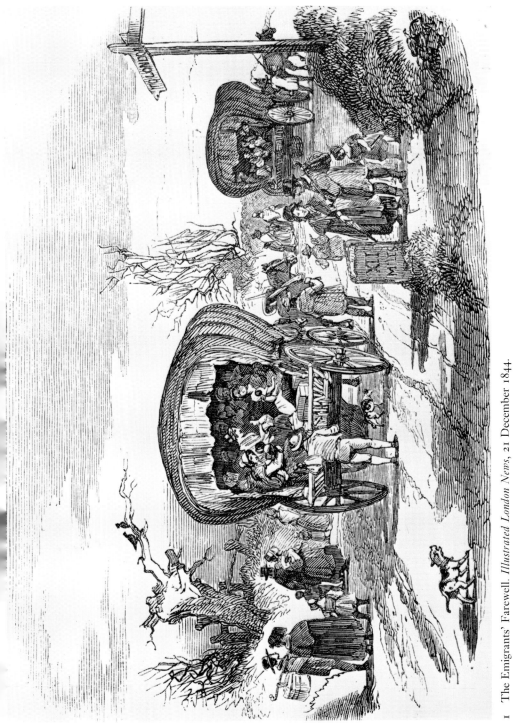

1　The Emigrants' Farewell. *Illustrated London News*, 21 December 1844.

2a The passenger broker's office
Illustrated London News, 10 May 1851.

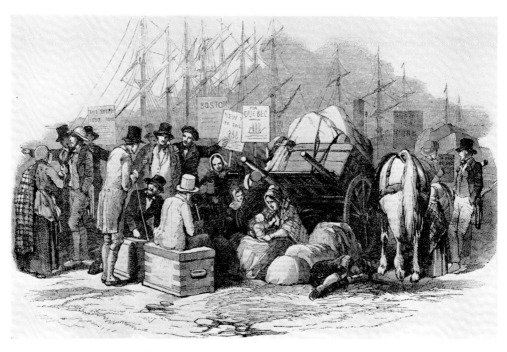

2b Emigrants at Cork. *Illustrated London News*, 10 May 1851.

3a Embarkation. National Maritime Museum.

3b Departure. National Maritime Museum.

4a   Emigrants on deck. National Maritime Museum.

4b   The Steerage. National Maritime Museum.

deputies were consulted only on business that directly concerned them; and the other house of the Landtag was made up of knights.[1]

One other force was operating by the 1870s. In the early years of that decade, emigration from the German Empire as a whole was running at the rate of 219 per 100,000 of population. The proportion in Silesia was 58, in the Rhineland 60, in Saxony 78, in Westphalia 95, and in Brandenburg 115. The south-western districts of the old emigration had proportions very close to the national average. Certain other provinces had far higher rates: Oldenburg 327, East and West Prussia 329, Hanover 247, Schleswig-Holstein 460, Mecklenburg-Strelitz 481, Posen 531, Pomerania 695, and Mecklenburg-Schwerin 944. Such figures reflect a pattern of industrialization and urban growth. Purely agricultural regions, and especially those dominated by the large estate, were sending out great numbers of emigrants: urban and industrial zones were absorbing a far larger proportion of the population increase of immediately surrounding provinces. By 1890, a further stage was reached. In the forty years following 1871, the urban sector in Germany's population rose from one-third to three-fifths, and cities of more than 100,000 people increased some 12 million. In the twenty-five years before 1907, the agricultural population fell slightly, while workers in trade and transport, mining and manufactures, and their families, rose by 14 millions. Population was now being drained away from the north-eastern farming areas to the industrial zones. While the rankings of provinces' ratios remained similar down to the Great War, the magnitudes became very much smaller. By the late 1890s, the ratio for the Empire was 53/100,000: by the period 1910–14, no more than 32/100,000.[2]

The picture, of course, has been painted with strokes much too broad. Small districts, individual villages, no doubt differed widely. Account has to be taken of the work of Hamburg and Bremen agents advertising the improved shipping of their ports. Letters poured in from America, telling of the fortunes of friends who had settled there. Nor should attention be limited to economic factors more or less measurable. Like Scandinavia and Holland, German states experienced conflict between established churches and devout people who resented rationalist tendencies and insisted on the importance of conversion, the value of devotional reading of the Bible, and

[1] Lowell, *op. cit.*, I 308–33 (Prussian local government), 364–8 (the Mecklenburgs).
[2] William H. Dawson, *Industrial Germany*, 10–16. Useful migration figures are in Willcox and Ferenczi, *op. cit.*, II 349–51: between 1840 and 1910, the eastern provinces lost half their natural increase by migration, within Germany or overseas. *Parl. Papers 1893–4*, XXXIX, Royal Commission on Labour, Part II 133–7 and map on 149, shows the move from the north-east to cities as early as the late 1880s. An interesting close-up view of internal migration is Koellmann's chapter on the population of Barmen, in David V. Glass and D. C. Eversley, *Population in History*, 588–607.

the importance of the laity. In Prussia and several other states, these grievances were connected with resistance to a reorganization of religion under state influence, combining Lutheran and Reformed into single churches, to the scandal of those to whom Reformation differences were real. There is some evidence that people of this kind, like the Old Lutherans, were pioneers in the emigration from the eastern regions, though their example would not in itself have produced a mass movement, had not other and more universal conditions been present.[1]

<h2 style="text-align:center">IV</h2>

The facts and figures thus far set down tell much about the forces shaping emigration. Population pressing upon resources, paucity of alternative local opportunities, the growth of the United States and the spread of knowledge about that country, improvements in European and Atlantic transport: these were the influences at work. But it was people who emigrated, people who moved not as pawns in a game but as individuals who made judgments in the light of their understanding of the world around them. This is the side of emigration history which can never be fully known. There is room here for religious fanaticism, for desire to escape family or citizen's obligations, for personal disappointments, for ambition, optimism, or despair. People moved when, in their own minds, they decided that the way of life they wanted, whether viewed as a standard of living or a good society or a godly congregation, could better be promoted by going to America than by staying at home. Had it not been for the underlying forces analysed here, they would not have reached the point of making such judgments, or if they had, they would have been unable to act on them. But they could make mistakes, could be swayed by neighbours' views, could be victims of moods. Rather than trying to disentangle all these multiple reasons for emigrating, it is better to assume a somewhat composite, undifferentiated set of reasons. Above all, we ought to recognize how little we can ever know.

A British student of emigration would be happy to say that important clues could be found, significant gaps in the evidence filled, from the records of his own country. Doubt begins, however, when he observes how little attention to his problems has been paid by earlier authors. In his great *Economic History of Modern Britain*, Sir John Clapham devotes five or six pages to emigration in each volume. Hansen's *Atlantic Migration* has no more than a dozen pages on Britain. Books, such as those by Johnson and Carrothers, which seem wholly concerned with British emigration, prove to

[1] Andrew L. Drummond, *German Protestantism since Luther,* esp. Part I chapter 4 on Rationalism, Part II chapter 2 on the Prussian Evangelical Church.

be little more than descriptions of government policies, or of private projects which produced very small results. None of this means that the writers were incompetent. It means, rather, that evidence about British emigration is in a state quite remarkably unsatisfactory for an advanced country, the pioneer in development towards the modern industrial way of life.

We know, with some certainty, the characteristics of British economic and social life in the nineteenth century. Industrialization occurred early, beginning with textiles. By the middle of the century, half the population was urban. From that time, there was a tendency, in many places, for rural population to show an absolute decline. Those who were left on the land were not peasants, but landlords, farmers and labourers, together with craftsmen performing services for those groups. Industry, and the export of manufactures, went on growing throughout our century; but from the 1880s it is possible to detect, overall or in some sectors, some slowing down, some reluctance to innovate, some surplus of labour. Britain was overtaken, as an industrial producer, first by the United States, then by Germany, though in the field of overseas investment she remained in the lead. During the same period, population as a whole continued to grow very fast. While France grew from 36·5 millions to 41·5 millions between 1850 and 1910, Britain almost doubled, from 22·3 millions to 42·1 millions. As late as the 1880s the birth-rate was still 33/1,000. It fell to 24/1,000 before the Great War; but the death-rate, a little below 20/1,000 in the 1880s, fell to about 15/1,000. The resulting natural increase averaged some 15/1,000 a year in the 1870s, and remained as high as 11/1,000 even in the first decade of the twentieth century. This meant an annual surplus of births in the 1880s, for example, of some 400,000 a year, a high proportion of these people coming into the labour market in the years around 1900. Unlike Germany, Britain was not a sufficiently dynamic industrial society to absorb such numbers. Instead, there was a net loss, by emigration, of almost two millions between 1871 and 1911; and the peak of emigration was reached just before the Great War.[1]

Despite certain difficulties of definition, we know the fluctuations in British emigration. Figures were high either side of 1850, though for those years separation between British and Irish cannot be guaranteed. They were high around 1870, very high in the 1880s, very high again in the decade before the Great War. Such peaks represent from half of one per cent to nearly one per cent of population emigrating in a year. This is considerably higher than the German peaks, but much lower than the peaks for Ireland,

[1] *Cambridge Economic History of Europe*, VI Part I, 61; William Ashworth, *Economic History of England, 1870–1935*, 41–2, 191; John H. Clapham, *Economic History of Modern Britain*, III 448; John Saville, *Rural Depopulation in England and Wales, 1851–1951*.

Norway, or Italy. In 1851, Ireland sent out more people than did Britain in 1882, from a population not much more than one-fifth as large; and even in 1912 Italy, with a population several millions smaller, sent more emigrants overseas, as well as 300,000 to other countries within Europe.[1]

The causes of such fluctuations are clear enough. Each boom in overseas investment stimulated such economic development as to attract people who were surplus to Britain's economic needs at home. In between such booms, investment in home industry and construction increased, and the equivalent 'surplus' tended to pile up as urban and industrial population.[2]

The relative attraction of the several emigration fields is also clear. In the 1830s, British North America was often in the lead. In the early 1850s, the Australian colonies, with their gold rushes, were most prominent. For several decades the United States was the favourite destination – 50,000 in a peak year of the 1850s, 100,000 in one of the 1880s – though in the 1870s Australia, and in the 1880s both Canada and Australia, took substantial shares. In the early 1900s, and again after the Great War, Canada took the lead, though in a few years Australia too was ahead of the United States. The broad reasons for these changes are easy to see. From about 1840 to about 1890, the scale of the United States involved such opportunities for British emigrants as to outweigh any but the most special booms elsewhere. After that, however, America's demand for skilled labour could more and more be met from domestic sources, and for unskilled labour from southern and eastern Europe. At the same time, with the help of British investment, Canada experienced a long period of expansion, and just before 1914, after a very long depression, Australia enjoyed a boom.[3]

With a rather wider margin of probable error, something can be said about the occupations of British emigrants, in general and in relation to the several countries to which they went. Discounting business and professional men, a high proportion of whom were travellers rather than emigrants, three main categories can be found in emigration to the United States. Between 1876 and 1880, nearly 15,000 British farmers emigrated, between 1881 and 1885 nearly 18,000, and in the following five years some 19,000, though after that a rapid decline set in. The American census of 1890 found more than 90,000 British-born farmers surviving, though some of them, no doubt, had worked their way up from a lower status. From one-fifth to one-third of British emigrants were counted as skilled workers, and this meant from 50,000 to 100,000 in each five-year period. The remainder fell

[1] Figures are conveniently presented in Brinley Thomas, *op. cit.*, 282.
[2] *Ibid.*, esp. Part III.
[3] *Ibid.*, 57, 304.

into the category of labourers and servants; and American figures for the same years suggest that these two sub-divisions commonly stood in the ratio of three to one.

This is not the whole story. In years of booming emigration to America, the proportion of labourers and servants rose above sixty per cent. In one of low emigration, like the later 1890s, the figure fell below forty per cent. In other words, rapid economic growth in the United States did not merely draw in more immigrants: it provided an especially large number of opportunities for the lower grades of worker. Further interesting features emerge if our view is broadened to include the other receiving countries. In the last quarter of the nineteenth century, the United States was always the destination of something like three-quarters of all emigrating labourers and servants from Britain, commonly of two-thirds of the farmers, and of three-fifths to two-thirds of skilled workers. Such were the effects of the scale of that country's growth. From the mid 1870s to the mid 1880s, however, Australia took most of the farm labourers, its opportunities reinforced by assistance plans. In the late 1880s, when more than 86,000 farm workers emigrated in five years, the United States took most of them. Australia usually took one-fifth of the farmers, Canada as many only in 1886–90 and 1896–1900, when total numbers were small. From 1903, Canada was a rival of the United States in taking the agricultural classes, and was far ahead from 1911: Australia drew ahead of the United States immediately before the Great War. Throughout those years, Canada was far ahead in taking labourers, though Australia took very few. As for skilled workers, the United States kept its lead until 1910, when Canada went ahead and Australia rose to a strong third place.[1]

Occupation figures can be looked at in yet another way. If we compare the relative position of certain categories of worker in the emigration, and then in the total employed population of Britain, interesting results appear. Even in the years of high emigration of the early twentieth century, skilled workers as a group emigrated less than their numbers in the population would lead one to expect; and of engineering and metal workers this was particularly true. The discrepancy was greater still among transport workers. General labourers and farm workers emigrated in disproportionately large numbers, even in the 1890s; and this played a substantial part in the halving of the number of farm labourers between 1851 and 1911.[2]

[1] *Ibid.*, 60–61, 268–72; and 62–7 show differences between England, Scotland and Wales. Because of the way in which passenger lists were compiled (the raw material of the printed statistics), it seems to me likely that the category 'labourer' was always overstated.
[2] N. H. Carrier and J. R. Jeffrey, *External Migration: a Study of the available Statistics, 1815–1950*, 126, set against the emigration figures.

Beyond this, information must come from sources less complete. On individual industries, a good deal of work has been done, based on the trade press and governmental sources within the United States rather than on emigration figures. Rather obviously, such sources involve a bias in favour of skilled workers; but no one denies the importance of that group, particularly in American industry in the third quarter of the nineteenth century. The central finding is that British skilled workers tended to move to the same occupation in the new country that they had practised in the old. Cotton and woollen workers moved from the North of England to New England, miners from South Wales to Pennsylvania, granite workers from Aberdeenshire to Vermont, pottery workers from Staffordshire to Ohio, Cornish copper miners to copper, iron and lead deposits in Michigan and elsewhere. Many such people moved back and forth across the Atlantic as the relative movement of the trade cycle suggested that earnings would be better on one side or the other.[1]

Various forms of sampling can add a little to our knowledge. The practice, especially in the Middle West in the later part of the nineteenth century, of compiling county histories with large biographical sections, can enable the scholar to see further into the lives of many British emigrants than any statistical or industrial source permits. Thus one can begin to see how many people were already mobile before emigrating, and how many industrial workers were able to change, or change back, to life on the land after reaching America. The bias is obvious, in that only the more successful settlers were recorded in this way; but there is no reason to suppose that the bias varies greatly from time to time or from place to place; and in this field every scrap of evidence has value.[2]

However much sampling is done, we shall still know little about the precise grade of employment that emigrants had occupied within an industry. We shall be unable to estimate their exact standard of living. We may remain unable to say whether they had been employed in a primitive or an advanced sector of an industry. Except where Cornish miners or Welsh tinplate workers became so numerous as to leave clear traces on American records, we may seldom know whether emigrants came from a rising or a declining British trade.

Such considerations should make us cautious about the whole study of

[1] Rowland T. Berthoff, *British Immigrants in Industrial America*, 32, 38, 54–5, 58, 78–81; Frank Thistlewaite, 'The Atlantic Migration of the Pottery Industry', *Economic History Review*, Second Series, XI (1958), 264–78.

[2] Important work on this subject will soon be published by Dr Charlotte Erickson. Some sources even permit, for the small sample, analysis of districts of origin, e.g. rural and urban distribution, which, in general, the passenger lists, and therefore the printed figures based upon them, do not contain.

emigration. There are limitations of comprehensiveness and accuracy, even in statistics better kept than those of British emigration. Some emigrants, highly skilled, were aiming at an industry abroad where their talents were even scarcer and better rewarded. Some were reacting to the movements of the trade cycle. Some were reacting to a particular dislocation in their lives, for example a wage-cut or a strike.[1] Others may have been trying to get back to the land after a period of disillusionment in industrial towns. Others again may have responded to family troubles, or taken advantage of a remittance or a prepaid ticket sent by some friend. All these possibilities we ought to project from the study of British emigration to that of emigration as a whole, recognizing that many details, in the interplay of broad economic movements and individual circumstances and calculations, are not known and can never be known.[2]

[1] Berthoff, *op. cit.*, 20–1, 32, 65, 70.

[2] The reader should be warned that my chapter does not exhaust the range of possibilities in Europe. One country did not experience the intense pressure of population which I have emphasized so much. France's population rose from $27\frac{1}{2}$ millions at the beginning of the nineteenth century to $36\frac{1}{2}$ millions in 1850 and then, with Alsace-Lorraine lost, to nearly 40 millions on the eve of the Great War. The Revolution had changed the social organization of agriculture; and although technical progress was far from dramatic, there was plenty of fertile land to which a free peasantry could feel attached. Any surplus of country people could be absorbed in industry, in towns, or in North Africa; and the urban population grew fast in the second half of the century. Few Frenchmen left French territory altogether, and those who did seem to have come mainly from the mountainous fringes of the south-east and south-west. Evidently the political upheavals of the century had little effect on emigration: perhaps institutions offered the discontented opportunities for change at home. See the rather unsatisfactory section in Willcox and Ferenczi, *op. cit.* I 105–14, 672–85, II 201–18.

CHAPTER THREE

South-Eastern Europe
Drawn In

'Italy is for us whoever gives us our bread.'
> Labourers in the Simplon Tunnel, quoted Robert E.
> Foerster, *The Italian Emigration of our Times,* 22.

'Here one is a dog, in America a gentleman.'
> Slovak peasant, quoted Emily G. Balch, *Our Slavic*
> *Fellow Citizens,* 118.

Towards the end of the nineteenth century, new areas of Europe were brought within the pattern of Atlantic migration. In the year ending 30 June 1882, when more than 648,000 Europeans entered the United States, 250,000 of them came from Germany, more than 100,000 from Britain, 76,000 from Ireland, 64,000 from Sweden, 29,000 from Norway, 11,000 from Denmark. Norway's contingent was almost as large as Italy's, the same as Austria-Hungary's, and far bigger than Russia's. Twenty-five years later, when, at the all-time peak of its immigration history, America received 1,200,000 people from Europe, the British Isles, Germany and Scandinavia combined sent little more than 200,000. Austria-Hungary now contributed a third of a million, Italy nearly 286,000, Russia a quarter of a million, and even the Balkans 70,000. Americans began to speak of a 'New Immigration' as a social problem. More modern writers, while rejecting such nativist implications, are inclined to discuss the concept of 'peasant Europe'. Neither expression sufficiently describes the variety of what is known to have occurred, nor the uncertainties that persist.

I

The classic treatment of peasant life is to be found in the introduction to Thomas and Znaniecki's great book *The Polish Peasant in Europe and America.* That life was governed by traditional obligation and by a desire for stability, not by the wish to innovate, to maximize profit, or to raise the standard of living by the ceaseless multiplication of wants. The centre of obligation was the family and its land. Each member of the family was expected to contribute labour; each was entitled to a living. The family's head was the temporary steward of a perpetual inheritance. Marriage was negotiated between families, and its material terms were so arranged as to permit the partners to continue life at the traditional level or within reach of it. A small number of families made up a village, with institutions, conventions, and obligations of its own. Beyond family, farm and village lay a less familiar and a less friendly world. Higher social classes, governments, law, all touched peasant life from time to time. Their operations were to be endured, evaded or, if possible, by influence or bribes, used for family ends. Life in the family, and life within formal external institutions, went on surrounded by the world of nature, in part deeply familiar, in part mysterious. In one aspect, it was the local environment, over which men had rights, but to which at the same time they owed the obligation of responsible behaviour. In part, however, it was capricious and violent, with secrets to which a few wise men and women had access. Anyone who worked hard, who observed Christian rites as well as magical prescriptions, might hope for good fortune; but even he knew, and was resigned to, the ultimate arbitrariness of fate.[1]

On such a basis of practice and belief stood a superstructure of detailed observance, which to the urban, modern and sophisticated student seems to display considerable uniformity over many parts of Europe. In the 1860s, a traveller in Transylvania witnessed a wedding. Several couples were married at the same time, and elaborate invitations were carried to all the relatives. Simple gifts were exchanged between brides and grooms. The service was followed by a long feast, each dish prescribed by custom, in the preparation of which the whole village had taken part. On the second day, each bride appeared in the different clothes laid down for matrons, and with hair cut short.[2] In the Greek district of Euboia, forty years later, another traveller described another wedding. The bridegroom and his friends took mules to the bride's village. Collecting her, they formed a procession. It was headed by a piper; the bride's male relatives accompanied her; and the mules carried her dowry of rugs, quilts, distaff and spindle. The ceremony comprised betrothal, followed by the Orthodox crowning for the marriage itself; and afterwards the young men fired a salute outside the church. The bridegroom went first to his house: the bride followed. Arrived there, she smeared honey on the door, then hurled a pomegranate against it, hoping for good

---

[1] William I. Thomas and Florian Znaniecki, *The Polish Peasant in Europe and America* (two-volume edn), I 87–315. See also Wayne Vucinich, ed., *The Peasant in Nineteenth-century Russia*, chapters 1 and 3.
[2] Charles Boner, *Transylvania, its products and its people*, 489–95.

5

luck if the seeds stuck fast. The door opened, she received bread and salt, touched water and oil, and only after that was she lifted over the threshold. Inside, she sat with her dowry around her. She was required to remain silent during the feast that followed. Five days later, her father gave another feast and dance.[1] Although scholars agree that economic foundation and social tradition both began to crumble towards the end of the nineteenth century, and that a new emphasis came to be placed upon the small family unit, on personal choice, on individual success, on economic calculation, yet survivals of the older order could be found even in the era of Herbert Hoover and Ramsay Macdonald. In Carniola in 1932, dowries were still carefully considered, a matchmaker was employed, and a wife was chosen with an eye to the suitable management of property, though because of the economic depression the feast was curtailed to a single day. At about the same time, a death in the family was the occasion for another set of rituals, though a visitor from America was carefully told that these no longer reflected beliefs. Candles and prayer-book were placed near the corpse, and a bowl of holy water allowed callers to sprinkle it. The dead man's hands were clasped round a crucifix; in the pockets of his best clothes were placed pipe, tobacco-pouch and snuffbox, together with a few coins. The mirror was turned round. Outside the door was placed a tub of water so that Death could wash his scythe. At an all-night party, the guests played dominoes and ate ham, sausage, horseradish, bread, and fruit, and drank cider, prune brandy, or wine.[2]

While the attachment to family and land was widespread and long-lasting, and while peasant practices long continued to mingle the magical and the Christian, there were many differences from one part of the continent to another. Just as there was little similarity between the terrain of the High Tatra and that of the Hungarian central plain, between the limestone hills of Croatia and the marshes at the mouth of the Danube, so each region, each ethnic group, each village, had its peculiarities of housing, dress and custom. In the Transylvania of the 1860s, Germans were living in roomy brick or stone houses, while neighbouring Roumanians were in wattle huts in which 'you probably do not perceive a single thing in which iron has been employed. It is exactly the architecture that a shipwrecked mariner . . . would resort to . . . All that is used is what nature alone furnishes.' Not only did ethnic groups live at different material standards: they were exclusive in marriage, entered into political controversy, and kept alive the memory of past wrongs.[3]

[1] William Miller, *Greek Life in Town and Country*, 91–4. See also Lucy Garnett, *Balkan Home Life*.
[2] Louis Adamic, *The Native's Return*, chapter 2, 68–74.
[3] Boner, *op. cit.*, 239–40, 251–60.

Even if ethnic divisions were absent, regions could still look different. Northern Slovakia had two-storey wooden houses, with galleries round the first floor, and with overhanging and steeply sloping roofs of slate or tile. Further south, stone buildings were common, whitewashed and roofed with thatch.[1] Villages preserved distinctions. Their girls, for example, had recognizable styles of apron and girdle. As late as the end of the nineteenth century, village styles could be found even in an area as small as the island of Corfu.[2]

II

This characteristic peasant life, as commonly described, depended on the possession of land, and on some predictable stability in the standard of living. Great numbers of Europeans, however, were landless, or almost so. The stability of their existence was threatened by massive changes during the century, though the combination of factors, and their relative weight, were far from identical from place to place.

Greatest of all these common features was the rise in population. Its causes, indeed, and much of its timing remain less clear than in north-west Europe, for not all the countries of the region kept accurate statistics until very late in the century. The latest study of Italian population claims that early in the nineteenth century natural increase per annum was of the order of 3/1,000. In the early 1870s, when epidemics and famines had become less destructive, the rate was a little over 6/1,000. A decade later it was 11/1,000, for the death-rate fell from 30/1,000 to under 20/1,000 in the forty years before the Great War, while the birth-rate began to fall significantly only halfway through that period. Even with massive emigration, Italy's population rose by more than six millions between 1880 and 1910; for an excess of births of some 200,000 in the late 1870s turned into one of 350,000 a quarter of a century later. Congress Poland's birth- and death-rates were of similar magnitude and changed in much the same way. Population rose by one million between 1850 and 1870, by considerably more than two millions between 1870 and 1890, and by nearly three and a half millions between 1890 and 1910, emigration notwithstanding; and by the later date natural increase was running at something like 150,000 a year. There were regions of eastern Europe with very different rates: birth-rates well over 40/1,000 and death-rates at first not much lower. But if, as in Hungary and elsewhere, the death-rate fell below 30/1,000 by 1890, while the birth-rate fell only slightly, natural increase rose to formidable proportions. In Hungary,

[1] Robert W. Seton-Watson, *Racial Problems in Hungary*, 352–7.
[2] Boner, *op. cit.*, 49–52, 581–2; Miller, *op. cit.*, 92.

indeed, population rose by two millions in the 1880s alone; and a similar rate of increase went on into the present century, until reduced by emigration. In Galicia, the rate of natural increase went from 4/1,000 in the 1850s to about 15/1,000 in the early years of the twentieth century. Even when statistics are available, one cannot expect to find any uniform turning-point; but the nearest to one was probably the 1880s. In Croatia-Slavonia, a dependency of the Kingdom of Hungary, population was almost stationary in the 1870s, severe cholera epidemics twice sending the death-rate above 40/1,000. Once these were past, population rose by 200,000 in each of the next three decades, despite emigration. Dalmatia and Bosnia-Herzegovina showed similar patterns. Russia took only one census, in 1897; but estimates suggest a very rapid population increase from the later decades of the nineteenth century. The autonomous province of Finland's population, more continuously recorded, rose from two to three millions in the thirty years before 1910.[1]

The effects of such increases depended on a region's natural resources and upon its social and political system. One characteristic, however, was more or less universal in eastern Europe. Overwhelmingly people depended upon agriculture; and whereas in north-west Europe, and in Italy too, rural population stopped growing at or before the middle of the century, in eastern Europe it went on increasing long after 1900.[2] The result, it may be suggested, was that local opportunities were likely to be insufficient to cope with early population increase; and that, even if towns or industries began to grow, or agriculture began to be improved, thereafter, nothing that could be done was likely to suffice for the huge numbers coming onto the labour market from about the end of the nineteenth century.

As population rose in eastern Europe, a very widespread phenomenon was fragmentation of landholding. There were, indeed, districts where woodland or pasture could easily be taken into cultivation: such a shift from livestock to arable can be seen both in Serbia and in Croatia-Slavonia.[3] Elsewhere, peasants' efforts to preserve the unity of holdings, whatever the inheritance laws may have said, were at odds with economic realities. In some regions, conditions remained tolerable for a good proportion of peasants: in Bohemia, about 1900, some twenty per cent of them held from

---

[1] *Cambridge Economic History of Europe*, VI, Part I, esp. 61–2, 68–9; Gustav Sundbarg, *Aperçus statistiques internationaux*, 64; David V. Glass and D. C. Eversley, *Population in History*, 101–35, J. Hajnal's chapter 'European Marriage Patterns in Perspective'.
[2] *Cambridge Economic History of Europe*, VI, Part II, 605–6.
[3] Doreen Warriner, ed., *Changing Patterns in Emerging Societies*, 288, 307–8; *Cambridge Economic History of Europe*, VI, Part II, 619–20. The migration of more than four million peasants from central Russia to Siberia (Donald W. Treadgold, *The Great Siberian Migration*) may be regarded as a special case: an opening-up of new land, distant but within the same political jurisdiction.

35 to 70 acres, and another fifteen per cent from 14 to 35. In Bulgaria, on the other hand, fewer than four per cent of holdings exceeded 50 acres; nearly thirty-five per cent were of $12\frac{1}{2}$ to 50; and of the remaining small farms, 100,000 at least seem to have been of less than $2\frac{1}{2}$ acres. In Serbia, most peasants held between 5 and $12\frac{1}{2}$ acres; and in such a country even these farms might be held in scattered plots. In Carniola, more than half the holdings were of less than $12\frac{1}{2}$ acres: in Dalmatia eighty-seven per cent fell into that category. Of all regions, the one most notorious for fragmentation was Galicia. In 1900, only some 1,500 holdings exceeded 50 acres; half a million were of $7\frac{1}{2}$ to 50; 600,000 were between $2\frac{1}{2}$ and $7\frac{1}{2}$; and more than 200,000 were smaller still.[1] Such holdings, except perhaps in vineyard districts, could not sustain a family.

Such generalizations assume peasant ownership after Emancipation; and in many places, Bulgaria and Serbia above all, this was a fact. In Italy, however, a variety of tenures existed, some of them much less likely to promote attachment to the land. Some men, whom we are tempted to call peasants, operated their land on annual tenancies. Some were share-tenants with landlords finding much of the capital, and willing to renew contracts from one generation to another. Others, working on a share system, found all capital themselves and had to renew the arrangement at frequent intervals. There were small plots under peasant ownership. Peasants might hold different pieces of land under different contracts at the same time. Landlords might be active managers, or absentees leasing their whole estates to rapacious middlemen – in which Sicily somewhat resembled pre-Famine Ireland. Other estates were simply worked by gangs of labourers.[2] Landlessness was widespread, too, in Prussian Poland and in Hungary.

Hungary provides a clear example of what could happen when there converged the forces of population growth, economic modernization, and class rule. Holdings of the smallest size were most important in Transylvania, those of middle size between the Danube and the Tisza. Over the Kingdom as a whole, in 1895, well over half of all holdings were of less than 7 acres, and another third of between 7 and 28. Yet such tiny farms comprised but a small proportion of the land area. Nine per cent of all Hungary's land was in estates of more than 14,000 acres; thirty per cent in those of 1,400 to 14,000; twelve and a half per cent in those of 280 to 1,400; fifteen

[1] Will S. Monroe, *Bohemia and the Czechs*, 349; and *Bulgaria and her People*, 288–95. Jozo Tomasevich, *Peasants, Politics and Economic Change in Yugoslavia*, 203–9. Emily G. Balch, *Our Slavic Fellow Citizens*, 138. J. Zubrzycki, 'Emigration from Poland in the Nineteenth and Twentieth Centuries', *Population Studies*, VI (1952–3), 253–5.
[2] J. S. Macdonald, 'Agricultural Organization, Migration, and Labour Militancy in Rural Italy', *Economic History Review*, Second Series, XVI (1963), 61–75.

per cent in farms of 42 to 280 acres; leaving only one-third of the land for the huge number of small farms. By 1914, the biggest estates had increased their share; those of middle rank had declined somewhat; the smaller ones had changed little in relative importance. At the same time, there were some two million labourers with no land at all. Nor did political institutions hold out promise of any trend towards greater equality: quite the contrary. Local and national government alike was in the hands of a very small class. Few people were entitled to vote, and those few exercised their privilege on open hustings.[1]

It was for reasons such as these that wide differences could be observed between the standard of living of the higher and lower classes. In the second quarter of the nineteenth century, travellers were recording their impressions of the rambling but comfortable mansions of the Hungarian gentry, the abundance of their food, and the retinues with which they travelled, when peasants were lucky to have two rooms and a kitchen in their cottages. Some Croat cottages lacked chimneys, though there were magnates in their province with parks around their mansions in the English style, men who travelled by coach-and-four with liveried outriders, and whose families dressed in the fashions of Vienna or Paris. In Roumania, the nobles' homes might have kitchens with hearths a dozen feet across, stables for twenty or thirty horses, while the eighty or a hundred people in the household might include a dozen cooks and a servant for each child. Peasants, meanwhile, lived off maize porridge, fruit and milk: 'they dress like the Dacians and feed like the first men.'[2] Europe changed in many ways in the following generations. Extreme inequality, however, persisted, from Posen to the Banat, or, for that matter, in Apulia, where the elegant villas of estate owners, white with red-tiled roofs, stately trees, and fountains in the gardens, stood in vivid contrast to the labourers' wretched huts, with their earth floors, hole in the roof instead of chimney, stones for seats, and straw for beds.[3]

III

Peasants, of course, did not always confine themselves to managing flocks or

[1] Scott M. Eddie, 'The Changing Pattern of Landownership in Hungary, 1867–1914', *Economic History Review*, Second Series, XX (1967), 293–309; Seton-Watson, *op. cit.*, 240–3, 250–68.
[2] G. R. Gleig, *Germany, Bohemia and Hungary in 1837*, III *passim*; John Paget, *Hungary and Transylvania*, I 287–90; Warriner, *op. cit.*, 332–3, 156–7, 170–7.
[3] Constantine M. Panunzio, *The Soul of an Immigrant*, 23–4; and compare Phyllis H. Williams, *South Italian Folkways in Europe and America*, 38–40. Although Louis Felberman, *Hungary and its People*, was designed to present as pleasant a picture of the country as possible, 159–63 shows the very low standard of living among peasants *c.* 1890. As late as the 1930s, Adamic, *op. cit.*, 38–9, found Croat peasants burning torches indoors, possessing neither candles nor oil lamps.

tilling fields. Slovak cottages were likely to have hanks of flax hanging from their ceilings, looms prominent in the living rooms. In Carniola, peasants made hats, linens, lace, and rugs, and carved wood.[1] Elsewhere, they might perform local services as a part-time job, as did Francisco Zapponi, share-cropper in Campania, who carried wood and stone for neighbours with his mule-cart.[2] Carrying services could be on a far larger scale. Long-distance carting was carried on over the plains of Galicia, across mountain passes in Croatia, and, by Jews, in the western provinces of Russia.[3] In search of a living, the inhabitants of some relatively barren district might stay away from home for longer periods. Just as, early in the nineteenth century, Irishmen had travelled to English and Scottish harvests, so, at the beginning of the twentieth, half a million Italians moved from their southern provinces northwards to harvests or building work, Bulgarians from mountain districts to neighbouring plains or into Turkish Thrace, and Slovaks and Galicians to the wheat fields of the Hungarian plain. Posen and other eastern parts of Prussia attracted great numbers of young labourers, of both sexes, from Galicia and Congress Poland – half a million a year on the eve of the Great War.[4] More specialized workers engaged in similar wanderings. Bulgarian carpenters went to neighbouring countries: so did Serbian masons, while Slovaks travelled as wire- and glass-workers. Women from the Greek islands went to Athens as nursemaids and cooks. Marble workers from the same places were to be found in Roumania and Egypt. Italians went as labourers, or as skilled construction workers, to the Alpine tunnels, to the Suez canal, to the fortifications of Bizerta, to Balkan railways, and, later, into German industry.[5] At that point, the movement was approaching the borderline of permanent emigration.

Occupations such as these suffered heavy blows as Europe became modernized. Countries might impose restrictions on the movement of foreign craftsmen. Mechanization, as in Hungary, might reduce the number of days' work open to migrant labourers.[6] Even more important were the effects of railways. In the short run, their construction gave jobs to thousands of peasants or labourers. When in full operation, however, they undermined much local carting business, as in Carniola and Croatia and among the

---

[1] Seton-Watson, *op. cit.*, picture facing 88; Warriner, *op. cit.*, 358–9.
[2] *50 Congress 1 Session, House Misc. Doc. 572*, Part I, 93–100.
[3] Balch, *op. cit.*, 175; Johann G. Kohl, *Austria. . . .* 444–5; *Parl. Papers 1903*, IX, Royal Commission on Alien Immigrants, Major Evans-Gordon's report following Q. 13,349.
[4] Robert F. Foerster, *The Italian Emigration of our Time*, 532–3; Warriner, *op. cit.*, 247–8; Geoffrey Drage, *Austria-Hungary*, 313; Zubrzycki, *op. cit.*, 257–9.
[5] Warriner, *op. cit.*, 264–7; Adamic, *op. cit.*, 115–20; Balch, *op. cit.*, 97–9; Miller, *op. cit.*, 228–30; Foerster, *op. cit.*, 171, 175–6, 194–6, 207–15.
[6] Balch, *op. cit.*, 99: Eddie, *op. cit.*, 308.

Jews of western Russia; and it was even claimed that Dalmatian coastal shipping suffered.[1] Railways, too, linked hitherto remote regions with Europe's industrial zones. Whatever the long-term effect on the standard of living, in the short run competition undermined cottage industry. As early as the 1870s this was being felt in Galicia and Carniola; and the same process was observed in Bulgaria somewhat later.[2]

Faced with such problems, some inhabitants of Europe's countryside could find opportunities opening up in large cities. Austria's urban population trebled between 1843 and 1900. The number of people living in towns of 10,000 to 20,000 people quadrupled; while inhabitants of towns above that figure increased more than fivefold. In half a century, Vienna grew from 431,000 to almost two millions. In Hungary, Budapest grew at a similar rate. Just as Vienna drew in people from Bohemia, and from the provinces towards the Adriatic, so Budapest's mills and distilleries, waggon works and boatyards, iron works and machine shops and electrical industry, had a similar effect on rural districts. In Congress Poland, Warsaw quadrupled in population between 1850 and 1900, and the textile city of Lodz grew tenfold between 1870 and the end of the century.[3] Migration to towns, participation in an industrial revolution, might have serious disadvantages for new workers with a rural background, as they experienced new factory discipline and a new degree of overcrowding. Under certain conditions, a European peasant might feel that his uprooting, if it were inevitable, would better take him to America, with its higher rewards, even if industrial work rather than land lay ahead. More important, it must be emphasized how limited was the scale of urban growth in eastern Europe, how patchy the map of industrialization. Hungary, and the countries to the south and east, all had fewer than twenty per cent of their population urban in 1900. At about the same date, Austria-Hungary's per capita use of iron, at 68lb a year, was less than a quarter as great as Germany's or Britain's; yet Russia's and Italy's figures were lower still.[4]

Hardship, in fact, was so severely felt that in several regions of Europe outbreaks of protest occurred. Rural labour unions, some of them with a

---

[1] Balch, *op. cit.*, 175, 185, 194–5; Warriner, *op. cit.*, 355–8, Major Evans-Gordon's report in *Parl. Papers 1903*, IX, Royal Commission on Alien Immigration, following Q. 13,349, and esp. 525–6 in the manuscript pagination; I. M. Rubinow's report on Economic Conditions of the Jews in Russia, *61 Congress 3 Session, Senate Doc. 748*, esp. 290–1, 312, 328 – one-third of Russia's Jews were in trade, so the repercussions of the changes here discussed were bound to be severe.
[2] Balch, *op. cit.*, 135–7, 153; Warriner, *op. cit.*, 267–73; Monroe, *Bulgaria*, 300–2.
[3] Sundbarg, *op. cit.*, 26–8; Balch, *op. cit.*, 81; Drage, *op. cit.*, 74–5; Warriner, *op. cit.*, 98–102; Guillaume Vautier, *La Hongrie économique*, 41–2.
[4] Sundbarg, *op. cit.*, 20–1; Witt Bowden, Michael Karpovich and Abbott P. Usher, *Economic History of Europe since 1750*, 383.

revolutionary ideology, could be found in Apulia and in Sicily in the 1880s and 1890s. In 1897, labourers in Hungary fought a strike so serious that the government, in an effort to restore stability, brought in a rudimentary welfare programme. In Roumania, as late as 1907, a large-scale peasant rising took place.[1] Yet, given the institutions of the time, the relative weight of the social classes, the odds against successful protest were very great.

IV

Economic hardship was not the only burden men had to bear. Throughout the century, ethnic differences were important, and in places the resulting conflicts became increasingly severe. The ethnic map reflected in part, as in eastern Hungary, very early migrations and settlements of Germans. In part, throughout the region, it reflected economic specialization. In Bulgaria in the 1890s, Edward Dicey saw that townsfolk wore the 'dull, sombre, monotonous garb of the West,' but that, on market days, peasants arrived, walking beside their ox-carts in leggings and sheepskin coats, followed by women in embroidered jackets, layers of petticoats, and a sort of turban round their heads. 'You can realize,' he commented, 'that the East, after all, lies very close at hand.'[2] Elsewhere, far more than a simple contrast between country and town, primitive and modern, was involved. Towns were largely inhabited, trade was largely carried on, by people different in ethnic origin from those of the surrounding country. In a Slav country, townsfolk might be Germans. In Roumania they were likely to be Greeks and Jews. In other parts of the Balkans they might include Macedonians. In western Russia, Jews were very prominent in small towns.[3] Consciousness of such differences tended to grow. Intellectuals took the lead, exploring medieval history to revive the glories of long-extinct empires, and studying traditional poems and stories to raise peasant dialects to the dignity of literary languages; but some understanding of these developments seems to have filtered down to the common people.[4] This was especially likely to happen when hitherto submerged nationalities aroused, by their new consciousness, the hostility

[1] Macdonald, *op. cit.*, 67, 73; Ignatius Daranyi, *The State and Agriculture in Hungary*, 193–209. Warriner, *op. cit.*, 200–3.
[2] Edward Dicey, *The Peasant State*, 48–9.
[3] Johann G. Kohl, *Austria*, 427, 438, 443–4, 446, 465 (all on Galicia); Warriner, *op. cit.*, 91, 170–7; 314–18, 330–1. Emile de Laveleye, *The Balkan Peninsula*, 28, found a Croatian town in which Jews owned the bank, the hotel, and 14 of the 16 shops.
[4] Oscar Jaszi, *The Dissolution of the Habsburg Empire*, 248–67, 271–82; Robert A. Kann, *The Multi-National Empire*, I 131–41, 196–215 (Czechs), 271–83 (Croats), 309–17 (Roumanians), 326–32 (Ruthenians), while the clash between these and the dominant Germans and Magyars is the theme of Vol. II.

of a master race which was itself undergoing a fierce national revival. This was especially true of Hungary. In Slovakia, Croatia, and Transylvania, Magyar rule was discriminatory, local languages being forbidden public use, newspapers suppressed, intellectuals imprisoned, elections interfered with, and public employment and higher education being almost monopolized by the ruling race.[1] In Roumania and Russia, the most obvious discrimination was practised against Jews. In both countries, their economic life was restricted, their higher education hampered, while from time to time the lower classes were encouraged by their superiors to use physical force against them. After the assassination of Alexander II especially, Jews in Russia suffered restrictions on landownership and liquor-selling, quotas in the universities, expulsion from Moscow, and, between 1882 and 1906, several pogroms. Struggling to maintain even a low standard of living, conscious of hostility around them, threatened by violence, many Jews could see no hope for the future under the Czars. Some turned to trade-unionism, others to revolutionary agitation, or to Zionism.[2]

One further point may be made. Given the low standard of living of peasant Europe, the exactions of government became a heavy burden. This may have been particularly true in the newly-founded states of the Balkans, where the whole apparatus of independent monarchy, parliament, bureau-cracy and army had to be set up.[3] But everywhere, in relation to resources, taxes were high. Military service, too, was a feature of all countries. Where government was oppressive to minorities, as in Hungary, or riddled with incompetence, favouritism and corruption, as in Italy, burdens seemed especially hard to bear.[4]

V

Against such a background, though at different times and in different local circumstances, breaking-points occurred, when a few individuals decided to quit Europe. Once this had taken place, other people's minds were stirred to reflection upon their lot. To the example of movement by the few was soon

---

[1] Jaszi, *op. cit.*, 278–82, 328–31, 441–6; Seton-Watson, *op. cit.*, esp. 240–86 on politics, chapter II on education, and chapter 15 on the press. See also his *Absolutism in Croatia.*

[2] On Roumania, see Samuel Joseph, *Jewish Immigration to the United States, 1881–1910*, 69–77; while Michael Davitt, *Within the Pale*, 55–6, gives a specimen of a newspaper article developing the ritual murder theme. On Russia, see Harold Frederic, *The New Exodus*; Davitt, *op. cit.*; Norman Cohn, *Warrant for Genocide*, on the Protocols of the Elders of Zion; and, in general, Semen M. Dubnow, *History of the Jews in Russia and Poland.*

[3] Tomasevich, *op. cit.*, 143–4, 169–70; Monroe, *Bulgaria*, 300–2. Theodore Saloutos, *The Greeks in the United States*, 6–7, 13, shows that some taxes were still farmed in Greece at the end of the nineteenth century, in the fashion of the *ancien régime* in France.

[4] Lowell, *op. cit.*, I 150–231, and Norman Douglas, *Old Calabria*, chapters 5, 12, 33, are both relevant.

added their news of America. Men therefore came to see their grievances more clearly. They could see an alternative to life at home. Even those whose difficulties were not acute might become so influenced as to float with the stream, once the current had become strong.

As early as the 1850s, the Czech districts of Austria began sending emigrants to the United States, local tradition suggesting that artisans had been the pioneers, with peasants from relatively barren lands following. The movement grew through the following decades, and down to the 1870s the remaining Habsburg lands played very little part.[1] In that decade, perhaps following the example of some particularly adventurous individual, perhaps following a handful of Germans or Jews, movement began from Galicia and Slovakia. In the former province, dislocation produced by the railway seems to have contributed to the continuation and widening of the emigration.[2] In the 1880s, Croatia became affected. There and in Slovakia, emigration spread from district to district as though by force of example, though from time to time reinforced by such local crises as crop failures. The earliest people to depart did not sell their land; but once they became sure of their prospects in America they were likely to return home, collect their families, and then arrange the final break.[3] In the last quarter of the century, Greeks also began crossing the Atlantic as emigrants. A single leader can be identified, in the person of Christos Tsakonas, who went first to Piraeus from his home in Sparta, then to Alexandria, and finally to the United States, whence he returned in 1875 to persuade neighbours to accompany him westward.[4] In western Russia, the pogrom of 1882 stimulated a small migration; and the expulsion from Moscow nine years later reinforced the Jewish minority's disillusionment with Czarist rule.[5] By the 1880s, too, Italians were moving in appreciable numbers, both to Latin America and the United States. Precise local circumstances are seldom clear; but the failure of a local movement of protest might have an effect, as apparently it did in Sicily after the suppression of the *fasci* movement in 1893.[6]

What is seen, in such a sketchy narrative, is a delicate balance between several forces of persuasion. The economy of some classes in some regions was being undermined, the standard of living threatened. Opportunities were beckoning from across the sea. Against such forces were working a

[1] Walter F. Willcox and Imre Ferenczi, *International Migrations*, I 588–9; Balch, *op. cit.*, 71.
[2] Balch, *op. cit.*, 100–101, 135–7.
[3] *Ibid.*, 101, 106, 177–9.
[4] Saloutos, *op. cit.*, 24.
[5] Frederic, *op. cit.*; Mark Wischnitzer, *To Dwell in Safety*.
[6] Macdonald, *op. cit.*, 67–8, 73–4; Foerster, *op. cit.*, chapters iv to vii.

widespread attachment to land. Yet not everyone had land; and the landless, or those whose tenure was precarious, or those whose position was complicated by minority status, might prove far more rootless than the classic peasant. Janos Kovacs, with six acres under a mortgage, a few farm animals, and a family to support, concluded that he must soon be reduced to the ranks of labourers; and since in Hungary such men could 'earn only enough for bread and water... There was but one hope, America.'[1] From such beginnings, emigration could become a habit. Emily Balch, early in the twentieth century, talked to a Czech who had six children in America, as well as other relatives. A Croat schoolmistress told her that half her village seemed to have crossed the Atlantic.[2] For Slovaks as for Swedes, the journey could seem so much a routine that single girls were quite willing to undertake it.

VI

It is time to look again at the figures, especially those of the early twentieth century. Emigration from Russia, from Austria-Hungary and from the Balkans was overwhelmingly to the United States, though in the last years before the Great War Canada began to take a share.[3] From Portugal, emigration went chiefly to Brazil. From Spain, it went largely to Cuba in the nineteenth century and the very early twentieth, then largely to Argentina, the residue going to Cuba and Algeria.[4] Italian emigration was far more complex. As late as the mid 1880s, European countries made up the principal destination, when the annual total was of the order of 100,000. As the total grew – 200,000 from about 1890, 300,000 from the mid 1890s, half a million in most years from 1900 – the Americas became more important. But until 1901, Latin America was more important as a destination than the United States, and Brazil the most important country. More than 160,000 Italians went there in 1888, and over 100,000 in several other years. In the present century, the United States drew ahead, and Argentina moved into second place. In 1907, when nearly 300,000 Italians went to the United States, over 78,000 went to Argentina and only 21,000 to Brazil; but in 1906, 1910 and 1913 Argentina took more than 100,000. Even then, however, European countries took great numbers of Italian emigrants – over 276,000 in 1907, for example.[5]

[1] Robert E. Park and H. A. Miller, *Old World Traits Transplanted*, 84.
[2] Balch, *op. cit.*, 63–6, 185–6.
[3] In particular, often 10,000 and occasionally 20,000 a year from Austria-Hungary – Willcox and Ferenczi, *op. cit.*, I 364–5.
[4] *Ibid.*, I 844, 850–53. The Argentine half (in round figures) of the Spanish emigration exceeded 100,000 in 1910, 1912 and 1913.
[5] *Ibid.*, I 543, 550, 820, 828–31. In general, the emigrants from northern provinces were more

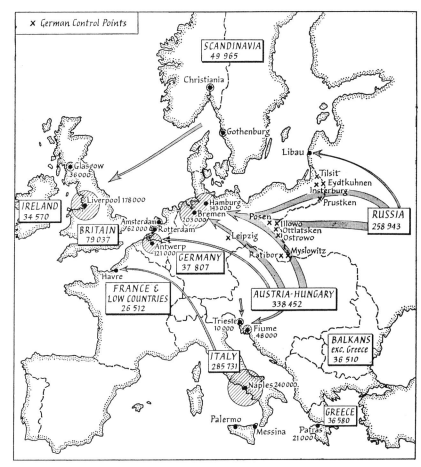

Map 4 EUROPEAN EMIGRATION
        TO THE U.S.A., 1907

Emigrants, of course, did not come equally from all districts of these countries, nor from all social groups. It is a sound generalization to regard emigration as high when it exceeds one per cent of population in a year, as it often did from Ireland and Norway. A considerable number of districts of eastern and southern Europe exceeded that figure for brief periods. Wasa province of Finland did so in the years just before the Great War. Earlier in the twentieth century, several districts of Slovakia and Galicia did so. From 1910, Spain as a whole exceeded one per cent, and Portugal even more so. As for Italy, in the years just before 1914, only Liguria and Sardinia had rates below one per cent; Latium, Emilia and Tuscany slightly exceeded that figure; most southern provinces had rates of more than two per cent, and Venetia slightly exceeded three per cent. Such high figures, moreover, were sustained for quite long periods.[1]

Most emigrants went in their teens or early adult life. Except among Russian Jews, the proportion of males was very high, highest of all among the Balkan peoples. Those who were married before emigration left their wives at home. The proportion of children was low. All this suggests that emigrants were uncertain whether their move would be permanent. Many returned home and stayed there. Many others, intentionally or otherwise, fell into a pattern almost seasonal.[2]

Occupation figures are seldom detailed enough to make possible an accurate analysis of social composition. Most emigrants, of course, were from rural origins; but from what ranks in rural society did they come? Only a few broad generalizations seem possible. Jews were more likely than most to be urban, skilled and industrial in their origins. Little more than one-seventh of Italian emigrants, however, to all destinations in 1907, could be described as industrial workers, and about one-ninth of Hungarian emigrants to the United States. Italians could mostly be classified as agricultural or construction workers, the former predominating in emigration that was more than seasonal, and among emigrants from southern provinces. Almost half of the Hungarian emigrants of 1907 were classified as farm workers, another tenth as general labourers, less than one-twelfth as farmers. Russian emigrants, in the strict ethnic sense of the term, were usually small peasants or landless labourers; but from Finland peasants and their

---

likely to go to European countries or Latin America, the great majority of southerners to the United States: Foerster, *op. cit.*, chapters viii–xii (Europe and Mediterranean lands), xiii–xvi (Latin America), xvii–xx (United States) – on 29–32, 244, he points out how much of the migration was seasonal or short-term.

[1] Balch, *op. cit.*, 103–5, 134; Willcox and Ferenczi, *op. cit.*, II 446, 532.

[2] Willcox and Ferenczi, *op. cit.*, I 396–8, 432–47, 476–7.

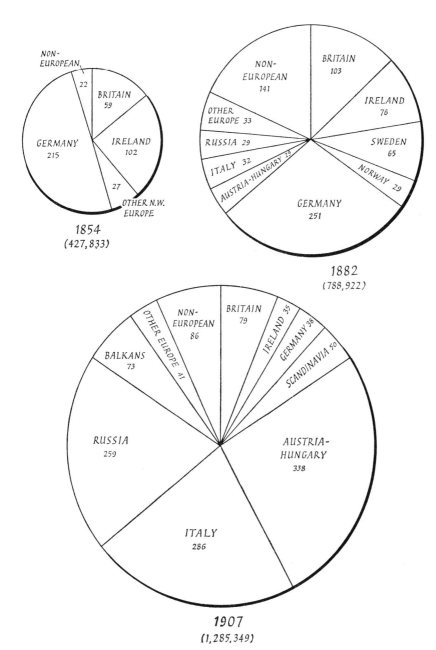

NON-
EUROPEAN
22

BRITAIN
59

GERMANY
215

IRELAND
102

27

OTHER N.W.
EUROPE

1854
(427,833)

NON-
EUROPEAN
141

BRITAIN
103

OTHER
EUROPE 33

IRELAND
76

RUSSIA 29

SWEDEN
65

ITALY 32

AUSTRIA-HUNGARY 29

NORWAY 29

GERMANY
251

1882
(788,922)

OTHER EUROPE 41

NON-
EUROPEAN
86

BRITAIN
79

IRELAND 35

GERMANY 38

BALKANS
73

SCANDINAVIA 50

RUSSIA
259

AUSTRIA-
HUNGARY
338

ITALY
286

1907
(1,285,349)

Diagram 1   American immigration:
three peak years
(*figures within circles in 000's*)

children, rather than labourers, predominated.[1] As far as the highly imperfect figures go, the impression given is one of emigration of the most vulnerable and least prosperous classes from the countryside, and in particular from the less fertile and more crowded regions.

One other aspect can be singled out. In Hungary and in the Russian Empire, as well as in the Balkans, emigration was particularly probable among ethnic minorities. Early in the twentieth century, Hungary's population was made up of 45·4 per cent Magyars, 14·6 per cent Roumanians, 11 per cent Germans, 10·5 per cent Slovaks, 8·7 per cent Croats, 5·5 per cent Serbs, and a few other groups so small as to be negligible. In the emigration of 1907, however, considerably fewer than one-third were Magyars, and until a few years before that date their importance had been far less. Germans made up about one-sixth and Roumanians one-ninth, figures roughly comparable with their ranking in the whole population. Serbs were more than one-fifteenth, Croats more than one-twelfth, and Slovaks more than one-sixth; and down to 1900 Slovaks had made up half of all the Hungarian emigration. Most emigrants from Roumania were Jews. Half the Bulgarian emigrants came from Turkish Macedonia. Almost as many Greeks came from Ottoman territory as from the Kingdom. Russia provides the best of all examples. Of her quarter of a million emigrants in 1907, 115,000 were Jews and 73,000 Poles, though at the census taken ten years before these groups made up no more than 4 per cent and 6·3 per cent of the Empire's population. Most of the remaining emigrants were Lithuanians, Finns and Germans. Barely 17,000 were Russians by ethnic origin, though that people numbered 66·8 per cent of the population in 1897.[2] What cannot be said with certainty is how far such people emigrated because of institutional discrimination, and how far because of economic hardship. Self-conscious minority status should probably not be discounted too much.

In so large a part of Europe, with such diverse local characteristics, it is easy to lose sight of essentials. A closer look at one region may help clear the mind; and the one chosen is that dealt with by Thomas and Znaniecki. Poland, of course, had no political unity during this period: Galicia was under Austrian rule, Congress Poland under Russian, and a third substantial section under German. From the earliest known figure in the nineteenth century down to the last recorded before the Great War, Galician population doubled, that of Prussian Poland trebled, that of Congress Poland quadrupled; but the increase in Galicia was concentrated in the latter part of the nineteenth century. Discrimination played some part in emigration

---

[1] *Ibid.*, I 718, 823–6; II 457, 531–3, 551.
[2] *Ibid.*, I 483–9; II 416, 424–5.

from Congress Poland – against Jews, of course, but also against the Uniates or Greek Catholics. On the other hand, industrial growth could absorb much of the surplus rural population down to about 1900. After that year, industrial growth slowed down; and there were always certain northern provinces, almost purely agricultural, that provided an especially large share of emigrants. Although great numbers from Congress Poland went to Germany for seasonal farm work – 200,000 a year, and more than 300,000 in 1913 – overseas emigration continued to rise. Galicia, on the other hand, had almost no modern industry, subdivision of land was acute, and damage to cottage crafts from foreign competition was severe. The result was a quarter of a million seasonal emigrants to Germany each year, half of them young women, and a million overseas emigrants in the forty years before the Great War, more than one-quarter of the natural increase. Prussian Poland, with an agriculture operated by landlords and labourers, had in its social life the additional complication of government hostility to Polish culture and Polish landownership. Movement out of the region was extremely high: sometimes more than half the natural increase. Yet the movement was different from that of other parts of Poland. Emigration to the United States was more important before, not after, 1900. More and more, after that date, it was superseded by migration to the industrial regions of Germany, to which went, in the period 1872–1913, more than half of the million and a quarter people who left their homes.[1] Only German industry, in those years, was booming in such a way as not only to cut its own nation's emigration almost to nothing, and to reverse the migration pattern of the eastern provinces, but at the same time suck in workers, on a seasonal or permanent basis, from several other countries.

Most Europeans, of course, stayed at home, enduring their hardships or making their adjustments as best they could. Yet the pressures here analysed impressed themselves on millions of minds as real. What is more, they continued to do so again once the Great War was over; and the reduction of emigration in the later 1920s was brought about by a change in American, not European, minds.

[1] Zubrzycki, *op. cit.*

6

CHAPTER FOUR

News of America

All of them are going to someone; not quite strangers they; someone has crossed the sea before them. They are drawn by thousands of magnets and they will draw others after them.

Edward A. Steiner, *On the Trail of the Immigrant*, 44.

When Gustaf Unonius landed at New York City in 1841, he and his companions were surprised to discover that 'we knew far more about conditions both in Iowa and Illinois than did the native Americans with whom we conversed through an interpreter'. Half a century later, the American consul at Bremen reported that 'the Germans have maps in their pockets and point out just the place of their several destinations'; though the same official admitted that 'the Polish emigrants . . . do not understand where they are going . . . because it is all "America".'[1] If emigration arose from the combination of Europe's discontents and America's opportunities, yet the movement could take place only when the alternatives were clearly pictured in men's minds. Such visualizing could come about from casual information in the newspapers, from a variety of printed propaganda of a more or less highly coloured kind, or from informal communication between individuals and families across the Atlantic.

I

Although, even in north-west Europe, literacy was far from universal in the middle of the nineteenth century, newspapers were to be found in public houses and workingmen's clubs, their contents spread by those who could read them. Such papers carried news of America, political events and economic conditions as well as sensational episodes of everyday life. For people of rather more elaborate education, large numbers of books were published by travellers to America. A recent writer estimates that at least fifty were brought out in the German states between 1815 and 1850. In the

[1] *A Pioneer in Northwest America 1841–1858: The Memoirs of Gustaf Unonius*, I 37; *52 Congress 1 Session, House Misc. Docs., 19 & 20*, 251, Special Consular Reports on European Emigration.

quarter-century before the Civil War, more than two hundred appeared in Britain.[1]

Such works were designed to convey their writers' opinions and to make money, rather than to promote or deter emigration. From the 1830s, however, magazines began to appear, specializing in the discussion of emigration, sometimes to further a single theory, or expound the advantages of a single country, but often to exploit the widespread interest in the subject and to sell copies. In Britain, during the 1840s and 1850s, the emphasis in the *Colonial Gazette*, the *Colonial Magazine and East India Review*, the *Colonial Magazine and Commercial-Maritime Journal*, the *Emigration Record and Colonial Journal*, and, best of all, the short-lived *Sidney's Emigrant's Journal*, was on the colonies rather than the United States. Since there were as yet no German colonies, American emphasis was far greater in the *Deutsche Auswanderer* and the *Allgemeine Auswanderungs Zeitung*. From 1839, Johan R. Reierson's paper in Christiansand also published news and arguments about emigration.[2] More systematic were guide-books. Some, like Gottfried Duden's *Bericht über eine Reise nach den westlichen Staaten Nordamerikas*, Ole Rynning's *True Account of America*, Reierson's *Pathfinder for Norwegian Emigrants*, and John Regan's *The Emigrant's Guide to the Western States of America*, based their accounts on personal experience.[3] Others were more pedestrian and encyclopaedic, like Wiley and Putnam's *Emigrants' Guide* of 1845, and John Cassell's *Emigrants' Almanack* of 1849.[4] In the German states, more than a hundred guide-books can be listed between 1827 and 1856, as many as eighteen in 1849 alone, and more than a dozen in each of four other years. Traugott Bromme's *Rathgeber für Auswanderungslustige*, of

[1] Allan Nevins, *American Social History as recorded by British Travellers*, esp. 3–26, 111–38, 283–307; Mack Walker, *Germany and the Emigration*, 62, 122, 152. Sweden had one famous work of travel, in Fredrika Bremer's *Homes of the New World* (1853). On literacy in Britain, see Robert K. Webb, *The British Working Class Reader*, esp. chapter 1; and on German village reading clubs, Marcus L. Hansen, *The Atlantic Migration*, 149–50. Once emigration had started, American newspapers might be sent back to the home country: Vilhelm Moberg, *When I was a Child*, 12, 17–18, mentions this, and the phenomenon must have been widespread. This is perhaps the most convenient place to note that some of the subject-matter of my chapter is outlined, and many valuable references are given, in Merle Curti and Kendall Burr, 'The Immigrant and the American Image in Europe, 1860–1914', *Mississippi Valley Historical Review*, XXXVII (1950), 203–30.

[2] Walker, *op. cit.*, 128–9, 137–8; Theodore C. Blegen, *Norwegian Migration to America*, 157. All the British magazines mentioned may be found in the British Museum.

[3] Duden's book, published in 1829, was translated by G. Bek in instalments, *Missouri Historical Review*, XII and XIII (1917–19). Ole Rynning's book, 1838, was translated by Professor Blegen in *Minnesota History Bulletin*, II (1917) and summarized in *Norwegian Migration to America*, 88–104. The same book summarizes, 243–7, Reierson's *Pathfinder for Norwegian Emigrants*, 1844. Regan's book appeared at Edinburgh in 1852.

[4] In *Birmingham Journal*, 6 April and 19 October 1850, H. W. Howe, agent for various Liverpool passenger brokers, advertised a 'Standard Library . . . Every work on emigration sold or lent out to read', and announced an Emigration List, with titles of all works published. Cassell's pamphlet sold at 4d., Wiley and Putnam's *Guide* at 2s. 6d.

1846, contained, in addition to more general information, a chapter on the resources and prospects of each state. It listed, for example, twenty-eight types of tree growing in Illinois, discussed prairie farming, demonstrated the rapid growth of population, and mentioned the great number of schools and colleges.[1] In later years, guide-books might come from emigration agencies, concerned with the sale of tickets, and therefore closely involved with steamship and railway companies. Such was the book published by 'Americus' in 1869, *Where to Emigrate and Why*, which contained accounts of journeys and their costs, and of wages in the United States.

When, in 1840, the Colonial Land and Emigration Commissioners came into existence in Britain, their foundation document used these words to describe the spirit in which they were to spread information:

> ... care being of course taken to present such facts in the most precise and determinate form, unaccompanied by any superfluous comment, and still more to strip them of any language calculated to work on the imagination, or to interfere with the calm and dispassionate exercise of their own judgment on the part of those whom you may address.[2]

No doubt intentionally, this was the exact opposite of the tone of contemporary commercial propaganda. Most emigrants who read books and pamphlets were exposed to the influence of agencies which, in order to sell land, or ocean passages, or seats on American trains, and to sell them in the face of intense competition, felt it necessary to practise the most colourful and persuasive arts they could command.

Advertisements for sailing ships, on the whole, were simple and informative, if enthusiastic. In 1853, for example, Bowman, Grinnell and Company said:

> The ships are nearly all new, constructed with particular regard to strength and durability, and commanded by captains of undoubted nautical skill, experience, and humanity. The good health which has been particularly remarked always to prevail among the passengers on board them affords a convincing proof that everything calculated to ensure the convenience and comfort of the emigrants has been strictly adhered to.

All brokers made such claims, adding that they would store luggage free, transfer money to America, and sell tickets valid for interior destinations. The principal deceptions they attempted were to express tonnages according to the formula giving the most reassuring result, and to convey the impres-

[1] Walker, *op. cit.*, 62 note. Bromme's book is in the British Museum. George M. Stephenson, *Religious Aspects of Swedish Immigration*, 488–91, lists fifty Swedish guide-books, only a few of which can be ascribed with certainty to railroad or steamship interests.
[2] Quoted by Fred H. Hitchins, *The Colonial Land and Emigration Commission*, 48.

sion that all ships for which they found passengers were under their direct control and sailed on regular schedules.[1]

In the same period, American land companies played their part. Setting up agencies in Britain, issuing handbills, placing advertisements in newspapers, publishing pamphlets of their own and, in one instance, a newspaper, their propaganda mingled elements of fact and eloquence. One tract of Texan land was advertised in 1853 by stressing that 'a number of respectable English farmers are now settling on the property, and the whole tract has been carefully examined by a resident Scotch farmer and horticulturist, and pronounced to be of one uniform quality and of the best description.'[2] Another publication appealed to the spirit of adventure:

> The rust of inveterate habits – the contentedness of inaction – the prejudices of education – the narrowness of local views – all vanish before the freshness and the enterprise that must ensue from emigration to entirely new scenes and fields of action.[3]

A complex argument was used in 1851 in an attempt to sell land in Virginia. Congenial company would be provided by British emigrants about to sail; settlers' welfare would be carefully safeguarded during the first few years; and 'you will, with the blessing of Providence, see your labours crowned with lasting plenty and independence.' The appeal was addressed to farmers and working men, who were exhorted to contrast American prospects with the hardships of life in Britain:

> Do you not read in the maintenance of war prices for land, of free trade prices for produce . . . Do you not read in the repeal of the Corn Laws and Navigation Laws, a measure that brings foreigners to your markets and enables them to undersell you at your own doors, the alternatives of emigration or the workhouse? . . . Then look to Virginia.[4]

Other advertisements, within the United States, featured town-sites. The promoters of the 'city' of Nininger, Minnesota, pointed to the advantages of surrounding fertile farm land, water-power for industry, and easy transport

[1] *Liverpool Mercury*, 1 March 1853; *Birmingham Journal*, 17 September 1853. On the distinction between regular 'packets' and 'transient ships' see Francis Wyse, *America, Its Realities and Resources*, I 7, and *The British Mechanics' and Labourers' Handbook*, 30–1.
[2] *Birmingham Journal*, 1 January 1853. The newspaper was the *Universal Emigration and Colonization Messenger*, 1850, issued by the land company of the same name.
[3] Wilbur S. Shepperson, *The Promotion of British Emigration by Agents for American Lands*, 24, quoting David Hoffman's *Views on the Formation of a British and American Land Company*, 1848. Shepperson's little book deals mainly with examples from Texas and Virginia. All these topics are summarized in his larger work, *British Emigration to North America: Projects and Opinions in the Early Victorian Period*, 29–31, 51–60, 86–93, 166–79.
[4] *Birmingham Journal*, 12 April 1851. Remarks on land companies' work in Europe are in Marcus L. Hansen, *The Immigrant in American History*, 198–9.

by steamboat and train. A journal was established, with a German edition. An arrangement was made with a steamship company, for through tickets from Britain. Posters were addressed not only to would-be settlers but to all who might carry them; for 'all railroads and steamboats giving this card a conspicuous place, or gratuitous insertion in their cards, aids the emigrant and forwards their own interest.'[1]

II

From time to time, certain public authorities were active. In Britain, the Colonial Land and Emigration Commissioners worked from 1840 until the 1870s to combat misrepresentation and fraud. Irregularly but with some frequency, they published substantial pamphlets called *Colonization Circulars*, with some emphasis on the colonies, of course, but with information on the United States. In 1886, the Emigrants' Information Office was set up, and this survived until 1918. It commented publicly on the demand for labour in all parts of the Empire, placed circulars in hundreds of public libraries and other institutions, and offered regular and free distribution of literature to workingmen's clubs and even to individuals who might apply.[2]

The American Federal government did much less. Between 1864 and 1868 it encouraged the immigration of contract labourers. Consuls co-operated with the American Emigrant Company in sending miners and others from Scandinavia. Later, however, officials found it more difficult to establish a policy that satisfied them. It was easy enough to translate the Homestead Act into the local language, as did the consul at Bergen in 1863; and it was obviously quite proper to publish a factual guide-book, as did the consul at Newcastle seventeen years later. It was proper to advise emigrants as they picked their way through conflicting advertisements; but it was much harder. Consuls were suspicious of much of the propaganda. They knew that the European governments were often hostile to it. Yet, naturally enough, they wanted to promote the interests of American enterprises.[3]

[1] See the photograph in Allan Nevins, *The Emergence of Lincoln*, I 310. A partner in the enterprise was a man later prominent in the history of reform movements in the United States – Martin Ridge, *Ignatius Donnelly*, 17–27. The project foundered in the depression of 1857.

[2] Among many other examples of the Commissioners' work, see the advice to emigrants posted in principal ports, reprinted as Appendix 51 to their annual report, *Parl. Papers 1865*, XVIII. Summaries of early publications of the Emigrants' Information Office appear in a report from the American consul at Manchester, *49 Congress 2 Session, House Exec. Doc. 157*, 460–2, which on 501–20 prints a few in full. See also the Memorandum on the History and Functions of the Emigrants' Information Office, *Parl. Papers 1907*, LXVII 459–70; and an example of a local notice in *Grimsby News*, 7 January 1908.

[3] Charlotte Erickson, *American Industry and the European Immigrant, 1860–1885*, chapter 1; Florence Janson, *The Background of Swedish Immigration*, 156–99, 233–47; Theodore C. Blegen, *Norwegian Emigration to America: the American Transition*, 415–17; Evan Jones, *The Emigrants' Friend*; *U.S. Consular Reports*, II (1881), 702, V (1882), 123–5, both from Aachen.

States did far more. Each was likely to conclude that its growth and prosperity depended largely upon the contribution that immigrants could make in settling its land and building up its industry. At one time or another, therefore, a high proportion of states organized propaganda to plead their cause.

The smaller New England states made a few efforts after the Civil War. In 1870 Maine employed an agent in Sweden. In 1889 Vermont had the American minister to Sweden distribute pamphlets. These provoked counter-propaganda from the agents of western railroads and other interests, and few immigrants seem to have been attracted by these means.[1]

Southern states worked hard to encourage immigration, conscious as they were of having fallen behind in the economic race.[2] One example will suffice. In 1879 a pamphlet defended Georgia's summer climate, underlined the political, religious and educational advantages of residence there, and proved to its writer's satisfaction that its death-rate was only half that of Michigan. County-by-county descriptions were reinforced by letters from settlers; but it is noticeable that almost all of these had come from other parts of the United States, not from Europe. Local communities gave support. In 1876, the Chamber of Commerce of Rome, with no more than six or seven thousand inhabitants, issued a pamphlet which asked the question, 'Why go to the far-off West or South-west, and settle in the wilds,' when abundant opportunities could be found in a settled region. There followed praise of the city, which, named Rome 'on account of its seven hills, sits like a Queen of Beauty, the great commercial centre of the finest bodies of agricultural and mineral lands on the continent of America.' This, let it be added, is only the beginning of two pages of description, filled with every cliché of Southern or any other nineteenth-century rhetoric.[3]

One border state, Missouri, was advertising in 1880. Its pamphlet included railroad and steamship notices, and its Board of Immigration offered to send information free to any part of the world. For fifty dollars, it claimed, a British immigrant could reach a state where 'forty million people can subsist in plenty and comfort.' For less than $300, a forty-acre farm could be secured by a first payment, a log cabin could be built, and implements and livestock bought. Missouri offered the advantages of a settled com-

[1] Harold F. Wilson, *The Hill Country of Northern New England*, 160–1.
[2] Rowland T. Berthoff, 'Southern Attitudes towards Immigration, 1865–1914', *Journal of Southern History*, XVII (1951), 336–9; C. Vann Woodward, *Origins of the New South*, 297–9; Carl Wittke, *We Who Built America*, 108–11. In 1870, an Immigration Convention was held at Charleston, S.C., to discuss such topics as railroad lands and steamship services.
[3] *Georgia, from the Immigrant Settlers' Standpoint*, published under the direction of the State Commissioner of Agriculture; *North, or Cherokee Georgia, Advantages to Emigrants and Families with Small Capital*, 17, 21, 25–6.

munity, yet land at moderate prices could still be had. The climate was 'a golden mean between the extremes of cold in the north and the heat of the south, thus rendering its temperature highly adapted to promote the prolific principle in man and nature.'[1]

California relied on unofficial agencies. Railroad magnates helped to found, in 1869, the California Immigrant Union, which sent agents both to Europe and the eastern United States. At about the same time, the Los Angeles and San Bernardino Land Company was advertising in Europe and America, to sell farms carved out of Abel Stearns' ranches. In the early 1880s, members of San Francisco's Board of Trade founded the Immigration Association of California. Beyond this, the state relied on the work of private boosters, like the Benjamin C. Truman who, in 1876, published *Semi-Tropical California*.[2] Similarly, an immigration society existed in Montana as early as 1872, while three years later there was founded the Big Horn and Eastern Montana Colonization Society. Wyoming relied upon its railroads, and on the printing of extra copies of its governors' reports. In Washington, however, where the same methods were prominent, and where both real estate companies and local immigration companies were at work, a Board of Immigration existed from 1875, fourteen years before statehood.[3]

Colorado likewise became active during its territorial period, with a Board of Immigration, correspondents in each county, and a pamphlet published in 1872. A full description was given of farming opportunities, stock-raising, mining, and railroads built or building. 'Garden vegetables,' the pamphlet proclaimed, 'attain an enormous size.' Twenty-five newspapers were 'evidences of the intellectual refinement of the people of Colorado,' for happily 'the rough and desperate element . . . has been thoroughly rooted out.' Colorado, too, was a summer resort, the 'Switzerland of America'. The back page summed up the entire message:

> Those who are restless in their old homes, or who seek to better their condition, will find greater advantages in Colorado than anywhere else in the West. Our mining resources offer inducements which no state east of the mountains can present, and for stockmen and agriculturists Colorado can make a better exhibit than any other region. The climate possesses peculiar charms and those in failing health, or invalids can find here a sure panacea for nearly every human ill.

[1] *The Commonwealth of Missouri*, esp. 10, 38, 42. Railroads were selling land, at prices rather high but payable over a period of years; and they offered thirty-day exploring tickets, the fare being refunded to anyone buying land.
[2] Robert G. Cleland, *The Cattle on a Thousand Hills*, 170-1, 204-5; Glenn S. Dumke, *The Boom of the Eighties in Southern California*, 32, 203-4; John Higham, *Strangers in the Land*, 16.
[3] Harold E. Briggs, *Frontiers of the Northwest*, 452-3; Earl Pomeroy, *The Territories of the United States*, 23; Arthur J. Brown, 'The Promotion of Emigration to Washington, 1854-1909', *Pacific Northwest Quarterly*, XXXVI (1945), 3-17.

The poor should come to Colorado, because here they can by industry and frugality better their condition. The rich should come here, because they can more advantageously invest their means than in any other region. The young should come here to get an early start on the road to wealth, and the old should come to get a new lease of life, and to enjoy their declining years in a country unequalled for its natural beauty and loveliness. In short, it is the Mecca for all classes and all conditions, and we confidently recommend it to the thoughtful examination of the public.[1]

Most active of all were the states of the Middle West, and especially the group west of the Great Lakes.[2] Each state set forth the attractions of its climate, Iowa's pamphlet of 1870 including a purple passage on the Indian Summer. Although none of them made claims as sweeping as those of Colorado, each was concerned to stress its good health record. Minnesota announced a death-rate between a quarter and a third of Europe's, half the American average, and, most important, lower than Wisconsin's. Fertility of soil, naturally, was a prominent feature of all such propaganda. Wisconsin described the abundance of its improved farms at prices up to $45 an acre, its railroad lands further north, averaging $2·50, its public lands at $1·25, and its remaining homesteads. Minnesota stated that a farm in the Red River valley could be bought and equipped for less than $500. Such information, often presented county-by-county, seems to have been factual enough. Opportunities for workers were not overlooked, and tables of wages were often printed.[3]

No state confined its appeal to material advantages. Wisconsin emphasized how full were the political rights of newcomers. An alien could vote after merely declaring his intention of becoming a citizen and completing one year of residence, and he could run for most public offices. Iowa, where aliens could not vote, gave them full property rights. Schools, churches and newspapers were advantages which states were proud to stress, and Minnesota pointed out that several of the papers were in immigrant languages. The same state remarked that the very fact of varied immigration was an advantage to later comers, for no one need lack the company of his own people. Finally, all states were at pains to point out the wide opportunities which the future held. Minnesota, it was said, could support five million

---

[1] *Colorado, a Statement of Facts*, 21, 23–5, 32, and back page.
[2] Indiana and Michigan had only modest programmes, and Illinois none at all: William L. Jenks, 'Michigan Immigration', *Michigan History Magazine*, XXVIII (1944), esp. 69–92; Maurice G. Baxter, 'Encouragement of Immigration to the Middle West during the Era of the Civil War', *Indiana Magazine of History*, XLVI (1950), esp. 34–6.
[3] The description in this and the following paragraph is based on three pamphlets: *Iowa, the Home for Immigrants* (1870), *Minnesota, the Empire State of the New North-West* (1878), and *Wisconsin, What It Offers to the Immigrant* (1879), all of which are in the British Museum.

people: this two years before a census which recorded fewer than 800,000. The possessor of capital enjoyed advantages, the same state admitted; but nowhere on earth could 'unaided muscle, with a plucky purpose, reap greater rewards.' Minnesota's appeal was addressed:

> To Labouring Men, who earn a livelihood by honest toil; to Landless Men, who aspire to the dignity and independence which comes from possession in God's free earth; to All Men of moderate means, and men of wealth, who will accept homes in a beautiful and prosperous country . . . It is well to exchange the tyrannies and thankless toil of the old world for the freedom and independence of the new . . . it is well for the hand of labour to bring forth the rich treasures hid in the bosom of the NEW EARTH.

Iowa's pamphlet had a similar message. In the Middle West, men could achieve independence, whereas in the Eastern States or in Europe 'the great majority . . . must live out their days as dependent labourers on the land of others.'

Within this region, states competed one with another. Wisconsin suggested that Minnesota had greater distances, fewer railroads, and, from time to time, was subject to natural disasters. Minnesota replied with its claim to a lower death-rate. If official publications made such claims, newspapers were more brutal in their language. When Dakota was first settled in the 1860s, Iowa and Minnesota editors printed articles on droughts, grasshoppers, blizzards and savage Indians. One such piece described a 'poor Dakota cripple who has lost both legs and an arm during one of the winter storms'; and when a few discouraged settlers drifted east, their stories were at once printed under such headlines as 'Another Survivor of Plague-stricken Dakota Reaches Town'.[1]

Middle-Western states, however, did not finance such campaigns lavishly or consistently. Wisconsin's Commissioner of Immigration worked for no more than a few years in the 1850s. The Board of Immigration set up in 1867 lapsed during the depression a few years later; then in 1879 another came into being. Minnesota did little until 1867, though its Board was then busy for more than a decade. Iowa had a Commissioner just before the Civil War; then a Board which worked for only three years from 1870; then another in 1880, also active for no more than a short period. With legislatures so parsimonious, it was particularly important to direct energies and funds

[1] Harold E. Briggs, 'The Settlement and Development of the Territory of Dakota, 1860–70', *North Dakota Historical Quarterly*, VII (1932–3), 127–8. Similarly, when in 1870 Ezra Meeker wrote his *Washington Territory West of the Cascade Mountains*, he remarked: 'The discouraged husbandman from the parched plains of California . . . is amazed to see the green grass of our bottoms and the luxuriant growth of everything planted, recollecting the scorching heats and droughts he has left behind him, and that but a few days' sail distant,' Brown, *op. cit.*, 9.

wisely. All states, of course, were interested in attracting settlers from neighbouring American communities. Newspaper advertising was a central feature of this effort: Wisconsin placed items in 900 American papers during the 1850s. The long pamphlets, too, must have been read largely by Americans. Yet all were eager to receive foreigners, and here the problem was more complex. An economical method was to try to tap the flow of immigrants at seaports or inland distribution points. Wisconsin's early Commissioner worked at New York City, seeking to establish relations with consulates, shipping companies and welfare agencies, though he also sent some of his pamphlets to Europe. Iowa began by using the same method. In 1854 Wisconsin sent an agent to Quebec, where he made arrangements with a steamboat company to forward immigrants. Trying to persuade the newcomers to use this service, he came into competition with representatives of other companies, a rivalry which, as he reported, was dissolved in conviviality at the nearest bar as soon as the immigrants had made their choice. Minnesota had an agent at Quebec in 1867, then, like Wisconsin, at Milwaukee and Chicago; but there was also a man at New York, who negotiated with steamboat and railroad companies for cheap rates. With competition so active, attempts were made, from time to time, to reach out to Europe itself. Only Minnesota sent men abroad. Hans Mattson went to Sweden. A less celebrated agent went to Bremen, whence he reported his visits to twenty-three shipping offices and fifty-seven emigrant boarding houses, and complained that shortage of funds compelled him to make all these journeys on foot. Another method, however, was found, at once more economical and more precise. In 1867, Wisconsin set up not only its Board of Immigration but county committees, whose task was to compile mailing-lists of the friends and relatives of existing settlers. Minnesota had a clerk who worked full-time on a similar project and on translating propaganda publications. The lists once drawn up, pamphlets in English, Welsh, German, Dutch, Norwegian or Swedish could be sent to Europe.[1]

[1] Several valuable studies have been written on the machinery of immigration propaganda: Theodore C. Blegen, 'The Competition of the Northwestern States for Immigrants', *Wisconsin Magazine of History*, III (1919), 3–23; Marcus L. Hansen, 'Official Encouragement of Immigration to Iowa', *Iowa Journal of History and Politics*, XIX (1921), 165–92; Theodore C. Blegen, 'Minnesota's Campaign for Immigrants: Illustrative Documents', *Yearbook* of Swedish Historical Society of America, XI (1926), 60–1, 72–3. See also Karl E. Erickson, 'The Emigrant Journey in the Fifties', Norwegian-American Historical Association *Studies and Records*, VIII (1934), 68–9; and Hans Mattson, *Reminiscences*, 97–111. Mattson's efforts were opposed by a Nebraska agent, a letter from whom, to a newspaper, is quoted in Everett Dick, *The Sod House Frontier*, 188. Edith Abbott, *Historical Aspects*, 129–32, quotes from a report of Wisconsin's commissioners, 1853, and, 167–72, from the 1871 report of the Minnesota Board. That Minnesota's prize essays of 1866 were printed is proved by their appearance as item 271 of Goodspeed's Book Shop (Boston, Mass.), *Americana, Catalogue 536*. Iowa's first Commissioner's work was supplemented by a Dubuque Immigrant Association, which tried to influence local newspapers against the wiles of Minnesota.

There were many links between public authority and commercial enterprise. While state pamphlets, like that of Minnesota, included much railroad advertising, railroad propaganda praised the surrounding communities. The first Michigan agent appointed was a man already representing large landowners in the state. The Burlington agent in Chicago, in 1870, also acted for steamship companies; and the railroad paid fees and expenses to Edward Edginton, about to sail for Britain as agent of the Iowa Board, for work he might be able to do. In the 1880s, the Wisconsin Central's land agent became unpaid European agent for the state. Dakota, too, had agents with mixed interests. Although the territory sometimes had an official organization, most of its propaganda during the 1880s was distributed through the immigration departments of railroads.[1]

III

Railroads were important as promoters of immigration because they commonly had large acreages of land to sell. Before the Civil War, the one great railroad active in this direction was the Illinois Central. With two and a half million acres at its disposal, it brought in some thirty thousand families, beginning in the 1850s. Its advertising was directed largely towards the older states: names of farmers being obtained from merchants and circulars sent to them, notices placed in newspapers, or in post offices, or in New York street cars. Appeals were addressed, also, to Europeans as they arrived in the United States, either at the ports or at such cities as Chicago, St Louis and Quebec. More than that, newspaper articles and pamphlets were prepared for Europe, and agents were sent to England, the German states and Scandinavia. Oscar Malmborg, who travelled briefly in Scandinavia in 1854 and more thoroughly in the winter of 1860–61, reported that his notices were read with others from the pulpit after a service, and later the parish hall was crowded with farmers who had come many miles to hear him. Some of his hearers shortly afterwards auctioned their stock and implements and sold their land. Malmborg arranged transport for them, handed them literature, and had the ship's captain promise to draw up a list of likely purchasers of Illinois Central land.[2]

[1] Jenks, op. cit., 69; Richard C. Overton, Burlington West, 260, 360; Blegen, 'Competition of Northwestern States', 22–3; Hansen, 'Official Encouragement', 175; Herbert S. Schell, 'Official Immigration Activities of Dakota Territory', North Dakota Historical Quarterly, VII (1932–3), 5–24. As soon as North and South Dakota became states, in 1889, they equipped themselves with organizations to promote settlement.
[2] Paul W. Gates, The Illinois Central and its Colonisation Work, esp. chapters 9 and 10; A. A. Stomberg, ed., 'Letters of an Early Emigration Agent in the Scandinavian Countries', Swedish-American Historical Bulletin, III (1930), No. 2, 24 and passim.

The Hannibal and St Joseph, which also had a land-grant in the 1850s, had an agent in Scotland after the Civil War. The Kansas Pacific, Missouri Pacific and Santa Fe all issued booklets. In 1875, the last-named employed a foreign-born agent, C. B. Schmidt, to visit Russia to arrange for Mennonite immigration; and on his way back he toured Austria, Germany and Switzerland, appointing local agents as he went.[1] Early in the 1880s, the Wisconsin Central published a sixty-page booklet, describing the American system of land-sales, giving data on crop yields, and presenting the political and religious rights which the Constitution guaranteed. Land was selling at about $5 an acre, payable by instalments; and anyone who, within a prescribed time, bought forty acres was entitled to a refund of his rail fare, together with reduced rates for the carriage of his livestock, implements and household goods.[2] Very early in its career, the Union Pacific was claiming to advertise in more than 2,000 newspapers in North America and Europe. A quarter of a century later, it was advertising Idaho. 'Imperial in extent,' Idaho (like every other state, as the reader of such literature is likely to sneer) had the lowest death-rate in America. Specimen budgets demonstrated that farmers' profits were high; yet it was also claimed that businessmen could lend money at from twelve to eighteen per cent.[3] The Southern Pacific had agents at Chicago, New Orleans and New York, as well as in London. It maintained hostels for immigrants in Texas, sold land-seekers' tickets, and distributed a wide range of literature, with such titles as *California, the Cornucopia of the World*.[4] In the years after the Civil War, at least eleven Southern railroads were trying to attract immigrants to that unpopular region.[5]

The Burlington system, whose nearly three million acres lay in Iowa and Nebraska, was intensely active, either through its own land departments in the two states, or through land companies in which its officers had a major interest. It offered tickets to prospective settlers and generous rebates to those who bought land. It arranged lectures, exhibitions, and tours for newspaper editors. It put up red, white and blue posters at railroad stations and docks. In 1875 and 1876, the Burlington published a monthly news-

[1] Overton, *op. cit.*, 111–13, 291, 359; Paul W. Gates, *Fifty Million Acres*, notes to 235–7 and frontispiece (a Kansas Pacific broadside); Carl B. Schmidt, 'Reminiscences of Foreign Immigration Work for Kansas', *Kansas Historical Collections*, IX (1905–6), 485–97 – the reason for all this activity, apart from the land sales themselves, is summed up, 487, in the words, 'A quarter-section of land in grain will produce eight car-loads of freight'.
[2] *Wisconsin Central Railroad Lands*.
[3] Overton, *op. cit.*, 291; *The Resources and Attractions of Idaho*.
[4] Edna Parker, 'The Southern Pacific Railroad and Settlement in Southern California', *Pacific Historical Review*, VI (1937), 103–19.
[5] Berthoff, *op. cit.* 333–4.

sheet, *The Iowa and Nebraska Farmer*, with annual editions in German, Czech, Norwegian and Swedish; and in 1882 it put out a sixty-four page publication, *Heart of a Continent*. Between 1870 and 1875, a campaign was mounted in Britain. Edward Edginton, who also worked for the Iowa state Board, drew up a list of London and provincial newspapers, and agricultural publications, in which advertisements might usefully be placed. He ordered a large consignment of showcards, handbills, and circulars, including one large type with a map. Many of these he distributed on trains, in boarding houses, and in ships about to leave for America. In the following year, the Burlington appointed a European Commissioner and an Agent-General; Edginton went to Glasgow; Nebraska's agent in London agreed to work also for the railroad; and paid agents were soon set up at Birmingham, Manchester, Bristol, Leicester, Dublin, Londonderry and Queenstown. A thousand sub-agents, working on commission, were soon appointed. A travelling exhibition was arranged, with photographs and crop samples. Throughout, the appeal was to farmers, who were encouraged to emigrate in groups, to form agricultural colonies, rather than as individuals. At the same time, Frederick Hedde worked at Hamburg for the Burlington as well as for Nebraska. Once immigrants had reached the West, they found hostels to accommodate them during their tours of inspection. As soon as they had settled, they were encouraged to write to friends in their former homes.[1]

At least equally active was the Northern Pacific, which had vast areas to sell in Minnesota and further west. Like other railroads, it set up subsidiary land companies. It had agencies at Omaha and Topeka, and in California. It established links with New England agencies for the relief of the unemployed. It had temporary accommodation for immigrants. At ports and inland centres, posters were put up. The Northern Pacific published a monthly magazine, *The Northwest*, and a booklet called *The Pacific Northwest*. Such publications were scrutinized by the company's highest officers, for in 1880 President Billings ordered an edition destroyed as being both misleading and ungrammatical. In Britain, the newspaper *Land and Emigration* was issued between 1871 and 1873. From the Liverpool headquarters, hundreds of thousands of posters, handbills and cards were sent to the more than 800 agents, most of them part-timers drawn from the ranks of shopkeepers. Literature was offered free to reading-rooms. Emigration societies were encouraged, and so was settlement in colonies, which would combine

[1] Overton, *op. cit.*, 251–62 (including an appeal to New Englanders by emphasizing churches and schools), 286–8, 336–40, 371–3, all on work in the United States; 308–21, 359–69, 432, 440, 445, 469–71, on work in Europe. *Sherborne, Dorchester and Taunton Journal*, 4 April 1872, shows the appeal to farmers; the Allan Line was cooperating in transport.

American prosperity with the amenities of village life. In Germany, Friedrich Kapp was briefly employed. To Scandinavia, the Northern Pacific sent Hans Mattson, a Swedish immigrant who had risen to the office of Secretary of State in Minnesota, and he stayed in Sweden four and a half years.[1]

The railroads' message can be summed up in the words of a Northern Pacific advertisement in a West of England newspaper. 'For the amount of a single year's rental in Great Britain, a British tenant-farmer may obtain in Minnesota the freehold of a large and productive farm.'[2] The keynote was not merely wealth: it was independence.

Like states and territories, railroads were engaged in competition. Frederick Hedde complained that the Northern Pacific and Union Pacific were both active at Hamburg, as well as agents of half a dozen states. In the same year, in the West of England, there occurred a miniature propaganda war. The Northern Pacific was trying to persuade groups from Somerset and Dorset to settle in Minnesota, and a Congregationalist minister, George Rodgers, went to examine the prospects for such a colony. At about the time of his return, there appeared a letter, painting in gloomy colours a picture of the 'fearful' winters of Minnesota, declaring the writer's duty to 'sound the alarm before 'tis too late,' and pointing out that the Union Pacific and the Kansas Pacific offered better lands in a more bearable climate. The next week came a rejoinder from the manager of the Northern Pacific's Land and Emigration Department. It claimed that the hostile letter came from a man who had applied for appointment as agent, to lecture in villages, and who, when rejected, had taken his revenge by working on behalf of rival organizations. Rodgers also wrote in defence of Minnesota; and after further controversy he and the London manager of the railroad addressed a meeting in the Corn Exchange at Yeovil.[3]

In 1891, American investigators found Thomas Cook and other British agencies distributing folders for the Chicago, Milwaukee and St Paul, while an agent in Antwerp was promoting the same railroad's *Homesteads for All*. By that decade, however, there was little railroad land left at prices European immigrants could afford, while the remaining homesteads were in districts unattractive to them. It was at this time that the Burlington transferred responsibility for advertising from its land department to its passenger department. When the Industrial Commission undertook its inquiry in

[1] *Land and Emigration*, esp. issues of November 1871 and January 1872; Ellis P. Oberholtzer, *Jay Cooke*, II 162, 296–307, 319; James B. Hedges, *Henry Villard and the Railways of the Northwest*, esp. 112–32; Thomas C. Cochran, *Railroad Leaders*, 255; Hans Mattson, *Reminiscences*, 118–37. The Northern Pacific worked closely with the Oregon State Board of Immigration.

[2] *Sherborne, Dorchester and Taunton Journal*, 13 June 1872.

[3] Overton, *op. cit.*, 269; *Sherborne, Dorchester and Taunton Journal*, 5, 12 and 26 September 1872.

1899, scarcely a trace of the railroads' work remained – the Chicago, Milwaukee and St Paul, for example, retaining but a single agent in Britain.[1]

IV

More and more, the railroads' place was taken by the transatlantic shipping lines. Much of their advertising was little more than announcement of their sailings and fares, and most newspapers came to include regular columns of such information. Auctioneers and various kinds of shopkeeper acted as local agents. In Germany 'almost every hamlet' was covered in this way. In England, places as small as Market Weighton and Driffield in Yorkshire, and Glastonbury, Ilminster and Bridport in the West Country, all had their sub-agents. The numbers reported were astonishing. About 1890, the five biggest shipping lines were said to have more than 3,600 such agents in the British Isles. The French line, C.G.T., had in France and Switzerland fifty-five principal agents, each with two or three hundred sub-agents. In the southern provinces of Italy, one hundred and sixty agents were said to be active, with four thousand sub-agents. Holland-America had nearly two thousand. About twenty years later, there were nearly two hundred agents and sub-agents in Sweden, some seventy of them connected with Cunard.[2]

In British guide-books, steamship advertising emphasized the size and stability of ships, the comfort of their accommodation, the length of their promenade decks, the care taken of passengers by stewards and stewardesses, and the fact that the cost of passage included 'an abundance of cooked provisions'.[3] In Sweden, the White Star line announced itself to be 'the favourite line of the Swedes,' with 'the world's largest and fastest steamers'; while North German Lloyd was stressing speed, Hamburg-America cheapness, and C.G.T. the possession of the shortest sea route.[4] Hints may be found, however, of more imaginative propaganda. Early in the twentieth century, an American traveller met a Greek returning to his home, and was shown poems praising America, and emigrant success stories.[5]

[1] 52 Congress 1 Session, House Exec. Doc. 235, Part I, 187–8, 213, 283; Reports of Industrial Commission, XV 537, 547.
[2] 52 Congress 1 Session, House Exec. Doc. 235, Part I, 12–13, 141–4, 283, 323, Part II 77, 90. Hull News and Sherborne, Dorchester and Taunton Journal are the newspapers used as illustrations. On Sweden, see Janson, op. cit., 233–47, 289–90: the country had had steamship advertising since the late 1860s.
[3] See, for example, the White Star and National Line advertisements in Evan Jones, The Emigrants' Friend, 235, 237.
[4] Vilhelm Moberg, When I Was a Child, 20; 50 Congress 1 Session, House Misc. Doc. 572, Part I 350–51 (the testimony of a former agent); Blegen, Norwegian Migration, 467, has a page of steamship advertisements; 52 Congress 1 Session, House Exec. Doc. 235, Part I 229, describes a Red Star booklet advertising rail connections to Antwerp from as far away as Reggio.
[5] Broughton Brandenburg, Imported Americans, 38.

Steamship advertising reached every corner of Europe. Posters from North German Lloyd could be found ornamenting cottages in Bohemia. Agents 'cover Italy as the locusts covered Egypt.' Advertisements could be found in Greek coffee houses and grocers' shops.[1]

V

The minds of discontented Europeans, however, were exposed to many cross-currents of propaganda, not all of which came from the United States or represented American interests.

European governments seldom attempted to prevent the emigration of their citizens, but often enough tried to dissuade them from leaving. In 1854, the Prussian government published handbills about the depression threatening the United States, while Saxony issued placards pointing to the Know-Nothing campaigns. In 1887 the Austrian Ministry of Interior sent instructions to local officials to oppose American attempts to recruit workers.

Wahre Jacob.]   [Aug. 25.

America draining the strength of Europe

In 1905 the provincial government of Croatia-Slavonia published warnings about American economic conditions. Any single scandal might reinforce the governments' general position, as when, in 1887, the Greek Ministry of Interior told local authorities to give full publicity to the hardships of the ocean voyage.[2] Semi-official argument, often containing patriotic appeals,

[1] Emily G. Balch, *Our Slavic Fellow Citizens*, 80; *52 Congress 1 Session, House Exec. Doc. 235*, Part I 290-96; George M. Stephenson, *History of American Immigration*, 71-2; Theodore Saloutos, *The Greeks in the United States*, 33.
[2] Hansen, *Atlantic Migration*, 304; *U.S. Consular Reports*, XXV (Nos. 89-91), 90, 381; No. 295, p. 281.

7

came from many sources: writers, clergy, and, just before the Great War, societies in Scandinavia.[1]

Europeans were exposed, also, to the competing claims of overseas countries. In the years after Waterloo, there was considerable publicity in favour of British North America, and even a little government aid for emigrants.[2] From the late 1830s, with the transportation of convicts to New South Wales abolished, funds from Australian land sales were used to promote emigration from Britain. Selection was sometimes in the hands of colonial agents, sometimes in those of settlers already in the colonies, sometimes in those of purchasers of land who were to be allowed to take their workers with them. Commonly, assistance was so graduated as to encourage the emigration of people especially useful to the new country: farm labourers, country artisans, domestic workers. Preference was also given to families and to single women, in order to balance the sexes in the face of the normal excess movement of single men.[3]

Some of the Australian schemes persisted until late in the nineteenth century, and were publicized in the *Colonization Circulars* and the emigration magazines. Increasingly, however, Canada and Latin America came to dominate the scene. By the 1880s, the American consul at Leeds was complaining that local people saw more about the Canadian West than about the United States. Twenty years later, Canada was spending up to a million dollars a year on advertising for immigrants in the United States itself, maintaining offices in sixteen cities, distributing literature, and allowing agents a commission of $3 for each farmer they sent across the border. Much of the effort, of course, continued to be directed to Britain. Booking agents strove to send out farmers, labourers, railway construction workers, and domestic servants. Successful farmers were sent back to Britain to lecture. While the government was active, the Canadian Pacific

---

[1] Blegen, *Norwegian Migration*, 81–3 (pastoral letter from Bishop of Bergen, 1837), 240–41 (a book of 1839), 254–5 (Rev. Dietrichson), 261–5 (a book of 1850), 318–20 (a satirical play by Wergeland); *The American Transition*, 471–3 (Society for the Restriction of Emigration, 1909); Franklin D. Scott, 'Sweden's Constructive Opposition to Emigration', *Journal of Modern History*, XXXVII (1965), 307–35, deals with the National Society against Emigration, 1907. Shepperson, *British Emigration to North America*, 179–84, discusses anti-emigration propaganda in Britain.

[2] Helen I. Cowan, *British Emigration to British North America: The First Hundred Years* (1961 edn.), chapters iii and iv. Blegen, *American Transition*, 357–82, describes Canadian attempts in the 1860s to attract Norwegians.

[3] Although Australian emigration is discussed at great length in the annual reports of the Colonial Land and Emigration Commissioners and in their *Colonization Circulars*, there is enough information in Robert B. Madgwick's excellent *Immigration into Eastern Australia*. For the situation later in the century, see Walter Hazell and Howard Hodgkin, *The Australian Colonies: Emigration and Colonization*: the authors were members of private emigration societies, as well as being on the committee of management of the Emigrants' Information Office. John S. Marais, *The Colonization of New Zealand*, shows rather similar developments.

railroad worked to dispose of its land grant. Its publication of 1890, *Free Farms*, consisted of a large map, folded into pamphlet form. On the reverse were closely printed pages of detail on each region of the prairies, together with the offer of a refund of fare to anyone buying 160 acres. In 1911, *The Canadian Settlers' Handbook* appeared in London as a semi-official publication. It contained estimates of the demand for many types of labour, details of wages, regulations applying to homesteads and land sales, calculations of the cost of successful farming, costs of travel, and lists of government agents and of 'immigrant offices and halls' in Canadian cities. It included also many advertisements of steamship and railroad companies, travel agencies, baggage insurance firms, and forwarders of furniture, as well as announcements by the Salvation Army.[1]

Latin American campaigns appealed mostly to southern Europe. Especially after the abolition of slavery in the 1880s, the Brazilian government favoured the organization of agricultural colonies, assisted immigrants with ocean and inland fares, allowed their possessions to enter free of duty, gave them very full civil rights, and made generous provision for the repatriation of widows, orphans, and men disabled at work. The attractions of climate and soil, the hospitable character of the people, the opportunities for work on estates or in factories, were all expounded in enthusiastic pamphlets, which also gave details about the system of government, coinage, the cost of land, and the official aid given to immigrants on arrival. A publication in Belgium, issued on the eve of the monarchy's downfall, extolled the virtues of the Emperor Pedro II, '*un des hommes les plus érudits de notre époque . . . Son amour de la justice n'a point de bornes; quant à sa générosité, elle est proverbiale.*'[2]

Argentina offered no assisted passages, but immigrants were guaranteed free lodging for a few days, and free inland travel. Official agencies helped them find work. Land was cheap and agricultural colonies were encouraged. To spread knowledge of all these advantages, propaganda was widespread. One booklet, published at Genoa in 1889, comprised more than 250 pages. It contained descriptions of Brazil and Uruguay as well as Argentina; printed all Italian laws relating to emigration; gave advice about the journey; and printed advertisements from agents and steamship companies. Another, issued in English at Buenos Aires in 1904, was profusely, if poorly, illustrated. More than 100 pages in length, it dealt with Argentina's geography,

---

[1] *49 Congress 2 Session, House Exec. Doc. 157,* 380; *61 Congress 3 Session, Senate Doc. 761,* 5–9, 25–6, 107–9; and there is scattered evidence in Norman Macdonald, *Canada: Immigration and Colonization, 1841–1903.* Homesteads were offered from 1872.
[2] Liévin Coppin, *L'Empire du Brésil au point de vue de l'émigration; Lo Stato di Rio de Janeiro nel Brasile; 61 Congress 3 Session, Senate Doc. 761,* 209–29. Frank Bennett, *Forty Years in Brazil,* facing 206, has a photograph of the immigrants' hostel, on an island in Rio de Janeiro bay.

climate (with temperature and rainfall maps), water supply, agriculture, mining, industry, railways, government, and education. It gave details of patent laws, trade-mark regulations, and postal services. Laws and regulations relating to land were printed in full, and the description of reception arrangements at Buenos Aires included a description of the Immigrant Home.[1]

VI

It is easy to describe the propaganda campaigns of governments and of business firms. It is much harder to estimate how effective they were, in determining the scale or direction of emigration.

Certainly the states of the Middle West attracted large numbers of immigrants from Europe. Michigan's foreign-born numbered 55,000 in 1850, 149,000 in 1860, 268,000 in 1870, and 387,000 in 1880. Wisconsin's totalled, for the same years, 110,000, 277,000, 364,000, and 405,000. Iowa's numbered 21,000, 106,000 204,000, and 262,000. Minnesota's total was 59,000 in 1860, 161,000 in 1870, and 267,000 in 1880. It is impossible to know how many of the immigrants reached the Middle West direct from their European homes, and how many after earlier settlement further east. Nor do the printed censuses tell us how many of the foreign-born of, say, 1860 were the same individuals recorded ten years earlier, though local studies find a conspicuously high rate of turnover in population during these years.[2] Before leaping to the conclusion that propaganda was therefore effective, four points should be noted.

The native-born population increased at a similar rate. Propaganda, which was directed simultaneously to Americans and foreigners, may have scored its successes principally among the former. The Burlington railroad, which in 1873 sold land in Nebraska to somewhat over 2,000 persons, recorded that barely one-sixth of them were Europeans, while the overwhelming majority came from adjacent, or at least nearby, states.[3]

It is interesting, also, to observe that the first decade's growth of foreign-born population seems disproportionate to the advertising effort deployed. In other words, the first rush of foreign settlement may have been independent of specific propaganda; and the rather slower, though still massive,

[1] Casimiro Marro, *Manuale pratico dell' emigrante all' Argentina, Uruguay e Brasile; Sketch of the Argentine Republic as a Country for Emigration; 61 Congress 3 Session, Senate Doc. 761*, 195–206. For another description of the immigrant hostel at Buenos Aires, see John A. Hammerton, *The Real Argentine*, 294–8 and photograph facing 4.
[2] Merle Curti, *The Making of an American Community*, and Stephan Thernstrom, *Poverty and Progress*, dealing with a rural Wisconsin county and an industrial town in Massachusetts.
[3] Overton, *op. cit.*, 381.

reinforcement that occurred later may have resulted not so much from further advertising as from informal and personal links between the first settlers and their friends in Europe.

Thirdly, the eastern industrial states were able to increase their foreign-born population enormously with no substantial propaganda either from governments or railroads.

Finally, the southern states, which in the last third of the nineteenth century made very considerable efforts, conspicuously failed to attract European immigrants.

Only two conclusions seem at all safe, and they are notably lacking in precision. Advertising campaigns by the states and railroads may have reinforced the natural advantages possessed by regions at an early stage of development, with an abundance of cheap land. Second, even if propaganda had no certain effect in attracting to the states that engaged in it an unusually large share of immigrants, yet the combined efforts of several states and many business firms may have had an effect on immigration as a whole. For Europe was saturated with information about America. Europeans' choices were clarified. America's advantages over its rivals were set forth. Europeans became acquainted with the ups and downs of American development, on which their opportunities depended.

VII

Among some emigrants, organized propaganda seems to have aroused a degree of scepticism. Discussing the qualifications needed for success in his work, Minnesota's Bremen agent said that it was important never to offer advice too enthusiastically.

> for the emigrant traveller, preyed upon by blacklegs and confidence men . . . from the moment he starts from his native city or village down to the day of his arrival at his final abode, is always on the alert for imposters and very apt to reject the true friend from fear of a snare.[1]

In 1881, the American consul at Aachen reported that many who came to his office were intelligent men who 'have received pamphlets from different societies . . . but are not satisfied with the information which these documents contain.' Intending emigrants might draw the conclusion which was expressed in a Polish letter of 1914. A man who had already crossed the Atlantic warned his friends at home against the advertising of shipping companies. They falsified news of American economic conditions so that

---

[1] Blegen, 'Minnesota's Campaign for Immigrants', 60–61.

they might continue to sell tickets. Therefore, 'let no one listen to anybody but only to his relatives whom he has here, in this golden America.'[1]

Letters had a more continuous flow than any organized advertising. They were much more precisely directed to individuals. They were inherently more credible, coming from known persons and including as they did a wealth of individual and local detail couched in familiar language. Yet their impact, like that of advertising, is hard to estimate. Few have survived. Those which we can read today may have survived because they were found usable for some more public, propagandist purpose, and may therefore reflect some degree of selection. The letters we can see cannot be guaranteed typical. We cannot know how many letters were sent – how many people, in other words, were intelligent, skilled, self-conscious enough to wish to transmit their opinions. Moreover, there is a strong regional bias in the letters that are available to the modern student. It may be, of course, that Scandinavians were especially articulate, and that links between emigrants and those at home were in those countries particularly well maintained. But the preponderance of Norwegian and Swedish letters accessible in print, not merely over letters in eastern Europe but over any in the British Isles, cannot be accepted as reflecting the flow that occurred. With all these qualifications in mind, however, it is still necessary to analyse such evidence as we possess.[2]

Many letters were designed to reassure those at home by showing the material advantages of life in America. From New Hampshire in 1821, a letter to England announced: 'We have now a comfortable dwelling and two acres of ground planted with potatoes, Indian corn, melons, etc. I have two hogs, one ewe and a lamb: cows in the spring were as high as 33 dollars, but no doubt I shall have one in the fall.'[3] Twenty-five years later, Welsh emigrants wrote to Aberystwyth about their farm, with its 'rich and fruitful' soil, abundant livestock, and proximity to neighbours from their own country. 'We can eat our beefsteaks or ham,' the writer went on, 'every morning with our breakfast.' Much the same thoughts can be found in the Somerset weaver's letter which, after dealing with the good food of upper New York state, asserted that in any store the writer can get 'as much brandy as I like to drink for three-halfpence.'[4] Emigrants from other parts

[1] U.S. Consular Reports, II 702; William I. Thomas and Florian Znaniecki, The Polish Peasant in Europe and America, I 774.
[2] Arnold Schrier, Ireland and the American Emigration, 162, states that two million letters a year went from America to the United Kingdom in the 1850s, and sometimes as many as six millions in the 1870s. Of course not all were written by emigrants; but it is easy to see how much we have lost.
[3] Wilson, op. cit., 16, quoting the London Monthly Magazine.
[4] Alan Conway, The Welsh in America, 101-2; Edith Abbott, Historical Aspects of the Immigration Problem, 77-8.

of Europe agreed. From Koshkonong, Wisconsin, in 1847, a Norwegian woman wrote: 'A breakfast here consists of chicken, mutton, beef, or pork, warm or cold wheat bread, butter, white cheese, eggs, or small pancakes, the best coffee, tea, cream, and sugar . . . and my greatest regret here is to see the superabundance of food, much of which has to be thrown to the chickens and the swine.' Three years later, a Swede wrote from Knoxville, Illinois a letter elaborating the theme 'the soil here is good and fruitful.' In 1896 a more positive comparison was made with the homeland. 'I had planned last Christmas,' the letter said, 'that I would spend this Christmas in Sweden – but when I gave more thought to the matter, what can one do in Sweden but work for sour bread and salt herring?'[1]

The same writer, however, said that 'Sweden has been and continues to be a slave land'; and many letters contained comparisons between Europe and America that went beyond material goods. From Kendall, New York, Gjert Hovlund wrote in 1835 of the farm he had cleared, of his good crops, and of his plans to move on to Illinois. His conception of America's advantages included also the absence of poor relief, low taxes, the election of officials, freedom of religion, and the lack of class distinctions. A similar mixture of ideas occurred in a Dutch woman's letter of 1846: 'Nearly all people eat meat three times a day . . . Arnhem can't compare with it. One sees no poor here . . . Schools are free . . . there are no taxes . . . The finery is great, one cannot discern any difference between the cobbler's wife and the wife of a prominent gentleman . . . nobody steals here . . . no night watchman. . . .' In the same decade a Welshman wrote that the traveller's first impression, on landing at New York, was of the inhabitants' neat and comfortable dress. 'The stranger is involuntarily led to inquire where are the working classes, the tattered and half-fed miserable-looking starvelings whom his eye was wont to rest upon whilst crossing the streets of his native land.'[2]

Social equality, religious freedom, political democracy appealed strongly to some of these writers, and they expressed themselves earnestly, sometimes in plain prose, sometimes with eloquence. 'The minister,' wrote one Norwegian, 'dresses just like members of the congregation. He wears no cassock in church, as in oppressed Europe, to call attention to differences in station in society. The same is true of lawyers and government officials.' 'Freedom

[1] Theodore C. Blegen, *Land of their Choice*, 263; and see also Ole Nielsen's account of his experiences as a farmer twenty years later, 409–12. Janson, *op. cit.*, 23, 141, has the Swedish letters. Compare the quotation from a British book of 1821, quoted by Hansen, *Atlantic Migration*, 163: 'Mr Malthus would not be understood here'.
[2] Blegen, *Land of their Choice*, 21–5; Bertus Wabeke, *Dutch Emigration to North America*, 117–18; Conway, *op. cit.*, 69–70.

and equality,' wrote a Swede in 1846, 'are the fundamental principles of the constitution of the United States.' 'There are no statutes,' wrote another five years later, 'which prohibit believing souls from meeting for edification.' 'I am living,' wrote yet another from Burlington, Iowa, in 1850, 'in God's noble and free soil, neither am I a slave under others . . . I have now been on American soil two and a half years, and I have not been compelled to pay a penny for the privilege of living. Neither is my cap worn out from lifting it in the presence of gentlemen.' In simple terms, a Norwegian summed up: 'Here, it is not asked, what or who was your father, but the question is, what are you.' More rhetorically, a Swede commented on Abraham Lincoln:

> How small and insignificant are the princes by the grace of God in Europe in comparison with this man, who began life as a simple working man and is now head of the world's largest and most powerful republic.[1]

A full generation later, in simple language again, a Russian Jewish girl commented that 'the cobbler and the teacher had the same title, "Mister", and all the children, boys and girls, Jews and Gentiles, went to school.'[2]

Not all letters were enthusiastic. Sickness, high prices, lack of community life in the wilderness, all were reported. So were frauds and, by Irish writers, anti-Catholic prejudice. Even those generally favourable to America had to admit the constant pressure to work to the utmost of a man's powers.[3]

None of the letters quoted comes from a guide-book or propaganda leaflet;[4] but all were published in newspapers, either because the writers so intended, or because some editor judged that his public would be interested in their contents. It is important, therefore, to consider such few letters as were genuinely private and which have been rediscovered, in distressingly small numbers, in modern times. Full treatment of this theme must await

---

[1] Blegen, *op. cit.*, 275–6; George M. Stephenson, 'When America was the Land of Canaan', *Minnesota History*, (X 1929) 240, 247, 252; his *Religious Aspects of Swedish Immigration*, 399; and his 'The Mind of the Scandinavian Immigrant', Norwegian-American Historical Association *Studies and Records*, IV (1929), 67: 'A Swedish *bonde* [freeholder], raised under oppression and accustomed to poverty and want, here finds himself elevated to a new world, as it were, where all his former hazy ideas of a society more closely conforming to nature's laws are suddenly made real and he enjoys a satisfaction in his life that he has never before experienced.'

[2] Mary Antin, *The Promised Land*, 148.

[3] Blegen, *op. cit.*, 86–8 (need for hard work, and for a reserve of resources during the year of waiting for crops), 173 (work is done in a day which would be expected to take three in Norway), 189–90 (analysis of the types of people likely to succeed and fail in America); Wabeke, *op. cit.*, 101; Conway, *op. cit.*, 70, 220–21; Schrier, *op. cit.*, 24–38.

[4] An example is *The Emigrant's Guide* (Westport, 1832), 67–136, containing letters mostly very simple and factual, but selected to encourage emigration from Ireland to North America. I have also omitted letters sent back by settlers in organized bodies, to rebut criticism and encourage emigration: see the 'Muskego Manifesto' in Blegen, *op. cit.*, 191–4, and Albert O. Barton, 'Norwegian-American Emigration Societies in the Forties and Fifties', Norwegian-American Historical Association, *Studies and Records*, III (1928), 23–42.

the publication of Dr Charlotte Erickson's book. The letters were written for such simple purposes as to arrange for the reunion of families, ask for money, or merely express the writers' loneliness and help them overcome it. Many of the writers were rural Englishmen, much concerned to preserve an accustomed status or to attain in America a degree of independence just out of reach at home. Once on land, they were likely to stay there, even if rather disillusioned. Other letters came from industrial workers, whose main concern was to move about until they could find the nearest equivalent to their accustomed trade. British emigrants as a whole were likely to preserve some separation from American society, some indifference to its public affairs, and a considerable clinging to the customs of the old country. There was no wild enthusiasm here, no attempt at ideological pronouncement, but sober realism.[1]

There seems no possibility of reaching even such tentative conclusions about other countries, least of all those of southern or eastern Europe. Most of the letters in Thomas and Znaniecki's great collection, for example, were written not in America but in Poland. All that can be said is that, exposed to the influence of letters and of organized propaganda, millions of Europeans came down on the side of optimism about America, at least in relation to the known conditions at home. Officials in the Netherlands understood this as early as 1847:

> Nothing avails to check this exaggerated tendency. For as long as the low cost of land in the New World, the cheap provisions, the high wages, the freedom from all taxation, etc. are much advertised, no warnings of the sad fate that awaits the poor who leave without any prospects can hold the crowd back and secure them against deception and disappointment.[2]

VIII

Other influences strengthened the message. The mere sight of emigration going on, of friends and neighbours departing, aroused men's interest. A reporter watching a party leave Nijmegen in 1847 wrote: 'All around one could hear conversations in which people approved of the plan, complained bitterly of the decline of the national welfare, and expressed the desire to flee the sinking fatherland.'[3] In peasant cottages stood photographs of those

[1] Meanwhile, see Dr Erickson's contribution, 'Agrarian Myths of English Immigrants', in O. Fritiof Ander, *In the Trek of the Immigrants,* 59–80. I have also seen her unpublished papers on agricultural and industrial emigrants' letters, presented to a seminar at the British Association for American Studies meeting, Exeter 1962.

[2] Wabeke, *op. cit.,* 102.

[3] *Ibid.,* 138. Compare the remark in the official publication of the Mormon Church in Britain, *Latter-day Saints' Millennial Star,* X 74 (1 March 1848): 'From the first day that they begin to sell their furniture and goods, the voice of emigration preaches loudly.'

who had emigrated, to be the focus of conversation and to give colour to the letters received.[1] More striking still was the impact of emigrants who returned in person. When Knud Anderson Slogvig went back to Norway in 1835, 'from all parts of the diocese of Bergen and from Stavanger people came to talk with him.' When Ansten Nattestad went home three years later, 'the rumour of my homecoming passed like a flame through the country. Within a few weeks letters came asking questions about America . . . Many travelled 20 Norwegian miles in order to talk with me about my trip.'[2] Three-quarters of a century later, and many hundreds of miles from Scandinavia, the effect was the same. In Italy, the popular attitude was summed up in the words, 'They come back arrayed like *signori*'; and an American visitor saw chairs all round the walls of the best room of a Sicilian house, to accommodate the people who came, each evening, to hear a returned emigrant's account of his six years in the United States. Men came back to Slovenia, in serge suits and black derbies, their suitcases bulging with gifts, standing treat in the wine shops and boasting of their experiences. After writing letters and sending money, a pioneer emigrant returned to Macedonia in his American clothes, to prove his affluence by presenting a chandelier to the village church.[3]

By such means, contacts were made and maintained, not merely in some general sense between two continents, but between members of single villages and single families. Many, no doubt, of the ninety-four per cent of arrivals at Ellis Island, who between 1908 and 1910 declared that they were joining friends or relations, did so to impress the officials that they were unlikely to become a public charge. Most, one suspects, were stating no more than the truth. 'There is probably hardly a locality,' reported British investigators from Hesse, 'between which and a corresponding locality on the American continent intimate relations have not grown up.' In 1890 an American consul, asking the causes of emigration from Naples, always received the answer, 'My friend in America is doing well and he has sent for me.'[4]

[1] Moberg, *op. cit.*, 10–11.
[2] Blegen, *Norwegian Migration*, 71, 102–3 (the distance equals 140 English miles). See also Carlton Qualey, *Norwegian Settlement in the United States*, 43, and Johan Bojer's novel *The Emigrants*, 23–4.
[3] Robert F. Foerster, *The Italian Emigration of our Time*, 417; Brandenburg, *op. cit.*, 91; Louis Adamic, *Laughing in the Jungle*, 3–6; Stoyan Christowe, *This Is My Country*, 20–29; Norman Douglas, *Old Calabria*, reports several encounters with these *americani*, with their energy, sense of superiority, and fluent use of such expressions as 'sons of bitches' and 'you bet'.
[4] *61 Congress 3 Session, Senate Doc. 756*, 361, 364–5; *Parl. Papers 1870*, LXVII, Part II 217; *52 Congress 1 Session, House Misc. Docs., 19 & 20*, 211.

CHAPTER FIVE

Calculations and Decisions

These (to Europeans) prodigal remittances serve to intensify the pre-existing impression that the new Canaan flows with more milk and honey than the old Canaan. When a letter comes into a German village bearing one or two hundred marks to some old frau the event is celebrated over the village beer and pipe, and in the halo the New World is transfigured – the more so when the girl working in the field and the man working in the shop compare their wages in marks with those American wages in dollars.

52 Congress 1 Session, House Misc. Docs. 19 and 20,
Special Consular Reports, European Emigration, 249.

In their reports printed in 1870, British consuls pointed to German villages, situated an hour's walk apart on either side of a small mountain, whose inhabitants not merely failed to intermarry, but never met; and Arnold Toynbee, in his *Industrial Revolution*, remarked that there were labourers in Devon who had never heard of Lancashire, where wages were double their own.[1] The statements, no doubt, were true; but they were far from the whole truth. Even among Europeans of the lowest class, even in the most backward regions, movement took place. In the larger empires, too, military service had the effect, if not of mingling ethnic groups, at least of carrying men into remote provinces in time of peace and into foreign countries during wars.[2] It is still true, however, that, in nineteenth-century European society, inertia was a force which the student of emigration must take seriously. People were accustomed to endure hardship. Their movements fell within a few traditional categories. However ample the information which spread across the continent, America could not at first seem other than remote. It was one thing to walk into a neighbouring province for the harvest, or, as a craftsman, undertake a *Wanderjahr*. It was quite another to cross the Atlantic.

Tensions and hardships prepared men's minds. Advertisements, books, letters pointed to the way of escape and improvement in America. In the middle of the century, a Roman Catholic priest, the Rev M. Lennon, told a

---

[1] *Parl. Papers 1870*, LXVII, Part I, 387, Report of H.M. Representatives . . . Tenure of Land . . . Europe; Arnold J. Toynbee, *The Industrial Revolution*, 70.
[2] Examples are in William I. Thomas and Florian Znaniecki, *The Polish Peasant in Europe and America*, I 515–26, 557–64.

Select Committee: 'Generally I read one-third of the letters for the poor people who cannot read, and see how the money is to be allotted.' In the 1890s, a Donegal schoolmaster was performing a similar function, sometimes translating a letter into Erse. At the opposite ends of Europe, the same thing could be seen. A young Jewish girl in western Russia, early in the 1890s, saw friends and relations pour into her home, day and night, to see the ticket which had arrived from America, to handle it, and to hear the accompanying letter read to them. In Macedonia, twenty years later, the arrival of a similar letter, enclosing money, 'robbed Selo of the tranquillity which it had enjoyed for centuries.'[1]

Such a combination of factors might cause a European peasant, labourer, or artisan to desire emigration. To translate desire into successful action, however, called for much thought; and destination, route and cost all had to be considered with care. A great deal of advice on these matters was in print. It is not, of course, suggested that every emigrant was able to follow through every single argument, or to arrive at the wisest of decisions.

In the days of sail, emigrants might await a vessel at a local harbour. They might travel, on the other hand, to one of the great seaports, where trade with America produced an abundance of shipping, and therefore brought the advantages of competitive fares and the minimum of delays. Patterns of trade might themselves dictate the place of arrival in America: much of Scandinavia's trade was with the St Lawrence, Havre was linked with New Orleans, and Bremen with Baltimore. Yet all major ports offered a choice. Ships left Liverpool, for example, in large numbers, bound for Quebec, Boston, New York, Philadelphia and New Orleans, though New York was always in the lead. An emigrant would consider the costs of the several journeys. He would think of the blocking of the St Lawrence by ice for several months, and of the lower quality of Quebec shipping; and he would set against these factors the ease of travel into the Middle West, once canals had been built, steamboat services organized, and, in the 1850s, a fairly continuous railroad constructed as far as Chicago.[2] People reaching the Atlantic ports headed for the Ohio and the Great Lakes. They could use the Hudson and the Erie Canal, or a mixture of railroads and canals leading towards Pittsburgh; and from the 1850s they could complete the whole of this part of their journey by railroad. Beyond, they could rely, first on

[1] *Parl. Papers 1852*, XIV, Q. 3484, 3490, evidence before the Select Committee on Outrages; Arnold Schrier, *Ireland and the American Emigration*, 40–2; Mary Antin, *The Promised Land*, 163–4; Stoyan Christowe, *This Is My Country*, 16–19.
[2] Theodore C. Blegen, *Norwegian Migration to America*, 350–1; and *Norwegian Migration to America: the American Transition*, 13–14; *Parl. Papers 1854*, XXVIII, 58–9; and for the background in Canada, W. T. Easterbrook and H. G. J. Aitken, *Canadian Economic History*, esp. chapter xii.

steamboats, later on railroads, while canals linked the Ohio and the Lakes. The difficulties facing them were the frequent changes of conveyance, the slowness of the journey, ice in winter and low water in summer, and, because of these natural conditions, the fluctuations in costs.[1] From the 1850s, when the whole of the Middle West as far as the Mississippi received a rail network, some of these inconveniences disappeared. The final possibility was to disembark at New Orleans and ascend the Mississippi and, if need be, its tributaries, by steamboat. The journey was both speedy and cheap. The disadvantages were delays at the mouth of the river because of sandbars, and steamboat accidents from snags, fire or explosion. These were taken lightly by most travellers, but everyone seems to have been impressed by the lower Mississippi's reputation for fever in summer.[2] After the Civil War, the Atlantic ports became completely dominant. Emigrants making their way west now travelled in special cheap cars, or whole trains, made up of obsolete rolling-stock and shunted aside for every superior train that passed.[3]

Seasons as well as routes had to be calculated by those intending to emigrate, and this remained true however much modes of transport and commercial systems changed. It was obviously inconvenient to cross the North Atlantic, or advance into the middle of Canada, in winter. On the other hand, it was always thought best to avoid New Orleans in the summer months, and in 1854 the city saw no more than two per cent of its arrivals in the third quarter of the year, nearly forty-three per cent in the fourth, and the remainder evenly divided between second and third. Elsewhere, however, seasonal figures reflect opportunities for work rather than factors of climate or health. Railroad and canal building, laying of streets, labour on the docks, in all of which many emigrants took part, were inevitably seasonal. The peak of migration on the North Atlantic was therefore likely to occur in spring, though there was a secondary rise in September and October. January was commonly the lowest month. When, in the twentieth century, more detailed figures were kept, the spring peak was found to be especially high for unskilled labourers; while, in November and December, large numbers of such men could be seen at the ports, on their way home.[4]

---

[1] It is sufficient to refer to Louis C. Hunter, *Steamboats on the Western Rivers*, and Harry N. Scheiber, *Ohio Canal Era*. Details of several such journeys, with references, appear in my chapter 7.

[2] *De Bow's Review*, VIII 376–8, XII 450, XV 294 (accidents); XIII 529–32 (sandbars, with a sketch of stranded vessels); I 81–2, II 348, III 252, IV 401, IX 245–6, XV 596–631 (epidemics).

[3] The first reference to emigrant trains known to me is in *Wiley and Putnam's Emigrants' Guide*, 131, in 1845. See also *Disturnell's Guide* of 1851, 32, 64; *Appleton's Railway and Steam Navigation Guide* (July 1856), 27, 35, 41, 45, 71; and advertisements in *New York World*, 1 May 1861, 1 January and 1 March 1863, and 6 June 1866.

[4] See monthly figures 1847–52, in *Liverpool Mercury*, 2 January 1852, 11 January 1853; quarterly figures for principal American ports, 1854, in *33 Congress 2 Session, House Exec. Doc. 77*; and monthly figures 1907–14, in Harry Jerome, *Migration and Business Cycles*, 216, 219. Taking the

Whatever the route chosen, movement cost money, and, since so many emigrants intended to secure work immediately upon arrival in America, it is logical to examine, first, the cost of the Atlantic crossing alone.

The fare for emigrants using sailing ships 'necessarily varies,' as a commentator put it in 1856, 'more or less on each ship.' The time of year, competition between ships, the calculations of individual masters and agents, all played a part. Advertisements of steerage passage used such expressions as 'on the most favourable terms', or 'at the lowest possible rates', while requesting a deposit of £1 to secure a berth. In 1853 a Liverpool passenger broker, accused of having failed to provide passage for some emigrants on the agreed terms, alleged in his defence, among other facts, that the rate had advanced 7s. 6d. between sailings.[1] Estimates published in guide-books, or stated before official inquiries, showed not so much single figures as a range. In 1840, for example, it was claimed that steerage on board the 'packets', ships sailing on a schedule, could be had for £5, on 'transient ships' for anything between £3. 10. 0 and £4. Nine years later it was thought that steerage from Liverpool to New York would cost £2. 10. 0, to New Orleans £3, and to Quebec between £3 and £4. In 1851 the estimate, including such provisions as the law required, was £3. 10. 0 to £4 for New York, and ten shillings more for Quebec. Four years later, Quebec's rate was said to be from five to fifteen shillings cheaper. In 1859 the situation was again reversed: Liverpool to New York cost £3. 5. 0, to Quebec, £4. 10. 0. These figures seem to have persisted until the middle 1860s, when sailing ships ceased to be important in the emigrant trade.[2]

Steamships, with regular sailings and a few big companies dominating the scene, allowed steerage rates to be advertised, though their uniformity was not complete. Five or six guineas was the common rate from Liverpool to New York, but newspapers early in 1890 quoted figures as low as £3. 10.0. From continental ports, $20 or $25 was normal; but momentarily, in 1894, the Bremen rate fell to $16.[3] Behind such fluctuations lay a struggle: not

---

monthly average of unskilled labourer arrivals as 100, Jerome found the March figure to be 169·3, April 173·5, May 150·2, June 113·8, July 69·4, October 86·6, and January only 52·9. A similar pattern is found in the Irish monthly figures, in annual volumes of *Parl. Papers* for the late nineteenth century and the early twentieth. Mark Jefferson, *Peopling the Argentine Pampa*, 185, 191, 198–9, shows the peak of immigration to occur in October, November and December, the spring and early summer in the Southern Hemisphere. *49 Congress 2 Session, House Exec. Doc. 157*, 265, reveals the effects in a country with emigration both to North and South America: among Italian emigrants, spring and autumn figures were fairly equal.

[1] *Latter-day Saints' Millennial Star*, XVIII 25 (12 January 1856); *Liverpool Mercury*, 4 January 1848, 13 March 1849, 9 September 1853.

[2] *British Mechanics' and Labourers' Handbook*, 25–31; *Colonization Circular*, February 1849, 3 April 1851, 3 April 1855, 3 May 1859, 3; *Aris' Birmingham Gazette*, 1 October 1849.

[3] Evan Jones, *The Emigrants' Friend* (1880), for advertisements; *50 Congress 1 Session, House*

now a struggle against the unpredictable effects of wind, or the unpredictable numbers of emigrants in relation to the supply of shipping, but a struggle between companies, alternating from unrestricted competition to manoeuvres to rationalize trade in their own interest. Hamburg-America and British companies reached agreement in 1886 to restrain the British share of Hamburg emigration in return for the German abandoning of Gothenburg. In 1888 an agreement was in force between the German lines and Red Star of Antwerp. In 1892, the same lines, together with Holland-America, formed the North Atlantic Steamship Association, to restrain competitive advertising and keep their share of traffic to the proportions of the 1880s. In 1902, Morgan's 'Trust' tried to broaden the scope of such control. In 1908, Cunard at last joined most of the other lines in fixing rates and sharing the traffic. Yet such arrangements were always exposed to rebellion, and lines were at times willing to accept short-term losses in the hope of turning long-term business in their own direction.[1]

Such published rates were not the whole cost of the emigrant journey. Emigrants had to reach the ports, pay for lodging, equip themselves, for much of the period, with bedding, utensils, and other articles for the voyage, and, in the early years, buy food to supplement the meagre provisions required by law. Reaching probably a total of £1, these necessities largely disappeared when the steamship arrived, and this fact in some degree offset the higher fares.

Great numbers of emigrants travelled when single, or as couples with their family still in the future. Those who already had children often found that the older ones were charged two-thirds of the adult rate, younger children half, while infants went for a nominal £1. If, then, the calculation is made of the total cost of reaching America for a man, wife and three children, it seems impossible to arrive at a figure much less than £18 under sail and £25 by steam. It would be rather higher for the ports of Germany and the Low Countries, and higher still for those who had to make a long journey across Europe before embarking.[2]

Emigrants planning to travel inland in the United States had to pay still

---

Misc. Doc. 572, Part I, 6, 18, 22, 25; *Hull News*, 4 January and 19 April 1890; *Cunard Passengers' Log-Book* (1893), 18; *Industrial Commission Reports*, XV, 104, 115, 117, 119 (1899 figures: Liverpool $25 to $27.50, Bremen $36.50, Antwerp $29.50, Naples $28, all to New York); Walter F. Willcox and Imre Ferenczi, *International Migrations*, II 329 (for 1913).

[1] *50 Congress 1 Session, House Misc. Doc. 572*, Part I, 10; *U.S. Consular Reports*, No. 295, 43-4 (for the rate war of 1904); Lamar Cecil, *Albert Ballin*, 44-62.

[2] Fourth-class rail fares were of course low. *52 Congress 1 Session, House Misc. Docs. 19 and 20*, 244, shows $12 from Milan to Antwerp in 1890; and the distance is very similar to that covered by millions of emigrants in the following quarter of a century.

more. Since all routes cannot be taken into account, it will be enough to concentrate on travel from eastern seaports to such a central destination as Chicago, adding, in later years, a few places further west. In the 1840s, the journey from New York City to Chicago was thought to cost about $14, travelling mostly by water. By 1852 the figure was more like $10.[1] By the St Lawrence route, in the 1850s, it cost from £1. 12. 0 to £1. 19. 0 to reach Chicago, and the figures changed little for many years.[2] The trip from Philadelphia to St Louis was likely to cost much the same as that from New York to Chicago, or a dollar more.[3] The river journey from New Orleans to St Louis, travelling on deck, cost no more than $2 or $3, though the emigrant had also to pay for his food.[4] From the late 1860s, costs cited in guide-books are for all-rail routes. Three specimens will suffice. In 1869, with Quebec as starting-point, it cost £1. 16. 0 to reach Chicago, £4. 7. 0 Omaha and Minneapolis ten shillings more, £10. 16. 0 San Francisco. Four years later, and starting from New York, the figures seem to have been higher. It cost $13 (more than £2. 10. 0) to reach Chicago, twice as much to Omaha or Minneapolis, and $60 (more than £12) to San Francisco. Still assuming travel by emigrant trains, the cost in the 1880s was a little higher; and it did not then change significantly until the Great War.[5]

Enough Germans, English, Scandinavians and others settled on land to make it worthwhile to examine the cost of establishing a farm. In the years before the Homestead Act, it is realistic to think of paying $100 for eighty acres, and after that, a log cabin, fencing, seed and livestock had to be provided, and the settler had to subsist until he could sell a crop. A writer with experience of pioneer farming in Illinois in the 1840s, but who had bought only forty acres, estimated the cost, including six months' food for four people, as $550. Doubtless many people managed with less, but it would have been at the cost of severe hardship: it was, for example, very advantageous to hire experienced Americans to perform some of the early work of preparing the land, work to which a European would be unac-

---

[1] *Wiley and Putnam's Emigrants' Guide*, 131; *Appleton's Railroad and Steamboat Companion*, 1847, 116, 160–1, 182; [Cassell's] *Emigrants' Handbook*, 49–53.
[2] *Colonization Circular*, May 1854, 31–2; *Parl. Papers 1857 (Session 1)*, X, Appendix 7, Report of Chief Emigration Agent, Quebec; 'Americus', *Where to Emigrate and Why*, 178–82.
[3] *Emigrants' Handbook*, 49–53.
[4] J. Calvin Smith, *Emigrants' Handbook*, 177. John M. Peck, *New Guide for Emigrants to the West* (1837), 379–81, states that emigrants could eat with the crew for 25c., that meals along a stage route could be had for 37½c., but warns that unpredictable delays could drive up costs.
[5] 'Americus', *Where to Emigrate and Why*, 172–82; *43 Congress 1 Session, Senate Exec. Doc. 23*, 184–92; Jones, *The Emigrants' Friend*, 42, 68, 101 (figures from Liverpool to final destination); Emory R. Johnson and G. C. Huebner, *Railroad Traffic and Rates*, II 120 (similar figures just before the Great War, with emphasis on the concessions to land-seekers).

5a   'Tea Water!'
Illustrated London News, 20 January 1849.

5b   Dancing between decks.
Illustrated London News, 6 July 1850.

6   Castle Garden: recruiting immigrants for the Union Army, September 1864
Radio Times Hulton Picture Library.

customed.[1] Against this formidable outlay, however, should be set the practice, very common among emigrants, of renting farms, or of working for others, acquiring relevant skills, and saving money from their wages in order to buy land of their own.

It is easy enough to estimate the costs of emigration: it is much more difficult to reach conclusions about the resources which emigrants possessed. Although figures exist for emigrants' occupations, they are far from reliable. Even when they do not overstate the category 'labourer', they never distinguish, in a trade, between the self-employed person and wage-earner, the skilled and the unskilled, the worker by modern and by obsolete processes, the overworked and the unemployed. The difficulty is even greater with the vast numbers of emigrants coming from the land. Contemporaries sometimes estimated that, in a certain ethnic group, there were percentages of freeholders, tenants, cotters, but this tells us nothing about the amount of land or other property they held, or what it was worth. We do not know what hidden resources emigrants possessed, in the form of savings from the wages of a secondary, and unstated, occupation, or from the cash part of wages largely paid in the form of accommodation and food. Nor can we compare those who went with those who were deterred by their difficulties: still less can we say whether the differences were those of material resources alone, or, on the contrary, of such personal qualities as courage, skill, enterprise, or optimism.

What is certain is that millions were not deterred, and that great numbers of these came from regions of Europe we should be inclined to call poverty-stricken. Not only did peasants and workers pay for the journey: they arrived in the United States with a small reserve of cash. Between 1899 and 1910, emigrants' declarations of resources, to the Ellis Island officials, averaged $31.39: it was more than $70 for British and Dutch, under $25 for South Italians, Roumanians, and most of the Slav peoples. They needed funds in order to prove that they were unlikely to become a public charge and so liable to be turned away. The funds, however, really were in their possession, and quite possibly they had more than they declared.[2] It remains to enquire how the emigrant journey was financed.

Public authorities gave some help. Agencies of the central government in Britain and Ireland sometimes founded settlements, and carried emigrants to them. The Poor Law authorities helped more than 20,000 to emigrate

---

[1] John Regan, *The Emigrant's Guide to the Western States of America*, 353. Allan Bogue, *From Prairie to Cornbelt*, 170, prints an estimate for railroad land in Iowa, 1870, which totals $515 for a small farm, or $800 if more elaborate machinery is desired.

[2] *61 Congress 3 Session, Senate Doc. 756*, 349 (immigrants had to declare whether they had less than $30, or $50 from 1903, and how much less), 358 (the figures).

8

from Britain, and more than 40,000 from Ireland, though not many of them went to the United States. Assisted passages, which benefited far more people, never applied to the United States, but only to the colonies, and especially to Australia. Indentured service, which had been so important in colonial days, was of course almost extinct in the United States by the 1830s. European governments undertook no financing of emigration. All that can be found is villages, which, in time of special crisis, might help their poor to cross the Atlantic.[1]

Some emigrants received aid from what may be called business sources. In the 1830s and 1840s, Irish landlords calculated that an immediate outlay for passage and a small sum for landing expenses would enable them to clear their land of unprofitable tenants, and begin the rationalizing of their estates.[2] This affected a few thousands, and only one country. More widespread, though still affecting small numbers, was recruiting by American firms. In the British Isles, Belgium, the German States, and Scandinavia, a few American factories sought workers with special skills, and brought them to America under contracts by which passage money was to be repaid from wages.[3] Serving industry, but motivated by the desire for an individual profit, was the *padrone*. Such a man established a network of personal contacts in his own country, recruited workers who bound themselves to him for a year, advanced their passage money for America, and secured it by having their fathers or other relatives give him a mortgage on their property, for a much larger sum. The system was to be found, late in the nineteenth century, in Italy and Greece.[4]

Private philanthropic agencies were active. In Britain, they were chiefly

[1] Helen Cowan, *British Emigration to British North America, the First Hundred Years* (1961 edn), chapter iv; Robert B. Madgwick, *Immigration to Eastern Australia, 1783–1851*; Stanley C. Johnson, *Emigration from the United Kingdom to North America*, 86–94; Oliver MacDonagh, in R. Dudley Edwards and T. D. Williams, *The Great Famine*, 352–9; Mack Walker, *Germany and the Emigration*, 75–6 (examples from Bavaria, Württemberg and Hesse).

[2] *Parl. Papers 1847*, VI, Q 1402–4, Select Committee of the House of Lords, Colonization from Ireland; Edith Abbott, *Historical Aspects of the Immigration Problem*, 124–5 (account by W. Steuart Trench, an agent); William F. Adams, *Ireland and the Irish Emigration to the New World from 1815 to the Famine*, 167, 216–17; Edwards and Williams, *op. cit.*, 332–40. Most of these people were assisted to go to Canada; but it is reasonable to suppose that, like so many of their contemporaries, they walked over the border.

[3] Charlotte Erickson, *American Industry and the European Immigrant, 1860–1885*, 17–22, 34–45, 133–4, 141–3. An example from the 1850s is in Ray Ginger, 'Labor in a Massachusetts Cotton Mill, 1853–60', *Business History Review*, XXVIII (1954), esp. 73–88.

[4] Robert Foerster, *The Italian Emigration of our Time*, 326, 391; Theodore Saloutos, *The Greeks in the United States*, 48–52. These true *padroni* must be distinguished from Italian and other agents who simply recruited within the United States on behalf of business firms, from the work of companies recruiting for themselves at the ports, and from the labour agencies attached to steamship companies, all of which found immigrants jobs but did not advance passage-money: Erickson, *op. cit.*, 70–72, 78–87, 99–103.

concerned with emigration to the Empire, and this was equally true of such early organizations as the Society for the Promotion of Colonization and the Fund for Promoting Female Emigration, and of later agencies like Mr James Hack Tuke's Fund, the British Women's Emigration Society, and, in one aspect of their work, Dr Barnardo's and the Salvation Army.[1] In the German States, the emigration of a few thousands, at most, was aided by the *Adelsverein* and less celebrated bodies.[2] Permanent Jewish organizations in several countries helped to set up a system to aid emigration from Russia, whenever a crisis occurred. They did so in the period 1869–73, in response to cholera and famine; in 1882 in response to pogroms in southern Russia; in 1891 after the expulsion of Jews from Moscow; and in 1904, after pogroms at Kishinev and elsewhere. Committees worked at the Russian borders, at transport centres in Germany, at the ports, and, less closely linked, in overseas countries. The relief system might last only a year, or a few years, lapsing and then reviving when the next blow fell. The scale, however, was impressive. In 1906–7 alone, more than 25,000 people received money, thousands more got clothes and medical care, and nearly a hundred thousand were guaranteed kosher food.[3]

Emigrants themselves could form organizations for mutual aid. As early as the 1820s, societies existed among working men in Renfrewshire and Lanarkshire, and in the city of Glasgow. The 1840s saw many such schemes, as far apart as London and Halifax. American railroads, in the 1870s, did their best to encourage the formation of similar groups. The principles were not exactly uniform, but one which was favoured involved a lottery, giving one member or a few the chance of drawing quickly upon a fund built up by the savings of a greater number. The principle was not confined to Britain. Early in the twentieth century it was observed in a Bulgarian village, the winners promising to repay, with interest, from America, the money they had drawn, so that others might benefit.[4] As a by-product of their main tasks, British trade unions sometimes undertook to assist members to emigrate. Iron workers, cotton spinners, engineers, carpenters were all

---

[1] Society for the Promotion of Colonization, *Report of the General Committee* (February 1849); Fund for Promoting Female Emigration, *First Report of the Committee* (March 1851); Eneas Mackenzie, *Memoir of Mrs Caroline Chisholm*, 137, 153–69; Johnson, *op. cit.*, 65, 73–80, 255–94.

[2] Walker, *op. cit.*, 82–5.

[3] Harold Frederic, *The New Exodus*, 273–94; Mark Wischnitzer, *To Dwell in Safety*, esp. 29–48, 71–82, 100–130. See also Samuel Joseph, *History of the Baron de Hirsch Fund*.

[4] *Parl. Papers 1826–7*, V, Q. 48, 133–5, 175, 638–9, 749–50, and paper following 2363; Wilbur S. Shepperson, *British Emigration to North America: Projects and Opinions in the Victorian Period*, 74 (note 124), 103, 113 (note 70); *Land and Emigration*, November 1871, January 1872; *61 Congress 3 Session, Senate Doc. 748*, 58–9.

involved, in addition to the celebrated Staffordshire potters in the 1840s – but the numbers aided were small.[1]

Most emigrants, however, relied on their own resources, or on those of their families and immediate friends. Probably many village craftsmen had cash savings. Other men owned land or could raise money from the sale of a leasehold. In the 1840s, Irishmen were selling off farms and stock, and were finding others willing to buy, even at the cost of going into debt, in order to provide for their sons. Once the Famine had occurred, contemporaries saw even heavier sales of homes and livestock.[2] A Dutch journal of the same period shows a man going through many formalities before being allowed to auction his farm, formalities designed to convince the authorities that he had settled with all his creditors and provided for any children he might intend leaving behind. Another Dutchman announced the sale of two horses, twenty cattle, fifty sheep, hay, and other articles. Yet another offered smith's equipment, farm tools, and furniture.[3] In Norway, freeholders were sometimes able to raise large sums for their farms: $7,500 was once recorded.[4] In Hesse, the inhabitants of two entire villages sold both private and communal property to a nobleman, and emigrated in a body.[5] Since the laws and customs of many parts of Europe required that the heir to a farm should compensate his brothers and sisters, the money, or goods which could be turned into money, might be used to finance emigration.[6]

Borrowing, too, was often possible. Examples can be found from the 1830s to the early 1900s, and from Ireland to Galicia. Relatives and friends, no doubt, were the people most often involved, guaranteeing, perhaps, as in Ireland, to pay an emigrant's passage within a year; lending money direct, free of interest, as in Galicia; or, as in Slovakia, acting as guarantor of a bank loan. Bank loans, of course, like loans from Galician Jews, involved the payment of interest, but some people were more fortunate. One Dutchman, in 1856, was able to borrow from the farmer who had employed him, then repaid him from America within a year. Another, a young apprentice,

[1] Charlotte Erickson, 'Encouragement of Emigration by British Trade Unions, 1850–1900', *Population Studies*, III (1949), 248–73; Shepperson, *op. cit.*, 94–9 and reproduction of one of the Potters' broadsides, facing 149; Harold Owen, *The Staffordshire Potters*, 72–81, 92–100.

[2] *Parl. Papers 1847*, VI, Q. 1877 a.; Edwards and Williams, *op. cit.*, 470 (note 11).

[3] Journal of James Moerdyke, in Henry S. Lucas, *Dutch Immigrant Memoirs and Related Writings*, II 415–16; and for advertisements of sales of property, see his *Netherlanders in America*, 139.

[4] Blegen, *American Transition*, 8. Johan Bojer, *The Emigrants*, 54–5, has an account of an auction. Florence Janson, *Background of Swedish Immigration*, 328, suggests that some emigrants from northern Sweden financed their move by selling their marginal farms to lumber companies.

[5] Walker, *op. cit.*, 76–7.

[6] *Parl. Papers 1870*, LXVII, Part I, 79–80, Part II, 133, 217, 226–7 – examples from several German states. See also Rigmor Frimmenshend, 'Farm Community and Neighbourhood Community', *Scandinavian Economic History Review*, IV (1956), 62–81.

repaid a master carpenter by working for him in America. Similarly, Sara Kools worked as a servant for five years, paying off her emigration debt of $24 as well as buying clothes for her marriage from her savings.[1]

A few were luckier still. A wealthy Dutch Seceder, Jannes van de Luyster, paid the debts of ten families of his poorer brethren in 1847, took their promises to repay, then set them up on land in Michigan to enable them to meet their obligations. Three years later, Joris Per Anderson, a Swedish farmer, helped his neighbours to emigrate and led them on their journey. In 1838, Ole Aasland, a wealthy Norwegian farmer, had done likewise, but required the people assisted to work for him.[2] Andrew Carnegie's family, to give one further example, emigrated with the combined proceeds of the sale of his father's looms, the withdrawal of a deposit in a friendly society, a friend's loan of £20, and an aunt's of £2.10.0 – loans repaid after two years in America.[3]

If money could be raised in none of these ways, one member of the family had to be used as pioneer. 'A son or daughter goes first, acquires some money, and sends it home . . . and the money which is sent takes over another member of the family, and at length the whole family go.' This, as was said in the early 1850s, had been the practice in Irish counties 'for many years'. Examples can be found in other parts of Europe, but the Irish gained a unique reputation for the efforts they made, even when in poorly paid work in America, to reunite their families.[4] Among Dutch settlers, examples can be found of small societies, formed in America among emigrant families, to finance the coming of friends and relatives from Europe.[5]

Remittances, in cash or in the form of prepaid tickets, undoubtedly became the mainstay of all but pioneer migration. This is true from end to end of Europe. Right through the nineteenth century, the Irish were active. Between 1847 and 1887, the recorded figure was £34,000,000, and very probably this was a considerable underestimate. Much of the money was used to support families at home, to pay their rent or buy livestock, or

[1] Oliver MacDonagh, *A Pattern of Government Growth*, 30; Jan W. Borman's journal in Lucas, *Dutch Immigrant Memoirs*, II 87–8, also 255–6, while I 92 has another variant, a woman who served as cook on the journey in return for her expenses. Thomas and Znaniecki, *op. cit.*, I 718, 930, have examples of interest payments. See also Emily G. Balch, *Our Slavic Fellow Citizens*, 108, 139; Blegen, *Norwegian Migration*, 123; Janson, *op. cit.*, 304.
[2] Lucas, *Dutch Immigrant Memoirs*, I 219–21, while 344 shows four families and a servant girl paid for by a pastor; 'The Early Life of Eric Norelius', *Augustana Historical Society Publications*, IV Part I (1934), 73–5; Blegen, *Norwegian Migration*, 108–9.
[3] Burton J. Hendrick, *Andrew Carnegie*, 36, 52.
[4] *Parl. Papers 1852*, XIV, Q. 4527; Irish emigrant letter printed in James Hack Tuke, *A Visit to Connaught*, 48; John F. Maguire, *The Irish in America*, 313–32. See also Balch, *op. cit.*, 72, on Bohemia.
[5] Lucas, *Netherlanders in America*, 491–2.

merely to provide for housekeeping. Much emigration was financed too, and enough money was sometimes sent for the wake, that all-night session of drinking, smoking, talking and dancing, followed by ritual lamentation as the emigrants set off.[1] Prepaid passages, too, were a major feature of business at the ports, as many brokers testified before Select Committees.[2] Into Norway, remittances, in the form of postal money orders alone, poured, by 1900, at the rate of half a million to a million dollars a year. In Sweden, the practice could become so much a routine that, by the sending of successive tickets, six or seven children in one family might go.[3] Late in the century Austria-Hungary received vast sums – supposedly more than $95 millions between 1893 and 1903, and over $80 million in U.S. money orders alone between 1900 and 1909 – and such figures never included notes enclosed in letters, or money taken by returning emigrants. Remittances were noted in Slovakia as early as 1891. Miss Balch was told that single emigrants often sent back to Slovakia $100 a year, and the figure given her in Croatia was somewhat higher. She noted, too, the practice in Galicia, of girls going to domestic service in America while their fiancés were in the army, sending them tickets when their term of service ended.[4] To Italy, the amounts sent were also large, more than $50 millions in money orders between 1900 and 1906, and perhaps as much as 500 million *lire* (nearly $100 million) in 1907 alone. An aged peasant told a British traveller early in the twentieth century, that many of his neighbours were receiving £3 a month from this source.[5] In the 1890s, the Hamburg and Bremen shipping lines were already seeing thirty to forty per cent of the emigrants they carried receiving prepaid tickets. An investigation at Ellis Island in the period 1908–10 led to the conclusion that 58 per cent of Jews had been helped by remittances or tickets, 38·6 per cent of the Irish, 35·5 per cent of the Germans, and over 27 per cent of the Scandinavians, while the lower figures for Italian, Slovaks,

---

[1] Arnold Schrier, *Ireland and the American Emigration*, 85–90, 106–20, 167–8.
[2] *Parl. Papers 1851*, XIX, Q. 505, 2812, 3625, 6236–9, Select Committee on Passengers' Acts; MacDonagh, *op. cit.*, 27–8, states that as early as 1834 one Liverpool broker did forty-five per cent of his business in remittances and prepaid passages.
[3] Blegen, *American Transition*, 462, 473; Vilhelm Moberg, *When I was a Child*.
[4] *52 Congress 1 Session, House Exec. Doc. 235*, Part I, 106 (for 1891); *61 Congress 3 Session, Senate Doc. 748*, 387 (for later figures); *Senate Doc. 753*, 283–5, states that in most countries of southern and eastern Europe, banks received advices of remittances, then mailed money orders to the persons named, which could be cashed at post offices. See also Balch, *op. cit.*, 114, 139, 183. Thomas and Znaniecki, *op. cit.*, I 757, prints a letter referring to $44 received from an aunt in America, half to be regarded as a gift, half to be worked off by the young man after his emigration.
[5] *61 Congress 3 Session, Senate Doc. 753*, 261–8, 275–9, has figures (e.g. 1907, $141 million through banks and $84 millions by international money order, the average transaction being respectively $35 and $21); *U.S. Consular Reports*, No. 300, 177; Foerster, *op. cit.*, 446–8; Norman Douglas, *Old Calabria*, 50. For Greece, see William Miller, *Greek Life in Town and Country*, 229, and Saloutos, *op. cit.*, 43.

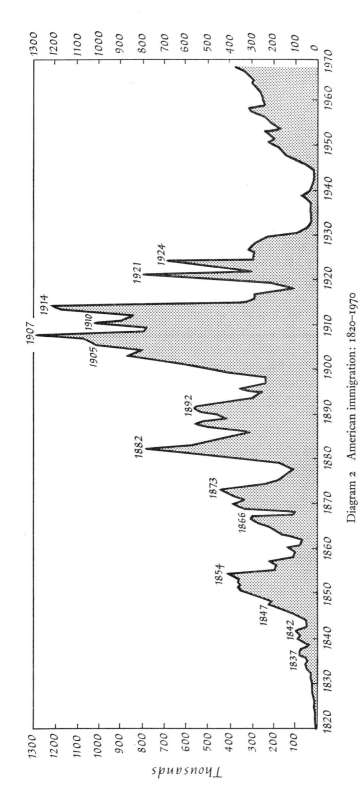

Diagram 2   American immigration: 1820–1970

Poles, and others, probably reflected the fact that such groups did not yet contain many well-established residents in the United States.[1] All in all, remittances were financing the emigration of millions, and it is important to remember that the later emigrants, from South and East Europe, were very largely single men, not the families for whom calculations were made earlier in this chapter. The practice became a familiar routine. Mid-nineteenth-century passenger brokers' advertisements offered facilities for emigrants to send their own money ahead to the United States. Forty years later, on the contrary, guide-books written for Italians were stressing the facilities which Buenos Aires offered for sending money home.[2] Not only were people helped to emigrate by this means: whenever money began to arrive in a district, interest in emigration grew, and local inertia was to that extent broken through.

Such emphasis on remittances serves as a reminder that emigrants' resources did not stay still. Nor did emigrants' estimates of the attractiveness of the United States. Even in the middle of the nineteenth century, news of American depressions became known in Europe. By the end of the century, news was fast enough, and transport systems allowed quick enough decisions, for emigrants to be able to respond in rather sensitive fashion to such economic changes.

The American economy experienced great fluctuations throughout our period. In the mid 1830s, there occurred a boom, marked by rapid public construction and wild speculation in land. It was followed by a crash, and by a depression which lasted well into the next decade. The early and middle 1850s saw renewed prosperity; and the panic of 1857 was soon succeeded, in the North, by a war-time boom. Only a mild recession followed the Civil War, but the boom which occurred around 1870 was soon followed not only by a crisis in 1873 but by prolonged depression. With short exceptions, the 1880s were prosperous. The panic of 1893, however, was followed by some of the worst years of the century. Renewed prosperity came between 1898 and 1907, then a crisis, and after then an improvement in conditions, broken by small fluctuations, down to the outbreak of the war in Europe.[3]

Such a description represents no more than an amalgam of stock-market quotations, business profits, and the like. The fluctuations, in real life, were of a different order. They involved, for working people, wage-cuts, un-

[1] *52 Congress 1 Session, House Misc. Docs. 19 and 20,* 265, 271, 273; while *61 Congress 3 Session, Senate Doc. 756,* 361, 364–5, has the 1908–10 figures.
[2] Harnden's advertisement is in *Liverpool Mercury,* 4 January 1848, and Tapscott's in 3 January 1851. Contrast Casimiro Marro, *Manuale pratico dell' emigrante all' Argentina, Uruguay e Brasile,* 84–6.
[3] Detailed description may be found in Willard Thorp, *Business Annals.*

employment, and short time, followed by severe hardship. In the 1840s, the mid 1870s, and the mid 1890s, in particular, American society was profoundly disturbed, discontent expressing itself in agitations for one or other of many brands of reform.

Reporting on conditions during the years either side of 1908, the Immigration Commission remarked:

> In periods of industrial activity, as a rule, the letters so circulated contain optimistic references to wages and opportunities for employment in the United States. . . . During seasons of depression . . . intending emigrants are quickly informed by their friends in the United States relative to the conditions of employment, and a great falling off in the tide of immigration is the immediate result.[1]

The argument is plausible, though somewhat beyond precise proof. Letters, after all, are likely to have had more influence than the propaganda of steamship companies or railways. Pretty certainly, remittances would vary with American conditions, and would reinforce mere advice. Their ebb and flow would affect, not merely the wish to cross the Atlantic, but the ability to set forth.

Certainly, immigration responded to American conditions. Great crashes were followed by sharply reduced numbers of arrivals. Long periods of depression were years of small immigration. Even small downturns in the economy, like that of 1886, were followed by reductions in the flow of people. This is not all. Fewer people arrived: more people left for Europe. Figures for this are not very accurate in the nineteenth century. When, in the present century, fuller statistics were kept, it is still impossible to distinguish between those who were going home disillusioned and those who were returning with their savings to demonstrate, to their European friends, their American success. It is clear, however, that between 1908 and 1924 about one-third as many people left the United States as entered it. It is equally clear that the several ethnic groups differed considerably in their proportions, the Jews being very unlikely to return to Europe, most of the southern and eastern Europeans showing ratios of more than half. Very broadly, groups with a high proportion of men were especially prone to a high rate of return, whether because of easy response to fluctuations in employment, or because of intentionally seasonal migration.[2] It is clear,

---

[1] Quoted in Isaac Hourwich, *Immigration and Labor*, 93–4.

[2] The procedure suggested in Willcox and Ferenczi, *op. cit.*, II 89, of assuming a ratio of returning emigrants diminishing steadily from the known figure of 1910 back to zero in 1820, is pure guess-work. There are fairly good figures in the annual volumes of *Commerce and Navigation of the United States*, of departures from American ports in accommodation other than 'cabin' (i.e. First class). Almost every year from 1869 saw more than 50,000 such departures, and every year from

too, that a slump was followed by a sudden exodus. Very early in 1908, to give but one example, newspapers at Grimsby were reporting the crowding of the North Sea steamboats with people returning across England to northern Europe. As many as 3,500 were said to have passed through the port in a single week-end.[1]

The relationship between economic conditions and changes in emigration, however, must not be made to seem too close. An ethnic group whose emigration was occasioned by disaster in Europe would pay rather little heed to economic fluctuations. Russian Jewish emigration, for example, was related far more to pogroms than to the trade cycle. Even more striking, and far more surprising, is the fact that the attractiveness of the United States showed a steady increase. In other words, troughs as well as peaks in emigration figures tended to become higher. The years 1905, 1906, 1907, 1910, 1913 and 1914 each saw the United States receive more than one million persons, though not all of them came from Europe. Yet the year July 1907 to June 1908, which saw the effects of a slump in the autumn of 1907, brought in 782,570 persons, an outstandingly high figure and one topped only by that of 1882 among the peak years of the nineteenth century. The off-years, 1909, 1911 and 1912, too, each saw the arrival of more than 750,000. Of the reasons for this, little can be said. European emigrants from more backward regions may have acted in ignorance. Very probably they estimated the American economy to be so superior in its scale, and in the breadth of its opportunities, that normal conditions in their homelands might be worse than a bad year in the United States.

1885 to 1894 saw more than 100,000. But the proportion of returns to arrivals varied greatly with the business cycle: years of good conditions and high immigration saw low rates of return: e.g. 1870, twelve per cent; 1882, eight per cent; and 1888, twenty-one per cent; while bad years with low immigration saw high ratios: e.g. 1875, forty-seven per cent, and 1894, fifty-three per cent. Jerome, *op. cit.*, 144, points out that in good years, when jobs were numerous, the proportion of males tended to increase. Remember, too, that some ethnic groups had proportions of males far above the 69·5 per cent average for all immigrants 1899–1910. The whole picture is complicated by intentionally seasonal migration. See Rowland T. Berthoff, *British Immigrants in Industrial America*, 52, 82 (masons, bricklayers, house-decorators, and mechanics); while *61 Congress 3 Session, Senate Doc. 756*, 359, notes that between 1899 and 1910, between 15 and 25 per cent of British and Irish declared each year that they had been in America before, similar proportions of northern Italians and Slovaks, and between 10 and 15 per cent of southern Italians, Germans, Scandinavians, and several Balkan peoples. P. 376 of the same document shows that 95·3 per cent of returning emigrants had been in the United States less than ten years. The fact that in 1908, 94 per cent had been there five years or less, but in 1909 and 1910 only about 70 per cent, may suggest that a depression not only brought about a large return, but most easily shook loose the newcomers.
[1] *Grimsby News*, 4 February 1908, and 10 June 1908, 12, 19 and 26 April 1910, for the more normal flow. Theodore Saloutos, in O. Fritiof Ander, *In the Trek of the Immigrants*, 199, mentions the special trains needed to carry returning emigrants to New York City in November 1907. As for the financial background, remittances through banks fell from $141 million in 1907 to $78 million in 1908, though curiously enough the flow of money orders was maintained – *61 Congress 3 Session, Senate Doc. 753*, 261–8, 275.

CHAPTER SIX

The Commercial System
and Government Regulation

Their comfort during the voyage must continue to depend chiefly on their own prudence, and that of the individuals who act on their behalf.
Parliamentary Papers 1831–2, V 6, Report of Commissioners for Emigration.

They see that all agreements between shipowners, agents, or masters, and intending emigrants, are duly performed. They also see that the provisions of the Passenger Acts are strictly complied with . . . They attend personally at their offices every day, and afford gratuitously all the assistance in their power to protect intending emigrants against frauds and impositions, and to obtain redress when oppression or injury have been practised on them.
Colonization Circular, May 1843, on the duties of Emigration Officers.

The agent must have a universality of talent, which few men possess; he must be a judge of the beams, the decks, and of the berths, and the best means of separating the sexes. He must be a judge of the sufficiency of the hospitals, and of the conveniences that are necessary to relieve nature, and of light and ventilation . . . The quantity and quality of provisions and water are to be determined by him . . . He is to be the judge of the qualifications of medical men . . . No man could possess all that knowledge.
Hansard, Third Series, CXII col. 69, W. Brown, Member for South Lancashire, 4 June 1852.

Emigrants found a business system which made their journey manageable, but it was an organization into which, at first, they fitted as a secondary element. Only in the 1850s did they at all commonly embark in vessels specializing in passenger traffic. Earlier, the ships that crossed the Atlantic – seldom exceeding 500 tons – delivered at the European ports cargoes of staves, cotton, tobacco, corn, wheat, beef and pork, then loaded for the westward crossing with iron, pots and pans, nails, salt, bricks, earthenware, glass, chemicals and, above all, textiles. And this was their main function.[1] To carry emigrants merely increased their owners' profit. Little trouble was taken to accommodate them, and less to care for them on the voyage.

[1] The generalization is based on the *Liverpool Customs Bills of Entry.*

As soon, therefore, as the number of people became great, the system was found to involve many abuses. Faced with these, governments were little disposed to interfere. They were likely to subscribe to *laissez-faire* theories in their treatment of business interests, and they knew that elaborate reforms, by driving up the cost of passage, might do their countrymen wishing to emigrate more harm than good.[1] Yet the scandals were such that, however unwillingly, government after government was forced to intervene.

I

Sailing-ships were usually owned in fractions, by the masters, businessmen, small investors, or the proverbial widows and orphans. An agent, or ship's husband, handled most of the business in port. Passengers were supplied by specialist brokers, of whom there were more than fifty at Liverpool in the 1850s. These operated a varied business. They provided ships with individual passengers, taking as their commission twelve-and-a-half per cent of the passage money. Alternatively, they chartered a whole steerage deck for a lump sum, then charged passengers in such a way as to make a profit.[2] To either system, passengers might be directed in two ways. Brokers advertised in newspapers all over the country, and this led to many advance bookings accompanied by a £1 deposit. Many emigrants, however, reached the port with no firm plans. Such people were encouraged to apply for passage either to the ship's master or to the broker, and it was the latter who was the dominant figure. But many of them were first accosted by runners, some of them attached to brokers' offices, many of them acting as freelances, who took them to the brokers and received seven-and-a-half per cent for their trouble. Often, they made an additional profit by running stores and lodging-houses for emigrants. Such runners were prone to use force or guile to get business, meeting trains and steamboats, trading on a glib tongue or an Irish brogue, snatching baggage in the confusion of station or dock. As one witness testified before a Select Committee in 1851, 'they are like so many pirates.'[3]

Passenger brokers did more than this central business. They stored

[1] *Parl. Papers 1826*, V, Q. 329 (Uniacke), Reports of Emigration Committee; *Hansard*, Third Series, XCVII col. 536 (Mounteagle).
[2] The fullest information can be found in *Parl. Papers 1851*, XIX, Select Committee on Passengers' Acts (note esp. Q. 2714–2812, Tapscott) and *1854*, XIII, Select Committee on Emigrant Ships. On the ship's husband, see Graham Willmore and Edwin Beedell, *The Mercantile and Maritime Guide*, 1042–3. Figures for brokers and runners (more than 200 of them, even after licensing had come into force) are in *Parl. Papers 1857 (Session 1)*, X 961, and *1857 (Session 2)*, XXVIII 306–7. See also William F. Adams, *Ireland and Irish Emigration to the New World from 1815 to the Famine* 76–9, 101–2, 126–7, 154–6, 203–5.
[3] See advertisement in *Liverpool Mercury*, 2 April 1845 and 1 March 1853; and the discussion in Oliver MacDonagh, *A Pattern of Government Growth*, 33–43. *Parl. Papers 1851*, XIX, Q. 1253

emigrants' baggage. They arranged the transmission of their money to America. They handled tickets prepaid by relatives abroad. A few of them, by the 1850s, had connections in Europe, by which they secured foreign emigrants and arranged their journey through London or Hull to Liverpool.[1]

Down to the 1830s, regulations were few, and only the British and American governments imposed them. The British Act of 1835 summed up typical rules of this early period by setting a maximum permissible degree of overcrowding; enforcing this by requiring a passenger list to be kept; insisting on bread and water sufficient to sustain life among the lawful complement for twice the average duration of the crossing; prescribing a medicine chest; requiring inspection of vessels by Customs officers; exacting payment to emigrants for maintenance while delayed in port; and compelling ships' masters to enter into a bond, of £1,000, to be forfeited if the provisions of the statute were broken.[2]

Far too much, therefore, was left to the knowledge and vigilance of people who were seldom experienced travellers and were often illiterate. At the port, the emigrant had to choose a ship. *Wiley and Putnam's Guide* of 1845, in general an intelligent publication, exhorted passengers to satisfy themselves about the quality of the ship's construction and accommodation, and to book passage only if master and mates bore a good character – all quite beyond their power to judge. At sea, the emigrant was at the mercy of captain and crew, as well as of weather. At the worst, as in the *Thomas Gelston* which reached Quebec in 1834, the crossing lasted nine weeks, and passengers were horribly crowded and short of food, but fortunately, 'a succession of fine weather enabled them to keep the hatches open – in a storm they would have smothered.' Twelve years later, the *Elizabeth and Sarah*, also from an Irish port, was eighty-three years old, overcrowded, ill-supplied with water, with temporary berths so badly constructed that some collapsed, and with 'excrement and filth . . . thrown into ballast, producing a stench which made it difficult [for officials at Quebec] to remain any length of time below.'[3] At best, the emigrant might encounter a master like Johan Gasmann, who set a watch at night as a precaution against fire,

(Hodder) and 3735 (Sabell) on runners' depredations, 4824 (Bramley-Moore) on shopkeepers' frauds, and 6673–7045 (Dalton) for a defence of the better lodging-houses, showing that they were already regulated by the Liverpool Board of Health.

[1] *Birmingham Journal*, 13 January and 24 February 1849 (Tapscott advertisements); *Liverpool Mercury*, 1 March 1853 (Bowman Grinnell advertisement); *Parl. Papers 1851*, XIX, Q. 2812 (Tapscott claimed 5,000 prepaid passages in six months), 2759, 3904 (Sabell).

[2] 5 and 6 William IV c. 53; Kathleen A. Walpole, 'Emigration to British North America under the Early Passenger Acts', M.A. thesis, London University, 1929.

[3] Quoted from *Montreal Advertiser* in William A. Carrothers, *Emigration from the British Isles*, 157–8; *Parl. Papers 1847*, XXXIX 44–5.

who had hatches open every fine day, who assisted ventilation by burning pans of coal below deck, who fumigated with vinegar, who had decks swept every day and scrubbed every third day, and who required passengers to air their bedding regularly.[1] Such masters, who might also organize, or encourage emigrants to organize, cleaning squads, and appoint cooks and stewards, were almost certainly rare.

II

In the 1830s, no more than thirty or fifty thousand people a year were likely to leave north-west Europe for the United States. In the late 1840s and the early 1850s, the number might exceed a quarter of a million. The strengthening of the protective system, during those years, may to some extent be regarded as a natural consequence of scale, more ships and more emigrants generating more abuses and more scandals that could not be concealed. Yet, in Britain at least, there existed men with a special interest in exploiting these circumstances in order to strengthen the protective code. From a modest origin – one man appointed at Liverpool in 1833 with very ill-defined powers – there grew up by the middle of the century a corps of Emigration Officers, at least one of them at each significant port of the British Isles. They were naval officers on half-pay, from lieutenant to captain in rank, whose salary was supplemented for the new work. From 1840, they came under the authority of the Colonial Land and Emigration Commissioners. They were charged with the tasks of providing information for emigrants, inspecting ships and stores, and protecting the inexperienced against victimizations and fraud. Their duties acquainted them with all the abuses of the emigrant trade. Their training inclined them to impose order and justice. With the Commissioners, therefore, they formed a powerful group striving to improve the law and its working. Their efforts, supplemented by the work of the Select Committees of 1851 and 1854, brought into being a long series of Passenger Acts, which, in turn, gave the officers the legal basis for day-to-day reforming action at the ports.[2]

[1] Theodore C. Blegen, *Land of their Choice*, 99–102. There was of course nothing original in this: Gasmann was adopting what had long been the best practice – see for example Alan Villiers, *Captain Cook, The Seamen's Seaman*, (Pelican edn), 123–6, 138.
[2] MacDonagh, *op. cit.*, 83–114, deals with the origins of the Emigration Officers. Fred H. Hitchins, *The Colonial Land and Emigration Commission*, esp. 38–49, describes the Commissioners' origins, and in later pages does much to analyse their annual reports. *Parl. Papers 1857 (Session 2)*, XXVIII 123–4, shows the entire establishment of Emigration Officers and subordinate personnel. *Colonization Circular*, 13 May 1843, has an early definition of the Officers' duties. Local opposition can be seen in *Liverpool Mercury*, 22 and 25 February 1848, 12 November 1850, 13 and 20 June 1851, 30 January 1852, and in MacDonagh, *op. cit.*, 111–12, 242–4, 254–6 (who also shows, 168–9, 174–5, 190–91, 284–5, how important an obstacle was Treasury parsimony).

Emigrants needed protection from runners, brokers and owners of shops and lodging-houses. In 1842, a Passenger Act required brokers to be licensed by Petty Sessions. Seven years later, they were ordered to find substantial sureties for good behaviour. In 1855, runners had to be licensed and badged, to signify that they were working for a broker. Emigrants needed to be assured of the ships' seaworthiness. From 1842, Passenger Acts entered into more and more detail on this. From 1847, each ship had to be inspected before Customs would clear it. Regulations came to deal, not only with structure, but with details of ventilation and lifeboats.

While at sea, emigrants needed guarantees for their health and welfare. Statutes became more and more precise about the height between decks, the size of berths, the separation of single men and women, the number of water-closets, and the medical precautions to be taken. From 1848, a surgeon had to be carried by any ship with a hundred passengers, unless additional space per person was provided. From 1852, the law said that, although small ships could still have that choice, any carrying five hundred passengers must have a surgeon on board. Space had to be set aside for a hospital. Even in 1835, Customs officers were supposed to inspect accommodation and stores, but for years afterwards it was assumed that emigrants would provide everything but breadstuffs and water for themselves. Significant changes began in 1848, after the disasters of the Irish Famine migration. Cooking facilities came under regulation. Then, in 1849, a fuller ration-scale was enacted: oatmeal, rice, potatoes, molasses, sugar, and tea. In 1852 other items were added, rations were to be issued daily – cooked when appropriate – and a ratio of ship's cooks to passengers was laid down.

It was not enough for emigrants to possess rights under the law: they needed to know that they possessed them. From 1842 a contract ticket had to be given them, and in time this evolved into a complicated document which even included the ration-scale. From 1848, an abstract of laws in force had to be displayed on board. Finally, emigrants were entitled to know that a procedure existed by which the law could be enforced, and by which they could obtain redress for injuries suffered. The Passenger Acts went into ever-increasing detail about this, proclaiming that foreign ships were as much subject to the laws as British, and giving emigrants the opportunity to sue for damages even when official prosecution was also undertaken.[1]

[1] The Acts are 5 and 6 Vict. c. 107; 10 and 11 Vict. c. 103; 11 and 12 Vict. c. 6; 12 and 13 Vict. c. 33; 15 and 16 Vict. c. 44. All but the last are summarized in Appendix I of *Parl. Papers 1851*, XIX. *Wiley and Putnam's Emigrants' Guide* (1845) advised people to take ham, pickles, and lime-juice; see also R. Druitt, *Medical Hints for Emigrants* (1850), 1–4. MacDonagh, throughout his book, argues that what seems the success of a statute often reflects no more than a temporary reduction in emigrant numbers, and that abuses appeared again in any boom year.

In 1855, a British statute was passed which marked the culmination of all these varied developments. It repeated the familiar provisions about bonds for shipowners, licence and bond for brokers, and added regulation of runners. It enacted many details about prosecution and penalties. It required, as had earlier laws, medical inspection of embarking passengers, the carrying of a duly inspected medicine chest, and a hospital of prescribed dimensions – and if more than three hundred people, including crew, embarked, a ship was to carry a surgeon. The law set out specifications for ventilation, lighting, lifeboats, and size of crew. Not only did it lay down that no more than two adult passengers could be carried for each ton, with two children of one to twelve years counting as one adult: it assigned a set number of square feet for each passenger, required more square feet on a lower than on an upper deck, and enacted that, exclusive of deck-houses, no more than two passenger decks should be fitted up. A passenger list, of course, was to be compiled. Single men were to be housed in a separate compartment. Water-closets were to number at least two, with two additional for each hundred passengers. Provisions, inspected before sailing, were to be enough for a voyage of seventy days in summer and eighty in winter. Their composition, including various permitted substitutes, included breadstuffs, vegetables, meat, salt, vinegar, tea, sugar, even mustard, all in prescribed weekly amounts, and cooked provisions were to be issued daily to the heads of messes of ten adults, into which emigrants were to be grouped. Each ship with a hundred adults was to carry a cook, a second if more than three hundred adults were on board. Any ship with more than a hundred adults was also to have a steward.[1]

By that date, an Order in Council tried to regulate conduct on board. It laid down the daily routine of meal-times, lighting and extinguishing of fires and lamps, sweeping of decks, airing of bedding, and cleaning of cooking utensils. It decreed Sunday worship. It forbade drinking, gambling, swearing, fighting, fouling the decks, and indecency towards females.[2]

III

These laws should be regarded, not as products of cold study, but as the result of strenuous and confused conflict: well-meaning observers agitating about emigrants' hardships, shipowners and brokers pleading innocence or

[1] The Act is 18 and 19 Vict. c. 119.
[2] The Order of 1848 is in *Parl. Papers 1847–8*, XLVII 349–50; that of 1864 in *Parl. Papers 1864*, XVI 594–6. Earlier suggestions by the Commissioners appeared in *Colonization Circular*, May 1844, 13–14.

7 New Orleans, 1853
Engraving from Frederick Piercy's drawing, in his *Route from Liverpool to Great Salt Lake Valley.*

8 St Louis, 1853
Engraving from Frederick Piercy's drawing, in his *Route from Liverpool to Great Salt Lake Valley*.

extenuating circumstances, Emigration Officers and magistrates recommending improvements in the law, then working to stretch the law's provisions when enacted. Enforcement was always hard. Several emigrant ships, carrying two or three thousand people, could leave Liverpool in a single day. The Emigration Officer's task, indeed, was sometimes thought beyond any man's powers.[1] Yet the Officers did much. They prosecuted offenders before the Liverpool stipendiary magistrate, who dealt out fines ranging from £5 to £50 and sometimes sent men to gaol. They acted as expert witnesses. They certified how much detention money was due to emigrants. Using their influence, they secured much money by settlement out of court. Often they won as much as £2,000 for emigrants in a year, once as much as £6,000; and in trying to guess the number of people aided, it is to be remembered that, as far as this represents detention money, it was made up of units of one shilling per day per person.[2] Provided that misdeeds occurred in port, or on board ships which for some reason had to put back to port, emigrants had a good chance of redress. On the other hand, medical measures were far from satisfactory. Inspection was carried out before embarkation by doctors, who were approved by the Emigration Officers and took a fee of £1 for every hundred people. As the emigrants filed past them, they detained for closer inspection anyone who at first glance seemed unwell. Those with trifling ailments could be treated before sailing, whilst more serious cases could be referred to a hospital or to the parish officers. Once inspection was completed, emigrants' tickets were stamped. Diseases affecting eyes, skin or scalp could probably be detected by such methods, and in justice to the doctors, children seem to have been scrutinized more closely than adults. Thoroughness, however, was impossible. London doctors were said to be examining, at times, at the rate of two hundred people an hour.[3]

Emigrants were less fortunate at sea. On the medical side, only the bigger vessels carried surgeons, for even when shipowners made genuine efforts to attract such men, there were never enough with qualifications and willing to sail.[4] Emigrants, therefore, were forced to depend, either on the traditional

---

[1] *Hansard, Third Series*, CXII col. 69 (Brown, the background of whose speech is described in MacDonagh, *op. cit.*, 242–4).

[2] *Parl. Papers 1847*, VI, Q.55 (Elliott), Select Committee of House of Lords, Colonization from Ireland; Hitchins, *op. cit.*, 141, 145, 152, 155. As for the stipendiary's work, I found 26 emigration cases reported in *Liverpool Mercury* between 1849 and 1854: theft, assault, frauds by brokers, runners and shopkeepers, and delays in sailing.

[3] *Parl. Papers 1851*, XIX, xiv (the Committee's report), Q. 812, 961–73, 1359–64 (evidence of Emigration Officers and Dr Lancaster); *1851*, XL 434 (Vere Foster's letter); *1854*, XXVIII 20–21.

[4] *Liverpool Mercury*, 28 April 1848, 7 January 1853 (two advertisements for doctors), 6 October 1854 (Dr Lancaster's opinion).

9

remedies of those around them, or on a doctor who might happen to be a cabin passenger, or on the master, working from experience or from some simple reference book. A guide-book assured its readers that 'the captains of the better class of ships are quite good medical men.'[1] In other directions, too, emigrants' welfare was imperfectly protected. When there were two decks, ventilation became difficult. Modern ships had large deckhouses, which made it hard for passengers to take exercise. As for berthing, probably few brokers, after 1855, would have testified, as did Tapscott in 1851, that single men were given upper berths and single women lower, as if it were an act of signal virtue not to put them together. Many, however, might still have agreed with him that to put single women in a separate compartment was to expose them to grave danger of molestation by the crew.[2] Certainly berths continued to be six feet square, with up to four adults allowed in each. With the larger ships of the 1850s, designed primarily for passengers, and with these largely American, everyone agreed that standards tended to rise.[3] It was none the less the primary duty of masters and officers to sail the ship, not to look after hundreds of emigrants, poor, often dirty in their habits, unaccustomed to the ocean, finding much of the diet unfamiliar and repulsive, and with their initiative weakened by seasickness during the early days.

The question remains, how far the law could be enforced at sea. Vessels carrying to Australia emigrants assisted by the government, and others bound for South Africa and New Zealand which imitated the system, carried matrons, and occasionally schoolmasters, appointed by voluntary societies. More important, they carried Surgeon-Superintendents who, in addition to medical duties, had the general oversight of passengers and who, making voyage after voyage, accumulated massive experience. Although their difficulties were great, with children falling ill, parents often obstinate and ignorant, and some troublemakers always to be found among so many people confined for months in so small a space, they seem to have won considerable success.[4] Such a system of control on the spot could not be reproduced on

[1] *Wiley and Putnam's Emigrants' Guide*, 58–9. The Board of Trade issued a *Ship's Captain's Medical Guide*. J. R. Beste, *The Wabash*, I 58–9, records that the master of his vessel set an emigrant's broken leg.

[2] *Parl. Papers 1851*, XIX, Q. 2555–6, 2572–3.

[3] *Parl. Papers 1851*, XIX, Q. 651 (Bunch), 1343 (Hodder). If, as was suggested in Q. 650, insurance companies scrutinized captains' records when fixing premiums, that was a further spur to efficiency. *Parl. Papers 1864*, XVI 15–16, Report of Colonial Land and Emigration Commissioners, shows that in the 1850s eighty per cent of Liverpool's emigrants embarked in American ships.

[4] Matrons were appointed by the British Ladies' Female Emigrant Society, schoolmasters by a subsidiary of the Society for the Propagation of the Gospel. They, and the Surgeon-Superintendents, are dealt with in *Parl. Papers 1857–8*, XXIV 419, *1859* (Session 2), XIV 15–16, and *1870*, XVII 133–6, Reports of Colonial Land and Emigration Commissioners. See also *Colonization*

the North Atlantic: there were too many ships and too few qualified men. The suggestion made in 1851, that former naval ratings, working as stewards, might have some disciplinary powers, was absurd. Quite apart from their inadequate qualifications for such a difficult task, such men would have had no standing, and, in a class-conscious age, could have commanded no respect from officers, crew, or the passengers themselves.[1] Enforcement, therefore, depended on prosecution or the forfeiture of bonds, and either required the procedure of a British court. Men well qualified to judge admitted that prosecution could not be employed against acts committed on the high seas in foreign ships, though as a matter of law the bond could have been put in suit.[2] The central difficulty, however, lay in producing evidence to set this procedure in motion. Obviously, no emigrant was going to return to testify about his grievances. There were no British courts in the United States. No procedure, unfortunately, was ever worked out by which evidence could be taken, by British consuls or American courts, to be brought back to Britain and used.[3]

It is true that the United States had passenger acts of its own – that of 1855, like its contemporary in Britain, being unusually complete. There was little difference between the two countries' laws, though American statutes explicitly gave masters power to make regulations for passengers, and imposed a fine of $10 on the owners for the death, during the crossing, of any passenger over eight years of age. The Act of 1855, however, was so badly drafted that the courts began declining to enforce some of its sections, and later held that none of them applied to steamships.[4] Even had the law

---

Circular, March 1847, 18–19; *Colonial Magazine and East India Review*, XXI 490–92; *Emigrants' Penny Magazine*, I 93, 129–33, II 168; *Canterbury Papers 1850–2*, 138; and *Emigration Record and Colonial Journal*, 3 January 1857, 3. In the Public Record Office, C.O. 208/298, as in admirable journal of the Surgeon-Superintendent of a New Zealand Company ship, 1842. A reading of Peter Cunningham, *Two Years in New South Wales*, II 215–95, which relates the experiences of several voyages as Surgeon-Superintendent of convict ships, convinces me that the organizers of Australian assisted emigration found it natural to adapt a well-tried system to new needs. See also A. G. L. Shaw, *Convicts and Colonies*, esp. 118–23.

[1] *Parl. Papers 1851*, XIX, xviii–xxii. MacDonagh, *op. cit.*, 141, 311–12, shows suggestions, in 1842 and 1857, for Surgeon-Superintendents on the North Atlantic; and, 312–13, for government investigators travelling in disguise, a proposal rejected as being an immoral exercise of power.

[2] *Parl. Papers 1854*, XIII, Q.5, has a statement by T. W. C. Murdoch, Chairman of the Colonial Land and Emigration Commissioners since 1847, which should rank as authoritative.

[3] *Parl. Papers 1851*, XXII 343–4, *1854*, XVIII 29–32, *1857–8*, XXIV 416–17, *1868–9*, XVII 135, Reports of Colonial Land and Emigration Commissioners.

[4] Statutes from 1819 to 1855 are collected in *61 Congress 3 Session, Senate Doc. 758*, 395–403. Pages 359–62, 367–8, of the same document deal with enforcement, as do *43 Congress 1 Session, Senate Doc. 23*, 11–12, 68–72, 78, and Friedrich Kapp, *Immigration and the Commissioners of Emigration of the State of New York*, 223. Professor Maldwyn Jones is working on a book which will put the entire subject on firmer ground.

been more satisfactory, and even had the courts taken a different view, practical difficulties would still have arisen. Once arrived in the United States, emigrants would seldom choose to suffer delay and expense in order to obtain redress. Rather, most of them would thank God for their survival and hurry on their way.

IV

The change to steam in the North Atlantic emigrant trade, in the later 1860s, introduced new elements, both technical and commercial, and these affected some five-sixths of all emigrants who ever went to the United States. Ships, obviously, became much larger. They were primarily passenger vessels, though their owners' attention was often directed to the comfort of the higher classes rather than of emigrants. They ran regularly. Crossings were much quicker. At the same time, steamships were organized in large, permanent groups, under the direct control of business firms – Hamburg-America, North German Lloyd, Holland-America, Red Star, C.G.T., Cunard, White Star, Inman, Guion, and the like. The steamship line, not the passenger broker, became the central institution, being, as it were, owner, ship's husband, and passenger broker all in one. This did not automatically produce amelioration in steerage conditions. At the very least, however, the ordeal was shorter. Government control, too, was easier, if there was the will to exercise it.

The steamship companies' advertising has been described in an earlier chapter. The agents and sub-agents who were responsible for local propaganda also sold tickets, taking commissions variously stated as from six shillings to three dollars. They were responsible, too, for giving information about the journey, and the companies always insisted, when asked by investigators, that emigrants were presented with the main points about America's restrictive laws.[1] As in other fields of business, competition was the rule. In 1888, in county Tyrone, 'one agent is fighting another who will sell the ticket.' Such men might also be auctioneers, helping to dispose of emigrants' property and thus taking a double profit.[2] Many of the emigrants, however, received prepaid tickets from America – a business handled, on

---

[1] *51 Congress 2 Session, House Report 3472*, 421, 447–8; *52 Congress 1 Session, House Exec. Doc. 235*, Part I, 12, 21, 283 (commissions), 112, 142–4 (Hamburg-America's instructions to agents), 141–2 (North German Lloyd's instructions); Part II, 77, 90 (further on commissions). A leading company could have principal agents (some no doubt concerned only with higher classes of passengers and with cargo) from Gothenburg to Palermo, from Manchester to Alexandria – see the diary in the Department of Shipping, Liverpool City Museum, entitled *White Star Line, General Information 1907*.
[2] *50 Congress 1 Session, House Misc. Doc. 572*, Part I, 337–41.

behalf of the lines, by a variety of offices in New York, by agents in back streets, and, as a sideline, by the German and Irish Societies whose main activity was welfare.[1]

Companies also helped emigrants during their journey. British lines organized the North Sea crossing for Scandinavians, their reception at Grimsby or Hull, and their crossing of England to Liverpool. Hamburg-America's officials met Scandinavian arrivals at Lübeck, to help them on the German stage of their expedition. The Compagnie Générale Transatlantique organized special trains from the Italian border to Havre. Balkan emigrants were met at each main station, and tickets pinned on them enabled successive agents to recognize them and forward them correctly on the next stage.[2]

At the ports, emigrants found further help. At Liverpool, where in the 1870s travellers still faced runners from lodging-houses who vied one with another in taking baggage from the railway stations, the leading companies, by the end of the century, succeeded in imposing a more orderly system. Officials met trains. Lodging-houses were under close control, and transport was organized from the stations to them. Cunard's complex of houses, early in the twentieth century, could accommodate 2,000 people at a time, in ten-bed dormitories, with good sanitation and food, provision of separate Jewish diet, and staffs of foreign origin who spoke the appropriate languages. Long before that, there were more modest houses where emigrants were charged a shilling a night for a bed, 'or one and sixpence for two persons sleeping in one bed,' sixpence for a plain meal, and a shilling for one with meat.[3] At Antwerp, about 1890, lodging-houses were charging from 55 to 75 cents a day, those at Bremen up to $2\frac{1}{2}$ Marks. Early in the present century, the Hamburg-America line went much further. It established what was in effect a large village, with its own railway station, churches and a synagogue. Emigrants had baths, and their clothes and luggage were disinfected. Medical inspection was arranged. Dormitory beds cost one Mark a day,

[1] 50 Congress 1 Session, House Misc. Doc. 572, Part I, 4, 52, 276–7, 282–3, 532–3.

[2] Parl. Papers 1882, LXII 87–99. Reports . . . Board of Trade and Local Government Board . . . Transit of Scandinavian Emigrants through the Port of Hull; 1903, IX, Q. 21713, Royal Commission on Alien Immigrants; 50 Congress 1 Session, House Misc. Doc. 572, Part II, 350–1; 52 Congress 1 Session, House Exec. Doc. 235, Part I, 122; A. G. Carlson's diary of 1891 in Roy Swanson, 'Some Swedish Emigrant Guide Books of the Second Half of the Nineteenth Century', Yearbook of Swedish Historical Society of America, XI (1926), 121–4; 'Excerpt from the Diary of Jacob Dolwig', North Dakota Historical Quarterly, III (1929), 204; Stoyan Christowe, This Is My Country, 32. Lloyd P. Gartner, The Jewish Immigrant in England 1870–1914, 34–7, shows the persistence of fraud.

[3] Parl. Papers 1903, IX, Q. 21444–6 (Medical Officer of Health, Liverpool); 52 Congress 1 Session, House Exec. Doc. 235, Part I, 9, Part II, 12; 61 Congress 3 Session, Senate Doc. 748, 86. At Glasgow, there were lodging-houses for Jews in 1890 – 52 Congress 1 Session, House Misc. Doc. 19, 279–80.

though superior hotels were available at a higher rate. Kosher meals were provided for the numerous Jews.[1]

Steamship lines found it profitable, from time to time, to enlist the support of governments, and to enter into agreement with competitors to divide the traffic.[2] A close-up view of one sector of the emigrant trade will be useful in illustrating this and earlier generalizations.

Although the north-west ports dominated the field, Mediterranean traffic was large and growing fast. In 1903, nearly seventy vessels, of eleven lines, made more than two hundred crossings from Mediterranean ports to New York, carrying more than 200,000 passengers in the steerage. The same vessels carried more than 70,000 eastward. One fraction of the trade involved a British line. In 1904 Cunard reached an agreement with the Hungarian government, under the terms of an emigration statute of the previous year. A fortnightly westbound service was promised, with ships of at least 10,000 tons and a speed of at least $13\frac{1}{2}$ knots. Steerage passengers were to be embarked at Fiume, though empty space could be filled by others from Trieste, while first- and second-class passengers could be picked up elsewhere, including Italian ports. If, on the contrary, space was insufficient, the surplus of passengers were to go overland to Antwerp, and thence to Liverpool. Accommodation at Fiume, food, quantity of baggage carried free, and fares, were all specified. Food for emigrants was to be bought in Hungary. Whenever possible, officers and crew were to include men speaking Magyar. The company was to contribute each year to the Emigration Fund. The government, in return, promised group fares for emigrants on the railways.

This was only one of a cluster of agreements. Cunard took over rights formerly enjoyed by 'Adria', the Royal Hungarian Navigation Company. In return, Adria became Cunard's agents for the whole Kingdom, taking five per cent commission on steerage fares, after sub-agents' commissions had been deducted, and seven-and-a-half per cent on first- and second-class fares. Similar agreements were reached with agents in Austria, in respect of the Trieste trade, and in Naples and Palermo. Cunard had a dozen agents in Austrian cities and, in addition, some sort of agreement with Austrian Lloyd permitted that company's agents to sell Cunard tickets. Finally, the Fiume traffic was to be fit into a wider commercial network. In 1904, Cunard reached

---

[1] *52 Congress 1 Session, House Exec. Doc. 235*, Part I, 19-20, 109-11; *Industrial Commission Reports*, XV 97-9; and, on Hamburg, Major Evans-Gordon's report following Q. 13349 of Royal Commission on Alien Immigration, *Parl. Papers 1903*, IX, and *61 Congress 3 Session, Senate Doc. 748*, 99-102.

[2] *Parl. Papers 1870*, LXVII, Part I, 75, reports from Württemberg; Lamar Cecil, *Albert Ballin*, 44-62.

agreement with Hamburg-America, North German Lloyd, Holland-America, Red Star and C.G.T., accepting a volume of steerage business from Fiume equal to six per cent of the westbound total from northern Europe. The point, of course, was that its Adriatic venture was tending to divert trade from overland routes to the North Sea and the English Channel.

During the next few years, ships called at Trieste, Palermo, Naples and Gibraltar on their way to New York, taking from sixteen to twenty-one days on the crossing. The first year of the service showed the normal seasonal variation: heavy spring and autumn traffic westward, much smaller numbers in summer and winter. By 1906, however, much of this rhythm had vanished, and the five small ships were carrying always over a thousand, and sometimes as many as two thousand steerage passengers, almost all, as the agreement prescribed, from Fiume. Eastbound, only autumn and early winter showed comparable numbers, and most of these people disembarked, not at Fiume but at Italian ports. An American depression could change the pattern. From late 1907 to October 1908, westbound passengers numbered only from 200 to 400 in each ship; while from October 1907 to June 1908 most vessels carried over 1,000, and sometimes more than 2,000, steerage passengers eastward.[1]

V

During this period of rapid change, British and American law developed little. An American statute of 1860 laid down heavy punishment for seducing women passengers. A British law of 1863 abandoned many details irrelevant to steamships, while increasing the owner's bond to £5,000 to correspond to the larger scale of firms. The American law of 1882 seemed to go much further. It regulated ventilation, cooking facilities, sanitation, and hospitals on board. It gave adults and older children 100 cubic feet of accommodation, and 120 on the lowest deck. Food was to consist of $1\frac{1}{2}$ Navy rations, and the three meals a day were to be served at tables. Each ship carrying more than fifty passengers was to have a surgeon. No member of the crew was to visit the passenger space except on duty. The captain was to make rules for discipline and cleanliness. The fine of $10 for deaths was retained. Unfortunately, however, the law proved technically hard to apply to steamships of growing size and complexity, and American commentators of the next

[1] My description is based on a memorandum book, recently given by Cunard to the Department of Shipping, Liverpool City Museum. It lacks a title; but it must have served as a work of reference for someone in the company closely engaged in the Adriatic trade. *Slavonia*, *Pannonia* and *Ultonia* carried no more than 100 or 150 in the higher classes, *Carpathia* about 350. The only description, known to me, of a crossing in one of these vessels, *Pannonia*, is by Vay de Vaya and Uskud, nobleman and priest, who published it in *Living Age*, 252 (January 1907), 173–82. Unfortunately it is too generalized to be of much value.

generation were willing to admit that it had failed. The British law of 1894 did little more than codify existing rules. Early in the twentieth century, not earlier, competent legislation appeared. The British Merchant Shipping Act of 1906 permitted the Board of Trade to draw up rules, and these were issued two years later. They, in turn, were taken as the model for an American law of 1908. Taken together, the laws now forbade the accommodation of passengers on any deck wholly below the waterline; guaranteed them more space if housed on the lowest deck; laid down a minimum of promenade space for the steerage; and, in order to encourage shipping companies to provide amenities, allowed certain public rooms to be counted in the calculations about steerage passengers' space.[1]

Even in the middle of the nineteenth century, countries other than Britain and the United States were deeply involved in the emigrant trade, and their commercial system was very similar to that described at Liverpool. At Mainz, and in the towns of the southern German states, brokers from Bremen, Hamburg and Havre competed for business, sending agents along the main routes to meet emigrants, advertising in newspapers, or enlisting the aid of local tradesmen and innkeepers. As in Britain, such men transmitted money to America and received prepaid tickets.[2] Hamburg, Bremen and Havre all had lodging-houses catering for emigrants, those at Havre dealing primarily with Germans.[3]

As early as the 1830s, the beginnings of regulation can be seen. The men who drafted the Norwegian bill of 1845, which unfortunately was defeated, studied American legislation. Such research, however, was by no means essential. Since the system of handling emigrants was the same everywhere, abuses were the same, and the same remedies were called for. Naturally, it was the Hanseatic ports which pioneered the continental legislation, starting with ships and lodging-houses. By the 1850s, both Bremen and Hamburg required passenger brokers to enter into a substantial bond, to give emigrants a contract ticket, to refrain from selling tickets to inland American destinations, and to lodge and maintain emigrants detained in port. Both cities experimented with information services. At the same time, inland states – the homes of emigrants and the fields of activity of agents rather than the

---

[1] The British statutes are 26 and 27 Vict. c. 51, 57 and 58 Vict. c. 60, and 6 Edward VII c. 48. The American laws are printed in *61 Congress 3 Session, Senate Doc. 758*, 403–10: 368–9 deals with enforcement difficulties, and 455–7 prints the Board of Trade regulations. By that time, berths were single (about two feet wide) or double, instead of the old six-foot berths for four adults. From 1894, British law stated that man and wife, or two children, could occupy such a berth; American law, from 1882, permitted as a couple 'males personally acquainted'.

[2] Marcus L. Hansen, *The Atlantic Migration*, 197–8, 290–91; Mack Walker, *Germany and the Emigration*, 87–96, 137 note.

[3] Hansen, *op. cit.*, 187–8.

collecting points for embarkation – began to regulate passenger brokers, with Prussia trying to steer emigrants to German and Belgian ports where conditions were thought to be best. France and Belgium set up Emigration Commissions, and enacted a few rudimentary regulations about ships. France established information centres in a few principal cities. Both countries, finally, tried to ensure that foreigners in transit had enough money to meet their expenses up to embarkation.[1]

The flow of emigrants in several periods after the American Civil War exceeded even that at the time of the Irish Famine, and more and more European countries were drawn in. By 1890, Hamburg was a close rival to Liverpool, whilst Bremen, Havre, Antwerp, Rotterdam, Gothenburg were all important, and Mediterranean ports were beginning to ship appreciable numbers. By 1907, Liverpool was well behind Naples and Bremen in the number of emigrants embarked for the United States. The incentive to regulate steamship companies and their agents was therefore widespread.

In the 1860s, Norway experienced its first large-scale emigration and its first contacts with foreign steamship companies. It passed a law which tried to restrict the emigration of men owing military service, men deserting their families, and debtors; which licensed brokers and required a heavy bond; required police endorsement for each contract ticket; laid down the space to be provided by ships, and enjoined a passenger list as a check upon this; and began to prescribe rations. Sweden enacted rather similar laws.[2] In 1890 a Belgian decree concerned itself with licences, tickets, medical services for emigrants, inspection of ships, and the spreading of reliable information, and it even specified the menu for meals at sea.[3]

In 1897, a law of the Reichstag supplemented the rules of individual German States. The shipowner's bond was set as 50,000 Marks, nearly $12,000, and that of the brokers at 1,500 Marks. Those concerned with the emigrant traffic were to keep books in prescribed form. Contract tickets were to be issued. Emigrants' rights when delayed in port were clearly set forth, and companies issuing tickets had to insure themselves against these

---

[1] Theodore C. Blegen, *Norwegian Migration to America,* 224–37; Mack Walker, *op. cit.,* 290–2; Emile Legoyt, *L'Emigration européenne,* 189–94, 262–84; *61 Congress 3 Session, Senate Doc. 758,* 345–6.
[2] Theodore C. Blegen, *Norwegian Migration to America: the American Transition,* 224–38, 460–1: these enactments followed study of British, French and Hamburg laws. Florence E. Janson, *Background of Swedish Immigration,* 246.
[3] *52 Congress 1 Session, House Exec. Doc. 235,* Part II, 13–16 (Dutch law of 1869 and supplementary regulations), 17–19 (Belgian law). Walter F. Willcox and Imre Ferenczi, *International Migrations,* II 202–4, summarize the French laws of the 1860s. Even Switzerland passed a law – *U.S. Consular Reports,* XXVII 295–303.

obligations. There was to be medical inspection. Although the States were to provide officials at the ports, the Chancellor, through a council of fifteen members, was to exercise supervision. As for the ships, the law contained detailed rules on space, ventilation, heating and lighting, hospitals, and sanitation; required tables and benches for meals; laid down the size of berths and the amount of bedding; separated unaccompanied men and women; provided for ship's cooks to serve three meals a day, though they might recruit helpers from among the passengers; required a doctor and stewards; and underlined the authority of the captain.[1] From 1892, there were special rules for the eastern German frontier, arising from danger of cholera. Inspection centres were established for emigrants from Russia and south-eastern Europe. From 1902, a rather similar system operated, partly to ensure a monopoly of the traffic for the German steamship lines, partly to ensure that emigrants complied with the health requirements of America's restrictive laws.[2]

In some respects, however, it was Italy which had the most comprehensive rules. As early as 1888, agents were being licensed and required to find sureties, while in each province was set up a commission to which, it was hoped, emigrants would apply for advice and report their grievances. The system proved insufficient. Emigration continued to grow. Foreign ships were more and more involved – by the early twentieth century only two-fifths of Italian emigrants crossed the Atlantic in Italian ships, more than one-fifth in British, nearly one-fifth in German, and about one-sixth in French. In 1901, therefore, a law was enacted containing no fewer than 173 clauses, some of them long. It set up a Commissioner of Emigration, with a Council to advise him. He licensed all firms carrying emigrants, fixed rates of passage every three months, and levied a tax on tickets so as to build up a welfare fund. Every three or four weeks, an information bulletin was issued, while prosecution for misleading statements was envisaged. Local committees were to link the Commissioner with the public. At the authorized emigration ports of Genoa, Naples, Messina, and Palermo, lodging-houses were to be inspected. Rules were made for the conduct of emigrant ships, not only about space, ventilation, and the separation of the sexes, but about laundry

---

[1] The Act's early clauses are in *Industrial Commission Reports*, XV 696–9, those on steerage conditions in *61 Congress 3 Session, Senate Doc. 758*, 458–64. *U.S. Consular Reports*, XXVI 234, has a Hamburg law of 1887, and p. 235 states that local lodging-houses had notices, in seven languages, advertising the city's information service. *52 Congress 1 Session, House Exec. Doc. 235*, Part II 19–21, has Bremen's regulations of 1890.
[2] *Industrial Commission Reports*, XV 105–7; *61 Congress 3 Session, Senate Doc. 748*, 93–7, *Senate Doc. 753*, 29–31. *Senate Doc. 758*'s summaries show that the key American law, as to health precautions, was that of 1893. On the discriminatory aspects, see *U.S. Consular Reports*, Nos. 260–3, p. 217, and No. 296, pp. 116–17.

arrangements and the storage of food. Most radical of all, the Italian law required each ship to carry a doctor, usually a naval or military man, whose responsibility was to be emigrants' welfare as well as health. In other words, the Italians were applying, to their entire twentieth-century emigration, the system which, with the Surgeon-Superintendents, the British government had once applied to their official Australian emigration. The *commissario regio* was to be the senior doctor, a second being carried if passengers numbered more than 700. He was to take part in the initial inspection of the ship, supervise the issue of food on board, receive emigrants' complaints, adjust these, whenever possible, by discussion with the captain, and report any failures to reach a settlement to the consul in America or to the home authorities. His salary was to be paid by the shipping company, which was to be fined for any violation of the law proved as a result of a complaint. To emphasize his status, the law provided that 'he shall wear the regulation uniform and sit at the first-class table, taking place . . . to the right of the commander.' A further check upon the companies' standards was the provision that they were to compensate any emigrant rejected by the American authorities: American law already required them to pay their return passage.[1]

The last element in the system of regulation was inspection at European ports, as a result of the increasingly complex American health regulations for immigrants. Obviously it was more humane to prevent people from sailing than to reject them on arrival at New York. At Liverpool, Havre, Rotterdam, Trieste, Fiume, the Italian ports, and Patras, therefore, American doctors, or doctors selected by American consuls, worked with local doctors representing shipping companies or European governments. Elsewhere, such local inspection as took place had to take account of American law. In 1907, nearly 12,000 people were turned back from the German border control stations, and nearly 40,000 from European ports, leaving only 13,000 to be rejected at Ellis Island. It is interesting to note that the number in this total from any one port seemed to bear no relation to the type of inspection practised: evidently European doctors were working as effectively as American. Nor, relative to numbers, was there any preponderance of south and east Europeans among the people rejected.[2]

[1] Casimiro Marro, *Manuale pratico dell'emigrante*, has a first, official section, in which he prints the law of 1888. That of 1901 is summarized in Robert F. Foerster, *The Italian Emigration of our Time*, 477–82; its early clauses are in *Industrial Commission Reports*, XV 699–708; and those relating to ships are translated in full in *61 Congress 3 Session, Senate Doc. 758*, 464–85. The latter document, 379–85, contains an analysis, topic by topic, of European laws in force *c.* 1910: it shows how similar, under pressure of circumstances, they had become.
[2] The system at Liverpool is in Mr Schloss' report to the Board of Trade, *Parl. Papers 1893–4*,

No completely satisfactory judgment on all this can be passed. In the twentieth century, steamship companies seem to have acted independently in promoting certain improvements, for at any rate a proportion of emigrants, though laws gave them encouragement. On the other hand, travellers just before the Great War testified that much remained to be done to make steerage conditions tolerable. What cannot be known is how bad conditions would have been had no laws been passed.[1]

VI

Emigrants' difficulties did not end when they disembarked in the United States. At New York, in the 1840s and early 1850s, 'an army of 100 or more composed of runners, tavern-keepers, and peddlers come on board' each emigrant ship, in the hope of making a favourable bargain with the new arrivals. On the dock, a howling mob of porters fell upon them, with no interference from the police. Men solicited business for lodging-houses, for Hudson River steamboats, and for railways.[2] Immigrants might be cheated while exchanging money, or be sold tickets to wrong destinations, or be overcharged by cab-drivers, or if young women, be enticed into moral danger. Often the exploiters were men of their own country, relying on emigrants' trust in men of familiar speech who seemed to possess, unlike themselves, knowledge of American ways. One example may be cited. In 1847, a Scot arrived at New York City, bound for Ohio. Near the landing-place of the Albany steamboat he met a man claiming to be a forwarding agent. He paid four sovereigns for tickets for himself and three of his family – more than twice the proper fare. On board, he was soon relieved of three more sovereigns, on the pretext that his ticket would not carry him to his destination. At Albany, eight more were taken from him as another 'balance' of his fare, and fifteen for handling his baggage. An agent of St Andrew's Society brought him back and secured a warrant for the swindlers' arrest. The ringleader, however, had decamped, and when, somewhat later, he returned, this time it was the Scot who could not be found as a witness,

---

LXXI 9–12. Other European ports appear in *61 Congress 3 Session, Senate Doc. 748*; 71 shows 116,000 turned away from the United States between 1899 and 1910, about 1·3 per cent; 122 gives the figures for 1907; 125–9 has the Commission's generalizations about inspection.
[1] The whole subject will be treated at greater length in my chapter 8.
[2] *Parl. Papers 1849*, XI 572–4, prints material from the report of a Select Committee of the New York legislature. The first report of the Wisconsin Commissioners of Emigration is quoted in Henry S. Lucas, *Netherlanders in America*, 486–7. See Brigham Young's account of 1841, in *Latter-day Saints' Millennial Star*, XXVI 40–41 (2 January 1864) and J. R. Beste's of 1851, *op. cit.*, I 72–4.

the suspicion being that one of the guilty parties had persuaded him to leave town.[1]

Against such dangers, private welfare agencies offered some protection. In 1852, the Colonial Land and Emigration Commissioners can be found advising emigrants to consult, at New York, the British Protective Emigrant Society or the Irish Society. St Andrew's Society has already been mentioned. Later, French, German and Jewish organizations had some influence, as did the 'Bethel Ship' mission of the Scandinavian Methodist, O. G. Hedstrom.[2] At other American ports, similar societies existed. At New Orleans, Sisters of Charity ran a hospital, many of whose patients were immigrants. A Hibernian Society was in existence. Above all, the German Society, founded in 1847, operated an information bureau, met ships, warded off runners, helped secure food and shelter, and, on occasion, gave Germans small sums of money for steamboat passage on the Mississippi. Yet the persistence of runners was such that some disguised themselves as agents of the Society, necessitating the issue of special identity cards.[3] Boston had charitable organizations set up by each ethnic group. In the early 1850s, the Irish Immigrant Society had an agent to visit the ships, gave information about jobs, sold inland tickets, and helped immigrants who were seeking lodgings.[4] German societies existed at Baltimore and Philadelphia, as well as at such inland cities as St Louis, Cincinnati, and Chicago. Later ethnic groups engaged in almost equally widespread activity. There were Polish organizations at New York, Boston, Baltimore and Philadelphia. The Italian St Raphael Society had a house of refuge at New York and an agency at Boston.[5]

For some years, public authorities contented themselves with passing laws aimed at preventing immigrants from becoming a public charge. To that end, taxes were levied on immigrants, or bonds taken from shipowners.

[1] Quoted from St Andrew's Society report in John F. Maguire, *The Irish in America*, 192–3. The early pages of Vol. I of Gustaf Unonius' memoirs also have references to the numerous supplementary charges made for immigrants' baggage.

[2] *Parl. Papers 1852*, XVIII, Appendix 25. See also *Sidney's Emigrants' Journal*, I 4 (5 October 1848); *Liverpool Mercury*, 2 and 5 September 1851, printing advice from the New York Commissioners; Robert Ernst, *Immigrant Life in New York City*, 32–4; Janson, *op. cit.*, 132, 176, 180–1, 203–4. Edith Abbott, *Immigration: Select Documents and Case Records*, 144–7, prints a memorial from the German Society to the New York legislature, outlining the help given in providing medical aid and finding jobs.

[3] Alan Conway, 'New Orleans as a Port of Immigration', M.A. thesis, London University, 1949; John F. Nau, *The German People of New Orleans*, 13, 21–4.

[4] Oscar Handlin, *Boston's Immigrants*, 160–63; Robert H. Lord, J. E. Sexton, and E. T. Harrington, *History of the Archdiocese of Boston*, II 455–7.

[5] Carl Wittke, *Refugees of Revolution*, 54–6. Legoyt, *op. cit.*, 194, adds Boston, Charleston, St Paul, Milwaukee, and Galveston. See also Joseph A. Wytrwal, *America's Polish Heritage*, 187–90, 199–200; Rudolph J. Vecoli, 'Peasants and Prelates', *Journal of Social History*, II, 254, 258.

Supervising the operation of such laws was the sole function of Boston's so-called Municipal Superintendent of Alien Passengers.[1] It was fortunate that New York was the pioneer state in passing welfare laws, for in the middle of the nineteenth century two-thirds of America's immigrants usually landed there, and at the end of the century nearer three-quarters. Over the opposition of many politicians, the law of 1847 appointed a Commission, made up of nominees of the Irish and German Societies, the Mayors of New York City and Brooklyn, and six nominees of the Governor. Not only were they to give information, inspect ships, and support immigrants who got into difficulties, they were empowered to establish landing-places at which everyone should disembark. In 1848 a second law licensed lodging-house keepers, ticket-agents and runners. In 1855 the Commissioners used their powers to set up a single landing depot, buying for that purpose Castle Garden, a former opera house at the tip of Manhattan.[2]

Descriptions dating from the late 1860s and early 1870s show that quarantine continued to be administered from Staten Island. When, after medical inspection there, a ship reached its dock on the Hudson or East River, immigrants passed rapidly through Customs, then went to Castle Garden by barge. After being registered, they were able to change money, buy rail tickets, collect letters that might await them, write letters or telegrams, deposit valuables for a short time, and meet representatives of churches or welfare agencies, and any friends who might have arrived. As they left the building, they passed an employment agency. Throughout this process, men competent in several languages were at hand to help them. Runners were excluded. Officials were forbidden to recommend one route or transport agency in preference to another. Although, it is true, they might still find themselves molested at the gate, immigrants were now well protected by the Commissioners' organization.[3] It was copied, however, by no other port.

Twenty years later, the system had changed in no fundamental respect, but a few details became more fully described. By that time, the Commissioners were acting, under contract, as agents of the Secretary of the Treasury. The writing into law of prohibitions against certain categories of immigrant made it necessary to have inspectors board at quarantine, and work both at the docks and inside Castle Garden. The depot had a hospital for minor illnesses, while more serious cases, insane people, destitute immigrants and

[1] Handlin, *op. cit.*, 183–4. The laws are summarized in William J. Bromwell, *History of Immigration*, 199–205.

[2] *61 Congress 3 Session, Senate Doc. 758,* 768–99; Ernst, *op. cit.*, 29–30.

[3] Castle Garden's rules are in Kapp, *op. cit.*, 211–20, and a description of the depot and of Ward's Island can be found on 105–41. For other descriptions, see Maguire, *op. cit.*, 198–212; *New York Herald,* 7, 12 and 13 July 1866; and *Land and Emigration,* October 1872. For the employment bureau, see Charlotte Erickson, *American Industry and the European Immigrant,* 95–7, 192–4.

their children, were all cared for in institutions on Ward's Island in the East River, and after a year were turned over to New York county authorities. Facilities at Castle Garden were much the same as earlier. Rates of exchange were checked three times a day with Wall Street, and prominently displayed. Contracts were made with a dozen rail companies, but they operated a single office. A restaurant was run under contract, offering beer at 10 cents a bottle, coffee at 5 cents a cup, 2 lb rye loaves at 10 cents, slices of pie or 1 lb of bologna sausage at the same price, large sandwiches at 13 cents. Signs in many languages invited complaints. The employment agency still operated outside. Immigrants who intended staying in the city or neighbouring towns could have their baggage carried, for 40 cents a piece as far as 59th Street, for 50 cents further north in Manhattan or to addresses in Brooklyn, for 75 cents to Jersey City. Those proceeding to railroad depots on the Jersey shore, bound for the West, could go by waggon with their baggage to the Manhattan end of the ferries, though large parties were sent by boat.[1] Others again might lodge in boarding houses which were thickly concentrated in the neighbourhood, houses which were licensed by the Commissioners for a fee of $25 a year and were regularly inspected. One boarding-house keeper, Daniel Hamilton, testifying before a congressional committee, described his establishment as consisting of a dining room and two sitting rooms, with sleeping quarters, not mentioned in detail, for a hundred people. He sold prepaid tickets and changed money as side-lines, and he ran a bar – but he insisted that the business there was mainly in postage stamps.[2]

A committee sitting at the Barge Office in April 1890 was forced to adjourn to Castle Garden, so great was the noise of work being done to convert the place into a temporary immigrant depot.[3] Castle Garden was to be abandoned in that year, and the Federal government was to take direct control, but Ellis Island was not to be ready until the beginning of 1892. In the spring of its first year, Ellis Island was already being investigated for faults in construction. Quite incidentally, this inquiry provides the first evidence about the inspection and welfare system. After the familiar quarantine and Customs procedure, immigrants passed by doctors, and a matron who was concerned with pregnant women. Anyone who seemed diseased, or for any other reason aroused doubts, was taken aside for further examination.

[1] *50 Congress 1 Session, House Misc. Doc. 572*, Part I, 256–8 (on the small sums paid for concessions), 412; *51 Congress 2 Session, House Report 3472*, 49–82, 87, 105–21, 183–95, 208–12; *52 Congress 1 Session, House Report 2090*, 457, shows Castle Garden in 1890 with 48 employees costing little more than $43,000 a year. Ward's Island had a rather larger staff. Reports show various complaints, from incompetence of interpreters to the delays in running emigrant trains.
[2] *51 Congress 2 Session, House Report 3472*, 520–3.
[3] *Ibid.*, 153.

Immigrants then went before registry clerks, who at that time still had to write the answers to questions into ledgers, since ships' passenger lists were delivered to Customs and not to the Immigration officers until the statute of the following year. The details recorded were name, age, marital status, literacy, destination, money carried, health, occupation, and whether at any time an inmate of almshouse or prison. The ships' lists would have given several additional facts. The staff numbered more than a hundred, from a Commissioner at $6,000 a year and a Chief Physician at $2,500, down to watchmen and charwomen. The clerks, one of whom was said to have a smattering of ten languages, had such names as Eichler, Silberstein, Jahn, Szermer, Erdofy, Raczkiewicz, Hobberg, and Palmeri, as well as a few of more Anglo-Saxon appearance. After inspection, immigrants could take advantage of facilities for money-changing, rail tickets, telegraph office, restaurant, barber shop, and baggage-handling, all involving concessions, and all attracting accusations that those concessions were granted far too cheaply.[1]

The system changed little during the next twenty or thirty years, though after the fire of 1897 new and more solid buildings were put up, and gradually dormitories, hospitals and other structures were added to an island which was filled in to an area of twenty-one acres. Railroad companies organized in such a way as to send shiploads of immigrants by one line after another in rotation. The ships' lists came to be supplied to the clerks, whose duty it now became to ask immigrants questions, as they came forward in groups corresponding to a page-full. Medical inspection became highly systematic, each doctor in the line looking for one type of disease. Boards of special inquiry were instituted, three inspectors making a careful examination of all doubtful cases, with immigrants entitled to have a friend, though not a lawyer, to help. All this corresponded to the growing complexity of the exclusion clauses, as well as to the growing volume of traffic. Of the modest numbers rejected, ten to twenty per cent each year were sent home because of contagious diseases, about the same proportion for contract labour offences, and most of the remainder as likely to become a public charge.[2]

[1] The Barge Office interlude, with the system working essentially as before, is described in William Smith, *A Yorkshireman's Trip to the United States and Canada*, 31–5. Early reports on Ellis Island are in *52 Congress 1 Session, House Report 2090*, esp. 95–6, 332–5, 350–57, 397–409, 458–63, 794–5: the superintendent of construction, George B. Hibbard, had gained his experience running up barn-like barracks for immigrants on the Northern Pacific railroad. The next full account is Mr Schloss' report to the Board of Trade, *Parl. Papers 1893–4*, LXXI 12–30.

[2] *Industrial Commission Reports*, XV 84–101, 145–7, shows the Barge Office again in use. Allon Schoener, *Portal to America: the Lower East Side 1870–1925*, 22, quotes *New York Times*, 3 December 1900, stating that the new Ellis Island is about to be occupied. Railroad arrangements are in Emory R. Johnson and G. C. Huebner, *Railroad Traffic and Rates*, II 117–20. Exclusion figures are in *61 Congress 3 Session, Senate Doc. 756*, 367, 371. Accounts of Ellis Island in full

Immigration officials were likely to make broad distinctions between groups of immigrants, as their experience dictated. In 1899, investigators were told that a shipload of Mennonites bound for the Great Plains would pass through without difficulty. So would Irish girls bound for domestic service, 'and Father Henry takes them over to his Mission.' On the other hand, a shipload of Sicilians might pose a great number of health and contract labour problems, and boards of special inquiry might be sitting for days.[1]

Although charges of favouritism or corruption were never put forward, many outside critics objected to the harshness of the rules, the discomfort inflicted while awaiting examination, and the failure to give immigrants, or their American relatives, the reasons for administrative decisions.[2]

VII

Ellis Island, efficient and impersonal, was unique in the United States. A British investigator in 1893 found no such depots at Boston, Philadelphia or Baltimore, the other leading immigration ports. On board ship, or in some shed on shore, doctors and inspectors rushed through the procedures. At Boston, when he watched, there were no contract labour inspectors at all, and one day no doctor could be found, though he was told that any doubtful cases would have been held overnight for medical inspection next day. Complaints along these lines continued down to 1914. Although a statute of 1917 allowed it, very little was done to collect information for immigrants by state or federal action, and the Federal Division of Information acted as no more than a minor employment agency.[3]

Voluntary agencies, therefore, remained essential, and forty-one of them were represented at Ellis Island in 1908. One information office advertised itself in a circular printed in twenty-one languages. Each main ethnic group had at least one, Jewish agencies at New York amalgamating in 1909 as the Hebrew Sheltering and Immigrant Aid Society. Other organizations existed

operation include: Broughton Brandenburg, *Imported Americans*, 214–27; Edward Steiner, *On the Trail of the Immigrant*, 64–72; Edward Corsi, *In the Shadow of Liberty*, 58–9, 72–81; Stephen Graham, *With Poor Immigrants to America*, 41–9; the Public Health Report quoted in Abbott, *op. cit.*, 244–51; the committee report, just after the Great War, quoted in Lawrence G. Brown, *Immigration: Cultural Conflicts and Social Adjustments*, 192–3; and the British Ambassador's report in *Parl. Papers 1923*, XXV 810–20. A fine air-photograph is in Maurice R. Davie, *World Immigration*, 397. Philip Cowen, *Memories of an American Jew*, 186, says that on a single day in 1907, fifteen ships arrived, carrying 22,000 people – hence much delay. Interpreters were scarce, since they were paid on Ellis Island even less than in the law courts: one of them was Fiorello La Guardia, while working his way through law school – Arthur Mann, *La Guardia*, 44–6.
[1] *Industrial Commission Reports*, XV 95–6 (evidence of Assistant Commissioner McSweeney).
[2] See especially Kate H. Claghorn, *The Immigrant's Day in Court*, 324–5.
[3] *Parl. Papers 1893–4*, LXXI 30–47; Claghorn, *op. cit.*, 4–7; Davie, *op. cit.*, 465–6.
10

at inland cities, yet the Immigration Commission found many whose motives were low and whose operations were at best inefficient. Organizations competed for immigrants, took them to poor lodgings, found them work without proper inquiry into its nature. A few, as disguised investigators found, were perfectly willing, in full knowledge of the facts, to send young women to brothels.[1]

Inland travel, therefore, imposed many hardships upon immigrants. At best, there was confusion at railroad depots and discomfort in the special immigrant trains. There were unnecessary changes, long waits, difficulties in getting meals. At worst, there might be fraud and victimization. Just as, in 1870, Scandinavians at Chicago were being cheated at hotels, and charged for transfer of baggage which was already included in their tickets, and just as at New York an immigrant could be sold a ticket supposedly for Kansas City, and be left by the obliging cabman at the Third Avenue Elevated, so in the years before the Great War sellers of food parcels at Ellis Island were over-charging, sellers of common-form telegrams were failing to give change, coastal steamboats' crews were molesting women, girls were being lured from trains on the pretext of finding them work, and cabmen at Chicago were over-charging whenever a train arrived after street-cars had stopped for the night. Yet, as Grace Abbott alleged, the head-tax levied on immigrants, included in the fare they paid, was producing a surplus of millions of dollars each year, which might have been used to finance proper hostels at inland cities, and to organize inspection of the immigrant trains.[2]

[1] See Abbott, *op. cit.*, for long extracts from welfare agency reports, principally the Immigrants' Protective League of Chicago. The later pages of Claghorn, *op. cit.* describe a variety of legal-aid agencies to which immigrants might resort. On Jewish agencies, see Cowen, *op. cit.*, 95–101, 156, and Mark Wischnitzer, *To Dwell in Safety*, 121–2. The less reputable bodies are exposed in *61 Congress 3 Session, Senate Doc. 753*, 125–95.

[2] Report on Norwegian and Swedish Immigration by A. Lewenhaupt of the Swedish Embassy at Washington, in Norwegian-American Historical Association, *Studies and Records*, XIII (1943), 50–51; Robert Louis Stevenson, *The Amateur Emigrant* ('Across the Plains'), 81–4; Einar Anderson, 'The Voyage of the Immigrant and how it has Changed', *Swedish-American Historical Bulletin*, II (1929), 96–7; *61 Congress 3 Session, Senate Doc. 753*, 39–40; Cowen, *op. cit.*, 151–2; Grace Abbott, *The Immigrant and the Community*, 1–23.

CHAPTER SEVEN

The Journey Under Sail

It was Sunday, and they all deserve praise for starting at once to wash and putting on their Sunday best, after which they joined in prayer with much devotion. During prayer some of Mynster's 'Considerations concerning God's Omnipotence and Omnipresence' were read aloud, and before and after the reading a hymn was sung to the accompaniment of a flute and violin. In the evening there was much gaiety on board, with a great deal of music and dancing. Four members of the crew and four passengers played the violin and one of the crew played the flute. The merrymaking, the captain observes, was conducted in a very respectable and orderly fashion.

> Diary of June 1842, reprinted in a Norwegian newspaper, and quoted in Theodore C. Blegen, *Land of their Choice*, 96.

Soon after we got to bed the ship began to roll very hard and the sea and wind began to roar as if it was bent on the destruction of everything floating upon it. Betwixt 12 and 1 o'clock it was the worst it was so bad that we could scarcely keep in bed . . . The luggage belonging to the passengers rolled about and cans and pots were strewed about in all places and the noise all made was beyond description. There was screaming and praying in every corner and the sailors cursing and the waves rolling all over the deck all at one time. Amidst all the turmoil the grim monster Death entered and took away the life of a child.

> 'An English Settler in Pioneer Wisconsin: the Letters of Edwin Bottomley 1842-50,' ed. Milo M. Quaife, *Wisconsin Historical Society Collections*, XXV (1918), 25-6.

Of many of the factors thus far discussed, no one emigrant would have been aware, even though their existance shaped his course. It is now time to take a view closer to his own, and to show the events of the journey to America as he would have experienced them.

The years 1865 to 1870 saw the end of sail in the North Atlantic emigrant trade.[1] In those six years, more than forty per cent of the $1\frac{1}{2}$ million emigrants to the United States went from the German states, eighteen per cent from Ireland, twenty-eight per cent from the rest of Britain, seven per cent from Scandinavia, and nearly four per cent from other parts of northwest Europe. Only some 30,000 went from countries east of Germany and from

[1] *Parl. Papers 1868-9*, XVII 130-31, *1871*, XX 347, Report of Colonial Land and Emigration Commissioners.

the Mediterranean region, and this pattern of north-west European pre-dominance had existed for the earlier decades of the century, though single countries' shares changed from time to time. The broad picture of the emigrant journey is therefore clear. It began with many small streams, as it were, leading down to a few seaports. In 1854, for example, Liverpool saw about 150,000 (more than 20,000 of them foreigners) embark for the United States, Bremen 77,000, Hamburg more than 50,000, Antwerp 26,000, and Havre, quite exceptionally, 96,000, most of them Germans. That left only some 10,000 for all other ports, in the unlikely event that all the figures were kept with perfect accuracy. From these collecting points, people bound for the United States crossed the Atlantic to New York (328,000 arrivals in 1854, but not quite all of them immigrants), New Orleans (51,000), Boston (27,000), Philadelphia (15,000), and, in small numbers, Baltimore and Quebec.[1] Those who did not settle in or near seaboard cities made their way towards and along three great routes: the Great Lakes, the Ohio, and the Mississippi. Thence, finally, they dispersed into innumerable small streams again, seeking their final destinations throughout the eastern half of the huge country.

I

The story, however, began before any move was made. Emigrants with property, those who proposed travelling as a group, even those endowed with foresight and initiative, made preparations for the journey. Norwegian farmers' wives, daughters and servants worked through the previous winter making clothes. Meat was salted, bread baked, cheese carefully prepared, butter packed in kegs. The men spent the time making huge wooden travelling-chests with iron bands and locks. Parties of Dutch Seceders entrusted their more complex affairs to committees, handling every detail all the way to the carrying of surplus funds in specially made money-belts.[2]

Some emigrants were able to make short and easy journeys from home to port. In 1831, Rebecca Burlend and her family went by waggon from the West Riding to Manchester, then took the new railway to Liverpool, where ships' masts were 'crowded like forest trees on the sea further than the eye could reach.'[3] Many of the Irish could sail from local ports, for ships,

[1] Port figures of departures and arrivals can be found in *Parl. Papers 1854–5*, XVII, Appendix 2, Report of Colonial Land and Emigration Commissioners; Walter F. Willcox and Imre Ferenczi, *International Migrations*, I 613, 678, 693–4; and in *33 Congress 2 Session, House Exec. Doc. 77*.
[2] Theodore C. Blegen, *Norwegian Migration to America: the American Transition*, 7–8; Henry S. Lucas, ed., *Dutch Immigrant Memoirs and Related Writings*, II 52. Even later, in the steamship period, Warwickshire villages saw bed-linen, towels, brushes, and cutlery collected for emigrants to Australia, and large quantities of clothes made – M. K. Ashby, *Joseph Ashby of Tysoe*, 89.
[3] Rebecca Burlend, *A True Picture of Emigration*, 9, 16.

in small numbers, left Dublin, Belfast, Londonderry or Cork for Philadelphia New Orleans and Quebec.[1] Similarly, Gustaf Unonius, in 1841, went by carriage from Uppsala to Gavle, after sending his heavy baggage to the port in advance. Twenty years later, Gro Svendsen and her husband took ship near their home in Norway and sailed direct to the St Lawrence.[2] From Schleswig-Holstein, it was easy to reach Hamburg.[3] Dutch emigrants had journeys only a little more complex, going by waggon to the nearest river or canal, then by boat to the sea, or by steamboat from one port to the next, ending at Rotterdam or Antwerp.[4]

The simplicity of such journeys could be deceptive, and it might be sound advice to urge one's friends to go to a larger port rather than a local one, for, as one Irishman put it, 'you will find trading vessels sailing every day from Liverpool.' Yet this course, too, had its hazards, for although deck fares on the Irish Sea steamboats were never more than five shillings, and by competition were sometimes driven much lower, no amenities were provided. Apart from cabin passengers, goods and livestock had first claim in these vessels, and deck passengers were added afterwards to the utmost limits of capacity. One boat in the spring of 1849 carried 280 passengers, 240 cattle, 206 pigs, 19 sheep, and 4 horses. Such passengers were packed shoulder to shoulder, drenched with spray, with only difficult access to a single water-pump, 'while the whole deck was afloat with animal mire.' The master of one steamboat assured an investigator that when no horses were being carried, passengers were allowed into the stables on deck. Others paid extra to get into engine-room or forecastle – a concession available to very few, but worth while for a crossing that might last anything from fourteen to twenty-eight hours.[5]

Many Europeans necessarily made more elaborate journeys. Johannes Schweizer, in 1820, travelled down the Rhine valley in several stages, some on foot and some by boat. From Mainz to Cologne he used a wheat boat under sail, camping out on deck with a brazier, coal, and his own provisions.

[1] Sholto Cooke, *The Maiden City and the Western Ocean*, 134–6 and plate following 70. For the eighteenth century, see R. J. Dickson, *Ulster Emigration to Colonial America 1718–1775*, esp. chapters vii and x. A. L. Rowse, *The Cornish in America*, 81, shows sailings in the 1840s from such small ports as Padstow and Falmouth.
[2] *A Pioneer in Northwest America, 1841–1858: The Memoirs of Gustaf Unonius*, I 8–11; Theodore C. Blegen, *Land of their Choice*, 112.
[3] 'The Diary of Heinrich Egge, a German Emigrant', *Mississippi Valley Historical Review*, XVII (1930–31), 125.
[4] Lucas, *op. cit.*, I 132–3, 195, 420, II 91–2.
[5] John Kerr to Graham family, 1847, printed in *Report of Deputy Keeper of the Records, Northern Ireland 1960–5*, 95–6; Ernest B. Anderson, *Sailing Ships of Ireland*, 179–204 (the title is somewhat misleading); *Parl. Papers 1849* LI 397–431, Captain Denham's Report on Passenger Accommodation in Steamers between Ireland and Liverpool.

From Utrecht to Amsterdam he travelled in a boat pulled by horses.[1] German emigrants took similar routes, as probably did the peasants whom Carl Schurz saw leaving a village near Cologne in the 1830s, their waggon loaded with trunks and boxes, and a crowd of neighbours gathered to see them off. Others, however, from higher up the Rhine, could make their way to Strasbourg, load their baggage on waggons which had brought raw cotton to the Alsace mills, then go all the way to Havre, or speed their journey by taking the steamboat down the Seine from Paris. Later, prosperous travellers might reach Paris or Havre by train.[2] In the 1850s, Germans and Scandinavians were already crossing the North Sea by steamboat to Hull, en route for Liverpool. The same route was taken by a Czech emigrant in 1854, who had started by river from Prague to Leipzig, whence he took the train to Hamburg.[3]

II

Not until the mid 1850s did British and American laws give anything like comprehensive protection to emigrants and force shipowners to give anything like full service. In earlier years, during which four-and-a-quarter million emigrants embarked, passengers had to do much for themselves. They searched for lodgings, perhaps with prostitutes, as at Amsterdam, plucking them by the sleeve and calling 'come in, farmer'. They walked the docks, looking at ships and barks, trying to make up their minds, then making their bargains with captains or agents. Going on board they might find, as did Swiss emigrants in the 1820s and Dutch in the 1840s, carpenters hurriedly running up berths in what had been cargo space during the eastward crossing.[4] If they were more fortunate, they found a vessel with permanent passenger space: an open deck divided roughly into compartments, single men forward, families amidships, single women further aft, and right aft a smaller compartment giving privacy to a few people willing to pay extra for it – accommodation called 'second cabin' or 'intermediate'. Cabin passengers occupied the poop. The galley was part of a deckhouse.[5]

[1] Robert H. Billigmeier and Fred A. Picard, *The Old Land and the New: the Journals of two Swiss Families in America in the 1820s*, 39–70.
[2] Carl Schurz, *Reminiscences*, I 28–9; Edith Abbott, *Historical Aspects of the Immigration Question*, 96–7, quoting *Chambers' Edinburgh Journal*, 13 June 1846; Franz J. Ennemoser, *Eine Reise vom Mittelrhein . . . nach den nordamerikanischen freistaaten. . . .*, 1–17, but even he went from Mainz to Cologne by steamboat.
[3] Francis J. Swehla, 'Bohemians in Central Kansas', *Kansas Historical Collections*, XIII (1913–14), 470.
[4] Billigmeier and Picard, *op. cit.*, 70, 190–2; Lucas, *op. cit.*, II 431 (Adriaan Zwemer); Ennemoser, *op. cit.*, 17–22; Blegen, *Land of their Choice*, 36 (Johannes Nordboe, 1835).
[5] Cooke, *op. cit.*, frontispiece and 134–6 – *Elizabeth*, 770 tons, 1857. Gustav Koerner, *Memoirs*, I 260, has a brief description of such 'second cabin' or 'intermediate' accommodation, as has Fred-

Later still, two passenger decks were sometimes found, in vessels of 1,500 or 2,000 tons, capable of carrying 800 or 900 people.

Until the 1850s, only cabin passengers could rely on a supply of cooked food, utensils, and bedding. Swiss emigrants of the 1820s therefore laid in supplies of bacon, rice, peas, biscuit, potatoes, cheese, butter, tea, coffee, beer and brandy, or even such luxuries as lemons, figs, dried prunes and spices. In the following decade, Gustav Koerner's party provided themselves with hams, herrings, flour, eggs, vinegar, chocolate, tea, coffee and wine, with the ship supplying biscuit, rice and potatoes. A Norwegian contract ticket of 1848 made it the emigrant's duty to provide food for twelve weeks, the ship supplying only water and fuel. In the 1850s, Franz Ennemoser, after finding a German boarding-house and even before engaging passage, bought sugar, rice, potatoes, olive oil and wine.[1] He also bought pots and pans, a chamber-pot and a lantern. Authorities at that time would have added a barrel for provisions, a water-can, canisters for tea and sugar, and cutlery, and one of them assured his readers that all this, together with a few bedclothes, could be had at Liverpool for little more than twelve shillings.[2]

Ships loaded cargo, stores and passengers as long as possible, but even when everything was on board the voyage did not necessarily begin. Adverse winds could delay sailing-ships days or weeks. Gro Svendsen had time to go ashore for an Easter service, and dance on deck in the evening – and the ship sailed only two days later. Gustaf Unonius, however, could hear the church bells, but dared not leave his ship, riding at anchor in Gavle harbour, lest the wind change and the captain decide to come on board.[3] Even when conditions improved, it was often necessary to pull the ship out of harbour by steam-tug, from Liverpool, indeed, many miles beyond the Mersey.[4]

Passengers watched carefully astern, storing up memories of the land they were unlikely to see again. Gustaf Unonius was fortunate in having Sweden's eastern coast in sight for a long time, and passed many places familiar to him

---

erick Piercy, *Route from Liverpool to Great Salt Lake City*, 23, whose quarters were in a deckhouse. Unonius, *Memoirs* I 15–16, describes the highest class of accommodation: a cabin for him and his wife, another serving as dining-room and as sleeping quarters for two men, and the use of the main saloon in which a servant could sleep.
[1] Billigmeier and Picard, *op. cit.*, 72, 191; Koerner, *op. cit.*, I 261; Worm-Müller, *Den Norske Sjofarts Historie*, II (i), 602–3, kindly translated for me by G. K. Orton; Ennemoser, *op. cit.*, 20–2.
[2] *Parl. Papers 1851*, XIX, Q. 5153 (Hunter), Select Committee on Passengers' Acts; Vere Foster, *Work and Wages*, 8.
[3] Blegen, *Land of their Choice*, 112–13; Unonius, *Memoirs*, I 21. See also Billigmeier and Picard, *op. cit.*, 74; Lucas, *op. cit.*, II 92; *Parl. Papers 1851*, XIX Q. 732 (Lean).
[4] Koerner, *Memoirs*, I 264; Ennemoser, *op. cit.*, 37; Egge 'Diary,' *loc. cit.*, 125; *Parl. Papers 1851*, XIX Q. 2620–6 (Tapscott).

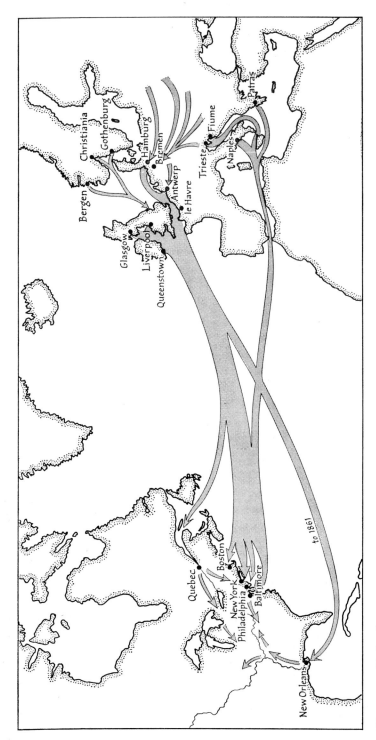

Diagram 3   Emigration routes

as a child. A few, later on, wrote poems about the experience. Gro Svendsen merely recorded that she saw the last of Norway 'far in the distance like a blue mist'.[1]

III

The crowded passenger deck, with its two tiers of six-foot berths each intended for several people, with its heaps of baggage, with nowhere to hang clothes and nowhere to eat in comfort, would have made even the smoothest crossing difficult. But for people unused to the sea, it was seldom long before sickness began. A storm could make things far worse. With hatches battened down, ventilation lacking, smells increasing, and no chance of getting meals even for the few who could have eaten them, with berths collapsing, kegs of drink stove in, bags of peas bursting, baggage soaked and broken up, the emigrants' lot was wretched. As the ship's pitching and creaking grew, landsmen's fears of danger mounted, but they could do little but pray.[2]

The first unpleasantness over, a routine could be worked out. Very probably, shipowners who gave evidence before official inquiries exaggerated the degree of order that prevailed, and when, in 1854, Emigration Officer De Courcy testified, he admitted that he was taking the captains' word for what went on, and had never himself travelled in an emigrant ship. Letters and diaries, however, show that, from time to time, passengers acted to ensure that life at sea was something better than a free-for-all. Equipment in the galley was never adequate for a full complement of emigrants. Only planning could make certain that everyone was regularly fed. Gustav Koerner observed a committee set up, with rules on the distribution of water and fuel, and on the taking of turns for cooking. The group of which Adriaan Zwemer was a member in 1849 saw a similar system, Germans and Dutch being separated. Firewood was issued daily. Cooking was supervised. Emigrants stood in orderly line for their food. No precautions, of course, could prevent the stove from being carried overboard in a storm. Zwemer noted, too, that a night-watch was organized, after a German had been found stealing. Two years later, in another Seceder party, cooks and assistants were named, grace was said before meals, and a chapter of the Bible was read afterwards.[3] It would be foolish to suggest that practices like these

[1] Unonius, *Memoirs*, I 23–4; Blegen, *Land of their Choice*, 114. See also Burlend, *op. cit.*, 16. Blegen, *Norwegian Migration to America*, 309, 315–16, prints poems relating to this experience, as does Henry S. Lucas, *Netherlanders in America*, 611–12.

[2] Burlend, *op. cit.*, 18–20; Billigmeier and Picard, *op. cit.*, 78–9, 207; Bottomley letters, 23, 'nothing but sea sickness and gruel making and emptying the chamber vessels'; Blegen, *Land of their Choice*, 105, 114; Alan Conway, *The Welsh in America* 28 (a letter of 1856).

[3] *Parl. Papers 1854*, XIII, Q . 5836–7 (De Courcy), Select Committee on Emigrant Ships; Koerner, *Memoirs*, I 269; Lucas, *Dutch Immigrant Memoirs*, I 195, II 96, 431–2. I have dealt with the quite exceptionally well organized Mormons in my *Expectations Westward*, chapter 9.

were common. Vere Foster thought that everyone would be in difficulties except 'the richer passengers who can bribe the cooks with half a crown now and then, the pretty women who can coax them with smiles, or . . . strong men who can elbow their way with their broad shoulders.'[1] There is much evidence to support him. The turmoil around the stoves reminded one writer in 1856 of the siege of Sebastopol. The weakest might get no cooked food at all. When force was not the rule, emigrants might persuade the ship's cook to prepare their meals, or at least give them a good place by the fire, giving him cash or drink.[2]

The problem of cleanliness may have been felt less acutely, but it was always present. There were water-closets of a sort, though few and in-conveniently placed, but no space or equipment was set aside for washing. Nor was the supply of water calculated with anything beyond drinking and cooking in mind. As for clothes, they could be washed only on the open deck, and in salt water. In such circumstances, a last-minute scrubbing before meeting the doctor at the American port was the best that could be hoped for.[3] If comfort and health were to be preserved, it was equally important that the passenger quarters should be kept clean. When passengers had to eat among their bedding and baggage, this would be essential, even in the calmest weather and with emigrants of tidy habits. Gangs were sometimes organized for the purpose, but it is quite impossible to say how widespread this practice was.[4] When the law came to require passenger stewards, to help care for the emigrants, these were commonly chosen from among the passengers themselves. Similarly, girls from the steerage might be hired as stewardesses for the cabin.[5]

Then, as now, one could cross the Atlantic with scarcely a sight of another ship, with no reminder of the land's existence apart from changes in the birds that flew alongside. Monotony was a feature of all crossings. Only a handful of emigrants could derive satisfaction from the beauty of a sunset,

---

[1] Foster, *op. cit.*, 22; and his letter to Lord Hobart on his own experiences, *Parl. Papers 1851*, XL 436.

[2] Billigmeier and Picard, *op. cit.*, 213 (tipping with schnapps); Burlend, *op. cit.*, 17–18; Bottomley letters, 22, 25; *Parl. Papers 1851*, XIX Q. 1117 (Hodder), 1859–61 (Welsh); Piercy, *op. cit.*, 25; *Latter-day Saints' Millennial Star*, XVIII 412 (28 June 1856); Blegen, *Land of their Choice*, 105; Conway, *op. cit.*, 26 (efforts to prepare Welsh dishes).

[3] *Parl. Papers 1851*, XIX, Q. 2083–5 (Prior), 2444 (Welsh); Lucas, *Dutch Immigrant Memoirs*, II 100.

[4] *Parl. Papers 1847–8*, XVII 49, Select Committee of House of Lords, Colonization from Ireland, has a letter from Stephen de Vere, introduced as evidence by T. F. Elliott, emphasizing the squalor; *1851*, XIX, Q. 3330 (Saul), 4599 (Rankin), 4996–8 (Hunter), 7355 (Murdoch), has other evidence. Blegen, *Land of their Choice*, 97, shows one ship's captain, in 1842, suspecting cholera, ordering fumigation with chlorine and vinegar.

[5] *Parl. Papers 1854*, XIII, Q. 1496 (Redmond); J. R. Beste, *The Wabash*, I 59.

or of moonlight on the sea.[1] Food at best was crude. No entertainment was provided by the ship. Day after day, for five weeks even if the ship proved lucky, passengers heard the creaking of timbers, the shouts of sailors, the wash of water against the hull, and lived their own closed, cramped life. Exercise was difficult, when the deck was cluttered with gear, boats, livestock, or deck-houses, and emigrants were so numerous. On the other hand, many of the passengers displayed a horror of fresh air, and even in their own interests it was hard to get them on deck at all.[2] Men and boys might spend time helping sailors haul at the ropes, and members of one Dutch party, who were carpenters, were enlisted to repair masts and bowsprit after a storm.[3] Women and girls, much of the time, sat on deck, with camp stools if they were lucky, but perhaps on benches with chicken-coops underneath, chatting or reading, wrapped in blankets on cold days. Marbles, cards and dominoes are mentioned in letters. So was dancing. So, too, was fighting, for example between Irish and Welsh.[4]

Certain breaks in routine were laid down by custom. Some sort of service was held whenever possible on Sundays, the emigrants washed and in their best clothes, a hymn sung to the accompaniment of violin or flute, a passage from some devotional book read. Children born on board might be baptized, the captain reading the service.[5] Certain nationalities, prominently represented among the emigrants, had festivals that were likely to occur during the crossing. Norwegians celebrated 17 May, with gunfire, a feast, and songs. Germans had St John's Day, 23 June. On board one emigrant ship in 1854, this coincided with the birthday of one of their number. Presents were given, and many bottles were opened, with toasts to the man himself, to the captain, officers, and ship, 'in fact everybody and every-thing'. The Fourth of July saw flags run up, salutes fired by the crew, a box of fireworks opened, and a pig killed and distributed to the passengers, while in the evening one party of Dutch Seceders gained permission to end the day with psalms.[6]

Births and deaths were both likely to punctuate the crossing. There is no certainty about the statistics, which, as regards deaths, may well include much understatement. Certainly one must not accept the famous year 1847 as normal, when at Quebec officials recorded nearly 17,000 deaths at sea,

---

[1] Billigmeier and Picard, *op. cit.*, 207; Burlend, *op. cit.*, 23–4.
[2] Burlend, *op. cit.*, 22; *Parl. Papers 1851*, XIX, Q. 5566–7 (Patey), *1854*, XIII, Q. 171 (Murdoch). Piercy, *op. cit.*, 25, and *Millennial Star*, XVIII 427 (5 July 1856), XXVI 7 (2 January 1864) describe the fresh air problem, the last reference being to Brigham Young's journal of 1841.
[3] Lucas, *Dutch Immigrant Memoirs*, I 291; *Millennial Star*, XVIII 413 (28 June 1856).
[4] Billigmeier and Picard, *op. cit.*, 196; Koerner, *Memoirs*, I 269; Conway, *op. cit.*, 24, 32–4, 43.
[5] Koerner, *Memoirs*, I 271; Blegen, *Land of their Choice*, 96, 114.
[6] Theodore C. Blegen, *Grass Roots History*, 55–7; Lucas, *Dutch Immigrant Memoirs*, II 96–8.

at quarantine, or in hospitals, out of fewer than 100,000 embarked. In the previous year, the figure had been 272 out of 33,000; and the year after it was to be 385 out of 28,000. A decade later, it was probably a good deal lower still. By the 1860s it was about one per cent of the passengers. What is equally certain, however, is that young children were especially vulnerable: on board the well-regulated Australian ships, where figures were probably very accurate, the death-rates of adults, children and infants were in the ratio 1:5:20, and the last-named represented an annual rate even worse than the appalling figure then prevailing on land.[1] Corpses were wrapped in sailcloth weighted with a bag of sand, placed on a plank, which was then tilted over the high bulwark, while captain or literate passenger read some sort of burial service. Gro Svendsen saw one baby buried in a coffin made by the ship's carpenter and partly filled with sand.[2]

With life in general so restricted and dull, even the most trivial episode seemed noteworthy. A child fell through a hatchway. The ship's cat was lost overboard. Cod were caught on the Grand Banks. Whales were seen, and icebergs. A German couple, unmarried but found too close together, were locked up for a night, then lectured by the captain. A German girl was suspected of becoming a captain's mistress.[3] Then, at last, occurred what every emigrant was bound to find exciting: the arrival of the pilot-boat – emigrants abandoning their dinner to rush on deck – the first lighthouse, the first glimpse of Long Island, the lights of Quebec, or the crowing of cocks and ringing of bells on the first morning in port.[4] Before landing, courtesies might be exchanged. The captain of one Norwegian ship treated his passengers to punch, while the mate gave an emigrant girl a prayer-book. On board another, emigrants took up a collection to buy the captain a gold watch.[5] There were, of course, examples of less happy relations between passengers and crew. Norwegian emigrant letters often complained of violence at the hands of English sailors. An Irish gentleman who travelled

[1] Mortality figures are printed annually in the Reports of the Colonial Land and Emigration Commissioners. I accept the Australian figures, but suspect the accuracy of those for the North Atlantic crossing, based as they were on what shipowners chose to report. Even American records of deaths, after the fine had been enacted, needed to take no account of younger children's deaths. Friedrich Kapp, *Immigration and the Commissioners of Emigration of the State of New York*, 241, prints sailing-ship mortality figures 1864–9. Canadian figures, for the years referred to, are in *Parl. Papers 1847–8*, XLVII 45, 383–403, *1849*, XXXVIII 45–6.
[2] Lucas, *Dutch Immigrant Memoirs*, I 308, II 53, 434; Blegen, *Land of their Choice* 113.
[3] Billgmeier and Picard, *op. cit.*, 77, 80–81, 199–200, 202–3; Lucas, *Dutch Immigrant Memoirs*, II 96; Blegen, *Land of their Choice* 110, 115.
[4] Unonius, *Memoirs*, I 26–30; Blegen, *Land of their Choice*, 115–16; *Millennial Star*, XXVI 478 (23 July 1864). Not all landings were so peaceful and charming: see accounts of the Irish Famine immigrants' arrival at Grosse Isle in 1847, the beach strewn with corpses and the hospitals filled to overflowing, in the Medical Superintendent's report, *Parl. Papers 1847–8*, XLVII, esp. 461–7.
[5] Blegen, *Land of their Choice*, 390; *American Transition* 27.

as an emigrant reported short weight and irregular issue of rations, and blows from the officers for anyone who protested – even the ship's surgeon was quarrelsome and violent.[1] We have no way of knowing how common was one extreme of conduct or the other, or whether some less eventful, more neutral relationship, usually prevailed.

IV

After a rather perfunctory medical inspection by doctors boarding from Quarantine on Staten Island, vessels sailed, or were towed, up New York harbour to their docks. Until the 1850s, runners were as much a menace there as at Liverpool. From 1855, the depot at Castle Garden, already described, brought the abuse fairly well under control. After their inspection, changing of money, buying of tickets, and so on, immigrants sought shelter in the city, if possible in boarding-houses run by people of their own nationality.[2] They might consult their welfare organizations. Most of them would need to make plans for a further journey.

Those bound for the New England states could board steamboats for Fall River or other ports, which in turn were linked to the railroad system. Five dollars to Boston was a normal fare, but competition could bring it far below that figure. The boats were more than three hundred feet in length, with freight and baggage on one deck, together with one large room for men, fitted with tables and three tiers of berths. Above were two saloons, one for ladies and couples, the other a smoking-room, and on either side were arranged cabins. Chandeliers, a piano, a barber's shop, were other features that travellers noticed.[3]

Immigrants heading for the West were likely to start their journey in a Hudson River steamboat. Johan Gasmann described his vessel as 'a beautiful floating hotel or palace', as it sped up a river crowded with traffic. The low standard fare could be reduced if travellers were willing to huddle on the lower deck amongst the baggage.[4] From the 1840s, it was possible to go from Albany to Buffalo by rail, but most people chose the Erie Canal boats. These craft were of several classes, differing in size, speed, comfort and cost.

[1] Blegen, *Land of their Choice,* 107; and Vere Foster's letter cited in note 1 p.138.
[2] Blegen, *Land of their Choice,* 261 – Jannicke Saehle wrote in 1847 of 'walking smartly' past the doctor. Billigmeier and Picard, *op. cit.,* 87.
[3] William Hancock, *An Emigrant's Five Years in the Free States of America,* 128 ff. Another short-distance journey is noted in Rowse, *op. cit.,* 111: Cornish immigrants of the 1830s who arrived at New York, went up the Hudson as far as Kingston, then took the Delaware and Hudson canal into Pennsylvania.
[4] Blegen, *Land of their Choice,* 155–7; Patrick Shirreff, *A Tour through North America,* 93; Hancock, *op. cit.,* 219–34; and Koerner, *Memoirs,* I 276 mentions a band that played on deck.

Dutch diarists found one type with a deck-house forming an eight-berth cabin. Others were so simple in design that women slept in the hold with the baggage, and the men on deck. Fairly typical of those used by immigrants was a boat with a single saloon, equipped with a table down the middle and sofas on either side. At night, sofas became berths, and an upper tier was arranged, fastened with ropes to the ceiling and hooks to the wall. A curtain was hung in such a way as to mark off a ladies' cabin at one end. The single wash-place was equipped with a common roller-towel. Low bridges made walking on deck hazardous at night. Low water was another inconvenience: passengers might need to disembark while extra horses tried to drag the boat over difficult places. Food was found at the numerous stops. Using such means, the journey along the canal was likely to take eight or nine days.[1]

Variations were possible. From the early 1850s, the Erie railroad opened a short route between the lower Hudson and the Great Lakes. There, the New York stream of immigrants met those who had entered North America by the St Lawrence, had travelled in one steamboat from Quebec to Montreal, and in others along the upper river and its associated canals.[2]

From Buffalo, travellers could go in a single steamboat all the way to Lake Michigan, taking about four days if the vessel made few stops for freight. There was comfortable cabin accommodation, but few immigrants occupied it. For them, the steerage might have three tiers of berths, most of them doubles and fitted with curtains. Outside were heaps of baggage with a narrow passage left between. Gustaf Unonius observed Germans with waggons and ploughs, harness and tools, tubs, furniture, candlesticks and clocks, which must have been transported at great expense. Eric Norelius took cabin passage, so crowded was his boat with Irish and freight. At Milwaukee, passengers ended their journey by landing in a small freight boat with open rails, drenched in anything like rough water.[3]

Increasingly, such journeys could be replaced by railroads, from Niagara to points opposite Detroit, from the Great Lakes across Michigan to Chicago, along the southern shore of Lake Erie, and, before the Civil War, all across

[1] Unonius, *Memoirs* I 60–82; Lucas, *Dutch Immigrant Memoirs*, many examples but see esp. Adriaan Zwemer's journal in II 438–40. Koerner, *Memoirs*, I 277, states that his party's baggage was so bulky that they chartered a slow boat for themselves alone.
[2] Blegen, *Land of their Choice* 169–70, 390–92; and, for grimmer experiences, Stephen de Vere's letter, *Parl. Papers 1847–8*, XVII 51. Remember, too, the overland migration from the Maritime Provinces, and journeys in coasting vessels, especially by the Irish, described in Marcus L. Hansen, *The Atlantic Migration*, 180–83.
[3] Unonius, *Memoirs* I 88–113; Lucas, *Dutch Immigrant Memoirs* I 309; 'The Early life of Eric Norelius. . . .', *Augustana Historical Society Publications* No. 4 Part I (1934), 109–10. Johan Gasmann, in Blegen, *Land of their Choice* 161–6, describes the scenery more than the vessel.

the Middle West as far as eastern Iowa or Missouri. Steamboats and canal boats continued, of course, to offer the advantage of low cost.[1]

Many immigrants landed at New Orleans, after their ship had been hauled by tugs over sandbars at the mouth of the Mississippi. No regulations of any consequence either aided or troubled them, though, especially if they were Germans, they could secure advice and modest financial aid from an exceptionally efficient voluntary society.[2] The journey upstream was rapid, easy, and cheap. Steamboats were palatial for those who could afford the great saloons, cosy staterooms, abundant meals, swarms of Negro servants, gas-light, and other amenities. Immigrants, here as elsewhere, were likely to be found, instead, on the lower deck, near machinery and freight, sleeping on bare boards, cooking at a single stove, drawing their water straight from the river, and expected at every stop to help carry fuel from woodlots on the bank.[3]

From the main river, passengers trans-shipped at St Louis for the major tributaries. One, in 1857, took a train for Jefferson City, planning to make a connection there with a Missouri steamboat. But most vessels had gone aground, and the only one at the landing-stage was already full when people rushed to it from the train in the dark. The fortunate ones who got on board found four sittings for meals and most of them had to sleep on the deck. Those who secured cabins were jammed in 'like stage coach passengers'.[4] Others might ascend the Illinois river, others again the Ohio. Steamboats on the latter river were much like those on the Mississippi in their arrangements. As they moved between flatboats carrying produce, and other steamboats, passengers could enjoy the privilege, if they wished to pay for it instead of fending for themselves, of eating at a second sitting with white members of the crew, while coloured servants or slaves 'satisfied their hunger on the veranda'.[5]

Immigrants on the Ohio were likely to meet others who had come south

[1] Lucas, *Dutch Immigrant Memoirs*, II 104–8 (in 1854 Johannes Remeeus went by rail from Albany to Buffalo, by steamboat to Detroit, by rail to Chicago, then again by steamboat to Milwaukee); Blegen, *Land of their Choice*, 392–3; and, for the Niagara suspension bridge, William Ferguson, *America by River and Rail*, 441, 455–8, whose train crossed it in 1855, its first year of operation (there is an excellent photograph, taken four years later, in Helmut and Alison Gernsheim, *Historic Events 1839–1939*, 9).
[2] Piercy, *op. cit.*, 28–30 and note, on sandbars; Regan, *op. cit*, 23–31; on aid, John F. Nau, *The German People of New Orleans*, 13, 21–4.
[3] F. Logan, *Notes of a Journey through Canada, the United States, and the West Indies*, 114–15; George Lewis, *Impressions of America and the American Churches*, 242; and on the whole subject, the first half of Mark Twain's *Life on the Mississippi*. The best modern treatment is Louis C. Hunter, *Steamboats on the Western Rivers*, esp. chapters 9 and 10.
[4] Erastus F. Beadle, *To Nebraska in '57*, 10–15.
[5] Burlend, *op. cit.*, 36–40; Shirreff, *op. cit.*, 267–72; T. L. Nichols, *Forty Years of American Life*, II 5–7.

from the Great Lakes by the canals constructed in the 1830s. Gustav Koerner went by this means from Cleveland to Portsmouth, Ohio, and thence by steamboats to Cincinnati, Louisville and St Louis. Canal boats could be comfortable enough, with a galley aft, a main saloon in which men slept at night, a separate ladies' saloon, and a small private cabin too, the deck above taking the baggage and serving as promenade. But they could become overcrowded, with people sleeping not only in temporary berths but on mattresses on the saloon floor, and horses could draw them only slowly on waterways hundreds of miles long.[1]

Immigrants, finally, who did not decide to stay in the river towns had to complete their journey on foot or by waggon, aided sometimes by such a new development as the Illinois Canal, but often setting out on rough tracks through the forest, finding lodging, if they were lucky, at inns which looked much like any other log cabins.[2]

---

[1] Koerner, *Memoirs*, I 279–83; Beste, *Wabash*, II 191–221, but he notes, I 158, that there were already railroads in similar directions.
[2] Unonius, *Memoirs*, I 154–62; Blegen, *Land of their Choice*, 70–3, 167; Hans Mattson, *Reminiscences*, 28; 'Early Life of Eric Norelius', *loc. cit.*, 111–17 (using canal boat from Chicago to Peru, Ill.); Heinrich Egge, 'Diary', 134 (reports crossing the Mississippi by steam ferry at Davenport, a year before the first bridge over that river).

CHAPTER EIGHT

The Journey by Steam

Most of those who go across the Atlantic in the steerage feed better, both as to quantity and quality, than they ever did before, and better too than, for some time at all events, they will do again.

Report on Emigrant Ships by the Sanitary Commission
of the 'Lancet' (1873), 28.

The steerage of the modern ship ought to be condemned as unfit for the transportation of human beings.

Edward A. Steiner, *On the Trail of the Immigrant*
(1906), 36–7.

Although, from the later years of the nineteenth century, emigration to America became significant in wider and wider areas of southern and eastern Europe, for the most part the predominance of the north-western ports continued. In 1891, some 110,000 steerage passengers embarked for the United States at Liverpool and landed at New York; nearly 82,000 started from Hamburg and 68,000 from Bremen; nearly 36,000 from Antwerp, more than 25,000 each from Rotterdam and Havre; 23,000 from Glasgow and about the same number from all other ports of northern Europe; and nearly 50,000 by British, French and Italian ships from Mediterranean ports. The figures given, for New York, amount to about four-fifths of all emigrants to the United States in the year.[1] In 1907, when emigration was almost three times as large, Bremen sent 203,767 people and Hamburg 142,794, nearly all of them from central and eastern Europe rather than Germany itself; Liverpool sent 177,632, about one-third of them foreigners; Antwerp and Havre were still important. Some Austro-Hungarian emigrants, however, now embarked at Trieste and Fiume; and Italians, more than 240,000 of them, were able to use Naples.[2]

[1] *52 Congress 1 Session, House Exec. Doc. 235*, Part I, 323. Arrivals at ports are in annual volumes of *Commerce and Navigation of the United States:* in round figures, 1891 saw 448,000 reach New York, 41,000 Baltimore, 31,000 Boston, and 26,000 Philadelphia. American and British figures cannot be taken as referring exactly to emigrants; and it is impossible to be sure how many foreign emigrants passed through Liverpool. British figures for 1891–1901, for what they are worth, can be found in *Parl. Papers 1902*, CXVI, Part II, 56–8.
[2] Port figures are in *U.S. Consular Reports*, No. 333 (June 1908), 91. Details of the ethnic composition of several major ports' emigrants are in Walter F. Willcox and Imre Ferenczi, *International Migrations*, I 593, 617, 716, 741.

I

Liverpool's emigrants included most of the English and Irish, and nothing new needs to be recorded about their journey to the port. They included also, however, almost all the Scandinavian emigrants, year after year. Figures for the 1890s ranged from 16,000 to 60,000 a year, the largest number from Gothenburg, though Finnish ports were becoming prominent at the end of the decade. In 1892, for example, Adolph Benson travelled to Osby by waggon, by train to Malmo, and by steam ferry to Copenhagen, boarding a ship there for Hull. The typical vessel was single-funnelled, 2,000 tons or less, and carried perhaps two hundred passengers. Agents of the Atlantic steamship companies brought emigrants to Christiania, Gothenburg and other main ports, and cabled to England when they had embarked. Soon after departure, they were given coffee, biscuit, bread, and butter. They slept on two shelves, in each of two or three dormitories, and occupied this accommodation for two nights. Breakfast and supper were much the same as their first meal, with salt herring sometimes added, while dinner was soup, meat, potatoes, and bread. Standards of cooking, sanitation and crew's services, varied greatly from ship to ship. The crossing cost £1.12.6., the last half-crown representing the cost of food. The ship's arrival off the English coast was telegraphed from Spurn Head. At Hull, emigrants were often allowed to wander ashore. When official disembarkation came, baggage was inspected, then transferred to railway trucks, while stevedores unloaded cargo, and hawkers tried to sell refreshments. Liverpool agents sorted emigrants into parties, took them for a meal to houses which were under contract, then put them on board special trains at the North Eastern station. The four-hour rail journey cost them 6s. 6d. A few shiploads, however, might be sent across the Humber Ferry to the Manchester, Sheffield and Lincolnshire line, later absorbed by the Great Central.[1] This was also the line used by emigrants arriving at Grimsby, from 8,000 to 19,000 a year during the 1890s, most of them from Gothenburg, but smaller numbers from Hamburg,

[1] Adolph B. Benson, *Farm, Forge and Philosophy*, 46; *Parl. Papers 1882*, LXII, 87–97, Reports received by Board of Trade and Local Government Board . . .Transit of Scandinavian Emigrants through the Port of Hull; *1903*, IX, Q. 21713, Royal Commission on Alien Immigration. The National Maritime Museum, in its collection of plans of ships built by Barclay Curle, has sketches of J. Currie and Company's *Rona* and *Thorsa*, 1884, 1,314 tons. Unlike the vessels described in the report, this had 2-berth cabins, a saloon, and a ladies' cabin, all somewhat forward of amidships, and open berths and a few tables for 146 emigrants, right aft, these people being provided with 4 W.C.s. A few Scandinavians, however, continued to travel through German ports. Thus P. P. Quist went by waggon and train to Malmo, by steamboat to Lübeck, by rail to Hamburg – 'Recollections of an Immigrant of 1865', *Swedish-American Historical Bulletin*, IV No. 3 (1931), 10–11; and A. G. Carlson travelled in 1891 through Kalmar, Lübeck, Hamburg and Bremen – Roy W. Swanson, 'Some Swedish Emigrant Guide Books of the Second Half of the Nineteenth Century', *Yearbook* of Swedish Historical Society of America, XI (1926), 121–4.

Rotterdam, Antwerp and other places. The railway company owned some of the ships. The short North Sea crossings seem to have been characterized by rather worse conditions than those just described, but at Grimsby itself the organization was at least as good as at Hull. Not far from the great tower which housed machinery for the dock gate, there was a pier on which stood a deserted railway station. This was used for the feeding and overnight accommodation of emigrants. As soon as possible, they were put on trains at the dock station a few hundred yards away.[1]

Met at the Liverpool stations by agents, and taken to lodging-houses associated with the steamship lines, emigrants and their baggage soon moved by waggonette to the dock. Often they embarked there, the ship's surgeon inspecting them at the gangway, with the Board of Trade doctor and, after 1893, the American doctor, repeating the process on board. After that, the crew were inspected, lifeboats were lowered for practice, and passengers of the higher classes could board later, by tender, when the ship had moved out into the Mersey. Alternatively, steerage passengers too might use the latter method, with medical inspection as they trans-shipped.[2]

Some Russian Jews also travelled through Britain. After his father had sold his house, after bedding, household utensils, a copper tea-kettle, and candlesticks had been packed, and after a farewell dinner had been eaten, the young Samuel Chotzinoff saw baggage sent in a cart to the wharf at Vitebsk, and the whole family embark on a paddle-steamer which, after more than two days and nights on the Dvina, reached Riga. Thence they took ship to Stettin, and thence another to London, though this was due to an agent's fraud and they had intended going straight to New York. They embarked at Liverpool a year later. Some twenty years after that, Stephen Graham watched Russians and Jews disembark at London from Baltic ports, their belongings in sacks upon their shoulders.[3]

Far more Jews, however, made for German ports. Mary Antin's family, early in the 1890s, had a crowd to see them off at Polotzk station, shouting blessings and advice. Like all emigrants, they passed through the control stations at the German border. There, medical inspection and fumigation

---

[1] *Parl. Papers 1902*, CXVI Part II 56–8; *1903*, IX, Q . 21713; Great Central publication *Per Rail* (1913); George Dow, *Great Central*, esp. II 147–69; an article in *Grimsby Evening Telegraph*, 4 August 1960, on the occasion of the old building's demolition; and interviews with local citizens with memories reaching back to the first decade of the twentieth century, Messrs Ayscough, Hudson and Westland.

[2] *52 Congress 1 Session, House Exec. Doc. 235*, Part I 9–11, Part II 12; *Parl. Papers 1903*, IX, Q . 21444–6; *61 Congress 3 Session, Senate Doc. 748*, 85–6; and a photograph in a rare book, Burke's *Photographs of Liverpool Street Life*, Record Office, Liverpool Public Library.

[3] Samuel Chotzinoff, *A Lost Paradise*, 39–45, and Lloyd P. Gartner, *The Jewish Immigrant in England 1870–1914*, 30–32, who both mention the smuggling of emigrants to avoid buying costly Russian passports. Stephen Graham, *With Poor Immigrants to America*, 3–4.

of baggage took place. A report in 1908 suggested that these installations were filthy, that no consideration was given to emigrants' comfort, and that they were persistently overcharged for food and drink. High standards, of course, were hard to maintain when, in a peak year, a hundred thousand people might pass through a single station.[1] Mary Antin, too, found fees charged at every stopping-place, so that many people were short of funds when they reached their port. During the rail journey through Germany which, as a child, she found so confusing, nothing was provided. Emigrants might rush to buy sandwiches, or run along platforms to obtain water, at a stop, or, if they were Jews, they might find refreshments handed to them, at Königsberg and other places, by welfare organizations of their own people.[2] After many hours they reached Bremen or Hamburg. The American consul at the former place wrote in 1881 that many emigrants were by that time desperate with anxiety about any further delay, so small were their resources. Lodging-houses, of course, existed at both ports. At Hamburg, as the volume of traffic grew, the Hamburg-America emigrant village provided a wide range of amenities at reasonable cost. There was even a band which played twice a day.[3]

German ports were also used by as many as two-thirds of the emigrants from Austria-Hungary. In 1898, for example, Jacob Dolwig left his home in the Banat, travelled to Temesvar with two relatives who were to help him sell property, then began a five-day rail journey through Arad, Hatvan, Oderburg, Ratibor (the control station) and Berlin, to Bremen. Five years later, an American consul reported 40,000 emigrants passing through Reichenbach in three months, bound for Leipzig and the ports, and all travelling in fourth-class coaches. Some ten years later still, Stoyan Christowe, who was bound for Cherbourg, wore a red button with a white star upon it, to identify him to agents all the way from Macedonia to the *Oceanic*.[4]

[1] Mary Antin, *The Promised Land*, 168–72, 174–5; *61 Congress 3 Session, Senate Doc. 753*, 29–31; *Senate Doc. 748*, 93–7, which points out that, in 1906–7, nearly 128,000 passed through the nine border stations between Russia and Germany, nearly 310,000 the four between Austria and Germany, and that 5·2 per cent were rejected at the former and 1·6 per cent at the latter; *U.S. Consular Reports*, XLIX 217, No. 295, pp. 44–5, No. 296, pp. 116–17. It was hard for Jews to make up their minds whether to endure this exploitation and discomfort, to leave from a Russian Baltic port, or to travel south of Germany to the Dutch and Belgian ports: Harold Frederic, *The New Exodus*, 269–73, 281–4, 293–4; Chaim Weizman, *Trial and Error*, 92–3; 443; Mark Wischnitzer, *To Dwell in Safety*, 37–49, 102–16.
[2] Antin, *op. cit.*, 173–4; Philip Cowen, *Memories of an American Jew*, 233–4; *61 Congress 3 Session, Senate Doc. 753*, 29–31.
[3] *U.S. Consular Reports*, II 784; *52 Congress 1 Session, House Exec. Doc. 235*, Part I 109–10; *Parl. Papers 1903*, IX 531, report following Q. 13,349; *61 Congress 3 Session, Senate Doc. 748*, 97–9.
[4] 'Excerpt from the Diary of Jacob Dolwig', *North Dakota Historical Quarterly*, III (1929), 204; *U.S. Consular Reports*, No. 297, p. 96; Stoyan Christowe, *This Is My Country*, 32 (13–14 gives a description of a Macedonian village send-off).

The journey to Fiume, of course, was less elaborate. It might, indeed, be a local train ride like one from a Midland town to Liverpool. Thus; early in the present century, emigrants from a Croat village went to confession, heard Mass, were blessed by the priest, made a round of farewell visits, and because they had to leave at 3 a.m. did not go to bed at all. The whole able-bodied population went with them in the train, returning after midnight. At the port, it was the custom for girls to buy small crucifixes and rings.[1]

The Sicilian emigrants' journey to Naples, to give a last example, illustrates the universal conflict between enlightened law and human incompetence or greed. Emigrants began by obtaining birth-certificates, which were sent by the village shoemaker, the local ticket agent, to Messina, where police checked for liability to military service, and then issued a passport. Only then could a ticket be sold. Departure was long prepared. Baggage was packed. Prayers for a safe journey were offered at a special service. Farewell calls were paid and family graves visited. A dance and an evening serenade were part of the ritual. At last, baggage was sent in carts to the nearest railway station, then the emigrants themselves, walking or riding donkeys, set off. The train carried them to Messina, where a Customs inspection took place, and where everyone passed through an agent's office to answer questions for a declaration form, corresponding to the questions American officials would ask. Already, however, spurious medical certificates could be seen on sale. Rowing boats, whose crews insisted on tips, took them out to a small and dirty steamer. After many hours without food, they reached Naples, where they were left for a long time in the blazing sun. The shipping line then issued ration-tickets, and, after another Customs inspection, all were sent to a licensed hotel, then to a restaurant for a meal of soup, stew, melon and wine, accosted as they walked by hawkers. Embarkation day saw bustle and confusion. After examination by an American consular official, the heavy baggage was carefully recorded and placed in the ship's hold. Men were selling grass ropes, to tie up bags which were already falling apart. Hand luggage was supposed to be taken in a small steamboat across the harbour for fumigation, but men were at hand to sell spurious labels and seals. Vaccination was then called for, but, again, certificates could be bought. Medical inspection by a port doctor, the ship's surgeon, and an American doctor from the Marine Hospital Corps was the last formal event, though sometimes a further check was made on board to ensure that documents procured by a fit man had not been transferred at the last minute to someone who was diseased. Emigrants then went on board, carrying baggage and rush-bottomed chairs bought at twenty cents for use on deck. Bumboats

[1] Emily G. Balch, *Our Slavic Fellow Citizens*, 183–5.

were thick along the ship's side, selling fruit, pipes, hats, medicines and lucky charms.[1]

II

In size and speed, steamships developed enormously between the Civil War and the Great War, but to focus on the most advanced vessels launched from year to year is to risk being seriously misled.[2] In the late 1860s and the 1870s, steamships on the North Atlantic still bore traces of the age that was vanishing, with their clipper bows and bowsprits, masts capable of carrying sail, and superstructures that were little more than deckhouses. Their gross tonnage rose from 2,500 to about 5,000, with a length of 400 feet to nearly 500, beam sometimes less than one-tenth of their length, a single funnel, and a single screw which had completely replaced paddles. Vessels like this carried from 150 to 300 first-class passengers, and from 1,000 to 1,500 in the steerage. A good westbound crossing saw an average speed of fifteen knots.

During the next decade, many such ships continued to be built, and the old ones continued in service. Some new ships, however, were in the range 5,000 to 10,000 tons, up to more than 550 feet in length, and often rather broader, proportionally, than before. Bows were now usually straight, masts nearer to simple poles, funnels were often two or even three. Most still had a single screw – the few with two sometimes reached speeds of twenty knots with reciprocating engines which had been much improved. Second-class passengers were now carried as well as first and steerage, and a distinction was becoming clear between liners intended for speed, luxury and prestige, and those concentrating on carrying the maximum of passengers, a high proportion of them emigrants.

The 1890s saw some slight increase in speed as larger vessels adopted twin screws. Superstructures were often two decks high. Twelve to fifteen thousand tons became common, and White Star's *Oceanic*, in 1899, reached 17,274. This vessel was 686 feet in length, with a beam of 68 feet; and she carried 410 first-class, 300 second-class, and 1,000 steerage passengers. Hamburg-America's *Pennsylvania*, on the other hand, 5,000 tons less,

[1] Broughton Brandenburg, *Imported Americans,* 110–76, and photographs facing 125, 162; *61 Congress 3 Session, Senate Doc. 748,* 113–20. The same document, 107–8, states that at Patras it was found necessary to stamp an indelible mark, changed from time to time without warning, on emigrants' wrists. For the older, casual system at Naples in 1891, see *52 Congress 1 Session, House Exec. Doc. 235,* Part I 256–7, 300–301.

[2] The entire summary is derived from Noel R. P. Bonsor, *North Atlantic Seaway,* the silhouettes at the end being particularly valuable. Bonsor seems to say, 133, that *President Lincoln* was first named *Brooklyn* and *President Grant, Berlin*; but I give the names on Harland and Wolff's plans of these vessels. As late as 1870, the Cunarder *China* certainly hoisted sail – *Diary of a Tour in America, by Rev. M. B. Buckley,* 4–5.

carried 162 first, 180 second, and no fewer than 2,200 steerage. Far smaller ships than that were still in service: the Anchor line, for example, had some of only 4,000 and 5,000 tons running between the Mediterranean and the United States.

The fifteen years before the Great War saw much more striking change. Three or four funnels, three or four screws, turbine propulsion, speeds of twenty-five knots, three-deck superstructures, all appeared. In 1907, Cunard's record-breaking *Mauretania* entered service. Her tonnage was 31,938, with a length of 762 feet and beam of 88, and she carried 563 first, 464 second, and 1,138 third, in conditions considerably better than the traditional steerage. White Star's *Olympic* of 1911, 45,324 tons, with a length of 852 feet and beam of 92, was the only vessel ever to carry as many first-class passengers as third-class – a little over 1,000 each – together with 500 second. Hamburg-America's *Imperator*, the biggest ship to go into service before war broke out, measured 883 feet by 98, had a gross tonnage of 51,969, and was designed to carry 700 first, 600 second, 1,000 third, as well as 1,800 steerage. These were the giants, and a few more typical ships must be mentioned. Such were *Saxonia* of 1900, 14,281 tons, with 164 first, 200 second, and 1,600 third, *Amerika*, 22,225 tons, with 386 first, 150 second, and 1,972 steerage, and *Nieuw Amsterdam* of 1906, 16,907 tons, with 417 first, 391 second, and 2,300 steerage. Hamburg-America's *President Grant* and *President Lincoln*, about 18,000 tons, were designed to carry more than 3,000 in the steerage, as well as small numbers in higher classes. At the same time, Anchor, Fabre, C.G.T., and Navigazione Generale Italiana, all put ships in service of little more than 10,000 tons, and Lloyd Sabaudo bought a few of not much over 5,000. Such vessels, of course, were still crossing the Atlantic at speeds well below twenty knots.

Even so, crossings from the north-west European ports seldom exceeded twelve days, and, from the Adriatic, twenty-one. The question that must be asked is, how far the favourable effects of this speed on emigrants' welfare was balanced by the great numbers carried, or by unfavourable factors in ships' design. Certainly, few people died. In 1880, only 269 did so, against 457,257 who landed (less than 0·06 per cent): 170 against 87,134 of those under fifteen, or nearly 0·2 per cent; 66 against 327,662 (0·02 per cent) of those fifteen to forty; and 33 against 42,441 (nearly 0·08 per cent) of those over forty. In 1885, the overall figures were 209 to 395,346, and, in 1890, 211 to 445,302, with a similar heavier mortality among children.[1]

[1] My figures are derived from annual volumes of *Commerce and Navigation of the United States*. A death-rate for all children equivalent to 70/1,000 per annum looks high; but remember that general death-rates of 20–30, and infant rates of 150–200, were then common in Europe.

Emigrants had of course been inspected, with varying degrees of thorough-ness, before embarkation. All ships carried hospitals and doctors, qualified men, even though it was admitted that the best were unlikely to go to sea, and that it was hard to guarantee the zeal with which they would perform their duties.[1] In studying emigrant conditions, therefore, it is discomfort that has to be looked for rather than deadly danger, but it is not easy to determine how severe that discomfort was.

A White Star advertisement, published in a guide-book in 1880, displayed a picture of a two-funnelled ship, praised the size and steadiness of every vessel in the fleet, and promised emigrants ample space below and above deck, ample wash-rooms and toilets that could be reached under cover, an abundance of cooked food served by stewards, and a stewardess to care for women and children.[2] Against this can be quoted the statements of many eye-witnesses. In the 1860s, Welsh emigrants were writing home about the predominance of tea, coffee and hard biscuit in the diet, potatoes 'more fit for pigs than for men', 'stinking codfish', the need to take one's own food or buy extras from the crew at inflated prices, the stewards' filthy hands, and the cramped berths where alone emigrants could eat. In 1879, Robert Louis Stevenson described the crowding and gloom of the steerage, stewards' and doctor's indifference to the sick, and British workers' discontent at the food, while the only indoor recreation space was around a hatchway, where there was a bar. A decade later, American investigators were hearing com-plaints about wash-rooms, absence of stewardesses, the rough treatment of emigrants by the crew, and the leaking of filth from a cattle deck into the steerage.[3] With such diverse impressions and claims on record, it is essential to examine evidence very closely, distinguishing between periods of time, types of accommodation, and routes. We cannot hope to verify what that veteran traveller Edward Steiner, himself once an emigrant, claimed before the Great War, that each steamship line had its own special character.[4] By looking carefully, however, at reports of official investigations, by check-ing these against plans of ships, and by comparing both with emigrants' own accounts, considerable objectivity can be achieved.

---

[1] *52 Congress 1 Session, House Exec. Doc. 235,* Part II 33–5 (Hamburg-America's instructions to ships' doctors); *House Report 2090,* 439–42 (an American doctor's comment on performance); *Industrial Commission Reports,* XV 105–7 (view of North German Lloyd agent at New York); Brandenburg, *op. cit.,* 197, 204.

[2] Evan Jones, *The Emigrant's Friend,* 235; and see 237 for a similar advertisement for the National Line.

[3] Alan Conway, *The Welsh in America,* 41–6 (three letters); Robert Louis Stevenson, *The Amateur Emigrant,* 11–12, 16–19, 33–6; *51 Congress 2 Session, House Report 3472,* 195–200, 400–404.

[4] Edward A. Steiner, *From Alien to Citizen,* 33–5.

9a   Boarding an emigrant train, Austria-Hungary (possibly Slovakia), early twentieth century
Edward A. Steiner, *From Alien to Citizen.*

9b   Inside an emigrant train, between Basle and Havre, 1883
Mansell Collection.

10a Dining room in the Hamburg-America Line's emigrant village, early twentieth century
Edward A. Steiner, *From Alien to Citizen*.

10b Emigrants leaving Liverpool lodging-houses, 1895, for the Cunarder *Lucania*
Burke, *Photographs of Liverpool Street Life*, Liverpool City Libraries, Record Office and Local History Department.

11a   A superior emigrant ship, Cunarder *Campania*, 1893
Liverpool City Libraries, Record Office and Local History Department.

11b   An inferior emigrant ship, Cunarder *Ultonia*, 1899, used principally between
Fiume and New York
Liverpool City Libraries, Record Office and Local History Department.

Emigrants on deck. City of Liverpool Museums.

13a   Third class dining saloon, White Star *Olympic*, 1911
National Maritime Museum.

13b   First class restaurant, Cunarder *Aquitania*, 1914
National Maritime Museum.

14a   Third class smoking room, White Star *Olympic*, 1911
National Maritime Museum.

14b   First class Palladian lounge, Cunarder *Aquitania*, 1914
National Maritime Museum.

15a Third class cabin, Cunarder *Aquitania*, 1914
National Maritime Museum.

15b First class state room, Cunarder *Aquitania*, 1914
National Maritime Museum.

16a   Ellis Island, 1923 (the reception building has the four cupolas)
Radio Times Hulton Picture Library.

16b   Ellis Island, 1907, entrance to reception building
Photograph by Lewis Hine, George Eastman House Collection.

III

American and British inquiries were held in 1873. The methods of investigation used by the Americans are by no means clearly shown in their report, but their findings are of interest. They found single men's accommodation separated, but not single women's, a watch kept at night on the passenger space, and occasionally a daily inspection by the captain. Wash-rooms and toilets were poor. British doctors and medical inspection they thought satisfactory. There were stewards and stewardesses, but, except for those of Cunard and White Star, they had doubts about discipline among the crews. The quality of food was poor, and it was kept poor by the prevalence of sales of food by the crews. One investigator who had certainly travelled in the steerage summed up: 'treatment is generally good, judged by the popular standard of what is due the poor and ignorant classes in return for value given by them.' The *Lancet* investigators travelled no further than Queenstown, and that only once. For the rest, they made a careful inspection at the docks, and questioned representatives of five leading shipping companies.

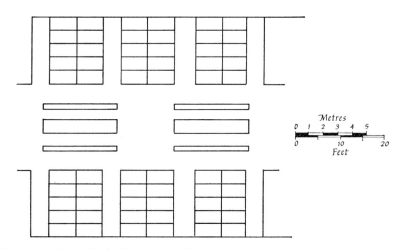

Diagram 4   Generalized ship plan, *c.* 1880

They found steerage accommodation consisting most often of compartments on either side of the ship, with twenty or twenty-four berths in two tiers, end-on to a narrow aisle. The centre of the ship, between these compartments, had tables and seats, the former sometimes hauled up to the ceiling when not in use. Toilets were on an upper deck, some old ships lacked wash-rooms, and ventilation was not very reliable. Stewards did some of the cleaning, and were helped by passengers. Cooks prepared three meals a day: breakfast and supper being bread and butter, porridge and molasses, and coffee; dinner usually soup, meat and potatoes. The investigators' conclusion has been quoted in this chapter's epigraph.[1] A similar judgment was passed by Joseph Chamberlain when, as President of the Board of Trade, he wrote a preface to a British report of 1881. He insisted that the proper standard of judgment was not the refined taste of the middle-class humanitarian, but comparison with 'the crowded cottage of the English labourer, the close, narrow garret of a workman, or the cabin of the Connemara peasant.' The report itself showed why Chamberlain should have thought this observation necessary. Some vessels provided no wash-places, others carried no matrons or stewardesses. The compartments described in 1873 were still normal, though some ships had larger dormitories. Division between single men, families, and single women was now standard practice. Steerage passengers provided their own bedding and table-ware. The White Star line had just introduced pantries, where tea could be made at all times. Doctors were always carried, and members of the crew patrolled at night. When considering wash-places and sleeping quarters, the investigators were likely to remark that emigrants seldom washed, and did not undress before going to bed, so that lack of privacy would not be considered a hardship.[2]

Half a dozen plans add to our knowledge of conditions in this period. That of Cunard's *Gallia*, of 1879, shows steerage W.C.s and a few of the familiar compartments, right forward. It does not show any other steerage accommodation, though it is known that 1,200 such passengers were carried. One whole deck is missing. A model of the vessel shows no such deck with scuttles, and the only conclusion possible is that one deck was provided for the vast majority of emigrants, right on the waterline and wholly lacking daylight. A similar arrangement seems to have existed for the 750 steerage passengers in *Servia*, two years later. More satisfactory plans exist of certain vessels, built by British shipyards for German lines. North German Lloyd's *Aller* and her two sister ships, of 1886, had emigrants' toilets and wash-places forward on either side of the winches, and amidships on the upper deck; a galley on the main deck forward, apparently for all classes; and dormitories on the lower deck, either side of engines and boilers, then right forward to the bows, accommodating from 72 to 304 each – about 780 emigrants in all, as well as small numbers in two higher classes, all in a five-thousand tonner. The curved forward end of the superstructure had a

[1] *43 Congress 1 Session, Senate Exec. Doc. 23*, esp. 145–7; *Report on Emigrant Ships by the Sanitary Commission of the 'Lancet'.*
[2] *Parl. Papers 1881*, LXXXII, 95–141, Reports . . . Accommodation and Treatment of Emigrants on board Atlantic Steamships; Chamberlain's preface is 95–7.

few seats under cover, with a stairway leading to the lower decks, and this may have been the nearest approach to a steerage public room. The plan shows no trace of dining-room or pantries. *Dresden*, two years later, was even smaller, and although her first- and second-class passengers were only a handful, she carried well over 1,800 in the steerage. They occupied the whole of the main and lower decks, which the plan labels uncompromisingly 'Cargo or Passengers', in twelve dormitories each with 100 to 200 berths, arranged to the extreme ends of the ship as well as round the top of the boiler-rooms. Not an inch of space was wasted. Tables and benches were arranged along the side of the hull in these compartments, but can have accommodated only a tiny fraction of the passengers. Stairways from each dormitory led to wash-rooms and toilets on the upper deck, some of them in deckhouses. The galley was on the same deck, amidships, so that food for the most distant passengers must have been carried down two stairways and along some two hundred feet of deck. Hamburg-America's *Normannia*, finally, which entered service in 1890, carried far more people in the higher classes, and only 700 emigrants, though it was a considerably larger ship. Steerage entrances, hospitals, wash-places and toilets were in a forward deckhouse and in the poop, and also in the poop was the galley. Berths were in open dormitories, which occupied the full length of the lower deck, and small open spaces in the middle of these were all that was available for eating. In all these vessels, it must be presumed that emigrants' only prom-enade space was to be found around hatchways and winches, very poor provision in ships only 400 or 500 feet in length.[1]

Such information comes to life in a long letter from one British emigrant. John F. Dixon travelled with two companions in 1871, on board the Cunarder *Cuba*. At Liverpool, they were careful to avoid the runners who were active around the railway station, and chose their own hotel. A man was found to take all their baggage on a hand barrow, though many were trying to do the job for twice the money, with horse and cart. They bought their tickets at the Cunard offices, and at the same time purchased straw mattresses, tinware, and salt-water soap, for a total of three shillings. On the appointed morning a cart took their baggage to the dock, and they went out to their ship by lighter. They found the twenty-berth compartments already described, and although stewards were at hand to assign berths, everyone in fact scrambled for his favourite place and tipped them afterwards so as not

[1] *Gallia*'s plan is in the 1878–9 revised edition of *Official Guide and Album of the Cunard Steamship Service*, following 28, while in 1965 a model stood in the Cunard Building, Liverpool. *Servia*'s incomplete plan is in a small booklet entitled *Cabin Plans*, in a box file for 1880–90 in the Cunard Building, and a model is in the Science Museum, South Kensington. Plans of the German vessels, which were built by Fairfield, are in the National Maritime Museum, Greenwich.

to be disturbed. The central space for meals was cramped. Assuming the usual fore-and-aft arrangement of berths in the compartments, two tiers and five rows on either side of the aisles, and assuming each berth to be two feet six in width, then, with the ship's maximum breadth forty-two feet, the central space could at no point have been more than about sixteen feet wide, and in places much less. Dixon took most of his own food, so that he does not fully describe the ship's meals, but he reports buying mineral water and beer from stewards, while other emigrants were trying to purchase left-overs from the first class. Seasickness was widespread – he himself once went sixty hours without food – and despite the use of chloride of lime the stench was severe. One storm threw food, utensils and people in all directions. Even the ordinary motion of the ship made it necessary for him to curl up in his berth and wedge himself in a firm position.[1]

I V

In 1891, William Smith crossed to New York in the White Star liner *Majestic*, nearly 10,000 tons and almost new. The First class, in which he travelled, had a smoking room in dark mahogany with plaster ceiling, a bar, a library and writing room, a barber's shop, a saloon sixty feet long in Renaissance style with a dome, state rooms with double beds, and many three-berth cabins. The Second class had a saloon and a smoking room. The steerage passengers, about 1,000 in number, he claims to have had a smoking room, family-size cabins, a few baths, and an open deck with seats along the bulwarks. If he observed correctly, this was the beginning of a genuine Third class, and this is the next strand of development to be traced.[2]

Progress was not fast. Cunard's *Campania*, of 1893, carried almost all her steerage passengers in dormitories on two decks, their portable iron berths arranged in irregular blocks, each compartment with a pantry, but with only a very few tables and benches for meals. One galley, twenty feet by twelve feet, was in the forecastle, and its two ranges, three boilers and two vegetable cookers were shared, it would appear, between passengers and crew. Another, though smaller, in the poop may have been shared between steerage and second class. For the thousand emigrants, the plan shows sixteen wash-basins and twenty-one toilets, though the latter seem to be

---

[1] 'An Emigrant's Letter from Iowa, 1871', *Bulletin* of the British Association for American Studies, New Series, XII and XIII (1966), 11–16. Wearing a money-belt increased his discomfort while in his berth.
[2] William Smith, *A Yorkshireman's Trip to the United States and Canada*, 1–16. *U.S. Consular Reports*, XXVI 234–5, states that some Hamburg-America vessels were providing cabins for 8 or 10 passengers as early as 1887.

rows of seats rather than separate compartments. Since they were situated in forecastle and poop, people needed to climb two decks by separate stairways from their dormitories, then walk sometimes 100 feet, sometimes as much as 250, a small part of the distance being open to the weather. On the other hand, the ship had enough four- and six-berth cabins for 120 people, though a six-berth cabin ten feet by six provided no more than standing space between the berths.[1] *Oceanic*, six years later, had steerage accommodation on a more generous scale. Dormitories were indeed provided for single men on two decks well forward, and for single women right aft, but there were cabins for families, and at least one public room existed, roughly furnished with tables and slatted wooden seats rather like one type of park bench.[2] With White Star's *Celtic*, two years later again, it seems fair to speak at last of a Third class. There were still six open compartments for a large proportion of the 2,350 emigrants, but the ship, first of the 20,000-tonners, also had cabins, one group for single men, one for families, and another for single women. Several entrances, wash-rooms and groups of toilets can be found on the plan, toilets amounting to about one for each forty-seven passengers. There were two public rooms, and although these were primarily for lounging, the fact that a pantry was attached to one of them may mean that people could take meals there. In addition, however, there was the striking innovation of two dining-rooms, stretching right across the ship, and capable of seating 479 persons at a time. The galley was immediately above.[3] Cunard's *Caronia*, of the same year, housed her first-class passengers

---

[1] *Campania*'s plan, on the scale of eight feet to the inch, was photographed for me, by courtesy of the Naval Architect's department of Cunard. *Cunard Passengers' Log Book* (1893), 55, devotes no more than eight lines to the steerage, but states that emigrants had the use of one promenade deck. A model is in the Science Museum, South Kensington.

[2] A not very detailed plan is in the Department of Shipping, Liverpool City Museum, which also has a complete photographic record from keel-laying to completion. Two of the three public rooms photographed I have been unable to find on the plan. *Southwark*, of the same year, built by Denny for Red Star, had small compartments with central eating spaces, like the arrangement so common in the 1870s and 1880s; but it provided about 240 people with four- and six-berth cabins. All but 23 'Special 3rds', however, lacked a genuine dining-room. This plan is in the National Maritime Museum.

[3] *Celtic*'s plan is in Harland and Wolff's offices, Belfast. Unfortunately it contains few details of dormitories or wash-rooms. *Virginian*, 1905, an Allan liner built for the Canadian run (National Maritime Museum), had two dining-rooms, two small lounges with padded seats, and two smoking-rooms with hard seats; but a substantial proportion of passengers were in spaces marked 'portable berths'. This description can also be found for the accommodation of about half of the emigrants in *Nieuw Amsterdam*, 1906 (Harland and Wolff), though 'steerage or cargo' is also used. These people had no separate dining space; but one large dining-room, a bar, and several pantries were provided for the approximately 1,000 people in two-, four- (the majority) and six-berth cabins, though the only galley was far distant. For 2,300 people, there were about 40 toilets, a similar number of wash-basins, and two showers. White Star's *Adriatic*, 1907 (Harland and Wolff) had 740 passengers in third-class cabins, more than 1,100 in dormitories. About 40 toilets and 60 wash-basins were provided, one or two decks above the sleeping quarters. The block of cabins for single

amidships, second-class aft, third-class forward. She had similar public rooms, and may have accommodated all her emigrants in cabins.[1] The much larger *Mauretania* had the words 'portable berths' on certain compartments in her plan, but a very high proportion of emigrants were in four- and six-berth cabins, with a very few two- and eight-berth. These were situated forward on E and F decks, and this grouping of the Third class forward became quite common, with First amidships and Second aft. A dining-room

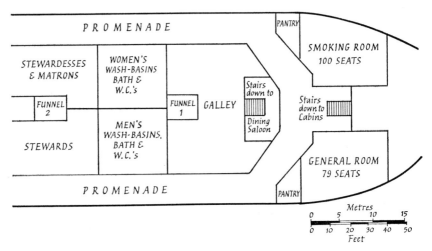

Diagram 5   *Mauretania*, 1907: part of C deck
          (Sketch from plan in Admiralty Collection,
          National Maritime Museum, Greenwich)

on D deck seated about one-third of the passengers. A General Room and a Smoking Room were provided on C deck. Entrances and stairways were of generous size. Toilets and wash-rooms were far better distributed than in earlier ships. A covered promenade, sixteen feet wide, was arranged on each side by the public rooms.[2] Like *Mauretania*, *Olympic*, 1911, was primarily a luxury vessel. Three dining rooms were provided for the Third class, a General Room, a Smoking Room, and a bar, though the only promenade space seems to have been among the winches on the open deck. All emigrants were in two-, four-, or six-berth cabins, and the inconvenience of their siting, at the extreme ends of the ship and scattered over four decks, was to

women had a matron's room nearby. A single dining-room seated 267 people; but two other public rooms, seating between them another 450, may have been used for meals. A covered promenade had rows of benches.

[1] A cut-away side view is in the Science Museum, South Kensington: the absence of a key is partly made up for in a description in Box File 1900–14 in the Cunard Building.

[2] This plan, the most beautiful in detail of any I have seen, is in the Admiralty Collection, in the National Maritime Museum. A model is in the Science Museum, South Kensington.

some extent offset by the presence of a fair number of showers and baths[1]. This was the highest standard attained by the Third class before the Great War. *Aquitania*, of much the same size, carried twice as many emigrants. They had a dining-room the full width of the ship around the casing of the third and fourth funnels, other public rooms, covered promenades forward and amidships, and an open one on D deck aft, but their four- and six-berth cabins (though there were a few larger ones) were so small that eleven were arranged across the hull at its fullest width of ninety-seven feet.[2]

From the end of the nineteenth century, we are fortunate in possessing photographic evidence to supplement ships' plans. They prove, of course, that the existence of third-class public rooms did not give everyone the luxury of, say, *Aquitania*'s first-class Palladian Lounge, with its elaborately patterned carpet, Ionic columns, and painted ceiling; her Restaurant two decks high; or her state-rooms with their twin beds, armchairs, and reproductions of eighteenth-century portraits on the walls. *Aquitania*'s third-class cabins were just large enough for six wooden-sided berths in two tiers, with wash-basins and a few hooks for clothes, or for ten or a dozen metal berths of the portable type, with wash-basin and a chest of drawers.[3] In such rooms, rivets, pipes and girders were clearly to be seen, and they were equally undisguised in many public rooms. This was true of *Oceanic*, whose dining-room had long tables and benches, and a row of clothes-hooks along the wall. *Olympic*'s smoking-room, too, was of the barest type, but her dining-room had tables for eight people only, and chairs. *Saxonia*'s dining-room, like others, shows white cloths on properly laid tables. One of *Mauretania*'s public rooms had swivel chairs, a ceiling, and even a few potted plants. On the other hand, promenade decks might be little more than odd corners, with a few wooden seats.[4]

These photographs are of empty rooms, but a few others show emigrants. Women and children on board *Oregon* sit on ladders or on the casing of pipes near the winches. In other vessels, great crowds stand shoulder to shoulder on deck.[5] Eye-witness accounts serve to clothe plans and photo-

[1] *Olympic*'s plan is in Harland and Wolff's offices, drawn to a smaller scale than most of the others mentioned. A cut-away side view is in the Science Museum, South Kensington.
[2] Small-scale deck-plans of *Aquitania* are in the *Marine Engineer and Naval Architect*, August 1914, which I was shown in the Cunard Building.
[3] A magnificent set of photographs is in the Bedford Lemere Collection, Box 3, in the National Maritime Museum.
[4] *Oceanic* photographs are in Department of Shipping, Liverpool City Museum; *Saxonia* and *Olympic* are in Bedford Lemere Collection, Box 1, National Maritime Museum; and *Mauretania* in the same museum's collection 'Travellers by Sea, 1900–1929'.
[5] The *Oregon* photograph is in the Department of Shipping, Liverpool City Museum. See also one of emigrants on *Lucania*'s deck, Liverpool City Library; the crowd among *Pennland*'s winches, Allon Schoener, *Portal to America*, 30; and the many (though not always good) photographs in Broughton Brandenburg's *Imported Americans*.

graphs with life. The young woman, whose reports were printed by the U.S. Immigration Commission, travelled in the Third class in 1908, though we do not know the ship. She started her crossing from Liverpool, certainly, and wrote of a medical inspection in the dining-room, and of the assigning of berths in such a way that people of one nationality were placed together. There were compartments capable of sleeping six hundred men when needed, but most emigrants were in two- and four-berth cabins on two decks. These were painted white, had good ventilation, and were equipped with electric light, a bell for calling the steward, hooks, mirror and a shelf. Bedding consisted of mattress, pillow and two blankets. The floors were cleaned daily by stewards. Numerous wash-rooms and toilets were grouped near stairways, usually one deck above the cabins, with tiled floors and soap and roller-towels. During her crossing, in a depression year, only two of four dining-rooms were in use. They had tables for ten or fourteen people, with white cloths, cutlery, bread and condiments all set out, and preserves at breakfast, while several times fresh fruit was issued. Kosher food could be had. Meals were at 7 a.m., noon, and 5 p.m., bouillon was served to women at 11 a.m., and they could get hot water, tea and coffee from a pantry, for themselves and their children, more or less all day. A bar stocked beer, soft drinks and tobacco. Stewardesses cared for children and for the sick. Like other members of the crew, they would do small favours for tips. The dining-room could be used as a lounge, red plush covers replacing the white cloths. Men could smoke in their own dining-room. A large open deck aft, clear of machinery and partly covered and enclosed, served as promenade. It was kept clean, lit at night, and had benches arranged at intervals. When music and dancing were going on, passengers might be allowed to remain there later than the usual 9 p.m. The interpreter on board was not very conscientious, but notices were posted in English, French, German, Norwegian, Swedish, Finnish and Russian. All the passenger accommodation was inspected every day.[1]

Five years later, a British journalist found very similar accommodation, though he was less impressed with certain aspects of Cunard's service: cabin wash-basins without water after the first day, and bath-rooms kept locked. Two open decks were available in good weather. One big dining-room was fitted with long tables, at which he saw emigrants sitting, Russians

[1] *61 Congress 3 Session, Senate Doc. 753*, 24–8. *Senate Doc. 758*, 427–8, another part of the Immigration Commission's Reports, has a White Star third-class menu of the same period. Breakfast had porridge, a cooked course such as fish or stew, potatoes, bread and butter, marmalade, tea and coffee; dinner consisted of soup, one cooked course different each day, potatoes and one other vegetable, and a different sweet each day; tea had a cooked course, sometimes cheese, with bread and butter and tea; while biscuits and cheese, or gruel, could be had later in the evening.

in sheepskins, Italians with black felt hats. Food consisted, he claimed, of 'mugs of celery soup . . . not a chunk of bread less than an inch thick; the hash of gristly beef and warm potatoes was what would not have been tolerated in the poorest restaurant.' He found British and Scandinavians expressing discontent at such diet, but admitted that emigrants from eastern Europe ate voraciously. Graham himself welcomed the fresh fruit which hawkers brought on board at Queenstown; and after a storm, he reported, stewards came round selling Bovril and ham and eggs. There were smoking-rooms for card-playing, and bars for beer. Medical inspections took place, and a hasty vaccination for those who needed it, but many people, as soon as they could return to their cabins, got their neighbours to suck out the terrifying vaccine. On Sunday, a Baptist clergyman organized a service in English. One night there was a full-scale concert. At other times, recreation included letter-writing, playing the concertina, dancing and much embracing in dark corners.[1]

V

While these improvements were being adopted, the old-style steerage was still in existence, for with emigration sometimes reaching a million a year there was a place for vessels whose sole purpose was to carry the greatest possible numbers, however closely packed. Cunard's *Ultonia*, which had been designed for the Liverpool-Boston run but soon became employed between Fiume and New York, had only a few dozen passengers in cabins. The major part of the ship, as its plan clearly indicates, could be used for cargo and cattle, or for steerage passengers. More than 1,400 could be accommodated, most of them in portable berths and all in large dormitories. There were no public rooms, and no dining space is shown. The only galley was in the forecastle, and was about fifteen feet square.[2] Three Hamburg-America liners, two of them sister ships, were considerably superior, but shared the preponderance of the steerage system. *Amerika* provided four-berth cabins for about 220 Third-class passengers, and gave them a dining-room which could have held all of them in two sittings. For the Fourth class, so-called, there were dormitories on three decks for some 2,000 people, several of them holding more than 200 and one more than 300. Galleys, each about twenty feet square and each with a tiny kosher kitchen attached, were in a forward deck-house and in the poop. The Fourth class had, it seems,

[1] Graham, *op. cit.*, 11–24, 34, 37–40.
[2] This plan was photographed for me in the Cunard Building, Naval Architect's department. Only ten toilets are marked, though others must surely have been improvised when the vessel was full of passengers. No other Cunarder was built to such a low standard. I should state here that I have found not a single interior photograph of the old-style steerage: nor am I surprised.

12

about forty toilets and sixty wash-basins. *President Grant* and *President Lincoln* carried rather more than 700 Third-class passengers in small cabins for two, four or six persons, and their dining-room could accommodate more than half of them. Food came from a galley less than twenty feet square, with a kosher kitchen. A General Room with promenade around it, and a bar, were also provided. For the more than 2,300 Fourth-class passengers, a similar galley and kosher kitchen were to be found, with a tiny canteen, in a deck-house forward. They had no public rooms of any kind, and they slept in compartments housing up to 300 persons each. For the Third class, there was one bath for men and another for women. For the entire 3,000 passengers, there were sixty toilets, about fifty wash-basins, and three showers, these facilities being arranged in six blocks.[1]

A final example can be the Italian vessel *Tomaso di Savoia*, built by Barclay Curle. Only 450 feet long, she measured 7,914 gross tons. Her rather more than one hundred First-class passengers had a dining-saloon, smoking-room, music-room, 'winter garden', and nursery. The hundred Second-class had dining-saloon only. Her 1,200 steerage had only two tiny dining-saloons, the larger measuring no more than twenty-eight feet by twenty-four. Galley and bakery, however, were more ample than in some other ships studied, and 'sale shop' and 'bread shop' are marked on the plan. The seven steerage compartments were on two decks; and stairways led to two blocks, containing together eight showers, twenty wash-basins, eighteen W.C.s, and urinals. Eight wash-tubs were provided, and a laundry was situated in the forward deck-house. All in all, one is surprised at how much could be provided in so small a ship, and how completely the 1901 statute was being observed. Apart from the laundry, the plan shows hospital accommodation, with separate space for infectious diseases. Among the first-class luxury suites is one for the *commissario regio*, one room fitted with brass bedstead. Next to the radio cabin is a chaplain's room, representing a quick response to a papal decision of 1906, to provide for emigrants' spiritual needs.[2]

It is essential to point out, once more, that such craft were at sea at exactly the same time as the majestic and famous *Mauretania* and *Olympic*.

Steerage accommodation was described by Broughton Brandenburg in 1903. The German ship in which he embarked at Naples carried an Italian naval surgeon who was responsible for welfare. He tasted the macaroni, beef, potatoes, bread and wine, visited dormitories during a storm, and supervised

---

[1] The plans are in Harland and Wolff's offices.
[2] The plan is in the National Maritime Museum. On chaplains, see Rudolph J. Vecoli, 'Peasants and Prelates', *Journal of Social History*, II 257.

the hospital. But while he had china dishes for his tasting, emigrants lined up with their mess-tins outside the forecastle galley, ate on the open deck, and washed-up in sea-water. The hard biscuit served for breakfast was sometimes mouldy. Supplementary food could be had from bumboats at Gibraltar, or from the crew when the *commissario* was not looking. Officers and crew, even the German ship's doctor, were impatient and brutal.[1] The Immigration Commission's investigator, who travelled five years later in the guise of a Czech peasant woman, was lucky to find a ship half empty, but she was none the less disturbed by what she found. The two-tier iron berths had only very low partitions around them, and although they had straw mattresses there were no pillows. The wooden decks were lightly sanded, but neither washed nor disinfected during the twelve days. Wash-rooms she found used indiscriminately by both sexes. No soap or towels were to be found, and the only water from the taps was cold and salt, yet stewards did their best to prevent women from taking water to the dormitories. The only baths were in the hospital. Women's toilets were separated, but they were arranged over an open trough, with an iron step and handles on each closet wall. At first filthy, they were later cleaned every night, then received a most thorough cleaning and disinfecting ready for American inspection. There were dining-rooms of a sort, though they were so stuffy that passengers ate on deck whenever possible, and there were no organized sittings, though anyone coming late would go without a proper meal. After food had been brought from a rather distant galley, passengers lined up for soup; then had meat and vegetables put in cans upon the tables, to be transferred to their mess-tins without the aid of serving-spoons; then lined up again for coffee. Breakfast was based on cereal, bread and jam; dinner on soup, meat or fish; supper on fish or meat with pickles. There was a separate galley and a separate cook for Jews. Coffee and bread were served in the afternoon; tea could be made; and there was a very profitable bar for drinks, fruit and sweets. Medical inspection was casual, passengers' cards being stamped for several days at a time, and although the hospital was well appointed, the doctor knew no Slav language and the nurse was untrained. About 4,000 square feet of promenade space was cluttered with machinery and showered with cinders from the funnel. It was hosed down each night, but since it had to be shared with the crew, further occasion was provided for what the young woman found the most trying part of the whole experience, the endless bad language, insults, and offensive gestures from stewards and sailors. During

[1] Brandenburg, *op. cit.*, 174–99 and photograph facing 38. He secured better berths for the women of his party by tipping a steward. On his eastbound crossing, he states (33–5) that he secured comfortable berths in the hospital, with the willing agreement not only of the sick-berth attendant but of the ship's doctor.

another crossing she made, in a ship carrying Third-class as well as steerage passengers, she found the crew better-behaved. Physical conditions, however, were much the same. Men had to fetch their own food. For women and children, stewards formed a line from galley to tables, passing cans of soup, meat, and vegetables from hand to hand, 'as pails of water are by a bucket brigade'.[1]

Edward Steiner, whose attack on the steerage has already been quoted, knew that emigrants accepted the social distinctions on board, regarding the captain as king, First-class passengers as nobles, officers and crew as army or police. He saw, too, that even in such crude conditions emigrants, who after all were mostly young people from backgrounds very far from comfortable, could find occasion for enjoyment. Harmonicas and accordions could always be heard. Dances were frequent. Each ethnic group had its characteristic songs, like the Slovak ditty he translates:

> Brothers, brothers, who'll drink the beer,
> Brothers, brothers, when we are not here?
> Our children they will drink it then,
> When we are no more living men.
> Beer, beer, in glass or can,
> Always, always finds its man.[2]

There is no way of estimating the proportion of emigrants who travelled under the two main sets of conditions here described. Only British vessels, setting out from British ports, seem to have gone over at all completely to the Third class, though many foreign ships housed some emigrants that way. It seems reasonable to guess, therefore, that the old steerage accommodated a substantial majority. Certainly the U.S. Immigration Commission held that view.[3]

VI

As in the days of sail, arrival in America caused intense excitement. If they came up New York harbour in daylight, emigrants pushed towards the rails to get the best view, lifting children up to see over their neighbours' shoulders. If they docked in darkness, they went on deck in the morning to find themselves in 'a kind of lake', surrounded by the tall buildings of the New World.[4] In either event, they got up early and tried to wash thoroughly.

[1] 61 Congress 3 Session, Senate Doc. 753, 13–23, 31–7.
[2] Edward A. Steiner. On the Trail of the Immigrant, 41–3.
[3] 61 Congress 3 Session, Senate Doc. 753, 6–13.
[4] Louis Adamic, Laughing in the Jungle, 40, and Stoyan Christowe, This Is My Country, 37–8, both recording experiences just before the Great War. Although the number of emigrants was much smaller, I saw something similar in 1950.

Men shaved. Women dressed children in their best clothes to meet fathers already in America. People tried to imagine the questions they would be asked on Ellis Island, or received coaching in the answers from those who had undergone the ordeal once before.[1]

The dock, which might be on the Jersey shore, was a scene of noise and confusion, as steerage passengers were separated from the higher classes, baggage was unloaded and sometimes lost, orders were shouted in unfamiliar languages and were reinforced by blows, and hawkers tried to sell fruit and cake at exorbitant prices.[2]

A ferry-boat then took them to the Island, and, since officials might have several boatloads to inspect in a single day, they might be kept waiting for hours. There followed a walk from quay to main building, then, suitcases, baskets and smaller bundles in hand, the clatter up the iron stairs which James Bryce described.[3] On the upper floor were found the corridors and waiting-rooms separated by wire fences, and along these corridors tramped the emigrants, now holding their medical cards to be stamped, while doctors lifted eyelids or ran their hands over scalps. After a wait on wooden benches, they came before clerks sitting at desks on little platforms, and, in some rudimentary form of their own language, were asked questions about their money, their relatives in America, or any other matter that seemed relevant.[4] Those who were fortunate enough to satisfy the officials could at once proceed, changing money, buying railroad tickets, perhaps buying a one-dollar box of food containing sandwiches, fruit and apple pie. They were ticketed anew for their several destinations.[5] Those less lucky might lose their baggage and would need to wait for a search. Others again might be kept overnight, in order to endure a further medical or other examination next day. For such people there were dining-rooms, with long tables and wooden benches, in which simple meals could be had, and dormitories with two-decker iron beds rather like the steerage from which they had come. One immigrant had a Turk in the bed beneath him who, at daybreak, jumped up, opened a big sack, took out a rug, spread it on the

---

[1] Brandenburg, op. cit., 200–202.

[2] Ibid., 208–11.

[3] Ibid., 212–15; Bryce, American Commonwealth (1911 edn.), II 481; photographs in Schoener, op. cit., 31–5, and three by Lewis Hine, George Eastman House, Rochester N.Y., negatives 10, 967, 6,803, and 2,507.

[4] Brandenburg, op. cit., 216–27, and photographs facing 227 and 230; Adamic, op. cit., 43–5; Christowe, op. cit., 41–7; Graham, op. cit., 41–7; Edward Corsi, In the Shadow of Liberty, 58–9, 72–81. See also the photographs in Schoener, op. cit., 36–7, whose portraits, 42, 48–9, very clearly show the benches; and Lewis Hine photographs, 3,767 and 3,769.

[5] Lewis Hine photograph 3,764 shows the ticketing in progress.

floor, and began his prayers. Whatever the delay, immigrants could still be cheerful, dancing to the accordion once more.[1]

Wherever they were going, another ferry-boat journey followed. On Manhattan, immigrants disembarked at the Barge Office, outside which they found a crowd of carts waiting to take their baggage.[2] Those bound for the Lower East Side needed little assistance: usually friends guided them the last mile or two. If they wished to stop only briefly in the city, lodging-houses were thick around the Battery, their names, or their owners' names displayed, an invitation to immigrants from every part of Europe from Ireland to Poland. Robert Louis Stevenson secured board and lodging for a dollar a day, and found satisfactory food, a bar, a simple but decent bed-room, and a place to wash downstairs and across a yard.[3]

Sooner or later, most of them moved on. As early as 1867 a guide-book listed some of the possibilities: a railroad depot for Albany at 4th Avenue and 26th Street; the Albany steamboat at the foot of Chambers Street to join the Erie railroad – for not until the early twentieth century were there tunnels beneath the Hudson.[4] On the Jersey side came much tedious waiting, in filthy rooms or by the side of the tracks, sometimes at night or in snow. Wrongly directed, immigrants might have to stumble with children and baggage from train to train.[5] Once on the move, progress was still slow, for all other trains took precedence on the line. Pittsburgh might take a day and a half to reach: Chicago always did. Meals, but hurried ones, could be had at stops, and newsboys also boarded, selling simple food and drink as well as papers. On the wooden seats, immigrants slept on overcoats or bundles. Stevenson has left an account of his twelve-day journey all the way to the Pacific coast. Few immigrants went so far, but whatever their destination, in mining community or steel town or Middle West farm, their arrival might give them the first chance of complete and comfortable undressing since their embarkation at the European port.[6]

---

[1] Lewis Hine photographs 3,982 and 10,273; Schoener, *op. cit.*, 38–9, 43; Adamic, *op. cit.*, 41–3.

[2] Schoener, *op. cit.*, 50–1. There is an unforgettable description of the ferry journey in the opening chapter of Henry Roth, *Call It Sleep*.

[3] Stevenson, *op. cit.*, 68–73; Frank Moss, *The American Metropolis*, III 270–2; and Brandenburg, *op. cit.*, 223–4, for an example of a cabman's fraud.

[4] Edward H. Hall, *The Great West*, 97.

[5] Stevenson, *op. cit.*, Part II 'Across the Plains', 81–4; *61 Congress 3 Session, Senate Doc. 753*, 39–40; Cowen, *op. cit.*, 151–2.

[6] Stevenson, *op. cit.*, esp. 84–108. See also the Dixon letter, *loc. cit.*, 18–19, and Jacob Dolwig's diary, *loc. cit.*, 206–7. W. F. Rae, *Westward by Rail*, is the story of a transcontinental trip, though not as an emigrant, in the first possible year, 1869, by the Niagara bridge, lighter for the train over Detroit river, bridge over the Mississippi, and steam ferry over the Missouri from Council Bluffs to Omaha. A good photograph of an emigrant train is in Kenneth O. Bjork, *West of the Great Divide*, between 210 and 211.

CHAPTER NINE

Immigrant Workers
and American Environments

The caravan seemed a miserably frail and lilliputian thing as it crept over the boundless prairie towards the sky line. Of road or trail there lay not a trace ahead; as soon as the grass had straightened up again behind, no one could have told the direction from which it had come or whither it was bound. The whole train . . . might just as well have been dropped down out of the sky.

Ole E. Rolvaag, *Giants in the Earth* (Harper Torch-book edition, 1964), 6.

The pavements along both sides of Hester Street are lined by a continuous double row of pushcarts filled with eatables of every kind agreeable to the palate of the Russian Jew. The latecomers among the vendors, no longer able to secure a place for their carts along the main avenue of the market, form an overflow market along the pavements of the side streets – Ludlow, Essex, Norfolk, and Suffolk. Here is a cart laden with grapes and pears, and the fruit merchant, a short, dark-complexioned, bearded fellow, clad as to outer garments in an old cap, a dark-blue sweater, and a nondescript pair of dirty-hued trousers, is shrieking at the top of his voice. 'Gutes frucht! Gutes frucht! Metziehs! Drei pennies die whole lot.'

New York Times, 14 November 1897, quoted in Allon Schoener, *Portal to America: The Lower East Side 1870–1925,* 55.

The Dutch settlers who, in 1846, landed on the eastern shore of Lake Michigan, faced a life of extreme discomfort and confusion. Some of them had to live under bedsheets hung on hemlock branches, in front of which a frame held the cooking-pot over the campfire. Log cabins, with very defective roofs, housed several families. The labour of clearing timber was hard and, for inexperienced people, dangerous. Deer, squirrels and raccoons damaged their early crops. The immigrants depended on outside sources for the simplest articles, like new cooking-pots or stovepipes. To reach the outside world conveniently, they had to hack paths through miles of forest; and when they reached existing roads they were mere rights-of-way, with swamps filled in, small creeks bridged, and stumps cut down to a height which a waggon could clear. This communication established, wood and bark could be taken out to exchange for provisions and equipment; mail carriers could get through with bags upon their backs; ox-waggons and, finally, stage-coaches, could arrive. More prolonged and systematic effort deepened a river and cut through a sandbar to make a small lake harbour. The mills that were needed for flour and timber could only be worked by water power, yet the dams which settlers constructed were again and again swept away by spring floods. In the end, though, a workable economy was organized, and a few comforts could be enjoyed. Log cabins replaced the more improvised shelters, and in turn were replaced by frame houses. With solidity came decoration: pictures of parents on the wall, or paintings, bought in nearby towns, on such patriotic themes as Washington crossing the Delaware. Churches and schools were founded and flourished.[1]

Sixty years later, Jews from Russia, Hungary and Roumania found their homes in the crowded streets of New York City's Lower East Side. Their five- and six-storey tenements, their fronts lined with balconies and fire-escapes, looked down on the mass of pushcarts, peddlers and customers, through which a few waggons might try to force their way, or children, hauling loads of old wood they had picked up for fuel. Everyone was barter-ing in loud Yiddish for old clothes and hats, legs of chicken, over-ripe tomatoes, single eggs and ounces of tea. A stranger, picking his way across a sidewalk crammed with boxes of goods from the shops, entered a dark hall, so dark that he might fall over a child, so dark that a little girl who had lost a toy could expect to find it when the gas was turned on in the evening. On each floor above the shop and street level was a landing with two toilets, large sink, and cold-water tap, and at either end two apartments of four rooms. To describe these as parlour, kitchen, and bedrooms would be misleading, for at night all rooms might be needed for family and lodgers to sleep in, chairs being pushed together to form beds for smaller children. The best room looked on to the street. The others – the kitchen with its highly ornamented iron stove, its work-table, the dining-table and chairs where the family could just find room to eat – and the smaller rooms had windows only on the airshaft which separated tenements. Some indeed lacked windows altogether, and district nurses needed to light candles before visiting patients. During the day, one room might be needed for some industrial task, like making trimmings for dresses, at which mother and quite small children would be busy. Intense summer heat, smells from the rubbish which piled up at the foot of the airshaft, noises from street

[1] Henry S. Lucas, *Dutch Immigrant Memoirs and Related Writings*, I 67–72, 93–5, 144, 160, 197, 288, 292, 439–48, 489–514; II 111, 117–28. On frontier roads, see also the description of the military road of 1835, from Green Bay to Prairie du Chien, Wis., in Francis P. Prucha, *Broadax and Bayonet*, 138–9.

17   Ellis Island, 1905, immigrants climbing the iron stairs to the reception hall
Photograph by Lewis Hine, George Eastman House Collection

18   Ellis Island, 1905, Italians in a waiting room
Photograph by Lewis Hine, George Eastman House Collection.

19a   Ellis Island, 1926, interpreting and recording
Photograph by Lewis Hine, George Eastman House Collecti-

19b   Ellis Island, 1926, ticketing for a railroad journey
Photograph by Lewis Hine, George Eastman House Collecti-

20 Ellis Island, 1905, music while waiting
Photograph by Lewis Hine, George Eastman House Collection.

and neighbours, bugs in the walls – all these were normal incidents of tenement life.[1]

Places, people and techniques were strikingly different. Yet both were communities of recent immigrants from Europe, seeking economic and other opportunities, concerned for the interests of their children, and facing the handicaps of being newcomers to American society. The point is absolutely central: immigrants had many aspirations, and disabilities, in common, and their varied European backgrounds marked them with many differences; yet their fate depended not merely on what they brought with them, but on the stage at which they arrived in the hectic rush of America's growth.

The broad shape of that growth is easy enough to grasp. In 1815, Massachusetts had almost no power-driven industry. In 1830 there were no railroads. There was no petroleum industry in 1850 and virtually no steel industry in 1870. In 1830, South Carolina had nearly as many inhabitants as Massachusetts, and Virginia far more. By the 1890s, the United States was the world's leading industrial nation. By the time of the Great War, half its population was urban and its railroad track stretched for a quarter of a million miles.

This is much too simple. There was rapid change within single communities, and not all of it was smoothly upward. A state might be largely backwoods at one census; two decades later its numerous improved farms might be pouring out wheat to a wide market; two decades later again it might be turning towards specialization in dairy products; and, like Wisconsin, it might have seen the rise and fall of a mighty lumber industry. Stages of growth overlapped. Cotton plantations boomed at the same time as Massachusetts mill towns. Pioneer farming survived, decade after decade, further and further west, if techniques were very different in the counties round the Catskills from those practised along the Red River. Farming continued to expand as America rose to industrial leadership, and food and raw materials dominated the export trade down to 1900. Industries which kept the same names were quickly transformed in their practical operation, with larger plant, more elaborate machinery, different grades of workers needed, and rapidly changing methods of management and ownership.

If the United States, on close inspection, ceases to be a single entity, so obviously does immigration. Some newcomers were farmers with capital,

---

[1] Moses Rischin, *The Promised City: New York's Jews 1870–1914*, esp. chapters 4 and 5; Robert W. de Forest and Lawrence Veiller, *The Tenement House Problem*, I, and esp. 112–13 and the numerous illustrations; Robert L. Duffus, *Lillian Wald: Neighbor and Crusader*, 73; photographs in Allon Schoener, *Portal to America: the Lower East Side 1870–1925*, 69–100 (streets), 221–44 (tenements); and other photographs, by Lewis Hine, in George Eastman House, Rochester N.Y.

some were skilled workers with all the value of great scarcity, many were general labourers who needed work immediately upon landing. Immigrant characteristics and American growth interacted to determine distribution of people. Then, towards the end of the nineteenth century, the broad character of immigration shifted, away from north-west Europe and towards people both less skilled, for the most part, and more foreign. Yet the 'New' immigration is a nightmare of American social thought, rather than a precise and adequate description of people. What did a Jew from Minsk have in common with an Italian from Palermo; and was he utterly different in his situation from an Irishman from County Cork half a century earlier? The answer is that they were immigrants, and that although they reached America at different times and places, all were needed by an expanding economy, which demanded especially unskilled and semi-skilled labour in huge quantities. Even this did not last. In our own day an economy based on oil and electricity, on the highway, on computer and jet plane, has come near making unskilled work as obsolete as the covered waggon.

Immigrants, it is true, themselves helped shape American development. They provided much of the labour on farms, in mines and in factories. They arrived at the age when they were about to reproduce themselves, so they played more than their part in swelling that huge national market on which economic growth depended. They did not, however, give many of the orders in this process, nor take many of the decisions. They were likely to start at or near the bottom. The advantage still lay with native Americans, or at least with immigrants' children born or educated in America. It is permissible, therefore, to stress the impact of American growth upon their fortunes – even, in some aspects, to view them as the victims of that growth.

This too may be a judgment with misleading implications. Immigrants may have been – in Professor Pollard's words applied to the Industrial Revolution in Britain – 'forced labour', people displaced, uprooted, pushed about, pressed into shape by the entrepreneurs and foremen of new industry.[1] Yet this was the whole truth neither about Britain nor about America. Nor should the facts cause us to overlook ways in which most of Europe was different from both these countries. It is utterly wrong to describe the free-enterprise capitalism of nineteenth-century America, in all its naked violence, and then compare it with a modern western Europe, saturated with the concepts of the welfare state, and equipped with administrators of notable honesty and skill. American capitalism did not beat everyone down, nor did it affect every district equally, and it existed in a relatively open society with a considerable degree of political democracy. On the other side

[1] Sidney Pollard, *The Genesis of Modern Management*, chapter 5.

of the Atlantic, there were regimes which lagged only a little behind in these respects. There were others that were efficient but class-ridden. Others again were oppressive, corrupt and incompetent. To find evidence of poverty, hardship, frustration and injustice in the lives of American immigrants is not to prove that they had been mistaken in quitting their European homes.

Through the jungle of infinitely varied detail a path towards clarity can be hacked by directing our attention to three short periods, points of time almost, which represent distinct stages of American growth, and by discovering how immigrants participated in certain typical occupations and environments.

I

Although the Dutch whose experiences we surveyed had a common origin and purpose, and enjoyed the advantages of an accepted leadership, far more examples can be found of pioneer life in which family or individual was the unit. In the middle of the nineteenth century, Hans Mattson arrived in the Middle West from Sweden, his journey from New York a mixture of steamboat travel, railroad, canal boat and waggon. He worked with his father and brother for a year, partly on a farm, partly on a railroad bridge over Rock River. As soon as the rest of the family had arrived, Hans and his father, accompanied by a married couple, went up the Mississippi by steamboat to prospect Minnesota. Finding a district with Swedish settlers, they claimed a plot of land, bought tent, stove, a yoke of oxen, and provisions, then put up a log cabin. So that they could buy more, they worked in a nearby village at chopping wood. Soon they built themselves a waggon, cutting solid wheels from an oak log. Lars Davidson Reque walked from Chicago to Koshkonong, Wisconsin, and bought eighty acres of government land, but before starting to farm he had to earn money, first on the Illinois Canal, then as fireman on Great Lakes steamboats, then as lumberjack and sawmill hand – and even as a farmer, he found it necessary to go to the Wisconsin lead mines in winter.[1] Many settlers, like Rebecca Burlend's family, and Gustav Koerner's, bought land already slightly improved by an American pioneer, with the advantage of some sort of dwelling already constructed. John Regan, who bought new land, rented

[1] Hans Mattson, *Reminiscences*, 28–47; Theodore C. Blegen, *Norwegian Migration to America: the American Transition*, 37–8. Joseph Schafer, *History of Agriculture in Wisconsin*, 87–9, points out how important farm work could be, especially at harvest, as a source of immigrants' earnings; and Merle Curti, *The Making of an American Community*, 147–9, 156–62, 180–87, shows how easy it was for a labourer to save money, then raise a mortgage from neighbours, who were confident of a rise in land values. Lucas, *op. cit.*, I 107–8, 334–6, 353, shows Dutch immigrants going to work for Americans in towns.

a home before building one of his own. All these people needed help in ploughing land for the first time – a job which local Americans were willing to perform for two dollars a day – and some hired help for their home-building. They bought livestock, and provisions for their first few months, then settled down to the tasks of growing corn and wheat, potatoes and other crops, selling them for cash or bartering them for food, clothing, or the simple scythes and cradles they needed on their farms. They made fences and constructed crude stables and barns.[1] Malaria, typhoid, cholera and smallpox made their lives harder, and they had to rely for help on their neighbours rather than on any expert – there was nothing unusual in Adriaan Zwemer's recording in his diary the deaths of four of his children.[2]

Experiences like these were repeated again and again as hundreds of thousands of Americans and immigrants moved west. Between 1830 and 1860, the population of Massachusetts and New York doubled, that of Ohio rather more than doubled, Missouri grew from 140,000 to 1,182,000, Illinois from 157,000 to 1,712,000, and Wisconsin, settled later, from 32,000 to 776,000. During the 1850s alone, half the nation's population growth occurred in the Middle West; Minnesota grew from 6,000 to 172,000; and the foreign-born inhabitants of the United States doubled in number, from two to four millions.[3] Translated into more concrete terms, this meant the crowding of settlers at the Mississippi and Missouri ferries, and the filling of every hotel bedroom, dining-room and bar-room as men waited for land offices to open. It meant the rushing for mill and town sites by anyone with superior knowledge – and this usually meant tough native American specu-lators like George Gale, who reached Trempealeau county, Wisconsin, with a career in law, politics and the militia already behind him at thirty-five, and who went on to buy land, lend money, invest in timber and railroads, and, after much lobbying, launch a new county.[4] It meant also the rapid growth of towns. Such places were centres of stage-services and often steamboat services too; they were centres of trade, of legal and other professional business, of religion, and of administration. In less than a year from its

[1] Rebecca Burlend, *A True Picture of Emigration*, 53–111; Gustav Koerner, *Memoirs*, I 291–300; Alan Conway, *The Welsh in America*, 101–2; John Regan, *The Emigrant's Guide to the Western States of America*, 61–5, 83–107, 165–7, 224, 339–42, 361–4; Allan G. Bogue, *From Prairie to Corn Belt*, 243–51 (analysis of William Sewall's diary of Illinois farming in the 1840s); Olaf M. Norlie, *History of the Norwegian People in America*, 135, 172.
[2] Blegen, *op. cit.*, 56–68; Lucas, *op. cit.*, II 458.
[3] Friedrich Kapp, *Immigration and the Commissioners of Emigration of the State of New York*, 234, shows that Ohio, Illinois and Wisconsin were among the five destinations most often declared by immigrants at Castle Garden, and that four other Middle Western states were among the top twelve.
[4] Erastus F. Beadle, *To Nebraska in '57*, 16; John B. Newhall, *Sketches of Iowa, or the Emigrant's Guide*, 57–8; Schafer, *op. cit.*, 31–40; Curti, *op. cit.*, 22–8.

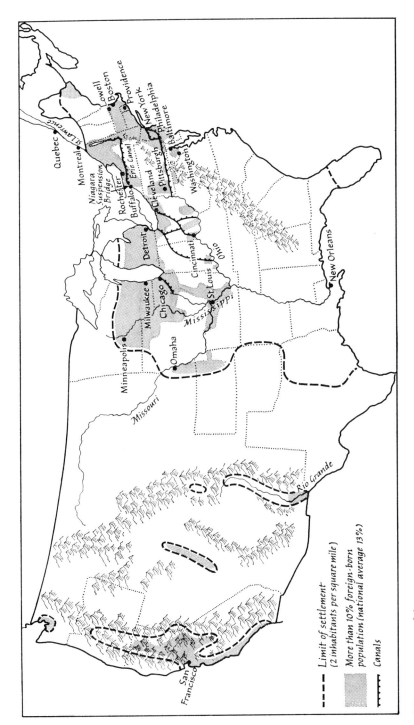

Map 5   U.S.A., 1860

Lowell
Boston
Providence
New York
Philadelphia
Baltimore
Washington
Quebec
Montreal
Niagara Suspension Bridge
Rochester
Buffalo
Cleveland
Pittsburgh
Detroit
Cincinnati
Milwaukee
Chicago
St. Louis
Minneapolis
Omaha
New Orleans
San Francisco

St. Lawrence
Erie Canal
Ohio
Mississippi
Missouri
Rio Grande

- - - Limit of settlement
(2 inhabitants per square mile)

More than 10% foreign-born
population (national average 13%)

Canals

foundation, Iowa City had a dozen stores and several hotels. Within four or five years, Mount Pleasant, not far away, had a hundred houses, eight stores, blacksmiths' and other artisans' shops, two hotels and a coffee-house. Six lawyers and three doctors were already in practice. A solid brick courthouse was the principal landmark.[1]

Most Americans still lived on farms or in towns no bigger than this, places too small to rank as urban in the censuses. During the 1850s, rural population rose from 19,648,160 to 25,226,803. Urban population, however, grew very fast, from 3,543,716 to 6,216,518. One and a half millions were in towns with fewer than 10,000 inhabitants each, another 900,000 in towns of 10,000 to 25,000. Many immigrants settled in bigger cities: over one-third of Boston's 177,000 people in 1860 had been born abroad, nearly half of New York City's 813,000, almost exactly half of Chicago's 109,000, and distinctly more than half of St Louis' 186,000.[2]

Irishmen could be found digging a canal from the Mississippi to Lake Pontchartrain, laying a railroad, working the jackscrews which compressed bales of cotton for shipment, and fighting with Negroes for New Orleans dock work.[3] They could be found making dams and digging canals to provide water power for the early textile towns of New England, helping build railroads, filling in the water to make extensions to Boston, constructing coastal fortifications, and working in such industries as textiles and glass. Usually labourers, some of them rose to be contractors in charge of portions of these large undertakings.[4] In Boston, more than seventy per cent of the foreign-born population were Irish. They made up one-third of the entire gainfully-employed population, but while they had no more than 356 of 2,053 carpenters, 81 of 695 printers, 132 of 3,676 clerks and 184 of 1,061 dealers in food, they had two-thirds of the 1,500 tailors, more than two-thirds of the 3,000 domestic servants, and 7,000 of the 8,500 labourers. They were newcomers, not only to America but to big-city life. They were poor, unskilled and unorganized. They needed to live close to their work, so old houses were subdivided, warehouses were converted into tenements, additional dwellings were put up in back yards, and cellars were used for

[1] Newhall, *op. cit.*, 83–5, 128–9 (and see 76, 112–17, for Burlington, a leading Iowa river town); R. Carlyle Buley, *The Old Northwest*, II 107 (Springfield, 1833, and see I 81–2 for the much bigger Detroit); Koerner, *Memoirs*, I 293–4 (St Louis). Beadle, *op. cit.*, 58–9, noticed a steamboat bringing furniture for a hotel.
[2] *Eighth Census*, Population, 608–15. The proportion in Philadelphia was lower than in Boston, and Baltimore's lower still, less than one-quarter. The census tells us nothing about the ethnic composition of small towns.
[3] Earl F. Niehaus, *The Irish in New Orleans 1800–1860*, 44–54.
[4] Constance M. Green, *Holyoke*, 27, 93; Donald B. Cole, *Immigrant City: Lawrence, Massachusetts 1845–1921*, 30; Carl Wittke, *The Irish in America*, 27, 32–9; Lord, Sexton, Harrington, *History of the Archdiocese of Boston*, II 83–4, 130–33.

human habitation, all constituting a threat to health which alarmed the city government.[1] In Manhattan – for New York City did not extend much beyond 42nd Street – there were 630,000 inhabitants in 1855, more than half of them foreign-born. Irish and Germans were the principal groups, in the proportions, roughly, of two to one. Of all immigrants who worked, more than twenty-two per cent were servants, laundresses and the like; fourteen per cent were labourers or porters; nearly thirteen per cent were already in the clothing trades; nearly nine per cent were in building. To arrange the figures another way, almost all the city's domestics, general labourers, shoemakers, tailors and stone-cutters had been born abroad, and far more than half its porters, draymen, carpenters and dressmakers. Only seven per cent of immigrant workers were in clerical or professional jobs, nearly as many were in retail trade. The two ethnic groups differed widely. Almost all the labourers and servants were Irish, and most of the porters and shoemakers. They had, however, only 4,171 tailors to the Germans' 6,709, only 1,817 dealers in food to 3,045, and only 2,135 clerks to 2,249, despite their great superiority in total numbers. For the same reasons as in Boston, most of the immigrants lived near the East River, where ships' bowsprits still spanned the quays to the warehouse roofs, though a few lived in Brooklyn at the other end of ferries.[2]

The Boston and New York figures are important, as showing where, in the American labour force, immigrants were likely to take their place, and what standard of living they were therefore likely to enjoy. For while a handful of skilled men could make $3 a day, and such large categories of craftsmen as masons, blacksmiths, engineers and printers $2, most artisans made no more than $1.50, most labourers, teamsters, and helpers of skilled men no more than $1, and women cotton-spinners little more than 50 cents. A single man, to be sure, needed to spend little more than $4 a week on board and lodging, but a family occupying four rooms would spend $5 or $6 a month in rent alone. Middle-class observers thought $10 a week the minimum for a decent living for man, wife and three children, and many families were larger. By that standard, a high proportion of working people, and an even larger proportion of immigrant workers, lived in want. Not only did they occupy the poorer-paid jobs to a disproportionate extent, they were concentrated in jobs that were subject to seasonal and other fluctuations.

[1] Oscar Handlin, *Boston's Immigrants* (1959 edn.), esp. 56–115, including illustrations, and map on 90; Edith Abbott, *Historical Aspects of the Immigration Problem,* 594–6 (report on cholera by the Boston Committee of Internal Health, 1849).
[2] Robert Ernst, *Immigrant Life in New York City 1825–1863,* esp. 40–47, 66–96, 163–5, 191, 197, 214–21. Since no federal census before that of 1870 printed occupation figures by ethnic group, Ernst makes use of a state census.

Many of them found it necessary to wander from place to place in search of work. Some, in the larger cities, pursued callings very like those of Mayhew's London, as rag-pickers, bone-gatherers, or newsboys without fixed address.[1]

II

A generation later, industrialization was in full swing. In years of such hectic growth as the 1880s, the construction of railroads and buildings, the sinking of mines, the operation of factories, the distribution of food and the running of homes, all multiplied opportunities for Americans and immigrants alike. A Welshman, even earlier, had put it, describing the growth of an iron town near Cleveland, 'the works rose like mushrooms. . . . After building the works they had to have workmen and they had to have houses.'[2] More than five million immigrants arrived during the 1880s, and after death and return to Europe had thinned their ranks, there were still nine million foreign-born in 1890. The children of the foreign-born numbered as many more.

Two and three-quarter millions of the surviving immigrants were Germans. Their number had grown by a million in twenty years, but their distribution had changed little. Nearly half of them were to be found in Illinois, Michigan, Missouri, Iowa and Wisconsin, and the most German cities were Milwaukee, Cincinnati and St Louis. The Irish numbered nearly two millions, about the same as in 1870, and nearly two-thirds of them were in the New England and the Middle Atlantic states. There were nearly a million Canadians living in the United States in 1890, those of French origin mainly in industrial New England, the British more scattered, but largely in Michigan and other parts of the Middle West. The English were nearly as numerous, widely scattered, and there were a quarter of a million Scots and a hundred thousand Welsh. Scandinavians were 900,000 strong, overwhelmingly in the region west of the Great Lakes: one-fifth of them were in Minnesota alone, one-seventh in Illinois, and more than one-tenth in Wisconsin. The remaining foreign-born population included rather more than a quarter of a million from other parts of north-west

[1] Report of a committee of the New York legislature on tenements in New York City and Brooklyn, 1857, in Abbott, op. cit., 633–4; Charles Loring Brace, The Dangerous Classes of New York (covering 1853–72); Edgar W. Martin, The Standard of Living in 1860, esp. 393–5, 409–10, 423, 428–9.
[2] Conway, op. cit., 220. The following are a few key figures for the 1880s: total population increase, 50 to 63 millions; increase in city population, 14 to 22 millions; increased railroad mileage, 70,000; growth in steel production, $1\frac{1}{4}$ million tons a year to $4\frac{1}{2}$ millions; coal production, 70 to 150 million tons a year. Yet half a million new farms came into existence; Kansas, Nebraska, Minnesota, and Texas, each gained half a million people, and the Dakotas not many fewer. Chicago, the greatest processing centre of the farming region, doubled in population to more than one million; Minneapolis, similar in its function, grew from 47,000 to 165,000.

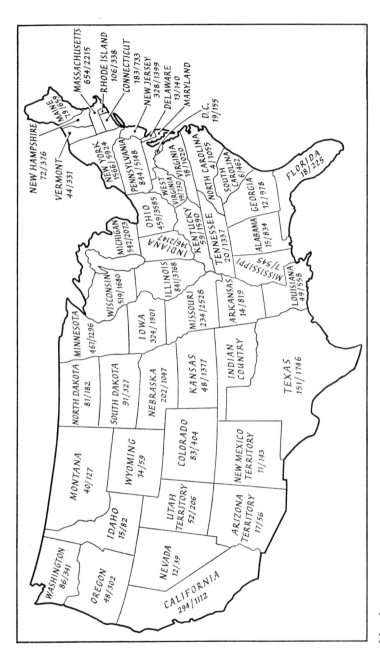

WASHINGTON 86/341
OREGON 48/302
NEVADA 12/39
CALIFORNIA 294/1112
IDAHO 15/82
MONTANA 40/127
UTAH TERRITORY 52/206
ARIZONA TERRITORY 17/56
WYOMING 14/59
COLORADO 83/404
NEW MEXICO TERRITORY 11/143
NORTH DAKOTA 81/182
SOUTH DAKOTA 91/327
NEBRASKA 202/1047
KANSAS 48/1377
INDIAN COUNTRY
TEXAS 151/1746
MINNESOTA 467/1296
IOWA 324/1901
MISSOURI 234/2528
ARKANSAS 14/819
WISCONSIN 519/1680
ILLINOIS 841/3768
MICHIGAN 542/2073
INDIANA 146/2147
OHIO 459/3585
KENTUCKY 59/1590
TENNESSEE 20/1337
MISSISSIPPI 7/545
LOUISIANA 49/558
ALABAMA 15/834
GEORGIA 12/978
SOUTH CAROLINA 6/462
NORTH CAROLINA 4/1055
VIRGINIA 18/1020
WEST VIRGINIA 19/730
PENNSYLVANIA 844/5148
NEW YORK 1566/5924
FLORIDA 18/225
D.C. 19/155
MARYLAND
DELAWARE 13/140
NEW JERSEY 328/1399
CONNECTICUT 183/733
RHODE ISLAND 106/338
MASSACHUSETTS 654/2215
NEW HAMPSHIRE 72/376
VERMONT 44/331
MAINE 79/659

Map 6 FOREIGN-BORN IN RELATION TO
WHITE POPULATION OF U.S.A., 1890
(figures in 000's)

13

Europe, three-quarters of a million from Austria-Hungary, Russia, Italy, and the Balkans (an increase of nearly 700,000 in two decades), and a hundred thousand Chinese. Taking the foreign-born together, their geographical distribution was strikingly uneven. The New England and Middle Atlantic states had four million foreign-born out of seventeen million white inhabitants; the North Central states, four millions out of twenty-two millions; the West, two-thirds of a million out of three millions. Elsewhere they were few. The South Central states had 300,000 out of $7\frac{1}{2}$ million whites, the South Atlantic states 200,000 out of $5\frac{1}{2}$ millions. The South Atlantic states, in other words, had fewer foreign-born than Brooklyn, and the entire block of states from Maryland to Texas, from the Ohio River to the Gulf of Mexico, had fewer than Manhattan, and not many more than Chicago.[1] At the same time, American cities differed greatly in the proportions of their foreign-born and in their detailed ethnic composition. Half of Fall River's population had been born abroad, nearly half of Lawrence's, nearly forty-five per cent of Lowell's, most of them still Irish, British and French-Canadian. New York City, i.e. Manhattan – had forty-two per cent foreign of its one and a half millions: Germans and Irish were still in the lead, but there were already more Italians and Russian Jews than English, and nearly as many from Austria-Hungary. Chicago's proportion was only a little smaller: Swedes, Czechs, Poles, Norwegians and British Canadians were all important, though English were significant, and Germans (161,000) and Irish (72,000) were well ahead. Milwaukee's foreign-born proportion was similar, but nearly two-thirds of it was German. San Francisco's proportion was about the same as New York's: the Irish were the most numerous, but there were more Chinese than Germans. Well behind, in their proportion of immigrants, were Boston, Philadelphia, St Louis, Cincinnati and Baltimore.[2]

Avoidance of the South needs no elaborate explanation. The remaining facts – the choice of city rather than countryside, of Middle West rather than New England, by one group or another; the rush of Scandinavians to a few states, such that more than eleven per cent of the Dakotas' population was Norwegian, and more than fifteen per cent of Minnesota's Scandinavian – these must not be seen merely as shadings on a map or figures in a table. They were in fact the product of thousands of decisions of individuals or groups, and of a good deal of chance.

In 1869, the high price of land in the old Dutch settlement of Pella,

[1] Half of them were in Maryland and Texas.
[2] *Compendium of the Eleventh Census,* I 469, II 600–611. In twenty years, Chicago's foreign-born increased by more than 300,000, New York City's by more than 200,000.

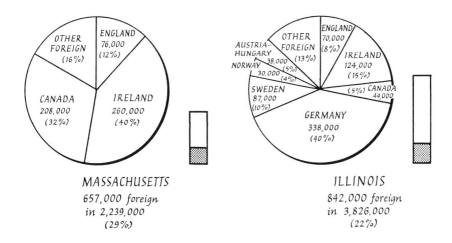

MASSACHUSETTS
657,000 foreign
in 2,239,000
(29%)

ILLINOIS
842,000 foreign
in 3,826,000
(22%)

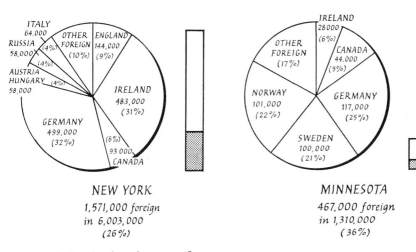

NEW YORK
1,571,000 foreign
in 6,003,000
(26%)

MINNESOTA
467,000 foreign
in 1,310,000
(36%)

Diagram 6   Foreign-born in states, 1890

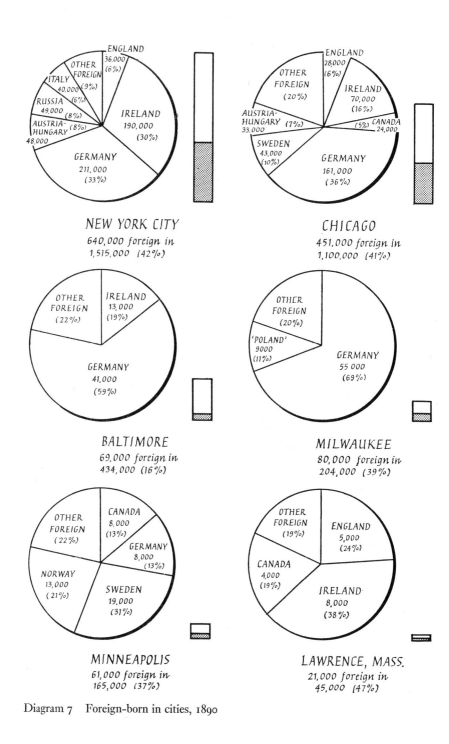

ENGLAND
36,000
(6%)

OTHER
FOREIGN
(9%)

ITALY
40,000
(6%)

RUSSIA
49,000
(8%)

AUSTRIA-
HUNGARY
48,000
(8%)

IRELAND
190,000
(30%)

GERMANY
211,000
(33%)

NEW YORK CITY
640,000 foreign in
1,515,000 (42%)

ENGLAND
28,000
(6%)

OTHER
FOREIGN
(20%)

IRELAND
70,000
(16%)

AUSTRIA-
HUNGARY (7%)
33,000

CANADA
(5%) 24,000

SWEDEN
43,000
(10%)

GERMANY
161,000
(36%)

CHICAGO
451,000 foreign in
1,100,000 (41%)

OTHER
FOREIGN
(22%)

IRELAND
13,000
(19%)

GERMANY
41,000
(59%)

BALTIMORE
69,000 foreign in
434,000 (16%)

OTHER
FOREIGN
(20%)

'POLAND'
9000
(11%)

GERMANY
55 000
(69%)

MILWAUKEE
80,000 foreign in
204,000 (39%)

OTHER
FOREIGN
(22%)

CANADA
8,000
(13%)

GERMANY
8,000
(13%)

NORWAY
13,000
(21%)

SWEDEN
19,000
(31%)

MINNEAPOLIS
61,000 foreign in
165,000 (37%)

OTHER
FOREIGN
(19%)

ENGLAND
5,000
(24%)

CANADA
4,000
(19%)

IRELAND
8,000
(38%)

LAWRENCE, MASS.
21,000 foreign in
45,000 (47%)

Diagram 7   Foreign-born in cities, 1890

Iowa, led to such discontent that a survey party was sent to the north-west of the state. They reached conclusions about soil, timber and other features of the district, and they observed that such was the rush of immigrants that they could enter the Sioux City land office, for information, only by a back door. When these men had reported at Pella, the group which was quickly sent to make purchases had to make a new search, for three weeks, before they could find unclaimed land that met their needs, then within the chosen area individual farms were assigned by lot. Families with their waggons made their nineteen-day journey to the new district the following year. Three years later, Norwegians from the Trondheim district, living in Iowa and Minnesota, made similar preparations for a move into Dakota Territory.[1] Business enterprise did something to influence movement. Dutch business-men who made a tour of Chicago, Milwaukee and St Paul railroad land, and bought 30,000 acres in Minnesota, advertised in Dutch-language news-papers, offered farms rent-free for a year, promised building material and help in constructing churches; then, when population still grew too slowly, they issued in 1889 a map, showing non-existent streets to give the appear-ance of a town.[2]

More commonly, the spread of population into new districts was spon-taneous, with the second generation of settlers in an older place, or late-comers to it after they had gained some experience of American conditions, moving on into the nearest area of known or assumed opportunity. Again and again, Norwegians did this from their early settlements in northern Illinois and southern Wisconsin, step by step through Minnesota and Iowa, into the Dakotas. By the 1880s, Dutch too were leaving north-west Iowa for Dakota lands, moving 'westward over the boundless prairie, by compass, like ships on the ocean', taking with them lumber and tools from the rail-head, and soon establishing a small but thriving village.[3] Accident, finally, could play a part. One Czech who had worked at farming and harness-making, with several stops on his way to Iowa, enlisted in the Union army. After the war, and marriage, he set off for Nebraska. Ruined there by prairie fires, he moved to Kansas where, in Ellsworth county, he found to his delight men from his old company of the Sixth Iowa Cavalry. He decided to settle in their vicinity, and did his best to attract other Czechs by writing to newspapers. Meanwhile, he bought eighty acres of railroad land, obtained eighty more of

[1] Lucas, *op. cit.*, II 217–19, 319–21, 379; and his *Netherlanders in America,* 334–9; Blegen, *op. cit.*, 502–3. Carlton Qualey, *Norwegian Settlement in the United States,* 151–2, prints an article from a Norwegian-language newspaper, praising the fertility of the Red River valley.

[2] Lucas, *Netherlanders in America,* 367–70.

[3] Qualey, *op. cit.*, has numerous examples; Lucas, *Dutch Immigrant Memoirs,* II 319–21, and *Netherlanders in America,* 377–8. Remember, again, the opening pages of Rolvaag's *Giants in the Earth.*

government land by pre-emption, and received valuable help from the Burlington agent. From 1875, settlers were pouring in.[1]

Chance was not only a rural phenomenon. In the 1880s, a group of Italians from near Milan were on their way to the mines of Calumet, Michigan. They went for a walk in Detroit between trains, heard Italian spoken in the street, entered into conversation, and were persuaded to stay.[2] In industrial districts, however, organized recruiting helped to shape the distribution of immigrants. Some of this was done at the ports, whether through the employment bureau at Castle Garden or private agencies. Such businesses existed in other cities too, supplying gangs of workers to lumber-camps, mines and railroads, with geography dictating that Chicago should be a particularly important centre. Any industrial city, however, gave factory owners opportunities for local recruiting. Newspapers could carry advertisements. The factory could display notices. Foremen would have their own contacts among their own favourite ethnic group. News of jobs would travel around homes and saloons.[3]

Whether the immigrant took the initiative or whether he was affected by some efficient organization, whether his destination lay in town or country, once a few members of his group had settled the way was open for the influences of letters and remittances to reinforce the concentration, through the piling-up of fellow-countrymen.

III

Even in the fiscal year 1890, more than 29,000 people describing themselves as farmers entered the United States, more than 8,000 of them from Germany, more than 4,000 from Italy, some 3,500 from Scandinavia, nearly 3,000 from Austria-Hungary, 2,453 from England and 1,525 from Ireland. It is safe to assume that many, at least of the the north-west Europeans, intended to pursue the same calling in America, joining the three-quarter million foreign-born farmers already there, or the quarter-million farm labourers.[4] Those who went straight to land, or who were now ready to

[1] Francis J. Swehla, 'Bohemians in Central Kansas', *Kansas Historical Collections*, XIII (1913–14), 470–79.
[2] John C. Vismara, 'Coming of the Italians to Detroit', *Michigan History Magazine*, II (1918), 118.
[3] The key sources are Charlotte Erickson, *American Industry and the European Immigrant 1860–1885*, and, especially for the less formal methods, Gerd Korman, *Industrialization, Immigrants and Americanizers: the View from Milwaukee 1866–1921*, chapter 1. For an example, see Stoyan Christowe, *This Is My Country*, 69, 85–6 – a coffee house and immigrant bank run by a former Sofia building contractor.
[4] *Commerce and Navigation of the United States . . . 1890*, 762–817. *Compendium of the Eleventh Census*, III 452–9, 532–9, shows 282,739 German-born farmers, 129,314 Scandinavian, 93,358

move into the West after earlier locations, could go most of the way by rail, even if, as one traveller alleged, the track 'was so rough the bell rang of its own accord'. A Welsh settler in Kansas reported in 1874 that the Santa Fe's trains were packed with immigrants, and that special trains often had to be run.[1] Then, as William Allen White's mother wrote in 1870, from a new Kansas town sixty-five miles beyond railhead, 'the streets are full of emigrant waggons all the time,' though 'emigrant' in this context might include old-established Americans from Illinois, Iowa or Missouri. Ten or a dozen years later, similar scenes were enacted in Dakota, crowds of prospectors leaving each small town at dawn, and returning to their stores and hotels at night after their search for land.[2]

Although, in the country just beyond the Mississippi, a log cabin was likely to be the settler's first home, it soon became a shed when he built a frame house, with earthen floor, bedroom and living-room, attic bedroom for children, and a lean-to 'summer kitchen'. Breaking the prairie and digging a well called for expert help. Then the farming routine was evolved. In spring, oats, sorghum, potatoes and corn were put in, work was done on the roads, and new ground was broken. In summer came mowing, harvesting of wheat and oats, then ploughing for winter wheat. In fall, apples were picked and potatoes dug, wheat was threshed, corn was cut and husked. Winter passed in taking hogs to market or butchering them at home, hauling corn from the fields, and mending fences. In the early days, implements were crude and cheap: one Norwegian family in Iowa paid only $35 for a waggon, $26 for a plough, and $40 for harness, and even after the Civil War's inflation a new waggon could be had for $90. After a few years of this farming, a man who survived hail, grasshoppers and other hazards could hope to buy more land, install a son or a tenant upon it, and build a new frame house with wooden floor and more rooms than his first. By that time the prairie was likely to be fenced, animals stayed on their own farms, and a district had trees for shelter, orchards, and fenced lanes. Many, however, moved on again. Further west, timber grew scarce, and the settler was likely to begin life in a sod house. One Dutch diarist records that such a dwelling called for a cash outlay of only $1.28, the cost of windows and a

---

Irish, 88,378 British, 54,797 British-Canadian. The distribution of labourers was not very different. We cannot know whether people who came in as carpenters were the same individuals recorded under that designation at subsequent censuses, though the probability is considerable: the chance of confusion is greater in the category 'labourer'. See Emily G. Balch, *Our Slavic Fellow Citizens*, chapter xv, for Czech and Polish farmers.

[1] Richard C. Overton, *Burlington West*, 282; Conway, *op. cit.*, 142.

[2] William Allen White, *Autobiography*, 20; Hamlin Garland, *A Son of the Middle Border*, 254–8.

door. Within, the sod of the walls was so shaped as to leave a rough bench, boxes were used as tables and cupboards, and beds and an iron stove were almost the only other equipment.[1]

Farming was, indeed, a commercial operation, cash sales being needed to pay off mortgages, buy equipment, and pay taxes. There were hired men on the frontier, men saving to buy their own land or men who had simply failed to rise. Teams of men toured with steam engines to hire for threshing. Yet it would be wrong to think of farming at this period as pure commerce, with loan companies, banks, merchants and labourers as the sole components. Ole Svendsen made his start in Iowa by borrowing from his father, after a spell of working for wages. In Illinois, Croft Pilgrim received a legacy, and although he hired masons and carpenters from time to time, his sons worked for him too, and he found it possible to share expensive implements with neighbours. Certainly members of the family worked. Hamlin Garland records his chores as a schoolboy: in the morning cleaning stables, currying horses, milking, pumping water for the animals, then, after school, putting fresh straw in stables, watering and milking again. A boy's summer involved turning cattle and horses on to the open prairie and bringing them back at night, and helping with the harvest, while smaller children kept the water jug filled at the corner of the field. Neighbours might volunteer help at critical periods, or would consent to work for pay. In short, many elements other than commerce entered into frontier life. The Reverend de Pree observed of his fellow Dutch: 'They helped build each other's houses and stalls; they watered each other's cattle; they took care of each other's children; they dug each other's graves.'[2]

Living was frugal. Sickness was frequent. Diaries and letters have toil as their major theme. Some settlers found themselves oppressed by the look of their environment, as well as by more material hardships. Garland, it is true, wrote with enthusiasm of the land's beauty in summer. On the edge of settlement, winter was very different. 'It is an iron country,' wrote a novelist of Nebraska, 'and the spirit is oppressed by its rigour and melancholy. One could easily believe that in that dead landscape the germs of life and fruitfulness were extinct forever.' Human landmarks were few: 'The great fact was the land itself, which seemed to overwhelm the little beginnings of human society that struggled in its sombre wastes.' A character in

[1] Garland's is a vivid account. See also Bogue, *op. cit.*, 253–8, 266–79 (analysis of diaries of Gro Svendsen and William Savage); Lucas, *Dutch Immigrant Memoirs*, II 237; Balch, *op. cit.*, 343–8 (a Czech family in Nebraska, settled after the father had worked for a time as a blacksmith at St Joseph, Mo.) For the background of Great Plains farming, see in general Everett Dick, *The Sod House Frontier*, and Gilbert C. Fite, *The Farmers' Frontier 1865–1900*.

[2] Bogue, *op. cit.*, 253, 259–66; Lucas, *Dutch Immigrant Memoirs*, II 239.

Rolvaag's masterpiece put it: 'It's all so big and open . . . so empty . . . Not another human being from here to the end of the world.'[1]

Such isolation did not last. As railroads advanced, towns came to be strung out along them. Yards around the depot held livestock awaiting shipment, coal and lumber just brought in – a single yard might handle several hundred carloads a year. Farmers brought their loads of grain to such towns, used feed barns and blacksmiths' shops, bought supplies at their stores, ate meals and took drinks, visited doctors, or prepared lawsuits against their neighbours. Such a town could grow fast. In its early days, it might have stumps thirty inches high in its main street, and holes knee-deep: a few years later, a flourmill, three sawmills, a brickyard, a furniture factory, seven stores, a livery stable, and two hotels, with eleven dealers in real estate, five lawyers, three civil engineers and three doctors, and supporting two newspapers and four churches. Such a place saw Grange picnics, county fairs, circuses, and Fourth of July parades. Often it had an opera house, with kerosene footlights or even gas chandeliers, which in a single year housed school exhibitions and graduation exercises, dances and amateur plays, lectures, acrobats and conjurers, a panorama of Ireland, a Roman Catholic festival, and a temperance meeting. In the advertising and speculation, the administration and justice and politics, the local merchants, lawyers and editors were deeply involved.[2]

IV

Although farmers continued to arrive in America, and although pioneers continued to move to the West, industry was bound to prove attractive to most immigrants, if only because they lacked capital. In the year 1890, nearly 45,000 of the new arrivals declared themselves to be skilled workers, and more than 139,000 to be labourers. At the census taken in that year, half America's coalminers had been born abroad, and nearly half its lumbermen. Immigrants provided, as we shall see, a disproportionately large number of factory workers and general labourers, but a very small number of white-collar workers. There are, of course, to be seen in the census figures wide variation between ethnic groups, and a modern statistician has made calculations which make the complicated facts easier to grasp. If an ethnic

---

[1] Willa Cather, *O Pioneers*, 15, 187–8; Ole E. Rolvaag, *Giants in the Earth*, 43.
[2] Lewis Atherton, *Main Street on the Middle Border*, esp. 28–9, 36–7, 138–40; Hamlin Garland, *Boy Life on the Prairie*, 137–50, 231–51. White's *Autobiography*, esp. 126, 356–7, emphasises editors in these small towns: the early chapters of Richard Lowitt, *George Norris, the Making of a Progressive*, deal with a lawyer's work, including as it did insurance, debt-collecting, land speculation, and of course politics.

group's share in one occupation is the same as its share in the entire labour force, then that group's Index of Relative Concentration in that occupation is 100. Hutchinson finds that, in 1890, all ethnic groups, except by a very narrow margin the Scandinavians, had an index of less than 100 in agriculture. In manufactures all scored more than 100, Scandinavians and Irish lowest, then British-Canadians, Germans 151, British 154, and French-Canadians 214. Only British-Canadians slightly exceeded 100 in the professions, though the British were very close. In domestic and personal service the British scored only 97, the Irish as high as 254, though more women servants were provided by Scandinavians and the French-Canadian figure for women was negligible. Individual occupations can be analysed in the same way. British and British-Canadians ranked low as labourers, Scandinavians, French-Canadians and, especially, Irish very high, the last-named 274. In coal mining, neither Canadian group made any significant contribution, and Germans and Scandinavians both score low, but the Irish index-number is 147 and the British 627 – they were in fact half the foreign-born miners. In iron and steel, the order is almost the same but the range is much smaller: British 278, Irish 247, Germans 123, Scandinavians 99, French-Canadians 84, British-Canadians 62. One last example may be given. Scandinavians and Germans provided very few women factory workers; British-Canadians scored 87, Irish 122 and British 261; but the French-Canadian index-number is 1,654 – the work, evidently, was the alternative to domestic service.[1]

It would be a mistake, however, to treat the city, manufactures, or even a single industry as a unit. Cities varied greatly in their ethnic composition, and therefore in the prominence of particular groups in occupations there. They varied, too, in their industrial structure, and each industry contained within its labour force a hierarchy of skill and reward.

Half the male cotton operatives had been born abroad, and forty-five per cent of the women; more than forty-five per cent of male workers in woollens, and over thirty per cent of the women. Many of the remainder were of foreign or partly foreign parentage. These people, who had crowded Lancashire railway stations to meet American agents in the 1860s, whose carts choked the roads from Quebec to New England in 1864, and who in 1879 piled their baggage high on Holyoke station on their arrival from the same province, went to work in towns dominated by one industry, or a cluster of closely related industries, often controlled by a handful of corpora-

---

[1] *Compendium of the Eleventh Census*, III 452–9, 532–9; Edward P. Hutchinson, *Immigrants and their Children 1850–1950*, 122, 124–31.

tions.[1] Four-fifths of the value of manufactures at Lawrence, Massachusetts, in 1880 was accounted for by textiles. At Lowell, cottons alone made up $19\frac{1}{2}$ million in a total of $33 million, and at Fall River they formed $14\frac{1}{2}$ million in $19 million. Such places were heavily foreign and overwhelmingly working-class. They had grown too fast for the development of amenities. Housing consisted largely of close-packed tenements. The whole scene was squalid and drab. Some towns had good sanitation – Fall River for example – but standards of health were as bad as in most industrial districts of Europe. In the 1880s, to take one example, the Massachusetts mill towns had infant mortality rates of about 200/1,000.[2]

Larger cities were more diversified in their industrial structure, though not necessarily more attractive to live in. In 1880, no industry contributed as much as one-fifteenth to the total value of Philadelphia's manufactures; only one in New York City, men's clothing, as much as one-eighth; meatpacking contributed one-third of Chicago's figure; and even Pittsburgh's iron and steel failed to reach one-half.[3] Immigrants from north-west Europe were prominent in most industrial jobs. At Pittsburgh, the Irish, British and Germans together had about as many workers in iron and steel as did native Americans, and the Irish had far more of the city's labourers. Chicago's labourers were largely Germans and Irish, who were strongly represented also among draymen, carpenters, masons and tailors. Boston's domestic servants were still largely Irish, and so were its labourers. In New York City, native Americans filled the ranks of the teachers, government workers, and clerks, but the foreign-born contributed nearly half the draymen, more than half the tailors and dressmakers, three-fifths of the carpenters and domestic servants, two-thirds of the masons, bricklayers, and traders, and four-fifths of the labourers. Germans were prominent among traders, carpenters and tailors, Irish among masons, draymen, servants and labourers, though they already had some government workers. The English provided, from their small total numbers, a considerable group of clerks.[4] Immigrants, it is clear, were still near the bottom of the economic scale, though they practised several skills and could offer some services even outside their own communities. They were weakly represented in any

[1] Erickson, *op. cit.·* 17–18, 59; Mason Wade, 'The French Parish and *Survivance* in Nineteenth-Century New England', *Catholic Historical Review*, XXXVI (1950–51), 173, an observation by Bishop de Goësbriand of Burlington, Vt. Green, *op. cit.*, 201–2.
[2] *Tenth Census*, Social Statistics of Cities, I 188–98, 227–41, 255–69; Cole, *op. cit.*, 21–2, 61–3, 70–73, 106–7, on Lawrence; and Green, *op. cit.*, 258, on infant mortality.
[3] *Tenth Census*, Social Statistics of Cities, I 594–6, 836–9, 871–2, II 511–13; though II 695 shows that flour-milling accounted for two-thirds of the manufactures of Minneapolis.
[4] *Tenth Census*, Population, 864, 870, 892, 895. The New York category 'other nationalities' already conceals Russian-Jewish garment workers.

occupation that called for fluent English, advanced education, familiarity with American business methods, and, therefore, aptitude for dealing with native Americans across counter or desk.

V

During the 1880s, labourers were likely to make $1.50 a day, teamsters $2, most skilled workers $2.50, and certain building and printing workers as much as $3. Male cotton workers seldom reached $1, however, and woollen workers seldom exceeded $1.50. Most skilled men in iron and steel earned $2 or $2.50; coal miners could expect $2.50 and their helpers half a dollar less; railroad engineers and skilled men in the shops exceeded $2 a day, firemen commonly half a dollar less. Over industry as a whole, the working day averaged eleven hours. Much, however, depended upon the number of days worked in a normal year, and upon the fluctuations in the state of business from one year to the next. There were men in heavy industry, it seems, who were steadily enough employed to earn $600 a year, but more received $400 to $450, and textile workers were more likely to get $250 to $300. There were women in big-city stores who made $400 a year, but most factory workers were lucky to reach $300. The proportions at the several levels can seldom be known. An investigation of a quarter of a million railroad workers, however, was made in 1889, and presents information of unusual precision. About one-sixth of the workers in the sample were employed 300 days or more in the year – white-collar staff, conductors, and engineers, who often made more than $900. About another eighth worked from 200 to 300 days; rather more between 100 and 200; and the remaining 113,000 can fairly be described as casual workers in this industry, whatever they did with the rest of their time. The income structure that resulted gave about 5,000 men more than $1,000 a year; and about 12,000 between $700 and $1,000; 26,000 from $500 to $700; and all of these could be described as very respectable working-class incomes. The 40,000 who earned between $300 and $500 were perhaps no worse off than most other industrial workers. But 55,000 earned between $100 and $300, and more than 100,000 casual workers earned, on railroads, less than $100.[1]

Such figures do not give the full picture of workers' lives. Deductions in coal-mining, the company store, the fortnightly or monthly payment of wages, led to special difficulties. In most industrial districts, on the other hand, immigrant families could raise their standard of living by taking in

[1] *Annual Reports of the Commissioner of Labor*, 1888 (women in large cities), 1889 (railroads), 1890 (iron, steel and coal), 1891 (textiles).

lodgers. In larger towns, and especially in the mill towns, several members of the family might work. The decade, fortunately, included no major depression, and since wages rose, especially in the last few years, and prices continued to fall, most people's real wages, however poor, were improving. As for the working environment, the growing scale of industrial plant brought problems of its own, with less personal management and many decisions taken in remote cities. Home environment varied greatly, from the shacks of new mining districts to the solid, though overcrowded, tenements of New York or the newer parts of Boston. Cities were still at a primitive stage of development, but the range from best to worst was enormous. In 1880, New York City, now covering most of Manhattan, was well provided with paved streets and horse-drawn streetcars. But only half Philadelphia's streets were paved, one-fifth of Chicago's, and one-sixth of Cleveland's, while Minneapolis was said to have no paved streets at all. Paving could mean many different things. Cincinnati used wooden or stone blocks, as well as macadam and cobble, and New Haven used, in addition, asphalt and 'about five miles hardened with oyster-shells, etc . . .' Standards of drainage showed just as wide a range. New York City and Boston had widespread sewage systems, to which most homes were connected, but below 14th Street sewers discharged into East River at the shore line, with noisome effects, while in Boston the tide washed sewage back to the shore close to the most populous districts. Half Chicago's homes had water-closets, and most of them were connected to sewers, but in Philadelphia less than one-sixth had closets, and many sewers were more than forty years old. At New Orleans, privies were the only form of sanitation, and the same was true of Baltimore, which 'so far as the question of drainage is concerned . . . is still in the condition of a small country town,' despite its third of a million inhabitants.[1]

Even such generalizations are not enough. Individual examples must be added if standard-of-living discussions are to become real. An immigrant in business might have freedom and a sense of opportunity, yet his enterprise might be so small as to make it a hardship, accepted only from a sense of pious duty, to distribute five dollars a week in small change to fellow-Jews who brought him sabbath greetings.[2] Another immigrant's standard of living

[1] Clarence D. Long, *Wages and Earnings in the United States 1860-1890*, esp. 35-6, 53, 61, 69-72, 94-5, 98. It is impossible to document the subject fully in such a book as mine. On working conditions, see Conway, *op. cit.*, 164-210, for contemporary Welsh descriptions of mining, unions and strikes; Clifton K. Yearley, *Enterprise and Anthracite*; Rowland T. Berthoff, *British Immigrants in Industrial America*; Korman, *op. cit.*, On urban environments, see *Tenth Census*, Social Statistics of Cities, I 131-2, 421, 563-4, 581-7, 812, 818-30, II 19, 288-9, 361, 380, 494, 508, 690, 693; and illustrations of working-class housing in Boston, in Sam B. Warner, *Streetcar Suburbs* 27, 48, 94, 100, 102, 137.
[2] Philip Cowen, *Memories of an American Jew* 87-8.

involved working all day in a sweatshop, sharing a room with two others at $8 a month, eating rolls and milk except, once a day, a restaurant meal of soup, stew, bread, pie and beer at thirteen cents – all in order to save for his wife's ticket from Europe. An even less fortunate man might pay fifteen cents for a bed in a lodging-house, or ten cents for a bed without covers, or five cents for the privilege of sleeping on a floor. Others again might be at home, making 3,000 cigars a week, working 'from they can see till bed-time'. Around such people was the jostle of the poorer sections of the metropolis, the pushcarts with their second-hand stockings, hats, spectacles, and tin cups, with the letter-writer and the horseradish-grinder busy on the sidewalk. The city's standard of living included also the heavy infant death-rate in summer: 'little coffins are stacked mountains high, on the decks of the County Commissioners' boat when it makes its semi-weekly trip to the city cemetery.' For grown-up immigrants, it might include, at the end, a journey to the paupers' burial-ground, to be placed in trenches three deep and shoulder to shoulder, to save space.[1]

VI

It would be unfair to end a survey of the period on this note. There were immigrants who made good. Cornishmen can be found entering the United States to undertake highly skilled work in mining, though they might easily move from country to country as opportunities arose. Skilled workers could rise to own mine properties, while some entered other types of business. One, the celebrated Richard Trevellick, became a labour leader in the third quarter of the nineteenth century.[2]

Among Scandinavians, there were many examples both of men arriving with special qualifications and of those rising from humble positions to prosperity and distinction. Edward Boeckmann entered the country in 1886 with medical training gained in five countries, and became an eye specialist. Luth Jaeger came in 1871, after a year of university study in Norway. He became an editor, deputy collector of internal revenue in Minnesota, had a real estate and insurance business, and was also an officer of a bank. John Peterson, a farmer's son, had already risen in Sweden to be super-intendent of railway bridge building when he came to the United States at the age of twenty-eight. Starting again at the bottom, as a labourer, he was soon a contractor, and went on to become city councillor, Republican committee man, and state senator. Others began with fewer advantages. Louis Almen began as labourer, became a railroad contractor, then went to

[1] Jacob Riis, *How The Other Half Lives* 45, 63–4, 85–6, 96–8, 102–8, 125, 132–3.
[2] A. L. Rowse, *The Cornish in America* 149–54, 171, 223, 268–9, 324–30.

college, becoming a pastor and editor of a church newspaper. August Darelius worked first on a farm, then as a clerk, studied law, started a legal practice, and became state assemblyman. Nils Haugen arrived as a child, worked on his father's farm, then in a lumber camp and a sawmill. After two years at Luther College he taught in a school, then studied law and became a court reporter. Later he became state assemblyman, railroad commissioner, and congressman, and narrowly missed nomination as governor of Wisconsin. Testen Johnson worked in Norway as a blacksmith in his early years, then farmed in Wisconsin and Minnesota, fought briefly in the Civil War, became county commissioner, assemblyman, and ended as state senator.[1]

The much larger German-American community provides further evidence. Reinhold Liebau had a long struggle as a Wisconsin farmer, but established himself in the end through hard work, attention to new methods, careful book-keeping, and learning English. His neighbours elected him road commissioner, member of a school board, and town clerk. Middle Western cities afforded wider opportunities. C. F. G. Meyer from Westphalia, an orphan when he came to America, was first apprenticed to a druggist. He changed to market-gardening, then bought and edited a newspaper, then became director of several banks. Henry Meier from Hanover started life in America by working on his father's farm. He drove a delivery waggon, then started a freighting business, became partner in a grocery, launched his own firm, and became president of an insurance company and a bank. Henry Ottensmeyer also began on a farm, then worked as a blacksmith before setting up a carriage and waggonmaking business. A carpenter, Matthias Herman, became a prosperous coffin-maker and undertaker. Gottlieb Neumeister from Württemberg was a cabinet-maker, but rose to be contractor for many public buildings in St Louis. Henry Schwartz worked in a drug store, studying as he did so, then went to medical school, crossed to Germany for further study and practice, and returned to the United States as practitioner and professor of medicine. To give one more example, Frederick Niedringhaus from Westphalia was a glazier, painter and tinner before his immigration, and worked at the last-named trade in America, but, going into business on his own, and inventing a new type of ironware, eventually he is said to have employed 3,500 men.[2]

[1] O. M. Nelson, *History of the Scandinavians and Successful Scandinavians in the United States*, I 366, 377, 392–3, 416–18, 423–4, 472–3, II 202–4.
[2] Robert E. Park and Herbert A. Miller, *Old World Traits Transplanted*, 87–91; random examples from the biographical volumes II and III of Walter B. Stevens, *St Louis, the Fourth City 1764–1909* – Forty-Eighters are intentionally omitted in my account. One could add, for a period only a little later, Italian examples from Andrew F. Rolle, *The Immigrant Upraised*, 248–50, 273–4.

Careers such as these called for unusual qualities of enterprise, energy and versatility, and no manipulation can make the evidence suggest that people so successful were more than a small minority of America's foreign-born.

VII

The British, Irish and German workers who still dominated the industrial scene in 1890 were building the opportunities soon to be presented to people from more distant parts of Europe; and the American, German, Scandinavian, Czech and British farmers would make it possible to feed them as they specialized in their industrial tasks.

Although more than forty-eight million Americans were still classified as rural in 1910, although there were still more than five-and-a-half million farmers and nearly four-and-a-half million farm workers, although the number of farms, their acreage and their value continued to increase, and although meat-packing, flour-milling, and lumber were among the five leading American industries, yet coal and steel, oil and locomotives, textiles and clothing, even automobiles and rubber, seem more characteristic of the country's economy on the eve of the Great War. During the first decade of the twentieth century, steel production rose from 10 to 26 million tons, coal from 270 to 500 millions. Urban population rose by twelve millions, and half of the increase took place in cities with more than 100,000 inhabitants each. Street-car mileage doubled, electric inter-urban railways, subways, tunnels under rivers, and skyscrapers were built in large numbers. The leading industrial states grew fast: New York gained two million people, Pennsylvania nearly as many, Massachusetts and New Jersey half a million each. What position could immigrants take up in this rapid development? There is only one way to answer the question. An admiring henchman once said of Al Smith that 'he could make statistics sit up, beg, roll over, and bark.'[1] Although I make no such claim, only a careful scrutiny of the figures can make the situation clear.

Of America's population increase, three millions consisted of the foreign-born who had neither died nor returned to Europe during the decade. There were now thirteen-and-a-half millions of them. One-seventh of the total population were foreign-born, but the proportion was nearly one-fifth in Pennsylvania and nearly one-third in Massachusetts and in New York. More than one-third of Boston's people, and Chicago's, were foreign, two-fifths of New York's, and even more of Lawrence's and Fall River's.

[1] Oscar Handlin, *Al Smith and his America*, 85.

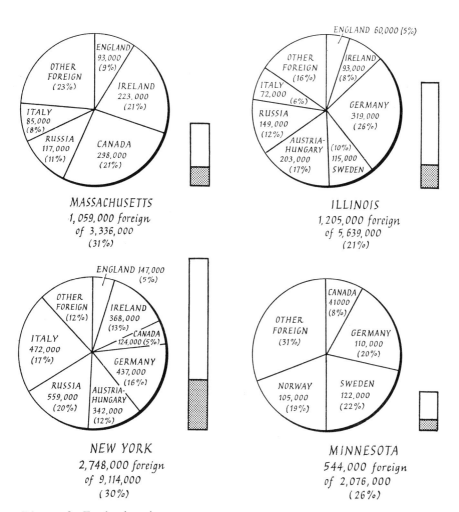

ENGLAND 60,000 (5%)

MASSACHUSETTS
1, 059, 000 foreign
of 3, 336, 000
(31%)

ILLINOIS
1, 205, 000 foreign
of 5, 639, 000
(21%)

NEW YORK
2, 748, 000 foreign
of 9, 114, 000
(30%)

MINNESOTA
544, 000 foreign
of 2, 076, 000
(26%)

Diagram 8   Foreign-born in states, 1910

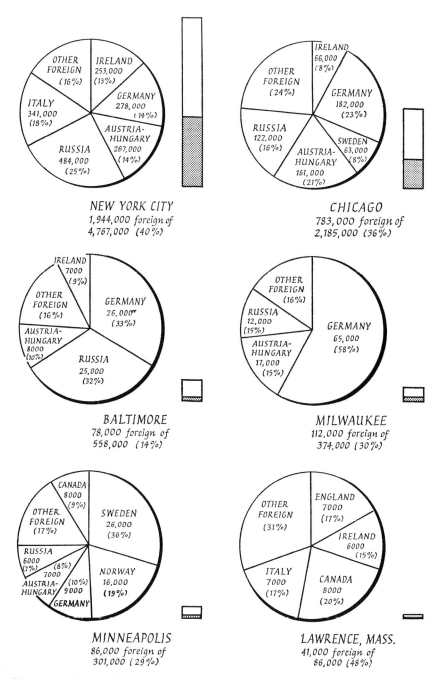

Diagram 9   Foreign-born in cities, 1910

The newcomers, too, were of different origin. In New York state there were now more people born in Russia and Italy than in Germany and Ireland. In Illinois, there were more from Austria-Hungary and from Russia than from Sweden, more from Italy than from England. In the decade, those born in Austria-Hungary and in Russia had each gained a million in the country's population, those born in Italy, 859,000. The five boroughs of the now greater New York City had gained more than 150,000 from Austria-Hungary, nearly 300,000 from Italy, more than 300,000, most of them Jews, from Russia. In 1910 nearly one-quarter of all the city's foreign-born had arrived within the previous five years, and in Manhattan, one-quarter of all those over ten years of age could speak no English. The new arrivals, obviously, were becoming concentrated in cities and industrial regions. More than seventy-two per cent of all the foreign-born in 1910 were urban, twice the figure for the American-born of native parentage, and twenty-nine per cent lived in cities with more than half a million people, nearly five times the native figure. The urban concentration of Italians was above this general average, and the urban proportions of the mainly Jewish Russian-born, in the East North Central, Middle Atlantic and New England states were ninety per cent and above.[1]

Immigrants made up a higher proportion of the labour force than of the population – about one-fifth of the thirty-eight million gainfully employed in 1910 – because of the ages at which they arrived and because of the higher proportion of their women who needed to work. No more than in earlier times, however, were they equally distributed among the occupations. The foreign-born had about one-fifth of all in wholesale and retail trade, though they had one-third of all labourers connected with trade, two-thirds of all junk-dealers, and five-eighths of all peddlers. They made up about the same proportion of those in public service, their high proportions among labourers and watchmen balancing their low proportions in the clerical and professional grades. Much lower proportions were found in the professions (under one-eighth), in banking (under one-tenth), in the Post Office (one-fourteenth), and in telegraph and telephone service (one-sixteenth). High proportions existed in domestic and personal service (one-quarter), steam and street railways (rather more than one-quarter), cotton mills (over one-third),

[1] The principal information comes from *Abstract of the Thirteenth Census*, esp. 92, 201, and from *61 Congress 3 Session, Senate Doc. 756*, Immigration Commission Reports, Statistical Review of Immigration, 420–21, 426. Most ethnic groups were more than half urban (English, Germans and Hungarians very slightly below that proportion) at a time when the national percentage was 45. Welsh, Danes and Norwegians, however, fell below 30 per cent. For the background of economic growth, it is enough to refer to *Historical Statistics of the United States* and to Harold U. Faulkner, *The Decline of Laissez Faire*.

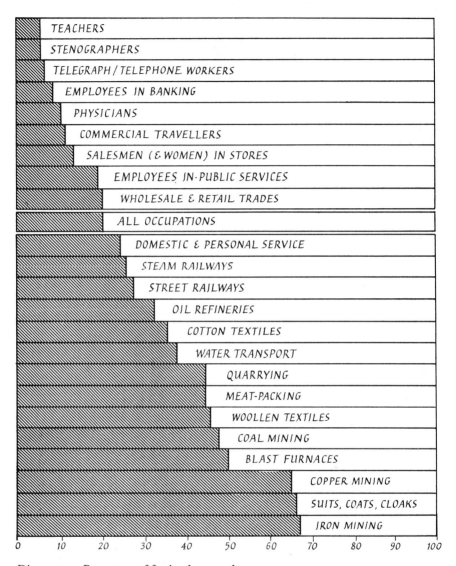

Diagram 10 Percentage of foreign-born workers, 1910

woollen mills (nearly one-half), coal mining (nearly one-half), blast furnaces and rolling mills, meat packing, tanneries and breweries (each at least one-half), iron and copper mining, and most garment trades (each about two-thirds).[1]

The category 'foreign-born', of course, is too simple. As at earlier times, ethnic groups had their areas of concentration, and the Immigration Commission Reports, though not the published censuses of the early twentieth century, make this clear. In agriculture were found fifty per cent of the male foreign-born Norwegians, thirty-two per cent of Czechs, thirty per cent of Swedes, twenty-seven per cent of Germans, twenty-two per cent of British-Canadians, eighteen per cent of the English, nearly fourteen per cent each of Irish and French-Canadians, about ten per cent of Poles, and so on down to six per cent of Italians and three per cent of those born in the Kingdom of Hungary. In mining, the proportions of Czechs, Canadians both British and French, Germans, Norwegians and Russian-born were exceedingly small, and of Irish distinctly low, but the industry employed nearly eight per cent of Poles, nine per cent of Italians, ten per cent of British, nineteen per cent of those born in Austria, and thirty per cent of those born in Hungary. As labourers were found only six per cent of the English, eight per cent of the Russian-born, ten per cent each of Norwegians and British-Canadians, thirteen per cent of Swedes, fourteen per cent of Czechs, and fifteen per cent of French-Canadians, but nineteen per cent of Austrians, twenty-two per cent each of Hungarians and Irish, twenty-nine per cent of Poles and thirty-three per cent of Italians. In the numerous other figures, we find the Russian-born very high in retail trade and in garment trades, French-Canadians very high in textiles, English and British-Canadians rather high in the professions.[2]

Our next step is to discover the level at which immigrants found work in American industry, for this helped to determine their standard of living and their status in American society. Four industries will furnish enough of the facts. In 1910, more than one-and-a-half million men worked on American railroads. The census of that year shows that the foreign-born, who were rather over one-quarter of all workers, provided one-fourteenth of ticket and station agents, one-twelfth of clerks and train conductors, one-tenth of engineers, but one-quarter of track foremen and more than half the

---

[1] The source is *Thirteenth Census*, IV, Population: Occupation Statistics, 302–431.

[2] The material in Immigration Commission Reports is conveniently summarized in Jeremiah W. Jenks and William J. Lauck, *The Immigration Problem*, 149–51. Some local differences, and many questions of levels of skill, are hidden in these figures. British and British-Canadians, as well as native Americans, formed most of the clerical workers, whose life in Boston's South End is described in Albert B. Wolfe, *The Lodging House Problem in Boston*.

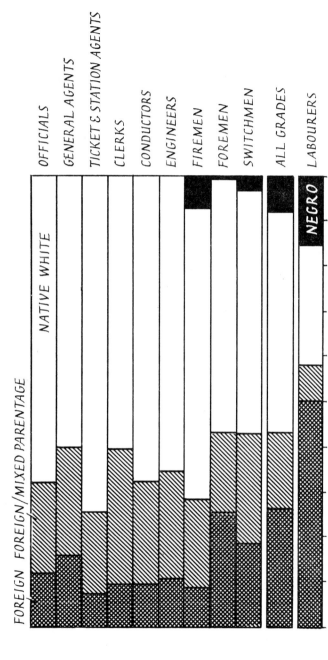

Diagram 11 Steam railways, 1910: percentage of foreign-born, foreign or mixed parentage, Negro, and native White

labourers.[1] In bituminous coal, fewer than one-third of foremen were foreign-born, but more than half the miners and labourers. In one large sample investigated about the same time, it was found that more than eighty per cent of the British had been miners at home, and more than half the Germans, Czechs and Irish, but only ten per cent of Poles, six per cent of Slovaks, and less than four per cent of any other group.[2] In blast furnaces and rolling mills, fewer than one-third of the foremen had been born abroad, rather more than one-third of the skilled moulders, but more than two-thirds of the labourers, most of whom had worked on the land in their old homes.[3] As for workers in cotton mills, rather more than one-fifth of the foremen were foreign-born (though pretty certainly far more of recent foreign ancestry), but nearly half the male spinners and weavers. At Fall River, among male workers in cottons, 1,009 out of 1,283 labourers were foreign-born, 1,003 of 1,366 spinners, 3,812 of 5,880 weavers; of the women, 1,859 of 2,520 spinners were foreign, and 2,724 of 4,996 weavers; and most of the remainder had at least one foreign parent. Despite the influx of southern and eastern Europeans into cotton mills, it was thought that one-tenth of the men and two-fifths of the women in the industry had been in some sort of textile work before immigrating, and for the British-born the proportions were fifty-seven and ninety-five per cent.[4]

Big cities offered a wider range of opportunity than did coal, steel or textile districts, yet the position of immigrants was not very different. Huge numbers of workers were needed to level and pave streets, dig sewers, put down streetcar tracks, dig foundations and erect homes and offices, generate electricity and gas. Great numbers were needed in factories, shops, and as servants in homes. The number of clerical workers grew rapidly from census to census. On the whole, however, immigrants, as before, stayed near the bottom.

New York City is example enough. Of its more than one-and-a-half

[1] *Thirteenth Census*, IV, Population: Occupation Statistics, 414–17. Many Negroes were also employed as labourers. The children of immigrants were better represented in the higher grades.
[2] *Thirteenth Census*, IV, Population: Occupation Statistics, 304–5; *61 Congress 2 Session, Senate Doc. 633*, Immigration Commission Reports, Immigrants in Industries, Pt. 1, Bituminous Coal Mining, I 44.
[3] *Thirteenth Census*, IV, Population: Occupation Statistics, 338–41; *61 Congress 2 Session, Senate Doc. 633*, Immigration Commission Reports, Immigrants in Industries, Pt. 2, Iron and Steel, I 41. John A. Fitch, *The Steel Workers*, 351–3, analyses the employees of Carnegie Steel in Allegheny county, Pa., March 1907: in a total of some 4,000, nearly 2,400 were American-born (though doubtless many were of foreign parentage), 533 British, 211 Irish, 283 German, 125 Scandinavian. There were 137 Slovaks, 116 Poles, and smaller numbers of Lithuanians, Magyars, Italians, and French-Canadians.
[4] *Thirteenth Census*, IV, Population: Occupation Statistics, 380–3, 555. *61 Congress 2 Session, Senate Doc. 633*, Immigration Commission Reports, Immigrants in Industries, Pt. 3, Cottons, 243.

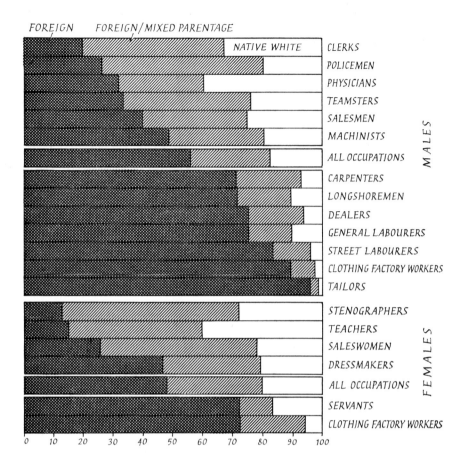

FOREIGN   FOREIGN/MIXED PARENTAGE

NATIVE WHITE   CLERKS
POLICEMEN
PHYSICIANS
TEAMSTERS
SALESMEN
MACHINISTS
ALL OCCUPATIONS

MALES

CARPENTERS
LONGSHOREMEN
DEALERS
GENERAL LABOURERS
STREET LABOURERS
CLOTHING FACTORY WORKERS
TAILORS

STENOGRAPHERS
TEACHERS
SALESWOMEN
DRESSMAKERS
ALL OCCUPATIONS
SERVANTS
CLOTHING FACTORY WORKERS

FEMALES

0   10   20   30   40   50   60   70   80   90   100

Diagram 12   New York City, 1910:
Percentage of workers foreign-born,
foreign or mixed parentage, native white

21a   Working on the New York State Barge Canal, 1909
Photograph by Lewis Hine, George Eastman House Collection.

21b   Living quarters, construction camp on New York State Barge Canal, 1909
Photograph by Lewis Hine, George Eastman House Collection.

23 Breaker boys at work at a coal mine, early twentieth century
Photograph by Lewis Hine, George Eastman House Collection.

a   Steel mills and workers' homes, Pittsburgh, 1909
Photograph by Lewis Hine, George Eastman House Collection.

b   Shaping rods under a trip hammer, Pittsburgh, 1909.
Photograph by Lewis Hine, George Eastman House Collection.

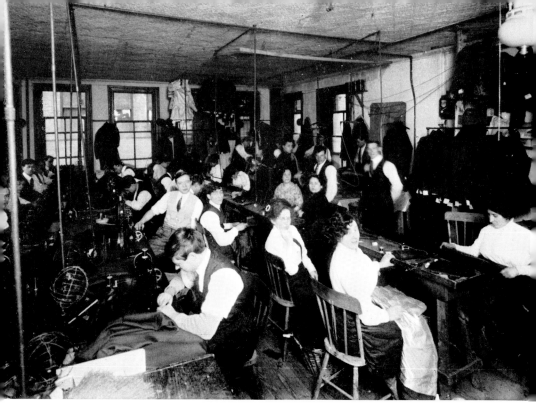

24a   Garment workshop, New York City, 1912
Photograph by Lewis Hine, George Eastman House Collection.

24b   Tenement work, early twentieth century
Photograph by Lewis Hine, George Eastman House Collection.

million male workers, rather more than half were foreign-born, and nearly half of its more than half a million women. The foreign-born made up nearly one-third of the physicians, rather more than one-quarter of the police. They were one-third of the teamsters and half the machinists. They were less than half the salesmen and less than one-fifth of the clerks. They made up, however, more than two-thirds of the longshoremen and almost three-quarters of the carpenters. They were nearly 17,000 of the 19,000 clothing workers in factories and all but 2,000 of the 49,000 tailors. They were 13,537 of the 16,618 street labourers and 27,406 of the 35,501 general labourers. The pattern among female workers was similar. Foreign-born ranked exceedingly low as teachers, stenographers, and saleswomen, very high as dressmakers (nearly half the total), clothing workers in factories (47,000 of 65,000), and domestic servants (81,000 of 113,000). There was of course much specialization among ethnic groups. Jews were peddlers, furriers, tobacco workers and, above all, garment workers. Italians were construction workers and labourers, bringing to the Hudson and East River tunnels, the subways, and the skyscrapers the skills they had already demonstrated in the Simplon tunnel and on public buildings in Rio de Janeiro and Buenos Aires.[1]

VIII

No certainty is ever possible in calculations about working-class standards of living, but if the position of immigrants in America is to be assessed realistically, some attempt has to be made to balance such factors as wages, hours, costs, housing conditions, and security over a period of years. The same industries and, for the most part, the same city, will furnish the evidence.

For a ten-hour day, coal miners about 1910 were earning $2 or $2.50. Since they did not work continuously through the year, their annual earnings were unlikely to exceed $450, and labourers would make substantially less. Just as it had been a generation earlier, their purchasing was dominated by the company store. Mine owners kept out hucksters who might compete, they were thought to charge unreasonable prices, and they were accused of keeping a man in work, or assigning him to a more or a less pleasant and profitable job, according to the patronage he gave the store. One Polish miner's budget showed fortnightly earnings of $41, a deduction of $9 for rent, a deduction of nearly $24 for store purchases, a charge of 50 ¢ for

[1] *Thirteenth Census*, IV, Population: Occupation Statistics, 571–7. I have omitted Negroes and Orientals. The W.P.A. publication, *Italians of New York*, 61–2, 70, shows Italians working on the subway construction of the 1890s and early 1900s, on the Bronx aqueduct, as ice-sellers and knife-grinders, among many other occupations. It is of some interest to see, in the Census, how far the New York immigrant jobs were done, at New Orleans, by Negroes.

the hospital and another 30 ¢ for sharpening tools. A company-owned house was half a two-storey building, wooden, painted a dull red outside, very imperfectly insulated, with four rooms, an outside privy, and its only water supply, very often, a hydrant in the street. Such houses were arranged in rows along the valley sides, the streets surfaced with coke ash, the drainage gutters on either side often choked with rubbish. School house, church, and store were the only larger buildings, and even they were scarcely landmarks in the smoke of railroads, coke ovens and other industrial installations. The environment was depressing. The work was dangerous. In 1907 more than 3,000 miners were killed on the job, and although the death-rate was roughly constant in relation to tonnage mined, it was rising slightly in relation to numbers employed, and was thought to be two and a half times as high as the British rate. State inspection systems were ineffective. The United Mineworkers Union was active, pursuing weekly pay, the eight-hour day, fair measuring of coal, safety, and the exclusion of child labour, the company store, and the Pinkerton men; but while the proportion of men organized was very high in Illinois, it was low in Pennsylvania and negligible in West Virginia.[1]

In steel, foremen might make $8 or $9 a day, highly skilled men leading gangs almost as much, and skilled men like crane drivers $4, but the mass of immigrant labourers, organized in groups each speaking one language, were paid nearer $2. A sample taken in 1907–8 at Pittsburgh found only twenty-three per cent in the range $2.50 to $5, and only five per cent above $5. Many steel workers had only nine months' employment, some only six, and a man was lucky to make $500 a year. For this, many worked a twelve-hour day, seven days a week, including Labor Day and the Fourth of July. Among the 70,000 to 80,000 workers in Allegheny county, there might be 200 deaths in a year, and countless accidents less serious. In one sample of 18,000 workers during six months of 1908, the company hospital had 231 in-patients and more than 1,600 out-patients. Not until the 1930s was the industry successfully unionized. Yet, as compared with coal miners, steel workers enjoyed several advantages. They had more freedom in housing and shopping, for in larger communities company control could not be so complete. There were likely to be more jobs for women and young people, given the existence in towns of industries other than steel. In larger places, immigrants might become traders – there were nearly 4,500 of them at

[1] 61 *Congress 2 Session, Senate Doc. 633,* Immigration Commission Reports, Immigrants in Industries, Pt. 1, Bituminous Coal Mining, I 322–3, 472–517. See also John Mitchell's testimony in *Industrial Commission Reports,* XII 30–58; Peter Roberts, *Anthracite Coal Communities* (including illustrations facing 120, 163, 346, of homes, evictions in the 1902 strike, and barefoot Slav children); John Brophy, *A Miner's Life,* 27–69.

Pittsburgh in 1910, and Polish saloon keepers were numerous in all steel towns – and their children might become salesmen or clerks. Most, of course, remained unskilled workers. They paid $10 a month for a four-roomed house. Many took in lodgers, who paid $2.50 a month for room and laundry and about $10 a month for the food which the housewife bought and cooked for them. This meant overcrowding, though seldom on the scale reported by one observer: a Bulgarian gang-boss and his family on the ground floor, twenty men upstairs accommodated in two-tier iron bedsteads, lunch-pails hung round the kitchen range, benches at an oilcloth-covered table, and the men eating stew and apple-cake.[1]

If steel workers were well paid for long hours, dangerous work, and a squalid environment, textile workers had safer and more pleasant work for low individual earnings, since many people of all ages above fourteen were seeking work, there were almost no unions, and employers were already facing competition from Southern mills. Families, however, were able to reach a respectable working-class standard of living, because more than one member could work, and the industry was less seasonal than some others. In the early years of the twentieth century, adult male workers born abroad were found averaging $9 a week in cottons, women $7½, boys and girls in their teens about $5½. Yet family income often exceeded $900 a year, and it was usually more profitable for wives to work in the mill than to take in lodgers. For rents ranging from $9 to $12 a month, families often had four or five rooms, but a quarter of them had six or seven. This was at Lowell. Nearby Lawrence was a worsted town above all, and wages were half a dollar a week higher. Some skilled workers, largely British, made $12.50 or more a week. Housing, on the other hand, was worse, an apartment in a company tenement, at $12 a month, being the standard home.[2]

Railroad engineers and conductors continued to be well paid and regularly employed, and many other workers were in skilled and tolerably rewarding grades. Section foremen and track labourers, however, were often

[1] *61 Congress 2 Session, Senate Doc. 633*, Immigration Commission Reports, Immigrants in Industries, Pt. 2, Iron and Steel, I esp. 329–418 (study of one Pennsylvania steel town); Fitch, *op. cit.*, 11, 57–71, 163, 177, 202–5, 301–5; Margaret F. Byington, *Homestead: the Households of a Mill Town, passim*, who emphasises that only these single men had much chance of saving money; 93–5 points out that, even with the help of the Carnegie Relief Fund, few families and men who were killed received $1,000, and only total disability lasting more than a year qualified for aid.

[2] *61 Congress 2 Session, Senate Doc. 633*, Immigration Commission Reports, Immigrants in Industries, Pt. 3, Cottons, 217–300, Pt. 4, Woollens and Worsteds, 741–92, deal (as comparison with the census proves) with Lowell and Lawrence. The labour of really young children, however, was no longer a significant factor in manufactures. *Thirteenth Census*, IV, Population: Occupation Statistics, shows some 10,000 children between ten and fourteen in cottons, under 2,000 in coal mining. There were 20,000 as newsboys and messenger boys, over 30,000 in domestic and personal service. There were three-quarters of a million in agriculture, most of them working on parents' farms; and the period saw some celebrated scandals in food-processing.

making less than $1.50 a day, for work that was bound to be highly irregular, and it was at this level that immigrants were especially numerous. Many such people were engaged in maintenance during summer alone. They lived in trains of box-cars, most of them fitted with bunks rather like the old steerage, one equipped as a dining car with benches, long table and lockers along the walls, and one as kitchen, where the cooks also slept. A gang-boss acted as interpreter and handled the commissariat, collecting on pay-day whatever money was required. Fuel, coal or old sleepers, was free. Each morning the men went to work on hand-cars, then, when the work grew too distant, the whole train moved on a few miles. When winter approached, everyone was taken back to Chicago and turned adrift.[1]

Because of their varied industries, big cities need to be considered separately. In Chicago, now with more than two million inhabitants, immigrants worked on railroads and streetcars, in the stockyards, as labourers and draymen, in tobacco and garment-making, much of the last-named being carried on in homes. In 1908, admittedly a depression year, the Immigration Commission found that nearly half the foreign-born workers it studied were making less than $400 a year, and three-quarters less than $600. Two-fifths of families had an annual income of under $500, two-thirds below $750, and one-sixth over $1,000. The most common housing consisted of two- or three-storey wooden tenements, built at the street end and also at the back of each lot. Four rooms made up the typical family home, running water was usually laid on, but the toilet was shared by more than one family. For this, the average rent was $9 a month. Many foreigners took in lodgers: some Sicilians were found living two families in one apartment. Immigrants moved easily from tenement to tenement, but few left their original district, even ten years after their arrival.[2] New York City is even better documented. Although there still existed districts of single-family brownstone houses, and although older wooden buildings survived, it was above all the city of tall tenements, in which four-fifths of its inhabitants lived. Immigrants commonly occupied three or four rooms at rents averaging $4 a month per

[1] *Industrial Commission Reports*, XVII 723, gives figures for 1900. For working conditions, see *61 Congress 2 Session, Senate Doc. 633*, Immigration Commission Reports, Immigrants in Industries, Pt. 22, The Temporary Labor Supply and its Distribution, esp. 333–43, 419–41; Stoyan Christowe, *This Is My Country*, 89–147 (a youth from Macedonia working in the West just before the Great War and during its early years); Rolle, *op. cit.*, 153–6, 226, 229–31 (Italian railroad labourers).

[2] *61 Congress 2 Session, Senate Doc. 338*, Immigration Commission Reports, Immigrants in Cities, I 250–329. *Hull-House Maps and Papers* has some ninety pages of investigation into Chicago slum conditions, but this dates from the previous decade. I am concerned with the general conditions of immigrant life, not with controversy over the Immigration Commission's sampling methods, sharply criticized in Isaac A. Hourwich, *Immigration and Labor*, 251–4. For a somewhat later view, see Edith Abbott, *The Tenements of Chicago*, esp. 249, 260–77, 343–62.

room. Between 1897 and 1901, a pioneer sociologist visited every dweller in a block on the Upper East Side, i.e. between Central Park and East River, some nine hundred persons in fourteen five-storey tenements. Germans and Irish were moving out, Jews and Italians were coming in. Crowding and noise impressed him above all. A woman could see across the airshaft the candles round a child's coffin in another apartment. The interviewer asked a question on one floor, received an answer, and had it corrected two floors up by a woman who had overheard. Families were visited by streams of peddlers, coal and ice dealers, janitors and landlords, social workers and church visitors, health inspectors and gas men. Police patrol-waggons, ambulances and fire-engines, newsboys and organ-grinders, provided background noise.[1]

New York's immigrants could work in many industries, but the garment trade, dominated by Jews, is of peculiar importance and interest. Within a generation, techniques had changed again and again. The balance shifted from custom-made to ready-made clothing. Sewing machines came to be operated by gasolene engines and then by electricity. Heavy irons were heated by gas and swung on moveable arms. Machines were developed for buttonholing and for sewing on buttons. Work became more and more minutely subdivided, so that skill and long apprenticeship became less important. Although, from the 1880s, state law tried to exclude work from the operatives' homes, many small workshops were no less crowded, and anything that could be called a factory was rare. Under pressure from unions, however, employment became more continuous, time-rates were common for women and girls, and for men complicated scales of piece-rates were worked out. At the beginning of the century, most workers had a 56- or 60-hour week. Men who were pressers, or assistants at various tasks, could make $500 a year, skilled men $600 or $700, and cutters, the aristocrats of the trade, $900 or more. Women earned less, but how much less varied greatly from job to job. Many immigrants, of course, were small employers rather than wage-earners, and there is no information about the profits of these small undertakings.[2]

Both the Immigration Commission and the Russell Sage Foundation examined living standards at this time. The latter, whose methods were more carefully thought out, surveyed some 400 families, half of them native Americans or immigrants of older-established groups, especially Germans

[1] *61 Congress 2 Session, Senate Doc. 338*, Immigration Commission Reports, Immigrants in Cities, I 159–244; Thomas J. Jones, *The Sociology of a New York City Block*, esp. 1–47.
[2] Jesse E. Pope, *The Clothing Industry in New York*, esp. 85–90, 124–7, 157–68, while 309–21 have specimens of agreements about piece-rates. See also Rischin, *op. cit.*, 55–69. There were of course Jewish doctors, dentists, lawyers, teachers, insurance men, editors, real-estate speculators, and shopkeepers, even at this early date.

and Irish, the remainder immigrants from southern and eastern Europe. With an average of five members, families differed greatly in their annual income. Seventy-nine made $1,000 or more; 116, $800 to $999; 151, $600 to $799; and a few under $600. The investigators thought $800 the minimum for a decent mode of life in New York conditions. Incomes above $700, they found, were reached either by taking in lodgers or by having wife or child at work. Remembering the typical occupations of recent immigrants, it seems reasonable to focus attention on the group making $600 to $799 a year. Taking broad averages, such families spent their money as follows: between one-fifth and one-quarter on rent, nearly half on food, one-eighth on clothes, the remainder, in very small amounts, on fuel, streetcar fares, medical care, insurance, and other items. An even sharper definition of immigrant life is obtained by looking at Jewish and Italian families within the same range of incomes. Italians were more likely to be living in two rooms, children sleeping in cots in the kitchen-living room. Jews spent more on fuel and light, on medical care, on contributions to religious and social organizations, and they tended to insure any property they possessed. Italians spent rather more on food, much more on cereals, fruit, vegetables, and alcohol to drink at home, but less than Jews on meat and fish. One Jewish family, with four children between six months and six years of age, bought in a week six quarts of milk and some condensed milk, 2 lb butter, a dozen eggs, $3\frac{1}{2}$ lb sugar, 6 lb potatoes, bread and rolls, beef and fish, minute quantities of cheese, dried fruit, and wine for the sabbath. The same family bought $\frac{1}{4}$ lb coffee and 2 oz tea, and although ice-boxes were standard equipment, the other food too was often bought in very small quantities. People in this class bought coal, never more than 1 cwt at a time, often in 25 lb pails for ten cents. They patronized ground-floor stores or pushcarts in the street. Adults and older boys resorted to public bath-houses. at any rate in summer. Children had a weekly bath in the kitchen wash-tub. In such conditions, misfortune or bad management easily led to squalor, Energy or taste could put oilcloth and a few pictures on the walls, and supply such amenities as musical instruments.[1]

IX

Immigrants shared with other workers considerable improvement in

[1] Robert C. Chapin, *The Standard of Living among Workingmen's Families in New York City*, esp. 39–41, 56, 70, 115–7, 156–60, 245–6. Gas for cooking and lighting cost a dollar a month in summer and two in winter. It is worth pointing out that, bleak though this life was in many aspects, it was very far removed from that of great numbers of British workers in the early years of the Industrial Revolution, their diet dominated by potatoes and bread.

measurable standards of living during the late nineteenth and early twentieth centuries. Recent investigation suggests a gain of fifty per cent in real wages between 1860 and 1890, in manufacturing industry as a whole, for prices fell rather steadily throughout the years after the Civil War, while wages either rose or fell less fast. If differentials between skilled and unskilled workers widened, then immigrants received less than their share of the benefits. Between 1890 and 1914, improvement was slower. Wages and prices both fell in the mid 1890s; both rose sharply between 1898 and 1903; both rose, but more slowly, until the depression of 1908, after which they rose once more until 1913, food prices going up especially fast in 1909 and 1910. Older writers held that gains were slight, if they occurred at all: the latest view is that living costs rose more slowly than used to be thought, and that over the whole period, and for industry as a whole, real wages may have risen rather more than one-third.[1]

Everything depends, however, on whether a particular group shared fully in the general advance. As in earlier periods, immigrants were in occupations exposed to a short or irregular working year. The Immigration Commission's investigations, for example, showed rather full employment in copper; in iron mining rather more than eighty per cent of men worked nine months or more in the year; in meat-packing the figure was somewhat below eighty per cent, in cottons about seventy per cent, while most anthracite mines worked 230 to 240 days a year.[2] Garment work was notoriously seasonal. General labourers were probably even worse off. Immigrants, in other words, were doubly in jeopardy: they had the lowest wage-rates and the least continuous work. Cyclical unemployment, uncertain in magnitude but undoubtedly severe in 1837–42, 1857–9, 1873–8, 1893–7, and 1921, bore heavily upon workers who were the last to arrive, those with the least skill, and living closest to the level of subsistence. Even the smaller depressions, like that of 1908, sent thousands rushing back to Europe. No public source gave a man satisfactory support during unemployment. If, on the other hand, he stayed in work, he might find compensation in the shape of lower prices of the goods he bought.

Whether in a safe or a dangerous industry, whether a labourer or a highly skilled man, the immigrant, like native American workers and workers in every other industrial society, was subject to a normal cycle of fortune characteristic of his class. Early in life he attained his maximum earnings,

---

[1] The most recent studies, prepared for the National Bureau of Economic Research, are Long, *op. cit.*, and Albert Rees, *Real Wages in Manufacturing 1890–1914*.
[2] *61 Congress 2 Session, Senate Doc. 633*, Immigration Commission Reports, Immigrants in Industries, Pt. 3, Cottons, 274; Pt. 11, Slaughtering and Meat Packing, 85–7; Pt. 17, Copper, 41; Pt. 18, Iron Ore, 331; Pt. 19, Anthracite, 619.

apart from broad improvements affecting his whole trade. This standard of living fell as children were born. It rose again as those children began earning, fell again as they left home. As he entered middle age, he might be down-graded if the job called for strength and speed, and his standard of living would fall still further if he lived long enough to retire. Such statements, however, are vague. They gain realism and force if they are filled in to show the upward and downward pressures bearing upon the standard of living of certain typical men. Let us assume, then, a worker at each of three dates, a man who never gets promotion, who marries five years after landing in America, has five children at two-year intervals, and has a working life of forty years.[1]

Arriving in the early 1850s, such a man experienced both rising wages and rising prices in his early working years, then wage reductions, short time, or unemployment in the depression of 1857, and further losses as his first children were born. If he remained a civilian during 1861-5 his wages soared, but prices rose almost as fast, and his later children were arriving. The War over, he enjoyed some years of prosperity, as prices fell faster than wages, and his first children began to work. In the mid 1870s, everything depended upon whether he kept his job. If he did, prices fell fast enough to offset reductions in wages. Between 1878 and 1884, employment was good, wages rose, and prices kept on falling, but his children began to leave home. With a possible setback in 1884-5, he continued to flourish, but in the early 1890s old age and economic depression hit him together, and his working life probably came to an end.

A worker drawn to the same specifications, who arrived in that record year of nineteenth-century immigration, 1882, gained in real wages through most of the first decade, though before the end of it children were beginning to arrive. From 1893 he was in grave danger of unemployment, though if he kept his job falling prices helped him. Soon after the birth of his last child, prosperity returned, jobs were easy to get and keep, and wages rose, but much of the gain was wiped out by rising prices, and his children were still dependent on him for their whole support. From 1903, however, his children began to earn, and apart from 1908 his position for some years was good. When the depression of 1913-15 came, his children were beginning to leave home, but soon came the war-time boom. The gains were of course partly cancelled by price-rises, and soon afterwards came the severe post-war slump. Since all his children had left home, and unemployment was very

[1] For this concept of the 'age-cohort' applied to standard-of-living studies, I am indebted to an article by R. S. Neale, 'The Standard of Living 1780-1844: a Regional and Class Study', *Economic History Review*, Second Series, XIX (1966), 590-606, which deals with the English city of Bath. Readers are invited to perform the exercise with workers entering the United States at other times.

probable, his working life might end before he could enjoy the gains of the 'New Era'.

A similar exercise is worth performing once more, with a worker arriving in the United States in 1907. Most of his children arrived during the Great War boom, but while they were still very small the 1921 depression inflicted desperate hardship. By the time the even worse depression of the 1930s arrived, one or two of his children were at work, but the scale of the disaster was so great that such factors no longer counted. On the other hand, larger programmes than ever before were launched to aid the unemployed, and he spent some months on the W.P.A. payroll, levelling ground for an airport and rebuilding a school. When better times came, the children were leaving home, but he was now likely to be backed by a union, the war-time boom benefited him greatly, and the process of readjustment after 1945, while not free from friction, was handled with unprecedented care for workers' interests. When, a little later, he retired, he found, unlike any of his immigrant predecessors, a pension that would help give him a minimum of comfort in his old age.

15

CHAPTER TEN

Immigrant Communities

... the dead man ... was a member of the Fratellanzo Calvallese ... and now a hundred of his brotherhood had left off work for a day to escort him to the Calvary Cemetery in Brooklyn. Each of them was dressed in black and wore in his lapel a black ribbon with silver letters. The men marched in double file; at the head of one was the green, red and white flag of Italy wreathed in crepe, and at the head of the other the stars and stripes of their new country. The procession was led by a brass band in brilliant uniform, the hearse was draped with flowers and followed by a second band. Then came the double file of the brotherhood, and after that closed carriages filled with women and children. Mass had been heard at the Church of Our Lady of Loreto.

Rupert Hughes, *The Real New York*, 332.

Immigrants were foreigners as well as workers, and they sought to perpetuate as much as possible of their European style of life, certainly as much as would enable them to feel safe in the unfamiliar American world.

'A map of the city,' wrote Jacob Riis of New York in 1890, 'coloured to designate nationality, would show more stripes than on the skin of a zebra, and more colours than any rainbow.'[1] The stripes were not distributed at random. Germans could be seen establishing blocks of settlement up the east side of Manhattan. A few Irish were still on the Lower East Side, though some of their districts had been taken over by Italians. English, French, Czechs and others all had their little zones of concentration. Above all, recently-arrived Jews were present in force.[2] Such national clustering was not the whole truth. A Jewish boy, it is true, could easily recognize an Italian district into which he had strayed, by the sight of certain sausages and cheeses in shops, of opera posters, and of lithographs of the Madonna with luminescent heart showing through her blue gown; but reality was more complex than that. The Italians of the Lower East Side were divided into Genoese, Calabrians, Sicilians, and so on, each group inhabiting a single city block, or filling the tenements which faced each other across certain streets. Jews clustered in the same way, according to their origin in Galicia, Roumania, Hungary or Russia, so that 'Rivington Street was only a

[1] Jacob Riis, *How the Other Half Lives* (1957 edn), 18.
[2] Kate H. Claghorn's report, 'The Immigrant in New York City', in *Industrial Commission Reports*, XV, esp. 470–74.

suburb of Minsk'.[1] In Chicago, a modern scholar claims to have identified no fewer than seventeen clusters of Italians, each one associated with a single district of the old country. The same city's Roumanians came chiefly from four villages of the Banat, and kept themselves quite separate from the few who had come from Bukowina. Chicago's ethnic map also included a large Czech district, commonly known as Pilsen.[2] By about 1900, many of Boston's Irish had already moved beyond the old densely settled districts. In those parts of the South and West Ends nearest the central business streets lived American, British and British-Canadian salesmen and clerks, single men occupying lodging-houses often converted from high-class residences, the marks of chandeliers still visible on the ceilings. Close to their humbler work could be found southern Italians, Syrians, Portuguese, and Jews, each with some corner of South, West or North End.[3] Each mill town had its Irish shanty district in the middle of the nineteenth century, then its French-Canadian streets, and half a century later its colonies of southern and eastern Europeans, equally localized, so that most of Lowell's Poles came from a small group of parishes near Vilna.[4] In the rural Middle West, similar patterns could be seen, with Wisconsin townships derived from a single German district, and with Norwegians settling according to the valley of their origin.[5] Such communities were likely to exert a pull upon the home villages, families becoming united and neighbours re-grouping for a considerable period of time.

Immigrants' lives were often made more difficult by their being new-comers settling in American communities which were themselves new or rapidly changing. In much of the rural Middle West, and in the mining camps of Pennsylvania and Michigan, the first immigrants found little that could be called a social structure – nothing more, in fact, than a business firm and the rudiments of a political and judicial system.[6] Some cities were little

[1] Alfred Kazin, *A Walker in the City*, 151 (he refers to the 1920s); Claghorn, *op. cit.*, 474; Moses Rischin, *The Promised City*, 76–8; Works Progress Administration, *The Italians of New York*, 18–22; Robert E. Park and Herbert A. Miller, *Old World Traits Transplanted*, 146–51, 201; Edward A. Steiner, *On the Trail of the Immigrant*, 175.
[2] Rudolph J. Vecoli, 'Contadini in Chicago', *Journal of American History*, LI (1964–5), 408; Park and Miller, *op. cit.*, 151–8; Christine A. Galitzi, *A Study of Assimilation among Roumanians in the United States*, 201, 225–9, 240; Edith Abbott, *The Tenements of Chicago*, 83–4.
[3] Robert A. Woods, *The City Wilderness*, 34–57, and *Americans in Process*, 40–41, 46–7 (maps). See also Albert B. Wolfe, *The Lodging-House Problem in Boston*.
[4] *61 Congress 2 Session, Senate Doc. 633*, Immigration Commission Reports, Immigrants in Industries, Pt. 3, Cottons, 230; Donald B. Cole, *Immigrant City*, 27–8; Constance M. Green, *Holyoke* 43–4.
[5] Reuben G. Thwaites, in *Industrial Commission Reports*, XV 538–9; Theodore C. Blegen, *Norwegian Migration to America: the American Transition*, 75–6.
[6] Rowland T. Berthoff, 'The Social Order of the Anthracite Region', *Pennsylvania Magazine of History and Biography*, LXXXIX (1965), 261–91.

better. Even native Americans found it necessary to improvise, setting up hospitals, secondary schools and fire services by efforts essentially private. Immigrants had special reasons for needing to do the same and more. They needed business institutions whose transactions could be carried on through the old language. They needed institutions of mutual aid to fill the void in American social welfare, a system of communications to link them with the old country and with fellow-immigrants in America. They needed churches which at one and the same time would offer them familiar rites and serve as a repository of language and tradition.

I

The group which, on a first commonsense view, must have had fewest language problems, must have felt least uprooted, alien and insecure, was the British, yet even this group built up, and for many years maintained, many institutions of its own. They included businessmen's clubs in big cities and workingmen's clubs in mill towns; clubs connected with clans and shires, with Cornwall, Shetland and the Isle of Man; cricket and golf clubs, and organizations for Highland games; public houses and grocers' shops to bring in delicacies from Scotland. The British imported the Odd Fellows and Foresters organizations for social security. They established newspapers. They celebrated the Queen's birthday and her Jubilee. Late in the day, during the Great War, their sense of solidarity was given new strength by the need to guard against Irish and Germans alike.[1]

Most ethnic groups felt far more radically separate. In 1910, nearly three millions of the almost thirteen million foreign-born Americans over ten years of age could speak no English. Manhattan alone had more than a quarter of a million of them, Chicago more than 180,000, several small New England textile towns more than 10,000 each.[2] The existence of dialects added to immigrants' problems, and immigrant women were likely to rely on the peddler or the corner store, in order to shop on a conveniently small scale, bargain in the accustomed way, and be readily understood.[3] Ethnic specialization was to be found, too, in places of accommodation and refreshment. Milwaukee's hotels bore recognizable national names: Cross Keys (English),

[1] Rowland T. Berthoff, *British Immigrants in Industrial America*, Part II.
[2] *Thirteenth Census*, I, Population, 1277–83. The situation had not been very different in 1890. By 1930, 4 per cent of foreign-born males over ten years of age, and 9 per cent of females, still spoke only their own language – Maurice R. Davie, *World Immigration*, 266.
[3] Sophonisba P. Breckinridge, *New Homes for Old*, 54–66, 122–8, deals sympathetically with immigrant housewives' problems. Louis Wirth, *The Ghetto*, 229, states that, for similar reasons, Poles came into Chicago's Jewish districts to trade, despite the hostility which in other respects characterized relations between the two groups.

Caledonian, St David's, Lakes of Killarney, and Zum Deutschen Haus. The New York Germans' Atlantic beer garden, with its orchestra, billiard tables, bowling alley and shooting gallery, was repeated in many cities. So, half a century later, was the Greek coffee shop – Acropolis, Parthenon, Venizelos – where compatriots could play cards, smoke, watch silhouette shows, hear music, and talk politics. Saloons were often run by immigrants who were rising from the ranks of manual labourers. They played an essential part in social life, for, as Charles Loring Brace put it, for the working man 'the liquor-shop is his picture-gallery, club, reading-room, and social salon, at once. His glass is the magic transmuter of care to cheerfulness, of penury to plenty, and of a low, ignorant, worried life, to an existence for the moment buoyant, contented and hopeful.'[1]

Immigrants needed help in other transactions. Many were illiterate even in their own language: so on New York's sidewalks the Jewish scribe could be seen, sitting in straw hat and shirtsleeves, a notice-board beside his desk. They feared the impersonal grandeur of banks: so men of their own nationality, sometimes no more than saloon-keepers, set up businesses which allowed them to deposit money, collect debts in Europe, send remittances or buy prepaid tickets for their friends, all in a congenial atmosphere, though often at the risk of careless or fraudulent business practice.[2]

When the reports of 1880 on streets and drainage are recalled, it does not seem surprising that public authority failed to provide more sophisticated forms of welfare. Some unions of skilled workers offered funeral and death benefits, and the few which also had sickness benefit, like the Cigar Makers and the German Typographia, had many immigrant members. Private charity and, at the end of the nineteenth century, the settlement houses, did something to help, but since they were run by native Americans or old-established immigrants they, too, might seem bureaucratic and remote.[3] Other aid was given, in less systematic but cheerful and informal fashion, by political machines. On the other hand, there were grave shortcomings,

---

[1] Bayrd Still, *Milwaukee*, 65; Robert Ernst, *Immigrant Life in New York City*, 124–5; Theodore Saloutos, *The Greeks in the United States*, 78–83; John F. Nau, *The German People of New Orleans*, 55–6, 63–8, 117–20; *Tenth Census*, Social Statistics of Cities, II 363 (showing Cincinnati's beer-gardens being abandoned in favour of others being developed in 'hill-top' suburbs); Hutchins Hapgood, *The Spirit of the Ghetto*, 38–43, 106–12, 297–312, for Lower East Side cafés catering for intellectuals; Charles Loring Brace, *The Dangerous Classes of New York*, 64–5.
[2] Philip Cowen, *Memories of an American Jew*, photograph on 290; Jerome Davis, *The Russian Immigrant*, 47–51; Edith Abbott, *Immigration: Select Documents and Case Records*, 498–509; and the Immigration Commission's special report on the abuses of immigrant banks, *61 Congress 3 Session, Senate Doc. 753*, esp. 203–29. Legal aid, too, was important; and Arthur Mann, *La Guardia: a Fighter against his Times*, 47–8, shows that the early legal practice of the celebrated Mayor of New York City consisted largely of cases on behalf of immigrants.
[3] Clifton K. Yearley, *Britons in American Labor*, 190–91; Roy Lubove, *The Quest for Social Security*, 18; Robert A. Woods and Albert J. Kennedy, *The Settlement House Horizon*, 40–72.

even after 1900, in the factory and mine legislation of states. Only just before 1914 did workmen's compensation laws and official employment agencies get going, and not until about 1930 did states begin to experiment with unemployment insurance and old-age pensions.[1] All this was important to the whole American working class. It was vital to immigrants, concentrated as they were in the lowest-paid and least secure jobs.

Each ethnic group felt the need to organize its own welfare institutions, the transaction of whose business also met some of the need for social life. Very early came organizations to aid immigrants recently arrived in New York, Boston, New Orleans, St Louis and elsewhere. Not much later came societies more permanently concerned with the group's insurance problems, like the two Irish clubs whose members came to blows in 1849 after a New Orleans Fourth of July parade.[2] Very numerous were small benefit clubs, connected with members' origin in a single district of Europe. Among the Lower East Side's Jews, in 1920, there were said to be more than 800 of them. Jewish clothing workers could be found paying 75 cents a month, to enjoy sickness benefits of $7 a week for three months, half as much for a further six weeks, or $400 payable to their families if they died. Smaller benefits than this might characterize another club, and the contributions too would be less. Others again raised the death-benefit by means of a special levy of a dollar on each member. A man with a particularly keen regard for his family's security could obtain a sum equal to his normal weekly wage, by joining several clubs, and still pay less than a dollar a week while at work. The committee of such a benefit club might meet in a tenement parlour, wrangling half the night about the expenditure of tiny sums. Another might assemble in a top-floor room of some more public building, its business disturbed by music from a dance-hall immediately below, and when it ended its proceedings members would pass, on successive floors, dance-hall, synagogue, and saloon, before reaching the basement restaurant where they supped on stew and beer.[3] Such institutions were equally popular among other ethnic groups. Those for Italians were usually connected with a village in the old country, and often had regular social as well as business meetings. Members commonly paid an initiation fee of up to $6, then dues of perhaps 25 cents a month. In return they received sickness benefits of $8 to $12 a week, but when a death occurred, a special levy was

[1] Lubove, op. cit., and John R. Commons and associates, History of Labor in the United States, III, are important authorities.
[2] Ernst, op. cit., 32–4; Earl F. Niehaus, The Irish in New Orleans, 117–18; Nau, op. cit., 20–24; Carl Wittke, Refugees of Revolution, 55–6.
[3] Jesse Pope, The Clothing Industry in New York City, 182–5; Park and Miller, op. cit., 127–8, 207; Steiner, op. cit., 168.

required. Italians took funerals far more seriously than did Jews, and apart from aiding the survivors such a club guaranteed a funeral costing perhaps $50, attended it in a body, and provided a monument. Similarly, Slav groups set up clubs, and in about 1908 one small Pennsylvania anthracite town had twenty for Lithuanians, seven for Ruthenians, and three or four for Slovaks, as well as societies with broader, patriotic aims.[1]

Immigrants needed ritual as well as economic security, and, to make their new life bearable, they wished to preserve features of their national tradition and culture. American institutions might sometimes be made to serve these purposes. An ethnic group might provide a volunteer fire or militia company, institutions which were prominent features of American city life, especially before the Civil War. From Charleston, South Carolina, to Bangor, Maine, Irish companies could be found, usually named for such a hero of Irish revolutions as Robert Emmet, but, in New Orleans, bearing the name of Montgomery, Irish-born commander in the American War of Independence. In the same city, the Germans maintained companies, the gorgeous uniform of one of them imitating that of the Prussian Guards; and more than dressing-up was involved, for German companies can be found in the Mexican War, and in the Civil War on both sides.[2] More commonly, however, immigrants had to work out their own practices and build their own institutions.

Very early in the life of an Irish community in America, a St Patrick's Day banquet and procession were likely to be organized. In New Orleans during the 1850s, the Germans held their *Volks- und Schützenfest*, a march of all social and benevolent societies, with bands playing and American, German and Swiss flags carried aloft, to a park where games and shooting contests were held. The Welsh Eisteddfod and the Italian Columbus Day celebrations arose from similar motives. In 1910, Greek Independence Day was celebrated in Boston, with American and Greek national anthems sung, the orator walking in procession carrying a silver cross and a Greek flag, and prayers offered for Greeks still living under Turkish rule.[3] Sooner or later, most ethnic groups developed societies covering the entire United States,

[1] John Daniels, *America via the Neighborhood*, 102, 197; Park and Miller, *op. cit.*, 129; *61 Congress 2 Session, Senate Doc. 633*, Immigration Commission Reports, Immigrants in Industries, Pt. 19, Anthracite, 677; Saloutos, *op. cit.*, 75-6. Milton L. Barron, *People Who Intermarry*, 85-6, notes that at Derby, Conn., Italians from each province had a separate undertaker, to guarantee the familiar observances; and Harry M. Shulman, *Slums of New York*, 174-201, emphasizes the Italians' suspicion of doctors and hospitals, along with their intensely narrow interests, focused on the family.
[2] Ernst, *op. cit.*, 127-9, 164-5; Niehaus, *op. cit.*, 56, 115-16; Nau, *op. cit.*, 123-4; Carl Wittke, *The Irish in America*, 52-9; and, for background, Marcus Cunliffe, *Soldiers and Civilians: the Martial Spirit in America 1775-1865*, chapter 7.
[3] Nau, *op. cit.*, 121-2; Edward Hartmann, *Americans from Wales*, 146-57; Saloutos, *op. cit.*, 105; Andrew Rolle, *The Immigrant Upraised*, 265.

characteristically with an insurance function, but also much concerned to promote education in the old language and national traditions. Because they were self-governing federations of local societies, and many men held office, immigrants were helped to develop their capacities. The Polish National Alliance was a prominent example.[1]

Books, too, helped in the building of ethnic sentiment, by describing the group's achievements, its contribution to the American Revolution and Civil War, and the exploits of its leading men. In its most extreme form, such patriotic purposes led to a claim to something like a monopoly of moral virtue. Faust's book on the Germans has such sub-titles as 'The best farmers in the United States', and he lists, as peculiarly German traits, honesty, devotion to hard work, sense of duty, and love of home.[2] The foundation, later, of historical societies, was backed by somewhat the same motives, though results were often more scholarly and objective.

Maintaining local links was for some people as important as fostering a sense of nationality. Before the Civil War, New York had Irish and German societies connected with regions. During the later nineteenth century, Rochester saw pageants organized by Bavarian and Swabian groups. Norwegian settlers formed organizations based on single valleys. Many Greek societies had similar ties.[3]

It was entirely natural for immigrants to employ newspapers to promote their solidarity as groups. In 1868, Brynhild Amundsen reached Decorah, Iowa, with his press and all his other possessions in two waggons.[4] Many foreign-language papers began in such circumstances, and many remained small and primitive in appearance, but even the smallest could print public notices in a language intelligible to their readers, advertise the group's banks, notaries and stores, and announce weddings and meetings. They could print European news, and, by being sent to the old country, they could preserve family and local ties. Irish and Germans were launching newspapers as early as the 1830s, Scandinavians from the 1850s, quickly followed by Poles, Italians, Czechs, Jews, Slovaks, Magyars, and many more.[5]

Best developed of all was the German-language press, which at its peak

[1] Joseph A. Wytrwal, *America's Polish Heritage*, chapter 7.
[2] Albert B. Faust, *The German Element in the United States*, esp. II xiii, 475.
[3] Ernst, *op. cit.*, 122, 243 note 22; Blake McKelvey, *Rochester: the Flower City*, 380; Blegen, *op. cit.*, 582–4; Saloutos, *op. cit.*, 75–6; and see Still, *op. cit.*, 276–7, for the names of Italian societies: *Liberta Siciliana*, *Vespri Siciliani*, etc.
[4] O. M. Nelson, *History of the Scandinavians and Prominent Scandinavians in the United States*, II 155.
[5] The principal authority is Robert E. Park, *The Immigrant Press and its Control*. For an earlier summary, see *Eleventh Census*, Manufacturing Industries, III 672–5. Wittke, *Irish in America*, chapter xix, deals with that group's press.

about 1890 had nearly 800 publications – three-quarters of all foreign papers in the United States. New York and Ohio had more than a hundred each, Wisconsin, Illinois and Pennsylvania each more than eighty, Iowa and Missouri each as many as forty. Some of them were mouthpieces of radical organizations, some of churches, others of farmers' interests, while yet others were aimed at immigrants from Schleswig-Holstein, Hesse-Darmstadt, Swabia, the Palatinate, or the Weser valley. A few were big-city dailies, like the *New Yorker Staatszeitung*, the *Anzeiger des Westens* of St Louis, the *Cincinnati Volksblatt*, and the *Wisconsin Banner*, which printed American and local news, advertisements, notices asking readers to contact friends in Germany, reports of Schiller festivals and music contests, arguments about the preservation of the German language, and a literary section with a serious classical German content.[1] Scandinavians had forty-nine papers in 1880, 130 ten years later, and they maintained something like that figure down to the Great War. Half of them were in Illinois and Minnesota, another quarter in Iowa, Nebraska and Wisconsin. Many were provincial in their orientation, and many were connected with some branch of the Lutheran Church.[2] In 1890, only ten Jewish papers were recorded, some of them printed in German. The number doubled by 1910 and doubled again by 1920. The emphasis was now on Yiddish, and Abraham Cahan's *Daily Forward* helped build it as a serious written language, achieving as it did so a circulation of 143,000, perhaps the highest of any foreign-language daily. Half the Jewish papers were printed in New York City, and more than another fifth in Chicago.[3] Much smaller groups were also active. Each ideology among Chicago's Czechs, for example – Catholic, Freethinker, Business, Socialist – was represented by its own newspaper.[4]

II

The immigrant community's central institution, however, was the church. The importance of religion to the newcomers needs no further proof. But since in America there was far more freedom than at home, and since the entire American tradition from the end of the eighteenth century favoured

[1] Carl Wittke, *The German-Language Press in America*: chapter 9 is on papers connected with special interests; p. 196 refers to those related to German districts; 217–30 discusses the contents of dailies.
[2] *Eleventh Census*, *loc. cit.*; Blegen, *op. cit.*, esp. 277–330; Finis H. Capps, *From Isolationism to Involvement: the Swedish Immigrant Press in America 1914–1945*, esp. 16–25.
[3] Rischin, *op. cit.*, esp. 115–30; Park, *op. cit.*, 166–92; and, for other excerpts from the Yiddish press, Allon Schoener, *Portal to America*, 245–56.
[4] Alex Gottfried, *Boss Cermak of Chicago*, 41–2. See Rolle, *op. cit.*, 264, on the Italian press in California, and Saloutos, *op. cit.*, 88–95, for the Greek press.

free competition in religion even more than in business, tensions that might have been accommodated within a state church became, in the new country, the occasion of separate organizations. Of this tendency to divide as well as grow, Norwegian Lutheranism furnishes a striking example.

Norwegians were often pioneers. Lacking, therefore, any apparatus of institutions in their first frontier days, they were forced to improvise. When there were no clergy, laymen had to conduct simple ceremonies. Thus, a funeral service would begin with the solemn hymn 'Who knows how near me is my death?' and after that a simple eulogy might be pronounced. Mourners filed past the open coffin, then went in procession to the grave, and as the now nailed-down coffin was lowered, further hymns would be sung. The burial completed, all said the Lord's Prayer, then returned to the settlement for a meal. As soon as a pastor arrived, he was expected to chant, throw earth on the grave, and preach.[1] Clergy at first travelled. The next step was to provide a resident pastor with a log cabin for a church or, on the Plains, a sod house.[2] In time frame buildings, then stone churches, followed. Norwegian Lutherans, however, though devoted to their faith, were far from united, either at home or in America. In Norway, after a period of Rationalist influence in church affairs, the early nineteenth century saw two opposing movements. One consisted of a return to the most orthodox Lutheranism of the century immediately following the Reformation, with formality of service and clerical dress, extreme precision of doctrine, an educated clergy, and a subordinate place assigned to laymen. The other was Haugeanism, an evangelical movement which stressed man's response rather than God's decrees, conversion experience rather than doctrinal theses, prayer-meetings and bible-reading and lay-preaching rather than clerical authority, free prayer by minister and laity rather than elaborate liturgical services.[3] Many of the immigrants favoured this latter approach, and some may have left Norway principally because they did so. While, therefore, early Norwegian history in America shows churches developing on ethnic lines – Scandinavians breaking away in 1860 from a synod partly of Germans and native Americans, then Norwegians breaking away from Swedes – most complexities of development concerned doctrine and church polity, and immigrants and pastors behaved less as Norwegians than as Lutherans.

In the 1840s, the Rev J. W. C. Dietrichson tried hard to impose a discipline

[1] Blegen, *op. cit.*, 223-4.
[2] See the photographs in E. Clifford Nelson and Eugene L. Fevold, *The Lutheran Church among Norwegian-Americans*, I facing 61, and Olaf M. Norlie, *History of the Norwegian People in America*, 173.
[3] An admirable survey of Lutheran traditions is in Nelson and Fevold, *op. cit.*, II 229-40.

of the orthodox type. All that was achieved, and it was after his return to Norway, was the establishment of a synod, called *the* Norwegian Synod, rather like the German Missouri Synod in its conservative emphasis and maintaining close relations with it. Against this there came to be ranged, first Eielsen's Synod, a congregationalist and evangelical organization, then Hauge's Synod in 1876, with a somewhat similar tendency. Two other bodies grew up, occupying an intermediate position: the Norwegian Augustana and the larger Conference. This three-fold division in principle and five-fold in organization did not exhaust the possibilities of dissension, for the Synod was rent during the 1880s by conflict over the doctrine of Justification, and split into 'Missourian' and 'anti-Missourian' factions. On the other hand, Conference, Augustana and anti-Missourians found it possible to come together in 1890 to form the United Church. In 1917, after negotiations far more prolonged, the United Church, Norwegian Synod and Hauge's Synod banded together as the Norwegian Lutheran Church of America.[1]

All these bodies used Norwegian in their services through most of the nineteenth century. All used Pontoppidan's eighteenth-century catechism. All sang Norwegian and German Lutheran hymns. All struggled to meet the pastoral needs of immigrants as they spread from Great Lakes to Pacific. All of them set up colleges, orphanages, homes for the aged, and hospitals. In the end, some sense of common culture and ethnic identity helped them overcome their doctrinal differences. But in the short run these were very real, and their nature can be seen very clearly if the Synod's liturgy is placed beside a description of the form of service of Hauge's followers. In the former, the opening prayer was read by a precentor while the minister knelt, clad in cassock, stole and white fluted collar. In the latter, the minister, in plain clothes, might call on a layman to extemporize a prayer. The former's elaborate succession of Kyrie, Gloria, Salutation, Collect, Creed and often, after the sermon, a full Communion service, was largely intoned, while at Epistle and Gospel the congregation stood. Hauge's Synod abbreviated the service, had no chanting and no prayers said by the minister while facing the altar and no uniform rule about standing, and at several stages permitted free prayer. Finally, it pronounced a general exhortation and a general assurance of forgiveness of believers' sins, whereas the orthodox body

---

[1] Nelson and Fevold are now the leading authorities, though their treatment of organization and daily life seems to me inadequate. Blegen, *op. cit.*, and Lawrence M. Larson, *The Changing West*, are also interesting, while Blegen's *Land of their Choice*, 139, contains an illuminating letter from Dietrichson. On the similar, though rather less contentious, history of Swedish Lutheranism, see George M. Stephenson, *Religious Aspects of Swedish Immigration*; and for divisions within a much smaller group, A. William Hoglund, *Finnish Immigrants in America 1880–1920*, 41–3, 92–103.

required individual confession and individual absolution before the sacrament could be taken.[1]

At the census of 1890, the United Church claimed more than 100,000 members, the Synod half as many, and Hauge's a mere 15,000. As far as their resources allowed, all of them were interested in secondary and higher education, though largely with a view to training clergy. On the question of elementary education, however, Norwegian opinion was divided. The majority stressed the value of a uniform, publicly financed system, which would leave congregations to attend to children's religious upbringing. They knew that their geographical concentration would often permit them to dominate the policies of school districts. The Norwegian Synod, however, fought this view, at any rate until the 1880s. Its members claimed that the public schools had low educational standards. Worse than that, they had no religion at their centre, so that the system 'of its essential principle must work in opposition to the Kingdom of God.'[2]

Almost certainly, a majority of German immigrants were Protestants, but they too were divided. A few brought with them the Reformed (Calvinist) tradition and maintained separate churches in America. Most came from states in which an Evangelical Church had been established, combining Lutheran and Calvinist elements under governmental control. A few, however, were already Lutheran rebels against such arrangements. Arrived in America, some Germans were content to join older Americans, and Scandinavians, in synods which tended to become rather fully americanized in language and doctrinal emphasis. Others, nearer the frontier, urged Evangelical unity as the best method of meeting a situation essentially missionary. This view was exemplified by the *Deutsche Evangelische Kirchenverein des Westens* of 1840, whose doctrinal statement accepted both Augsburg Confession and Heidelberg Catechism as far as the two agreed, and where they did not, 'we adhere strictly to the passages of holy scripture bearing on the subject, and avail ourselves of the liberty of conscience prevailing in the Evangelical Church.' Some Germans, however, took the opportunity of returning to the strict Lutheranism of the seventeenth century, as it had been before either Pietism or Rationalism had exerted its influence. It was this view that became the basis of the Missouri Synod, sternly orthodox, emphasizing clerical authority, and insistent on reinforcing church teaching by a system of parochial schools. By 1890, with more than 1,500 churches and a third of a million members, it was the largest Lutheran

[1] Nelson and Fevold, *op. cit.*, II 122–6, 342.
[2] *Eleventh Census*, Report on Statistics of Churches, 436–7, 469–78; Blegen, *op. cit.*, 263–6, 269–70; Larson, *op. cit.*, 121–46.

body in America, flourishing especially in the Middle West. Its nearest rival in size, the General Council, included Swedish, German and native American synods both in the Middle West and the East, and only a small proportion of its churches still employed the German language. The Joint Synod in Ohio, the General Synod, and the United Synod in the South, were all largely English in their language. Evangelical churches had a combined membership of no more than a quarter of a million.[1]

The Roman Catholic Church experienced no such doctrinal divisions, and the conflict over the power of trustees, bitter in the early nineteenth century, was an encounter between American democracy and an authoritarian hierarchy rather than an ethnic clash. In the problems of its growth, however, it was the most interesting of all religious bodies in America.

In 1815 the Roman Catholic Church had five dioceses; in the 1840s it had sixteen, with some 700 churches; by the mid 1860s it had forty-two dioceses and nearly 3,000 churches; and before 1900 it had seventy and some 10,000.[2] It was essentially a church for immigrants. At a time when the diocese of Boston covered the whole of New England and when only a handful of priests were at the bishop's disposal, missionary journeys were being made among Irish canal workers. A third of a century later the diocese of St Louis, at an early stage of its development, was reaching out in the same fashion to construction workers on the Hannibal and St Joseph and Iron Mountain railroads.[3] Travelling priests said Mass in private homes or in hired halls. Then, after house-to-house collections, donations from Catholic laymen or from sympathetic Protestants, and gifts of land from business corporations, the first permanent buildings could be put up, log huts sometimes in Kentucky, Missouri and Minnesota, an unplastered barn-like structure in Cincinnati, simple frame buildings in New England.[4] The next stage, very often, was the purchase of more elegant structures

[1] *Eleventh Census*, Report on Statistics of Churches, 401 ff. on Evangelicals, 437 ff. on Lutherans. A few years later, Chicago had 36 German Lutheran churches, 28 of them in the Missouri Synod, 23 Evangelical, and 2 Reformed, while some Germans belonged to the Methodist and other denominations – Albert J. Townshend, 'The Germans in Chicago', *Deutsch-Amerikanische Geschichtsblätter*, XXXII (1932), 114–18. On the Evangelical tradition, see Carl E. Schneider, *The German Church on the American Frontier* (the quotation is on 409).
[2] John Gilmary Shea, *History of the Catholic Church in the United States*, IV 715; *Eleventh Census* Reports on Statistics of Churches, 232. The *Statistical Atlas of the United States*, 1914, has charts showing that in industrial states Roman Catholics were from nearly one-half to nearly three-quarters of all affiliated to churches.
[3] Robert H. Lord, J. E. Sexton and E. T. Harrington, *History of the Archdiocese of Boston*, II 52–6; John Rothensteiner, *History of the Archdiocese of St Louis*, 50–58, 92–3.
[4] Shea, *op. cit.*, III 117–19, 156–9, 180–81, 201, 337–8, 387, 605; IV 127, 129, 160–61, 170–71, 238. Rothensteiner, *op. cit.*, 226–37; James H. Moynihan, *Life of Archbishop John Ireland*, 2–3. See also the reports on Chicago and Milwaukee dioceses in John T. Ellis, *Documents of American Catholic History*, 300–301, 357–67. Priests had to carry with them everything they needed for Mass.

from Episcopalians, Congregationalists, Unitarians, Baptists, Methodists, or Universalists, who were acquiring grander premises, moving to suburbs, or abandoning independent existence.[1] Only at that stage were resident priests likely to become established. Then, from the middle of the century, parishes were multiplied, as population poured into mill towns, or Boston, or St Louis. The city of Boston had sixteen parishes in 1866, fifty-one in 1907.[2] In much of New England, the major effort was directed towards catering for the Irish, but priests were secured from Quebec to set up churches for French-Canadian immigrants, so that by the 1890s there were more than eighty such parishes.[3] In Cincinnati and St Louis, much of the work had to be directed towards Germans, persuading religious Orders to send priests from central Europe, or sending experienced men to recruit secular priests or theological students, as did Joseph Melcher in Alsace-Lorraine, Switzerland and Bohemia.[4] Later still, similar measures had to be taken for Italians, Poles, or Portuguese from the Azores, and occasionally an Irish priest, Harkins at Holyoke, O'Reilly at Lawrence, helped in the formation of the new ethnic parishes.[5] Later still, original churches might be enlarged. Then came brick or stone, not only for grandiose cathedrals at Boston, Philadelphia and St Paul, built at vast cost, but for parish churches in such small industrial centres as Naugatuck. By the end of the century, it could almost be taken for granted that a new parish would have such a building from the start.[6]

It was not enough to multiply parishes and erect churches. The entire Church had to be brought to uniform and improved standards of piety and efficiency. Successive Councils of Baltimore not only recommended the creation of new dioceses and proclaimed Catholic doctrine: they expressed the hierarchy's concern for clerical discipline, laying down rules for dress and conduct, prescribing study, examinations, and retreats. Bishops were to control all church property, and were not to permit religious Orders to

[1] Lord, Sexton, Harrington, *op. cit.*, II, has many examples.
[2] Among many examples in the *History of the Archdiocese of Boston,* see II 535–47 on the district around Worcester, Mass., III 251–7 on Roxbury, and 296–308 on Lawrence and Lowell. John H. Lamott, *History of the Archdiocese of Cincinnati*, 126–70, is also useful, and so too is Rothensteiner, *op. cit.*, 681–92.
[3] Lord, Sexton, Harrington, *op. cit.*, III 202–15; but since their treatment contracts as more and more territory is taken from Boston diocese, it is important, for the remainder of New England, to consult Mason Wade, 'The French Parish and *Survivance* in Nineteenth-Century New England', *Catholic Historical Review,* XXXVI (1950–51), 163–89.
[4] Lamott, *op. cit.*, has appendices on the clergy. Rothensteiner, *op. cit.*, 6–15 (Melcher), 731–44 (on the Regulars), is also useful.
[5] Green, *Holyoke*, 334–6; Cole, *op. cit.*, 164.
[6] Lord, Sexton, Harrington, *op. cit.*, III 51–5 (Holy Cross Cathedral, Boston, the debt of $250,000 on which was paid off in less than twenty years); Shea, *op. cit.*, IV 58, 78–9, 468; Moynihan, *op. cit.*, 292; Constance M. Green, *Naugatuck*, 116–17.

become independent in their work. Church services and music were carefully regulated. The laity were encouraged to join societies which would deepen their religious practice. Rules were elaborated for mixed marriages.[1] Again and again the faithful were exhorted, and finally were commanded, to ensure for their children a Catholic education, in parochial schools wherever these could be set up. In 1873 a priest, editor of a Catholic newspaper, introduced a resolution at a meeting of the Irish Catholic Benevolent Union which insisted 'That the present system of public schools, ignoring all supernatural authority and making knowledge the first and God the last thing to be learned, is a curse to our country, and a floodgate of atheism, of sensuality, and of civil, social, and national corruption.' The hierarchy of course chose smoother words, expressing their desire 'that the Catholic youth may be instructed in letters and the noble arts, as well as in religion and sound morals . . . and kept free from that indifferentism which is now so rampant.' As far as their resources permitted, dioceses put up schools and brought in teaching Orders. Even if a full parochial system could not be launched, it was necessary to take a firm stand against the practices of a watered-down Protestantism, which were likely to be imposed in the public schools on all pupils, regardless of their family's faith.[2]

The Catholic history of western New York shows the entire development from frontier conditions to massive stability.[3] About 1820, priests were travelling from one settlement to another, officiating in courthouses and schools, and using local newspapers to announce their coming. After a few years, a permanent church was established at Rochester, and a little later, with the priest as an original member, a Hibernian Society was founded, to collect funds to relieve the poor and to care for orphans. When it was decided to build a new and bigger church, the priest hired waggon and driver, made a fund-raising tour as far as the Pennsylvania border, and himself contributed a year's stipend to the cause. While this was going on, a Methodist chapel was bought, to serve as a second church for the Irish, while for the Germans a brick building, probably a warehouse, was bought and converted, money coming partly from collections, partly from a mortgage on the property, partly in the form of a loan from a local Irishman. Help in paying off these debts was received from the Leopold Foundation in Europe.

---

[1] Peter Guilday, *A History of the Councils of Baltimore*. Lord, Sexton, Harrington, *op. cit.*, II 306–7, 430–31; III 25, 336–42, 383, 521–3, 541–7, shows diocesan practice.
[2] Joan M. Donohoe, *The Irish Catholic Benevolent Union*, 33. Frederick J. Zwierlein, *Life and Letters of Bishop McQuaid*, esp. chapter xxxii, has much evidence. See also Lord, Sexton, Harrington, *op. cit.*, II 582–606, 614–23, III 81–3, 114–29, 346–57; and Timothy L. Smith, 'Protestant Schooling and American Nationality 1800–1850', *Journal of American History*, LIII (1966–7), 679–95.
[3] Zwierlein, *op. cit.*, I: almost the entire volume deals with the early diocesan history of Rochester.

Current expenses, however, were met in the parishes. Pew-rents and collections provided the priest's stipend. Parishioners gave him firewood and vegetables, and contributed candles and other minor church equipment. A society was organized, whose members pledged themselves both to regular religious observances and to teaching in Sunday schools. A burial-ground was acquired, its $10 lots to be purchased by instalments, and soon the Germans had one of their own, on land given them by a farmer. In the 1840s, a loan of $2,000 from a bank enabled a second German church to be built. During that decade, too, the trustee controversy was finally settled in favour of clerical control of property, and strenuous efforts were made to start parochial schools.

By 1847, there were enough Catholics in the region to justify founding the diocese of Buffalo. One of the new bishop's first acts was to tour his territory. In several places he was able to hear confessions and celebrate Mass in churches, the one at Watkins Glen being a former Presbyterian place of worship, though elsewhere he used halls or private homes. During the years that followed, Rochester continued to raise funds for its local needs, contributed money for Buffalo's cathedral, and sent funds to relieve an Irish famine in 1863. The means used included shilling lectures, concerts and festivals, and church picnics which featured bands, races, and such competitions as climbing a greasy pole and chasing a shaved pig. The city's Catholics had societies which collected money and groceries for the poor. An orphanage was established and supported in the same way, the proceeds of a 'fair' greatly exceeding the modest subsidy paid it from the public school fund.

When Rochester received a bishop of its own in 1868, the city had ten Catholic churches and the same number of parochial schools, though only about 2,500 pupils attended them. Bishop McQuaid built a cathedral, and in the early 1880s launched a campaign to pay off its debt. Teams of collectors were organized, who tried to obtain weekly contributions of not less than ten cents. A year of such work raised $9,000. At this point, fifty-seven of the more prosperous Catholics pledged the sum of $25,000, if the remainder could raise a further $7,000, and in the second year of the campaign this was achieved. The bishop's other concern was education. After the injunction on this subject from the second Plenary Council of Baltimore had been reinforced by an instruction from Congregation of Holy Office in 1875, McQuaid issued a pastoral in 1878. Public schools, he insisted, could have no true religion: they were either Protestant or godless, their teachers drawn from any sects or none. Parents, of course, were under an obligation to teach their children the true faith, but the clergy could not escape their

25   Orchard Street, New York City, early twentieth century
Photograph by Lewis Hine, George Eastman House Collection.

26 Meal in a tenement, early twentieth century
Photograph by Lewis Hine, George Eastman House Collection

responsibility for watching the public schools for offensive practices as long as Catholic children had to attend them, and of bringing all such children into parochial schools as quickly as possible. Such a programme, in turn, necessitated recruiting men and women from Orders, then providing them with houses where they could live under their chosen discipline.

Everywhere, Catholics fought hard to secure the right to minister to the inmates of state institutions – soldiers' homes, orphanages, hospitals and the like – but they set up many such institutions of their own.[1] By 1880, for example, Philadelphia had two cemeteries, two hospitals and five orphanages, and at about the same date Boston had a hospital and three homes for various categories of children in need.[2] There and in many other places, charity of a more intimate, house-to-house kind was the speciality of the St Vincent de Paul Society.[3] To expand such activities, as well as build churches and train priests, imposed a gigantic burden on a laity overwhelmingly working-class, struggling at one and the same time to make a living, acquire houses, raise families, and save to bring relatives from Europe. Yet nowhere did the Catholic Church wait for its members to make good. Instead, projects were pushed forward, debts were incurred, and priests were then expected to make all necessary efforts to pay them off.

The parish was intended to become the centre of immigrants' life, and the Church early resolved to duplicate every institution of American society by some organization under its own control – in modern times all the way to Foresters and Boy Scouts.[4] A few examples may be given, from Polish communities. At New Britain, Connecticut, a priest first celebrated Mass for Poles in 1894, in an Irish church. A year later, the Poles had a wooden building of their own. By 1902 this had become the rectory and school, while a new church had been put up, costing no less than $150,000. By 1920 there were some 9,000 people in the parish, which was equipped with cemetery, orphanage, building societies and savings banks, cooperative workshop and printing office, as well as a school with an enrolment of 1,700 children and a house for the nuns who taught them. In a larger city, a Catholic parish could show an even greater complexity. At St Stanislaus Kostka, Chicago, in 1920 there were no fewer than seventy-four organizations, for all ages, some purely local, others branches of nation-wide societies. A group of women, for example, pledged themselves to uphold 'the prin-

[1] Zwierlein, *op. cit.*, III, chapters xxxiii and xxxiv; Donohoe, *op. cit.*, 171–207; Lord, Sexton, Harrington, *op. cit.*, II 630–47, III 358–78.
[2] *Tenth Census*, Social Statistics of Cities, I 814–16.
[3] Daniel McColgan, *A Century of Charity: the First Hundred Years of the Society of St Vincent de Paul in the United States;* Ellis, *Documents,* 289–90.
[4] Arthur E. Wood, *Hamtranck Then and Now,* 191, 238–40; priests even prevented the building of a Y.M.C.A. after a business corporation had given the land.
16

ciples of the Roman Catholic faith and national traditions' and to practise 'mutual aid and material assistance'. They took Communion together at Easter and on the Feast of the Immaculate Conception. When a member died, a sum of $75 was paid for funeral expenses, the society ordered a Mass, and all attended, hiring coaches or cars and guaranteeing $10 worth of flowers. In the same parish, thirty altar boys were uniformed as Papal Guards, to stand at Christ's grave at Easter, and take part in processions.[1]

Numerically, the Orthodox Church was far less important, but it had the loyalty of many members of the Greek and other Balkan communities, and of the handful of Russians. Like the adherents of other faiths, these people wished to preserve the special traditions in which they had grown up: the procession on Good Friday with a bier decorated with flowers, Saturday night Mass with the priest lighting worshippers' candles while all cried 'Truly He is risen', and the ceremonial breakfast of lamb stew, salad, cakes and eggs dyed red, to mark the end of Lent. Organization, however, proved hard. As soon as Greeks were in settled jobs, they were likely to launch a society to raise funds for a church, and to bring a priest from the old country. By 1910 there were some twenty organizations of this kind. But it was difficult to guarantee the priests' quality; factions often sprang up, representing different Greek villages; and from the time of the Great War the Orthodox Church was as much disturbed by dissensions based on old-country politics as was every other American Greek institution.[2]

It was not only Christians who faced problems of religious organization, conflicts of doctrine and loyalty, in the new American environment. In Chicago, Jews celebrated the Day of Atonement as early as 1845, in a room over a store. Next year they bought a burial ground, and six years later they had a synagogue (a frame building) and a benefit society. These were Jews from German states. Very soon Polish Jews started a distinct organization, and later still, Jews from Bohemia, Latvia and Hungary did the same. In New York City, for similar reasons, there were twenty-seven synagogues by 1860. The Jewish community's leaders were still German in origin, in New York as elsewhere. As the nineteenth century advanced, these people became prosperous, respectable, but also modernized in their Judaism, americanized as it were, with music, sermon, and Sunday services. The Reform movement brought in learned rabbis from Europe, paid them high salaries, and established them in fine buildings. In 1890 there were more members of Reform than of Orthodox congregations, and, although their

---

[1] Park and Miller, op. cit., 213–18.
[2] Saloutos, op. cit., 75–7, 83–5, 105, 245–56; W. Lloyd Warner and Leo Srole, *Social Systems of American Ethnic Groups*, 167, 176–92, gives a local example.

congregations were fewer, the former had more permanent buildings and their property was worth more than twice as much. Significantly, while no state had more than one-eighth of the Reform groups, almost half the Orthodox were in New York, and more than two-thirds in five industrial states.[1]

As early as 1869 in Rochester, an Orthodox synagogue came into existence in protest against the Reform development, and in the 1880s began the influx of Russian Jews. Some of these were devoted to Socialism rather than the traditional religion, and because of the pressures of economic life in America, even the Orthodox could not reproduce in their new home every detail of worship and study and Sabbath observance which had characterized the *shtetl*. They did their best, however, to build up familiar institutions They hired rooms over stores and workshops. At Holyoke a group of them bought a building from the French-Canadian society of St Jean Baptiste. At New Haven they took over a Negro church; in Brooklyn they acquired what had once been a farmhouse. Much later, a congregation at Newton, a Boston suburb, which happened to include carpenters and masons, built a synagogue for themselves.[2] Older men sometimes attended daily services. For most, the Sabbath was the time, not only of a ritual family meal but of services, the men in street hats and prayer shawls, going up to read from the raised platform, auctioning off the privilege of taking the most important passages, escorting each scroll back to the Ark. Chanting was done with bodies swaying. Women and girls were segregated, in a gallery if the design of the building permitted. Conversation, even family visiting, were likely to occur during service. Weddings were even more colourful, with procession, an embroidered velvet canopy held over bride and groom, an intoned service, the sipping of wine by the couple, and the grinding of the glass underfoot, all followed by dancing and lavish feasting.[3] To recall such details from contemporary descriptions, however, is to run the risk of exaggerating the scale of the congregations. Most of these were in fact associated with

[1] Wirth, *The Ghetto*, 157–87; Ernst, *Immigrant Life in New York City*, 137–8; *Eleventh Census*, Report on Statistics of Churches, 415–17; and, for background, Oscar Handlin, *Adventure in Freedom* and Moses Rischin, *The Promised City*. The Social Statistics of Cities volumes of the *Tenth Census* show that by 1880 New York City had six Jewish burial grounds, New Orleans four, and Philadelphia two. Cincinnati's cemetery had separate sections for three congregations, while Cleveland's five burial grounds included Hungarian, Austrian and Prussian, so named – I 587, 831, II 279, 368–9, 383–4, 587, 672.

[2] McKelvey, *Rochester: the Flower City*, 169–70; Green, *Holyoke*, 359–60; Rollin Osterweis, *Three Centuries of New Haven*, 340–41; Alfred Kazin, *A Walker in the City*, 44–6; Albert I. Gordon, *Jews in Suburbia*, 106–7.

[3] Woods, *Americans in Process*, 241–3, 279–80; S. N. Behrman, *The Worcester Account*, 147, 164–5; Samuel Chotzinoff, *A Lost Paradise*, 73–4, 152–6. Marshall Sklare, *Conservative Judaism*, 91–3, notes the attempt of that group to ensure decorum in services, in open reaction against the older tradition.

one place in eastern Europe: every member was a *lantsman*. By 1920, Manhattan had nearly 600 of them: a single area of twenty blocks of the Lower East Side had sixty. To each of them, the next synagogue had about it something alien – the people were outsiders, with strange accents and uncouth habits, like the Galicians who, as every Russian Jew was sure, 'had no taste, took cream with herrings.'[1]

III

Analysis of ethnic institutions in terms of the needs they served has value, but cannot convey the whole truth. It is now time to focus our attention on places of various sizes, so as to see what an immigrant community looked like as a whole.

In the Middle West and Texas, Germans had a few small towns virtually to themselves. Such was Hermann, Missouri, founded as a self-consciously German colony, though it never grew as its promoters had hoped. It could show a Lutheran church, a Catholic church, a German-language school, and a Freethinker newspaper, and held a *weinfest*, all before it had 1,500 inhabitants, though to be sure it served a surrounding agricultural district.[2] Germans were also prominent in big cities of the Middle West. In the 1840s, Milwaukee's Germans already had two newspapers, a benefit club, a school, a fire company, a beer garden, a Roman Catholic church, two Lutheran churches affiliated to different synods, a Freethinker organization, and music clubs which became federated in 1850. In the following decade came operas and plays in German, a *Turnverein*, and more Freethinker bodies. A May Festival was held in 1852. The victories of 1870 were celebrated, though Germans also observed the Fourth of July, and their volunteer companies fought in America's wars. German doctors organized as early as 1853. During the 1880s the large German community, which had already produced many office-holders, became more sensitive to hostile forces, and especially to the campaign against their language in schools. They founded a German Society in 1882, and paraded for a German Day in 1890, as gestures of solidarity. Theatres and newspapers continued to flourish until the end of the nineteenth century.[3] Very similar features appear at St Louis. The variety of institutions can be seen from even the most superficial study of the biographies of successful Germans, though no doubt men in that category were rather more likely than their humbler neighbours to be 'joiners'.

[1] Park and Miller, *op. cit.*, map on 201, 206–7; Kazin, *op. cit.*, 44–6.
[2] John A. Hawgood, *The Tragedy of German-America*, 115–24.
[3] Still, *Milwaukee*, 68, 79–80, 89–92, 115–30, 157–8, 225, 259–65.

John C. Biensieck, who ran livery stables and had fought in the Civil War, sat on the city council and was a member of the Grand Army of the Republic, the *Turnverein*, the Sons of Hermann, and the Sharpshooters. Mathias Herman, an undertaker, was a Roman Catholic, a member of three choral societies and of the Order of Harugari, and despite his faith, of the *Turnverein* as well. Gottlieb Neumeister, a contractor, was in the G.A.R. and *Turnverein*, was a member of a music society, and joined the mysteriously named 'Church of the Society of Practical Christianity'.[1]

Down to the 1880s, the Jewish community of New York City, led by men of German origin, spent lavishly to found hospitals and charitable institutions, like the United Hebrew Charities in the depression year of 1874. Their work was then greatly complicated by the arrival of large numbers from Russia, different both in the character of their Judaism and in their standard of living. The feelings of the older-established were far from purely welcoming, but they put forth a massive effort to found the Hebrew Immigrant Aid Society, the Educational Alliance, probation and prisoners' aid societies, and to operate the Baron de Hirsch Fund. The Alliance's gymnasia, showers, classrooms and meeting-rooms for societies were so much used that 'within twenty years . . . the marble steps were worn so thin that they had to be replaced.'

The life of the man who wrote those words illustrates very clearly the community's change in direction. Philip Cowen was born in New York City in 1853, son of a tailor from Prussia who had anglicized his name. Most of his friends had done the same, unless they bore such Sephardic names as de Sola Mendes or da Silva Solis. As a boy, he left the Lower East Side for Third Avenue north of 30th Street, the family's old neighbours thinking that 'we were going into the wilds'. After dabbling in several lines of business, Cowen launched in 1879 the *American Hebrew*. Apart from a few Hebrew literary items, the paper was in English, and aimed at a very serious tone. In the 1890s, Cowen moved to the Bronx. But by that time his life was becoming dominated by the problems of Russian Jews. He took part in charitable work and visited Castle Garden to give advice. From 1905 to 1927 he worked in the Immigration Service, visiting Russia in 1907 to report on *pogroms* and other conditions that lay behind the exodus.[2]

The new arrivals, however, were not content to be objects of charity, the source of which they distrusted as too American, imperfectly Jewish, almost alien. They preferred to rely on local benefit societies, though these were more clearly separated from the synagogue than had been the case in

---

[1] Walter B. Stevens, *St Louis, the Fourth City*: examples from his two biographical volumes.
[2] Cowen, *Memories of an American Jew* (the quotation is on 92).

the *shtetl*. In 1890 they formed the Hebrew Sheltering Society, in 1892 a loan society to help people set up in trades, then dispensaries and hospitals. More than 300 schools came into existence, most of them for part-time instruction in Hebrew, though the Orthodox found attendance disappointingly small. It must not be thought, however, that this old-style Judaism was the community's only strand of thought. Socialism, which was strong among Jews in Russia, flourished in the garment trades of New York, and by the early twentieth century such Jews were celebrating May Day, the French Revolution and the Paris Commune, the anniversary of the assassination of Alexander II, as well as Labor Day and the Fourth of July.[1]

Few ethnic communities existed in isolation, and many towns lacked a single dominant group.

Although Lowell, Lawrence and Fall River were far bigger and more famous, the diversity of ethnic groups in New England mill towns is almost as striking in Holyoke, Massachusetts. Its industrial plant was built by Irish workers in the middle of the nineteenth century, and soon after the state census of 1855 had recorded 1,657 Irish-born in the town, a Roman Catholic parish was organized. Just before the Civil War, French-Canadians began to arrive, and a few Germans came in after peace had returned. About 1870, when the population was half foreign, Irish, French-Canadians and Germans all had societies; the Germans had a Lutheran church; a French-Canadian parish had just been set up; and there was one parochial school. In 1873 came a Catholic hospital and an orphanage. By 1890 there were four parochial schools, one of them French, corresponding to the number of parishes which then existed. Within another fifteen years came two more French-Canadian parishes, a Polish parish with school, two Catholic high schools, a second Lutheran church, and two synagogues. During the Great War a Greek Orthodox church came into being. By that time, in round figures, there were 8,000 French-Canadians, 5,000 Irish, 4,000 born in Germany and Austria, 3,000 British, 1,700 born in Russia and Poland, and 1,400 from other foreign countries – and there were another 25,000 people of foreign or mixed parentage.[2]

---

[1] Rischin, *op. cit.*, 98–108, 148–68. The extraordinary proliferation of Jewish institutions is illustrated by figures compiled in 1921 – Breckinridge, *New Homes for Old*, 217, 313–32. Counting national organizations only, Lithuanians had 13, Czechs 12, Finns 11, Slovaks and Germans 8 each, Italians only 2. The Jews had no fewer than 86, linking people within a profession, organizing charities in America, fund-raising for Jews overseas; and many of them were for women.

[2] Green, *Holyoke* (population figures are summarized on 367–8). By the time of the Great War, Lawrence had its calendar marked not only by numerous Saints' Days, but by the birthdays of Robert Burns, Robert Emmet, von Humboldt and Schiller, and by commemorations of the Battle of the Boyne, the Polish Revolution, and the Armenian massacres – Cole, *Immigrant City*, 144–5 note.

In Pennsylvania, the small iron and steel centre of Johnstown deserves notice. By the first years of the twentieth century, the British, Irish and Germans were declining in numbers, though their second and third generations kept some interest in churches, societies and the surviving German newspaper. Italian-born inhabitants, on the other hand, increased in number from 400 to nearly 2,000 in the decade before 1910, and this figure understates the true number of individuals, when they arrived and went home and returned again so readily. Halfway through the period they established a church, in 1908 a newspaper, then a benefit society. There were very few people described as Russian-born, but Austrian-born grew from 923 to 4,736, and Hungarian-born from 2,017 to 4,563. A Roman Catholic church for Poles (presumably from Galicia) dated from 1900 and a benefit society from 1908. Magyars, Croats and Slovaks, however, contributed most of the institutions. The Slovaks had a Greek Catholic (Uniate) church in 1895 and another in 1908, a Roman Catholic church in 1902 and a Lutheran in 1903, as well as two benefit clubs which cannot be dated exactly. Croats had an Orthodox church in 1902 (perhaps they were really Serbs who had lived in Croatia-Slavonia), a Roman Catholic in 1903 and, surprisingly, a Greek Catholic in 1907, in addition to a political and social organization and two benefit clubs. Magyars had a Roman Catholic church in 1901 and a Reformed church two years later, three benefit clubs, and a music society.[1]

Rochester was a much bigger city with a far more diversified economy. As in most places, the earliest foreign groups were Irish and Germans. In the 1820s the former had a parish, in the 1830s the latter. A Lutheran church was set up in the 1830s, then a second Catholic parish and before the middle of the century a Reformed church. By the 1850s there were Catholic schools and academies, German Protestant schools, and a German newspaper. Soon after the Civil War, Rochester had seven Irish and five German Catholic schools and three for German Protestants, and another school was run by a rabbi. There was a French-Canadian parish, a Dutch Reformed church, a Reform synagogue, and a more Orthodox German synagogue, and in 1879 Russian Jews founded yet another. There were benefit societies and German music societies, and within a few years appeared both Catholic and Jewish orphanages. By 1890, a Polish parish existed, and an Italian club. The Germans had three newspapers (one of them specifically Roman

---

[1] *Twelfth Census*, Population, I 796–9; *Abstract of Thirteenth Census*, 213; *61 Congress 2 Session, Senate Doc. 633*, Immigration Commission Reports, Immigrants in Industries, Pt. 2, Iron and Steel, I 453, 468–71. Emily G. Balch, *Our Slavic Fellow Citizens*, facing 389, has photographs showing styles of church architecture ranging from New England traditional to unmistakably Slavonic, all the way, as it were, from Concord to the Kremlin.

Catholic). The Protestant schools had by that time closed. The German-born in the city numbered more than 17,000, there were more than 6,000 each Irish and Canadians, nearly 6,000 British, and some 1,500 Russian and Polish Jews, as well as another thousand Europeans of diverse national origins. German institutions continued to flourish, and even expand, down to the Great War, though, interestingly enough, the *Turnhalle* was sold to Italians. The Irish community was showing signs of decline, even the St Patrick's Day parade having been abandoned. By 1915, to select one more date, there were three Dutch churches and two Swedish, several Swiss clubs, at least eleven synagogues, two Jewish schools, a library, a home for the aged, several societies, and the Associated Hebrew Charities, all for no more than 10,000 Jews. The Poles had a parochial school, and branches of the National Alliance and the Socialist Alliance. Lithuanians had a church and club; Ruthenians had a Greek Catholic church; the Italians had a newspaper and fifteen clubs.[1]

Ethnic communities living thus side by side displayed differences of style. Descriptions of Boston's Italians about 1900 make much of their street life and their fondness for picnics in public parks. Their Jewish neighbours lived much more at home. Although the synagogue had its vital place, observers and Jewish writers alike dwell on the domestic Sabbath, with its traditional food and wine, and its fine candlesticks which even poor families were likely to have brought with them across the ocean. Such a description could quite naturally begin with the words: 'By sundown the streets were empty, the curtains had been drawn, the world put to rights,' though of course the participants were conscious of sharing the same ritual and the same ideas with Jews in homes throughout the world.[2]

There were differences of interest too, however similar the environment of several groups, and however much we may assign them all the role of victims of America's industrial growth. Competition for jobs played its part, as when Finnish miners clashed with Irish or Cornish. So did religious prejudice, as when French-Canadian newspapers launched attacks on Jews. Most old-established groups disliked Chinese and Japanese, and in California Irish labour leaders were prominent in the attack. Irish and English clashed over policies in the British Isles, and so did northern and southern Irish over religion. The Irish, indeed, were very often involved. As the nineteenth-century's first-comers to many parts of America, they wished to defend their gains, but because they had such a prominent role in politics

[1] Apart from the Censuses, see McKelvey, *op. cit.*, 39,150, 168–70, 276, 304, and his subsequent volume on Rochester, *The Quest for Quality*, 115–18, 146–56.
[2] Woods, *Americans in Process*, 224–44.

and the public services, they could attract the hostility of later arrivals, Germans, French-Canadians, Poles and others.[1]

IV

Nor was an ethnic group at all certain to be united within itself. On the contrary, striking examples can be found of competition between leaders and organizations. In particular, the ethnic church, which strove so hard to become the centre of group life, encountered rivals, institutions sometimes parallel, sometimes overlapping, but differing in their sense of priorities, in their interpretation of ethnic identity.

Irish-Americans, overwhelmingly working-class in the early years, were bound to be pursuing several objectives at the same time. They struggled to make a living, pressed for political recognition in an American city, contributed towards the building of their Church, and supported Ireland in its struggle for self-government and land reform.[2] It was not likely that all Irishmen would devote their energies equally between these programmes. Enthusiastic pursuit of one of them might have unfavourable repercussions on another: local political ambitions, for example, might gain from anti-British oratory which other Irish would enjoy, but might suffer if advocacy of violence in Ireland alienated large numbers of other Americans.

The campaign for Irish liberation was itself always divided. Throughout the nineteenth century there was tension between those who favoured constitutional methods and those who, like the Fenians, thought insurrection or terrorism unavoidable. There was tension, too, in the 1880s, between Parnell and his closest followers with their eyes upon Home Rule by Act of Parliament, and Davitt with his emphasis upon land reform as a way of raising the inert masses to united action. Both groups, of course, were interested in both kinds of reform. Priorities, however, were in dispute, and a man's sense of these could change with Irish conditions or British policy. As between Ford and Davitt on one side, Parnell, and O'Donovan Rossa and dynamite, the Irish in America could not easily avoid making a choice.[3]

Almost all Irish-American leaders would have called themselves Catholics. Many, however, were more immediately interested in nationalism than in the growth of the Church, and they were bound to recognize that, in Ireland

[1] Hoglund, *Finnish Immigrants*, 63; Wittke, *Irish in America*, 183–92; Cole, *op. cit.*, 88–91.
[2] Thomas N. Brown, *Irish-American Nationalism*, is an excellent pioneering work, regrettably brief. See also Geoffrey Blodgett, *The Gentle Reformers: Massachusetts Democrats in the Cleveland Era*, esp. 141–71.
[3] In addition to Brown, *op. cit.*, see William D'Arcy, *The Fenian Movement in the United States 1858–1886* Michael Davitt, *The Fall of Feudalism in Ireland*; Conor Cruise O'Brien, *Parnell and his Party 1880–90*.

and America alike, the Church's attitude to their cause was ambiguous. Greater independence from Protestant England was, indeed, something for which most prelates could feel sympathy. If, however, Home Rule meant the exclusion of Irish Catholic members from the House of Commons, with possible repercussions on Catholic interests in England, they might feel doubts. They felt hostility towards the operation of secret societies, Fenians as much as Freemasons, towards the use of violent methods, and towards threats to traditional doctrines of property. American bishops, after all, questioned not merely Fenians or Molly Maguires, but the Ancient Order of Hibernians and the Knights of Labor and the views of Henry George. Moreover they were sensitive to the danger of taking any stand that would label the Church, in the eyes of a majority of Americans, as dominated by foreign concerns.[1]

Above all, the hierarchy had priorities of their own. Freedom for the Church to function was more vital than the achievement of any particular political or economic reform. Protestant proselytizing was more dangerous than colonial oppression. Systems of self-government mattered less than an educational system fully under Church control, with bishops appointing teachers of Catholics, and prescribing books.[2] The Church felt itself less menaced by political hostility than by the ideological threats of the nineteenth century, the threats denounced in the Syllabus of Errors. Prelates were conscious of the need to stand firm against change. When Bishop Williams of Boston preached his last sermon before going to the Vatican Council in 1869, he felt able to say:

> This Council will give nothing new. If it gives us new articles of faith, it will only give us what has been believed from the beginning. We expect nothing new. The Holy Father shall rise and speak in the name of the Holy Ghost, and declare the belief of the Church. God will speak through him, and deliver to His people His eternal truths.[3]

Many possibilities of conflict therefore existed. Leaders of labour unions defended secret rituals as essential in a period of highly unequal struggle for recognition. Irish M.P.s openly resented the Curia's intervention against the boycott as a method in the struggle for land, and against the subscription

[1] Zwierlein, *McQuaid*, II chapters xxiv, xxviii, III chapter xxix, presents conservative views on secret societies and property. See also Henry J. Browne, *The Catholic Church and the Knights of Labor*.
[2] In addition to Guilday's summaries of decisions of successive Councils of Baltimore, see for the views of the hierarchy in Ireland, Donald H. Akenson, *The Irish Education Experiment*, esp. 99–101, 202–14, 250–74, 301–10, and Edward R. Norman, *The Catholic Church and Ireland in the Age of Rebellion 1859–1873*.
[3] Quoted in Lord, Sexton, Harrington, *op. cit.*, III 32–3.

for Parnell, arguing that the issue was political rather than a matter of faith and morals. This tension can be seen, too, in the Ireland of the 1840s, when the *Nation*, organ of Young Ireland, pleaded for a 'nationality which may embrace Protestant, Catholic, Dissenter, Milesian or Cromwellian,' and when the same paper supported the Queen's Colleges as essential to the development of an enlightened Catholic middle class. Looking back, Davitt bitterly condemned the quietism of priests during the Famine.[1] From all these examples, a nationalist current of opinion may be detected, about which the Catholic hierarchy felt serious doubts. It is scarcely too much to say that, against this current, Cullen in Ireland and McQuaid and Corrigan in America took up a recognizably similar stand.

Polish-America too saw a development of distinct and to some extent conflicting nation-wide institutions. Like the Irish, the Poles were concerned both with their development as a group in America and with the fate of a people in Europe, living under foreign rule. The early history of St Stanislaus Kostka parish, Chicago, whose activities in modern times have already been described, reveals a split between benefit society and ethnic church on the one hand, and an exclusively nationalist group on the other, which hastened to set up a separate church and for many years fought for lay control of property and funds. A modern scholar very fairly describes these events as meaning 'Polish Catholics battling Catholic Poles'. By 1880 there existed two organizations which sought to promote these distinct viewpoints throughout Polish-America. The Polish Roman Catholic Union in America was devoted to parochial schools, hospitals, orphanages, and so on, and because of its parochial orientation thought more of America than of the old country's political struggles. The Polish National Alliance looked more towards European events and towards Polish culture, less towards the Catholic Church. But all this was a matter of priorities, not of exclusive interests. Both organizations had big educational programmes, and ran insurance schemes, and neither opposed American citizenship.[2]

Catholicism with an ethnic emphasis versus extreme patriotism was not the only possible clash within an ethnic community. Among the Germans there was a current of thought aggressively hostile to all churches. As early as 1854, at Cincinnati, there assembled a congress of Freethinkers, which passed resolutions condemning legal oaths, Sunday-closing laws, religious exercises in public schools, slavery, and capital punishment, and supporting

[1] Gavin Duffy, *Young Ireland*, 80, 684 ff.; Davitt, *op. cit.*, 47 ff., 397–408.
[2] Victor R. Greene, 'For God and Country: the Origins of Slavic Catholic Self-Consciousness in America', *Church History*, XXXV (1966), 448–56 on Poles, and 457–9 for rather similar tensions among Lithuanians, Slovaks, Croats and Slovenes; Joseph A. Wytrwal, *America's Polish Heritage*, esp. chapters vii and viii.

homesteads and inheritance taxes. Longer-lasting, and prominent in most German communities, was the Turner movement. In Europe, this had been a Liberal and Romantic, as well as a nationalist movement, much given to poetry about freedom and the horrors of persecution and spies. In the American environment, it stood for physical fitness, for pride in German culture, and against Nativism, Prohibition, and slavery. A report of a spring festival at Jamaica Plain on Long Island shows them engaged in singing, gymnastics, feasting, and speech-making, and the description of the beauty of the scene and of the warmth of human joy ended with the words: 'What hopes crossed my mind at the sight of the charming green of the forest, only a German heart can fathom.' The Turners' halls could be found in every large city. Many of the members enlisted in the Union army, and the only part of Chicago's *Turnhalle* to escape the 1871 fire was a memorial, topped by an eagle and dipped flags, which classified members' names as '*Gefallen auf dem Schlachtfelde*', '*In Gefangenschaft zu Andersonville gestorben*', and '*Ertrunken*', the last-named being two soldiers and two sailors lost in the Ohio and Mississippi.[1]

In yet another group, conflicts derived from differences over degrees of americanization, and from political battles in the old country. The Panhellenic Union of 1907 tried to keep people Greek, to mobilize men for military service in campaigns to liberate fellow-Greeks from Turkish oppression – in short, it regarded Greeks as being only temporarily in America. On the other hand, the newspaper *Atlantis* strove to foster adjustment to American life. During the Great War, all this was overshadowed by the controversy between Royalists and Venizelists. As one regime succeeded another in the old country, as faith in the intentions of the Allies rose and fell, newspapers took sides, churches were split, and meetings dissolved in violence. With the republic firmly established, something like the earlier conflict reasserted itself. Early in the 1920s, the American Hellenic Educational Progressive Association and the Greek American Progressive Association were founded, the first a middle-class fraternal organization looking towards the wider American community, the latter more working-class, more purely Greek, placing more emphasis upon language and the Orthodox Church.[2]

V

So powerful were the tensions just described that, towards the end of the

---

[1] Adolf E. Zucker, *The Forty-Eighters*, 82–90, 97; Daniels, *America via the Neighborhood*, 140; and for background, Carl Wittke, *Refugees of Revolution*, 122–88.
[2] Theodore Saloutos, *Greeks in the United States*, 98–104, chapters vii to x, 246–56.

nineteenth century, the unity of the most disciplined of churches was disturbed.

Observers of Italian life in New York and Chicago often described the institution of the *Festa*. Electric lights were festooned across the streets, arches were put up, flags were draped across the front of buildings, concessions were sold for the privilege of having booths on the sidewalk. A special Mass was paid for, and people brought candles or plaques in token of gratitude for favours from their saint, or brought waxen images of bodily parts that had been healed. A procession, led by a priest, centred upon the saint's shrine, carried, then lowered from time to time so that children could kiss the image, and sometimes a blind child would ride for a few yards in the hope of a miracle. Finally, in one version, two children dressed as angels, and carrying armfuls of flowers, were slung on ropes to a position just above the shrine, where they chanted a long prayer. Elsewhere, festivities ended with a firework display. The atmosphere was very like that of the mountain festival in southern Italy, described by Norman Douglas. Based on an association related to a village in the old country, and designed to raise funds for it, the ceremonies appear to demonstrate a perfect blending of self-help, a very local patriotism, and the practices of traditional religion.[1]

On the contrary, many Italian men went to Mass at no other time. Many Italians felt that the Church was indifferent to their needs. The hierarchy did something for them, but they were reluctant to single out a new group for special treatment, or to seem to be building up the foreign-ness of a group of Catholics.[2] This attitude reflected, in large measure, sensitiveness to a wider crisis, in which Germans, Poles and Lithuanians were more prominent than Italians themselves.

For much of the nineteenth century, Germans were the second largest Catholic group in America. By their own efforts, supplemented by aid from the Leopold Foundation in Austria and the Ludwig Society of Bavaria, they built up parishes and related institutions. As early as 1847, the German Catholics of Chicago were asking for a coadjutor bishop of their own nationality, though their diocese was no more than three years old.[3] A few decades later, a much wider conflict broke out, largely as an expression of German resentment towards what they deemed an Irish-dominated Church.

[1] Park and Miller, *op. cit.*, 154–5; W.P.A., *Italians of New York,* 86–91. Compare, Norman Douglas, *Old Calabria,* chapter xx, and Louise Caico, *Sicilian Days and Ways,* 60–115.
[2] Rudolph J. Vecoli, 'Peasants and Prelates: Italian Immigrants and the Catholic Church', *Journal of Social History,* II (1968–9), 217–68. A Bostonian acquaintance once expressed this to me differently, by saying that the local Irish always thought Catholicism too good for the Italians.
[3] Bessie L. Pierce, *History of Chicago,* I 242. Beyond that, it is enough to cite Benjamin J. Blied, *Austrian Aid to American Catholics 1830–60* and Emmett H. Rothan, *The German Catholic Immigrant in the United States 1830–1860.*

Their views had some basis in fact. Of 210 bishops appointed before 1900, 174 were of foreign birth or recognizably foreign parentage. Ninety-nine of these were certainly Irish, thirty-five French or French-Canadian, and eight Belgian. Only nine were German, seven Austrian and four Swiss.[1] Analysis of the rank-and-file clergy in Boston archdiocese would produce rather similar results, though in St Louis and Cincinnati Germans were far better represented in the lower ranks.

In 1883, there visited the United States a German businessman, Peter Paul Cahensly, who had helped form both the *St Raphaelsverein* for the protection of German emigrants, and *Katholikentagen*, conferences of clergy and laity. Soon after his visit, a Catholic newspaper at St Louis began urging German parochial autonomy. By 1887 a German priests' association was in existence, and a German-American Catholic congress was being discussed. While some bishops viewed these trends with sympathy, Ireland of St Paul condemned them as separatist and hostile to true authority. In 1891 the *St Raphaelsverein* petitioned the Pope. They complained of neglect of immigrants' interests in America. They asked for more ethnic parishes, more priests speaking the appropriate languages, and seminaries in Europe to train them. They argued for bishops to lead each ethnic group. Ireland at once condemned this as 'German foreignism', and the Pope soon came to agree with the American hierarchy in its opposition to this type of federal structure for the Church. But because of a more general controversy over the degree to which the Church should merge itself in American society – in which Archbishop Ireland stood on the side of more assimilation – Catholicism in America remained disturbed for some years. Some separation was held essential if the Church was to maintain the institutions and practices called for by its dogmas, but there was little willingness to invite Protestant attack by stressing the appearance of being foreign. Small Polish and Lithuanian secessions took place, to found National Catholic Churches, but no wider disruption occurred.[2]

[1] My own computation from Joseph B. Code, *Dictionary of the American Hierarchy*.
[2] Documents are in Ellis, *op. cit.*, 476–9, 495–507, 533–43. The narrative is well presented in two articles by John J. Meng, 'Cahenslyism: the First Stage 1883–91', and 'Cahenslyism: the Second Chapter 1891–1910', *Catholic Historical Review*, XXXI (1945–6), 389–413, and XXXII (1946–7), 302–40. For the wider controversy about 'Americanism', see Thomas T. McAvoy, *The Americanist Heresy in American Catholicism*.

CHAPTER ELEVEN

Immigrants and Native Americans

Go and see in our public schools the children of German, Irish, Bohemian, and Italian parents, waving the Stars and Stripes on the glorious Fourth, and you will fully appreciate the meaning of my statement, that education is solving the problem.

Richard Bartholdt, 19 May 1896, *Congressional Record*, 54 Congress 1 Session, 5422 (House of Representatives).

. . . a large and increasing number of the weak, the broken and the mentally crippled of all races drawn from the lowest stratum of the Mediterranean basin and the Balkans, together with hordes of the wretched, submerged populations of the Polish ghettos. Our jails, insane asylums and almshouses are filled with this human flotsam and the whole tone of American life, social, moral and political has been lowered and vulgarized by them.

Madison Grant, *The Passing of the Great Race* (1916), 89–90.

. . . hirsute, low-browed, big-faced persons of obviously low mentality. Not that they suggest evil. They simply look out of place in black clothes and stiff collar, since clearly they belong in skins, in wattled huts at the close of the Great Ice Age.

Edward A. Ross, *The Old World in the New* (1914), 285–6.

I

Opponents of immigration became vociferous in the second quarter of the nineteenth century. They alleged that newcomers included an unduly high proportion of criminals, that they made excessive claims on charitable institutions, and that they damaged the standard of living of American working men. Since, too, they came from countries where free governments were unknown, they were ignorant as voters, and therefore could easily be manipulated by corrupt politicians. Recent immigrants, the *Native American* said in 1844, 'fill our large cities, reduce the wages of labour, and increase the hardship of the old settler.'[1] In the past, perhaps, immigrants had been men

[1] Quoted in Ray A. Billington, *The Protestant Crusade*, 200; see also 338, quoting *The Republic*, organ of the Order of United Americans, and Roy L. Garis, *Immigration Restriction*, 52–7.

of education, of self-reliance, and of honest purpose, in every way desirable. Now, however, they were 'the ignorant and vicious . . . the outcast tenants of the poorhouses and prisons of Europe.' Very probably they were deliberately exported by their governments 'to our loss and their gain.'[1]

Such attacks gained emotional force when associated with religious prejudice. The United States was at the high point of evangelical Protestant fervour. Yet at the same time, faced with the arrival of Irish and German immigrants, the Roman Catholic church was bound to make strenuous efforts towards expansion of its organization, bound, also, to protect its adherents, in education especially, from contamination by secular or heretical influences. Collision was inevitable, and immigrants became involved in the more general conflict, were accused, indeed, of disloyalty because members of an international church. The citizens of Sutton and Millbury, Massachusetts, who drew up a petition in 1838, invited Congress to inquire 'whether there are not now those amongst us, who, by their oath of allegiance to a foreign despotic Prince or Power, are solemnly bound to support his interests and accelerate his designs.' Washington county petitioned the New York legislature to investigate the work of the Leopold Foundation, which they suspected of working for 'the subversion of our civil and religious liberties'. Immigrants were attacked as part of a general campaign against 'Romish corruptions' and 'monkish traditions', familiar since the Reformation. The horrors of the Inquisition were rehearsed, pornographic pamphlets were circulated against alleged immoralities in convents, and other writings sought to prove the Papacy the Beast of Revelations. A speech delivered at Newark, New Jersey, in 1854 summed up by describing the Church of Rome as 'dripping with the cruelties of millions of murders, and haggard with the debaucheries of a thousand years, always ambitious, always sanguinary, and always false.'[2]

In the 1830s, no-popery activities took the form of petitions, pamphlets, sermons, and a few mob attacks on convents. In the next decade, a Native American Party sought to uphold the Authorized Version of the Bible as a school book, and to make more severe the requirements for naturalization. In the early 1850s, the Know-Nothings exerted much political influence in several states. Their national party platform in 1856 demanded twenty-one years' residence as a condition of naturalization, which in turn was to be the

---

[1] Samuel, Morse *Imminent Dangers to the Free Institutions of the United States* (1835), quoted in Edith Abbott, *Historical Aspects of the Immigration Problem*, 449–52. See also Billington, *op. cit.*, 326, quoting President Fillmore.

[2] Abbott, *op. cit.*, 738–9; Billington, *op. cit.*, 130 – and see also 53–4, 251–2, 266 (the Newark speech), 278, and titles of anti-Catholic works listed in his bibliography. Oscar Handlin, *Boston's Immigrants,* chapter vii, also deals with Nativism in this period.

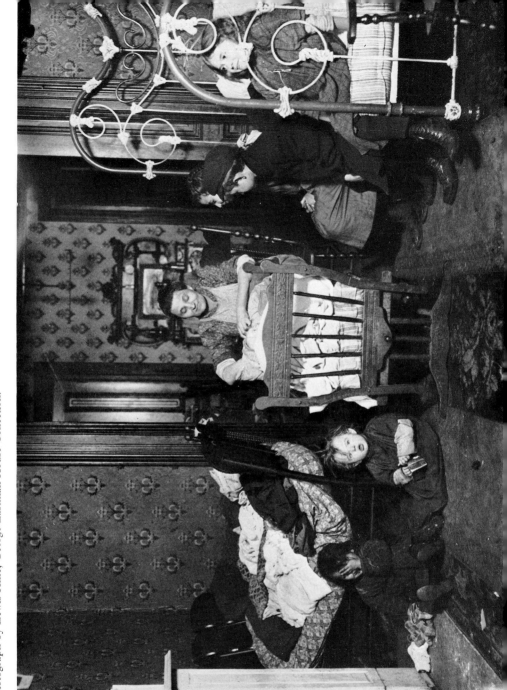

27   Tenement family and their beds, early twentieth century
Photograph by Lewis Hine, George Eastman House Collection.

28a   Washing dishes in a tenement,
early twentieth century
Photograph by Lewis Hine,
George Eastman House
Collection.

28b   Kitchen in a Chicago tenement,
early twentieth century
Photograph by Lewis Hine,
George Eastman House
Collection.

qualification for voting: the slogan was 'Americans must rule America'.[1] The issues the Know-Nothings emphasized, however, were soon overshadowed by Kansas and Nebraska, then by the Civil War itself.

II

Traces of similar arguments can be found in the years after the Civil War, as when Godkin wrote in the *Nation*, 1866, of people 'ignorant, credulous, newly emancipated, brutalized by oppression, and bred in the habit of regarding law as their enemy', who were readily admitted to the suffrage, to be manipulated by city politicians.[2] But although fears of immigrant radicalism might briefly emerge when revolution occurred abroad or labour violence at home, the two decades after 1865 were years of tolerance towards the immigrant.

In the 1880s there appeared signs of change. Instead of words of encouragement for immigration, or silence on the subject, party platforms came to contain restrictive utterances. The Democrats in 1884 attacked contract labour, the American Party in 1888 was strongly restrictionist, while the Union Labor Party urged Chinese exclusion. The Democrats of 1892 opposed contract labour and Chinese immigration, and the influx of criminals and paupers, all of which tended 'to degrade American labour and lessen its wages,' but condemned 'any and all attempts to restrict the immigration of the industrious and worthy of foreign lands.' In 1896, the Republicans urged restriction of a wider kind: 'For the protection of our American citizenship and of the wages of our workingmen, against the fatal competition of low-priced labour, we demand that the immigration laws be thoroughly enforced, and so extended as to exclude from entrance to the United States those who can neither read nor write.'[3]

Very little was done. A law of 1882 excluded convicts, idiots, lunatics, and those likely to become a public charge. Three years later, unions of skilled workers gained the exclusion of contract labourers. The real danger came from small numbers of highly skilled Europeans imported under contract. But to gain this limited end, supporters of the bill took advantage of resentment at the use of immigrants as strikebreakers, and of anti-foreign prejudice in general, to suggest that hordes of ignorant and improverished eastern Europeans were being brought in by employers, which was simply not true.[4] The categories of undesirables to be excluded were gradually

[1] Kirk H. Porter and Donald Johnson, *National Party Platforms*, 22–3.
[2] Quoted in Abbott, *op. cit.*, 648–50.
[3] Porter and Johnson, *op. cit.*, 65, 75–6, 84, 88, 109.
[4] Charlotte Erickson, *American Industry and the European Immigrant*, chapters 6 to 9.

'The American nation – a pretty darned crew'

extended during the next third of a century, but all of these could reasonably be defended by arguments about anti-social behaviour of a rather obvious kind, or physical and mental defects disqualifying the immigrant from any effective share in American life.

Even the no-popery tradition, revived in the late 1880s, had little impact on immigrants. The American Protective Association urged severe naturalization requirements, attacked parochial schools, and lobbied for public inspection of private hospitals and convents. It drew up lists of friends and foes among newspapers and politicians. It circulated to branches study-outlines on such themes as 'The Grand Army of the Papacy in the United States', 'The Vatican and Labor Unions', and 'The Jesuit Lobby in Washington'. Members spread wild rumours of papal conspiracy, even of shipments of arms to exterminate Protestants. But although one point in their programme dealt with restriction of immigration, in the interests of American workers, it received no particular emphasis.[1]

Had no other strands of thought been present but fear of labour violence,

[1] Donald L. Kinzer, *An Episode in Anti-Catholicism*, esp. 45–6, 49, 51, 82, 97, 202: chapter 1 deals with Roman Catholic policies which provided the occasion for this agitation.

of industrial competition, and of the Pope, it is probable that nothing further than the exclusion of small categories of undesirables would have been achieved, or even attempted. The 1890s, however, saw new ideas injected into discussion of immigration. The assertion that the frontier no longer existed, and the visible facts of big business and great cities, made some men dread that America might go the way of Europe, towards social rigidity and class conflict. This in itself tended to induce a less optimistic frame of mind, one in which people felt defensive about American institutions and American values. Stability, order and homogeneity came to be stressed more than ever before. The beginning of significant southern and eastern European immigration, and the onset of economic depression in 1893, made the danger seem more acute. But the new leaders of the restriction movement were not content to express vague prejudices. Men of education and high social status, resentful of threats to old-American predominance, they systematized their views in dogmatic theories about race. In their categories, the new immigrants were peculiarly inferior, peculiarly unfitted to contribute to American society, and such people, by one means or another, must be shut out.[1]

The method selected was the one mentioned in the 1896 Republican platform – the literacy test, applied to all adult immigrants, or to all men, and the test being literacy in the immigrant's own, European language. A bill of this kind was for the first time debated in Congress during 1896 and 1897, and although there were elements of parliamentary manoeuvre, disputes over technicalities of enforcement, and several interruptions and attempts to bring in irrelevant topics, the arguments in the debate were very clear, sometimes eloquent, sufficiently so to seem worthy of detailed treatment here.[2]

Although the debate occurred during a depression, economic arguments were secondary. Danford of Ohio called attention to the prevailing economic difficulties, and suggested that they portended a fundamental change in America's capacity to absorb immigrants. Johnson of California wanted to exclude all unskilled workers, and Lodge of Massachusetts, one of the leading promoters of the bill, admitted that as a personal opinion he would have

---

[1] Barbara M. Solomon, *Ancestors and Immigrants*, and John Higham, *Strangers in the Land*, 87–105 and chapter vi, give excellent accounts. See also Higham's article 'Another Look at Nativism', *Catholic Historical Review*, XLIV (1958–9), 147–58, emphasizing the fears of Irish economic and political competition, which were as real as no-popery prejudice.

[2] My account omits many details of argument; it overrides chronology in favour of the logic of debate; and it disregards all parliamentary manoeuvring. My footnotes give references to *Congressional Record*, I standing for the first session of the 54th Congress, II for the second. Since page numbers are continuous through each session, volume numbers need not be cited. I have identified Senate and House by S and H, though my text makes no distinction between the double debates.

been willing to end all immigration until better conditions returned.[1] Johnson of Indiana pointed out the absurdity of protecting American labour standards by a tariff, while allowing much more direct competition in the form of immigration.[2] Morse of Massachusetts, Taylor of Ohio, Hepburn of Iowa, all attacked cheap labour, though sometimes in conjunction with other arguments.[3] McCall of Massachusetts denounced the 'masses of men who either fester in the slums of our great cities or make predatory incursions into industrial centres, where they work for wages upon which American workingmen cannot live. The evidence abundantly shows that they habitually live in shanties, that they eat the rudest food, that they do not have even the most common sanitary appliances, that they expose themselves to all the diseases that are generated by filth. The American workingman cannot support churches and decently clothe his children and send them to school and enjoy any of the comforts of civilization, so long as he must come into this degrading competition.'[4] Against this, several speakers emphasized the contribution of past immigrants to American growth. Caffery of Louisiana claimed that large areas of America even now remained to be developed. Gibson of Maryland, in the most logical attack on the Massachusetts group, asserted that, despite immigration, wage rates were higher than ever before, and that in Massachusetts, with its numerous foreign-born, wages were particularly high. He insisted, too, that immigrants were often employed in work which native Americans would not touch.[5]

Most speakers, however, addressed themselves to a wider problem: not so much America's economic capacity to absorb foreign workers, as its cultural capacity to assimilate people of alien social background and political tradition. Johnson of Indiana put the case against the immigrants as follows:

> There may have been a time when we could assimilate this undesirable immigration – the ignorant, the pauper, and the vicious class. That time has passed. Annually there are coming to our shores large numbers of people who are utterly unable to discharge the duties of American citizenship. They add to our burdens and responsibilities without adding anything whatever to our energies and resources. They strain our public and our private charities, fill our charitable and penal institutions, and are a constant menace to our free institutions.[6]

Wilson of South Carolina took a similar view, though his special concern

[1] I 5481–2 (H); I 5420–1 (H); II 72 (S).
[2] II 1227 (H).
[3] II 1230, 1232–5 (H).
[4] II 1677 (H).
[5] II 1935 (S).
[6] II 1227 (H).

was that 'this mass of European corruption' might soon infect the South, to add to its burdens of 'the cyclone, the pestilence and the earthquake', and to take the place of the horrors of Reconstruction from which it had so recently emerged.[1] Corliss of Michigan brought forward another argument: 'I believe in a pedigree, not only in the animal, but in the human family.' The idea was applied by other speakers more directly to the matter in hand. Lodge himself claimed that the new immigrants were often temporary, that they were often paupers or criminals, that they stayed in city slums, whereas earlier arrivals from north-west Europe had helped to develop lands in the West. The latter were 'kindred peoples', and to them the literacy test would scarcely apply. 'The races most affected by the illiteracy test', he explained, 'are those whose emigration to this country has begun within the last twenty years and swelled rapidly to enormous proportions, races with which the English-speaking people have never hitherto assimilated, and who are most alien to the great body of the people of the United States.' The older immigrants were descended from 'the great Germanic tribes' which had become united in national character through 'more than a thousand years of wars, conquests, migrations, and struggles.' Purity of 'mental and moral qualities must be preserved,' for the new immigrants confront America with a 'great and perilous change in the very fabric of our race.'[2] This was a cultural and historical, not a purely biological, classification, but many regarded it as decisive, Johnson of Indiana insisting that Polish Jews were undesirable even though they were literate.[3]

Not all speakers agreed. Mahany of New York accepted the racial classification as scientific, but drew different conclusions, asserting that each race had its own distinctive contribution to make to world civilization.[4] Bartholdt of Missouri, chairman of the House Immigration Committee, and himself an immigrant only a quarter of a century before, began by accepting the literacy test as a simple way of excluding undesirables, though he stressed the contribution of former immigrants to American welfare in peace and war. Later, however, when Johnson had spoken, and when a clause about the choice of language seemed to discriminate against Yiddish, he reacted strongly to what seemed to him an unworthy imitation of the

---

[1] I 5470 (H).

[2] I 5431 (H); 2817–20 (S). Lodge thought it proper to argue, perhaps with his constituents in mind, that the Irish, though racially distinct, had been closely associated with England for a thousand years, and spoke the English language. It is doubtful whether this Anglo-Saxon status by association would have commended itself to patriotic Irishmen of that day. John A. Garraty, *Henry Cabot Lodge*, 140–5, 281–2, adds only a few details to our understanding of the Senator's views.

[3] I 1221 (H).

[4] I 5474 (H).

anti-Semitism of the despotic regimes of Europe.[1] Another speaker of German origin, Buck of Louisiana, took higher ground. He saw no logic in the attack on living in cities: these were centres of civilization, and people flocked thither to improve themselves. It was unfair to exclude those who had been denied opportunity in Europe. Many countries had once enjoyed a high culture, only to lose it under political or religious oppression. Those who would betray American citizenship would not be the honest though ignorant immigrants, but sophisticated freethinkers. This was not all. Immigrants would adapt themselves to American principles, because these 'are the principles of humanity; and every man who comes here comes to be an American, because to be an American is to be a citizen of the world. . . . If the immigrant is educated, so much the better; if not, he still brings his labour and his honest purpose.'[2] Gibson was equally optimistic about the American capacity to absorb newcomers. The Anglo-Saxon race had unique capacity to do so. 'You can tell the newly-landed stranger at first glance; but who shall discriminate between the native-descended immigrant and the son or grandson of him who landed forty years ago? The newcomers will not change us, but we shall change them.' Racial deterioration, he insisted against Lodge, worked from the top downwards, not from the bottom. Viewing their past triumphs, Americans should not falter in their confidence. 'Let all the peoples of the world who are industrious, vigorous and law-abiding come and join us in the development of a healthy, free, prosperous, and powerful population.'[3]

McCall had pleaded for a recognition of the principle that intelligence was the basis of free institutions. But Mills of Texas pointed out that the proposed test applied not to intelligence but to European social opportunity. Many were deprived of a chance to qualify, not from any fault of their own, but from the nature of the despotism under which they had the misfortune to live, and from which they wished to escape.[4] In his veto message, which was not overridden, Cleveland insisted that literacy was an imperfect index of capacity for citizenship. The bill threatened hardship to many people. Moreover, it was not needed. Immigration had fallen during the depression: with prosperity would come more people, but also more opportunities for them. Throughout American history, recent immigrants had come under

[1] I 5421–4 (H); II 1222 (H). It is worth pointing out that Bartholdt never suggested that immigrants had a cultural contribution to make. They provided manual labour, and the test of admissibility was willingness to work and willingness to 'identify with us and our institutions'.
[2] II 1225–7 (H). Buck pointed out: 'I have nothing to gain as a foreign-born citizen by opposing this bill. I have no friends that want to come here from foreign countries. They are all here. The bones of my parents repose in American soil. . . .'
[3] II 1935–6 (S).
[4] I 5476 (H); II 240 (S).

attack, yet their children had become most satisfactory citizens. All in all, the United States would do better not to depart from its traditions.[1]

III

Since there had been enough votes in the House, though not in the Senate, to override, it is surprising that it took twenty years to bring the literacy test on to the statute book. In 1907 a bill got as far as a deadlocked conference committee. In 1913 and in 1915, similar bills were vetoed by Taft and Wilson. Wilson argued that it was unjust to abandon the test of personal fitness for a test of social opportunity. In 1917, however, a further veto was overridden. By overwhelming majorities the Congress decided to set immigrants over sixteen (with certain exceptions for close relatives of citizens and admissible aliens) a short passage to read in a language of their choice.[2] It is important to try to explain both the delay and the final triumph of this form of restriction.

The lobbying of powerful Irish, German and Jewish groups, against further restriction, is part of the explanation. Even more important, probably, is the fact that, once prosperity had returned, there were powerful business forces favourable to free entry. In the absence of any severe pressures of economic circumstance, public opinion was hard to arouse in nativist directions. Opponents of immigration continued to rage against backward people who 'have entered our ports in less than one-quarter of the period which was required to put the barbarian hordes in practical control of Rome, and usher in what men speak of as the Dark Ages.' Many states discriminated against aliens. Oriental exclusion remained rigorous.[3] As to wider restriction, however, success long remained just out of reach, despite the over-representation in Congress of rural and small-town elements among whom nativism could be expected to be strong. Opponents of

---

[1] II 2667–8.

[2] Marion T. Bennett, *American Immigration Policies, A History,* 26–8, summarizes the Act. The Wilson veto is in *Congressional Record, 63 Congress 3 Session,* 2481–2. Arthur S. Link, *Wilson, The New Freedom,* 276, shows that the President privately regretted having to disagree with many of his friends, but felt himself pledged by his public utterances to resist discrimination. Link's earlier book, *Wilson, The Road to the White House,* 381–2, refers to a passage in Wilson's *History of the American People,* which spoke of 'sordid and helpless' elements from southern Europe, with 'neither skill nor energy nor any initiative of quick intelligence', which became embarrassing in his political career, and had to be repudiated.

[3] The quotation is from Daniel C. Brewer, President of the North American Civic League for Immigrants, 1916, quoted in Herman Feldman, *Racial Factors in American Industry,* 135. The background is discussed in Higham, *op. cit.,* esp. 74, 119–30, 161–83. See also Morrell Heald, 'Business Attitudes towards European Immigration, 1880–1900', *Journal of Economic History,* XIII (1953), 291–304.

immigration, of course, did not relax their efforts. They built up their case. The Great War put success within their grasp.

Between 1900 and 1908, party platforms were virtually silent on the subject of immigration, except for that of Orientals. Theodore Roosevelt's Annual Messages insisted on character as the criterion for immigrants. 'There is no danger in having too many immigrants of the right kind . . . But the citizenship of this country should not be debased.' People should be excluded who could not meet some educational test, who were of 'low moral tendency', or 'who are below a certain standard of economic fitness to enter our industrial field as competitors with American labor. There should be proper proof of personal capacity to earn an American living and enough money to insure a decent start under American conditions.'[1] In 1907, an Immigration Commission was set up, with three members from each branch of Congress and three presidential nominees. It spent four years in investigations, published evidence and report in 1911 in forty-two volumes, and, after pointing to several possible techniques for reducing the influx of temporary immigrants, unskilled workers, and people least assimilable, decided by a majority that the literacy test was most practicable.[2]

During these same years, and immediately thereafter, many books were written to express fears about the 'New' immigration. Perhaps the most cogent was *The Passing of the Great Race*, published in 1916 by the extremely conservative lawyer Madison Grant. Most of its pages are filled with an apparently objective account of the races of Europe, and particularly their migrations, though it is soon clear that the Nordic race arouses his keenest admiration. But the discussion is intended to have an American application. People should recognize, Grant argues, the fact of human inequality, and not be deceived by democratic dogmas. There are superior people, and these are in danger. They engage in wars and are killed; they engage in pioneering and perish before reproducing themselves; they withdraw from competition with inferior races, by failing to produce large enough families. The American pioneering stock of Nordic origin may soon become 'as extinct as the Athenian of the age of Pericles, and the Viking of the age of Rollo', because

[1] Theodore Roosevelt, *Works* (National Edition), XV 95–7, 245. After the fifth Message, no further interest in the subject is expressed. In private letters, Roosevelt fluctuated from time and time, and according to the person he was addressing: hostile to immigration when writing to Lodge in 1892, sober and statesmanlike when stressing the character test in a letter to Speaker Cannon in 1906, he was pointing to his own record of appointing members of minority groups to his cabinet, when he wrote to Lyman Abbott in 1908 – *Letters* (Elting E. Morison, ed.), I 291, V 285–6, VI 1042–3.

[2] Summarized in Jeremiah W. Jenks and William J. Lauck, *The Immigration Problem*, 359–65. Jenks had been one of the presidential nominees on the Commission. Other devices reviewed were exclusion of single men, a monetary qualification, and setting quotas based on the past immigration of the several ethnic groups. The procedures of investigation used, and the logic of analysis, soon came under heavy attack, notably in Isaac Hourwich, *Immigration and Labor*.

in their search for a labour force to bring about material prosperity, Americans have overlooked the hard fact of race. The true solution is to segregate races, for otherwise they 'ultimately amalgamate and in the offspring the more generalized or lower type prevails.'[1]

Not only conservatives wrote such books. By most standards of his day, John R. Commons was a progressive thinker. He found it possible, however, to call attention to the line that could be drawn across Europe, separating literate, economically advanced, democratic and Protestant peoples from those still backward and ruled despotically. He feared the coming to America, from the latter zone, of a 'degraded peasantry', who would bring about class divisions and endanger free institutions.[2] In the same political category, and indeed a teacher in the same university, was Edward A. Ross. Although he repeated the point about native and immigrant birth rates, most of his emphasis was placed upon economic competition and on evidence of social degradation among certain races. He discussed the largest old and new ethnic groups, in such a way as to suggest that the newest were ignorant and superstitious, filthy and coarse, harsh in their treatment of wives and children. Their parochial schools worked against assimilation. The Irish had come to dominate city politics, and although this had 'given our cities genial officials, brave policemen and gallant firefighters, it has also given them the name of being the worst-governed cities in the civilized world.' The plain fact was, in Ross' view, that northern Europeans (with some doubts about the Irish) were superior, and one sign of this was their better conduct, as compared with southern Europeans, in several recent disasters at sea. The newest arrivals were inferior to the pioneer stocks, and it was this that emerged as the author's test. Watching garment-workers in Union Square, New York, Ross found only 38 of 368 with 'the type of face one would find at a county fair in the West or South.'[3] In such statements, by a professor of sociology, are to be found the latest theories about race, devotion to the concept of national character, veneration equalling Theodore

---

[1] Madison Grant, *The Passing of the Great Race* (1918 rev. edn), esp. 12, 47–8, 73–5, 89–90, 222, 263.

[2] John R. Commons, *Races and Immigrants in America*. The first edition appeared in 1907, but he held the same opinions in the revised edition of 1920, which was still being reprinted ten years later.

[3] Edward A. Ross, *The Old World in the New*, esp. 123–4, 130, 133–4, 136, 259–63, 285–6, 295–6. The first expression of the argument about differential birthrates, by Francis A. Walker, is quoted in Garis, *op. cit.*, 219. For similar opinions to Ross's, see Prescott F. Hall, *Immigration and its effects upon the United States* (1906): on 42 he writes of the Armenians, 'Some of the Armenian merchants are fairly intelligent . . . On the other hand, many of the lower classes are extremely objectionable. Their standards of living and of morals are low, and they tend to form small colonies in manufacturing centres. Some take up the occupations of cigarette making and peddling. On the whole they are not desirable immigrants.'

Roosevelt's for the pioneer virtues, and a prejudice against the corruptions of popery and great cities which can only be described as Populist.

Characterizing all these opponents of immigration was not only a strong prejudice against many European and other races, but a profound pessimism about the capacity of the United States to absorb them. Henry P. Fairchild, writing in 1926, represented this view. He began with a discussion of race in the physical sense, making the familiar remark that mixture meant degeneration, but then turned in a rather different direction to discuss nationality, with traditions imbibed from childhood. He then posed the issue of one nationality's survival as against others. If American nationality were to survive, he asserted, 'The traits of foreign nationality which the immigrant brings with him are not to be mixed or interwoven. They are to be *abandoned*.' In fact, even this would not work, such was the natural solidarity of groups and the natural antipathy of one group towards another. The danger of non-assimilation would be averted only by reducing immigration to an insignificant scale. Fairchild's final plea was for the recognition of the supreme importance of preserving American values. The interests of the world demanded that America remain intact to perform its mission 'to point the way, to demonstrate the possibilities, to lead onward to the goal of human happiness,' through democratic organization. Any humanitarian policy which interfered with that mission was 'treason'. If immigration went on uncontrolled, it was American nationality that would lose 'all form and symmetry, all beauty and character, all nobility and usefulness' in the melting pot.[1]

IV

Thus far, it may seem fair to say that four factors influenced the rise or fall of movements to restrict immigration or to impose limitations upon foreigners already arrived in the United States. They would gain strength when immigrants were especially numerous, and when they deviated considerably from what older settlers might regard as the American norm. The flood of Irish Catholics before and after 1850 stimulated nativism for both these reasons. The campaigns would be weakened if the country were prosperous: businessmen might then welcome immigrant labour, and workers could afford to tolerate it. Restriction would seem particularly important, finally, at times of general social tension or crisis, when labour unrest, or disquiet about the consequences of industrialization or the growth of cities, made social unity seem something to be prized.

If such views are anything like correct, the period following 1917 might

[1] Henry P. Fairchild, *The Melting-Pot Mistake*, esp. 154, 246, 260–61.

be expected to have seen increased anxiety about immigration, and a renewed effort to reduce its scale. The existence of war in Europe, American involvement in that war, the influence of the Bolshevik revolution, the slump of 1921, all contributed to an acute sensitiveness to the danger of social division.

It is true that such feelings led to the constructive effort of 'Americanization'. Voluntary organizations, or public authorities, investigated immigrant life and provided classes and facilities for recreation. Some states enacted compulsory classes in English for people above school age. For a few years, the Committee for Immigrants in America, an immigration committee of the Chamber of Commerce of the United States, and a National Americanization Committee, were active. Even the Federal Bureau of Education had a Division of Immigrant Education.[1] From as early as 1917, however, these programmes came to contain an element of coercion. The National Americanization Committee began recommending that aliens who, within three years, failed to learn English and take out first papers, should be deported. The same attitude was expressed naively in Iowa: 'We are going to love every foreigner who really becomes an American, and all others we are going to ship back home.'[2] Soon, some alien radicals were deported. States began discriminating against aliens in certain kinds of employment, and enforcing English as sole language of instruction in the public schools.[3] More sinister were the anti-semitism of Henry Ford's *Dearborn Independent* and the activities of the second Ku Klux Klan. Imperial Wizard Evans asserted that 'we have taken unto ourselves a Trojan horse crowded with ignorance, illiteracy, and envy.' Remembering also the wave of rural and small-town puritanism which brought about Prohibition, it is safe to say that, in millions of minds, fear and hatred of the city, the foreigner, the Catholic, the Jew, the infidel, the radical, became linked.[4] Economic arguments were added, as when, fearing the dislocations of the demobilization process, the American Federation of Labor urged a total suspension of immigration for two years. The Republican platform of 1920 not only urged strict enforcement of existing laws, but stated the principle: 'The immigration policy of the United States should be such as to ensure that the number

[1] Edward G. Hartmann, *The Movement to Americanize the Immigrant*, is the authority. Harold Ickes, working his way through college, taught English to immigrants in a Chicago night-school – *Autobiography of a Curmudgeon*, 22–3.
[2] Quoted in Higham, *op. cit.*, 221.
[3] On this, and especially on deportations, see Kate H. Claghorn, *The Immigrant's Day in Court*, esp. 270–71, 277, 292, 298–304, 328–33.
[4] The quotation is in W. C. Smith, *Americans in the Making*, 162. See also William J. Simmons of the Klan, in John M. Mecklin, *The Ku Klux Klan: a study of the American Mind*, 102; Bishop Cannon, in Oscar Handlin, *Al Smith and his America*, 132; Prohibition spokesmen in Andrew Sinclair, *Prohibition: the Era of Excess*, 9–10, 19–20, 285; and for background, Higham, *op. cit.*, chapter x.

of foreigners in the country should not exceed that which can be assimilated with reasonable rapidity, and to favour immigrants whose standards are similar to ours.'[1]

The chairman of the Republican-dominated House Immigration Committee was Albert Johnson of Washington, a small-town editor who had gained a reputation for antagonism to the Industrial Workers of the World. He argued for suspension, with Jews from eastern Europe particularly in mind. The Senate insisted on a different approach. William P. Dillingham, who had been chairman of the Immigration Commission of 1907, now headed the Immigration Committee, and he revived an old plan of quotas based on the number of foreign-born from the several countries at the 1910 census. This view prevailed. The ratio was fixed at three per cent, to produce a quota of somewhat over 350,000; and exemptions for close relatives, and the exclusion of the Western Hemisphere from the quota system, ensured that total immigration would be far higher.[2]

The Dillingham committee's report on the bill emphasized the contrast between 'Old' and 'New' immigration. The former, it was alleged, came as families, became permanent settlers, distributed themselves throughout the country, acquired property, and accepted American citizenship. The latter 'has consisted largely of single men, it has gone directly to the cities and to the manufacturing centres, and has remained there. It has moved in racial groups and to a large extent has maintained them, and compared with the older immigration it, as a rule, shows a slighter tendency to become American citizens and the numbers who have gone to the land have been negligible.' Congressman McReynolds insisted that the newcomers' backgrounds prevented them from becoming successful citizens of a democratic nation, and pointed to the failure of orderly government in Latin America. Carl Vinson argued against the new immigrants as being different from 'our forefathers', the British and Irish who were 'ancestors of the real American people'. A few years later, Albert Johnson, writing the foreword to a standard book on the restriction campaign, expressed his convictions thus: 'Today, instead of a nation descended from generations of freemen bred to a knowledge of the principles and practices of self-government, we have a heterogeneous population, no small proportion of which is sprung from races that, throughout the centuries, have known no liberty at all, and no law save the decrees of overlords and princes.'[3]

---

[1] Porter and Johnson, *op. cit.*, 235–6.
[2] Bennett, *op. cit.*, 41–4; Garis, *op. cit.*, 142–6; and on Johnson, Higham, *op. cit.*, 177–8.
[3] Bennett, *op. cit.*, 48–9; Garis, *op. cit.*, 218, 220–21, and Foreword, vii. Compare John B. McMaster, the historian, on recent immigrants: 'The Declaration and the Constitution, the Fourth of July and the Twenty-second of February, Bunker Hill and Saratoga, Yorktown and New

It was Johnson who began to work towards an even more restrictive law. He was in touch with Madison Grant, while Dr Laughlin, a specialist in eugenics, provided him with data on the 'social inadequacy' of recent immigrants. John B. Trevor, formerly of military intelligence, was brought in to testify about dangers from radicals and Jews. Although the House Committee had decided to approve the plan based on two per cent of the foreign-born of 1890, Trevor's suggestion, for a calculation of the ethnic composition of the whole population in 1920, gained much support, since, by taking account of people of colonial descent, it opened up the prospect of limiting the 'New' immigration even more drastically. The Senate was divided between these two methods, and in the end the 1924 Act laid down restriction in two stages: the two per cent plan for three years, and the national-origins plan to begin in 1927, each aimed at producing a quota of 150,000. As in 1921, there were exempted categories in addition to the national quotas, and, as before, the Western Hemisphere was not subject to the plan. The voting on this bill is interesting. It passed the Senate 62 to 6 with 28 abstentions. In the House, it passed 323 to 71 with 38 abstentions: of the opponents, about half belonged to each major party; all but seven came from eight industrial states and 24 from New York; about half came from five great cities, 18 from New York City alone. In other words, congressmen voted against the bill only if they had foreign-born constituents.[1] When 1927 arrived, a quite different controversy broke out. It was suddenly appreciated that the new system, with its weighting of colonial and early Republican stock, would increase the British quota as compared with those of Ireland, Germany, and the Scandinavian countries. This was highly unwelcome to groups which were often anti-British on other grounds, and they agitated fiercely against the national-origins basis. All they could achieve was suspension of the plan, first for one year and then for another. It was now the South that was willing to go ahead, the other regions which provided majorities in favour of delay and reversion to some other plan. The House voted a further suspension in 1929, by 192 to 152, but since the Senate failed to complete action on a resolution, President Hoover was bound by the 1924 Act to proclaim the new quotas.[2]

Orleans, were instruments, days, and events of which they knew nothing and for which they cared nothing.' Quoted Edward Saveth, *American Historians and European Immigrants*, 182–3.

[1] Bennett, *op. cit.*, 51–8, and, on the exemption of the Americas, 61; Garis, *op. cit.*, 170–201, 240–51.

[2] Robert A. Divine, *American Immigration Policy, 1924–1952*, 26–7, 31–3, 36–50; and 52–61 deals with the failure of attempts to enforce a quota on Mexico. For a brief treatment of Swedish attitudes to quotas, as expressed in their newspapers, see Finis H. Capps, *From Isolationism to Involvement*, 110–14. Swedes worried about Scandinavian quotas, but were quite willing to restrict southern and eastern Europeans: Scandinavians were the backbone of America.

The Effects of the Quota Laws: American Immigration 1921–30

The numbers are those admitted, quota and non-quota. Very small regions and countries have been omitted. Source: *Historical Statistics of the United States* (1945 edn), 33, 35. Figures in ooo's.

Year	1921	1922	1923	1924	1925	1926	1927	1928	1929	1930
All Countries	805	310	523	707	294	304	335	307	280	242
Europe	652	216	308	364	148	156	168	159	159	147
Britain	51	25	46	59	27	26	24	20	21	31
Ireland	28	11	16	17	27	25	29	25	20	23
Scandinavia	23	15	34	36	17	17	17	16	17	7
Other North-west	29	11	12	16	9	9	9	9	9	9
Germany	7	18	48	75	46	50	49	46	47	27
Poland	98	29	27	29	5	7	9	9	9	9
Other Central	77	29	34	33	5	6	7	7	8	9
Russia & Baltic	10	20	21	21	3	3	3	3	2	3
Other Eastern	33	12	16	13	2	2	2	2	2	2
Italy	222	40	47	56	6	8	17	18	18	22
Other Southern	74	6	7	9	2	3	4	4	4	5
Asia	25	14	14	22	4	3	4	3	4	5
Canada	73	47	117	201	103	93	85	75	66	65
Mexico	31	20	64	89	33	43	68	59	40	13

By that time, acceptance of drastic restriction was almost universal: debate was on methods alone. The 1928 party platforms accepted the quota law, with no more amendment than pleas for precautions against splitting families. Only the Workers' (Communist) party, in section XIII of its long document, denounced the exploitation of immigrant workers by capitalists in league with the 'labor aristocracy' of the American Federation of Labor, and appealed eloquently for working-class solidarity.[1]

The result of the 1924 Act was to cut the total of immigration, to ensure that European immigration did not much exceed that from the Americas, and to impose drastic cuts in the movement from southern and eastern Europe. British and Irish quotas were more than enough to meet the demand, German and Scandinavian were about adequate, but elsewhere enormous pressure existed on the few places open. The 1920s, therefore, saw a compulsory reversal of the balance of 'Old' and 'New' immigration which had existed since the 1890s; and even before the Depression, American law had brought the great century of immigration to an end.[2]

[1] Porter and Johnson, *op. cit.*, 276, 289, 319–20.
[2] My table gives the salient figures to demonstrate what happened down to the Depression. On the later history of American immigration policy, see the books already cited by Divine (to 1952) and Bennett (to 1962). The Act of 1965 has substituted an economic criterion (limited by a uniform maximum for each nationality) for racially-biassed quotas.

CHAPTER TWELVE

Towards Assimilation

Who was I . . . I felt like a house inhabited by many strange people, unacquainted with each other, any one of whom might at any moment become my 'self'.

Joseph Freeman, *An American Testament*, 51–2.

On their arrival, immigrants inhabited, not merely the United States, but several worlds at the same time. They lived in a district of homesteads, or in a city ward, surrounded, most probably, by fellow-members of their own ethnic group. North-eastern Iowa was Norwegian, the Lower East Side of Manhattan was Jewish, South Boston was Irish and Boston's North End Italian. Yet they had the recent memory of an equally real and local community somewhere in the old country. Relations and friends were still there, and they followed its news as closely as they could. If these were worlds of direct personal association, the world of German or Irish or Italian nationality was not much more remote. Whether marching in a St Patrick's Day parade, secretly drilling with Fenian forces, flocking to hear Michael Davitt expound the Land League, or reading in the *Irish World* of the advancement to public office of their compatriots in other states, Irish immigrants felt themselves part of the history of Ireland, and part of an Irish-America in the New World.[1] Similarly, Germans were aware of having founded in America a special community, a special culture, while at the same time they celebrated the 1848 revolutions or Bismarck's triumph of 1870–71.[2] For Croats and Slovaks and Finns, too, a sense of national identity in the United States preceded national status in Europe, and indeed helped to achieve it. Immigrants inhabited at the same time a city, a state, a country, whose history and institutions affected their lives, and some of them had already judged these with approval before leaving home. Many immigrants, however, lived also in one more world, that of the Roman Catholic Church.

[1] I have sampled the *Irish World* only for 1878. See also William D'Arcy, *The Fenian Movement in the United States*; Michael Davitt, *The Fall of Feudalism in Ireland*, chapters xi, xvi, xix, xxx; James J. Green, 'American Catholics and the Irish Land League, 1879–1882', *Catholic Historical Review*, XXXV (1949–50), 19–42.
[2] Carl Wittke, *Refugees of Revolution*, 35, and *The German-Language Press in America*, 164–8, Bayrd Still, *Milwaukee*, 115; Rollin Osterweis, *Three Centuries of New Haven*, 284, 386–9; similarly, Italians in Virginia City, Nevada, celebrated 1870 – Andrew Rolle, *The Immigrant Upraised*, 244.

While growing rapidly in America, that Church was at the same time suffering territorial loss in Italy, defining its doctrines and practice, defending its position against nineteenth-century ideologies. German or Irish or Italian Catholics in America were necessarily involved, whether they were paying from meagre earnings to put up a handsome new church, listening to their priest's command to send their children to parochial schools, sending a contribution from Boston to aid Pius IX in 1849, or testifying sympathy and admiration for the same pontiff in 1871 and 1873.[1]

I

At varying speeds, each of these worlds changed. Italy and Germany became politically united. Much later, Poland and Czechoslovakia and most of Ireland became independent nations. To that extent historical agitations were brought to an end and one of the immigrants' worlds ceased to exist. The city in which they lived was transformed: Boston's Back Bay and more and more of the South End and South Boston were reclaimed from water, more streets and railways were constructed, old buildings were torn down and new ones put up. New occupations, new demands for skill and education, exercised their influence. With rising income and savings, immigrants might begin the move to new and less purely ethnic districts, or see their children do so, while their original American home became flooded with newcomers from other parts of Europe. In not much more than half a century, parts of Boston changed from Yankee to Irish, and from Irish to Jewish or Italian.[2] Similarly, the Catholic Church multiplied its churches and elaborated its parochial life, and instead of searching western Europe for trained priests, or sending its few American-born youths with a vocation to Montreal or Paris or Rome to be trained, it built colleges and seminaries, produced more and more of its own clergy at home, and by the end of the nineteenth century could support missions overseas.[3] Not every change, of course, was forward and upward. The lives of millions of rather recent Americans were affected by the disaster, in the 1940s, to central Europe's Jewish communities.

The immigrants' place in their surviving worlds changed too. They came to understand more about America, advanced themselves at work, became

[1] Robert H. Lord *et al.*, *History of the Archdiocese of Boston*, II 419; Mary A. Frawley, *Patrick Donahoe*, 113, 115–16.

[2] Together, Walter M. Whitehill, *Boston: a Topographical History* and Walter Firey, *Land Use in Central Boston* tell the story.

[3] Lord, *Archdiocese of Boston*, II and III, has abundant information on this process, which included some direct recruiting in Ireland and considerable reliance on seminaries in other American dioceses until late in the nineteenth century.

18

more accepted by neighbours outside their own group, made more and more successful political claims. Inevitably, therefore, their perception of the relationship between their worlds, of their relative significance, also changed.

Even more was this true of later generations – but as soon as the words are used, qualifications have to be brought in. Generations were not simple blocks, placed edge to edge in time. In each immigrant group, for half a century or more, original immigrants grew a little more American, their children became assimilated much faster, but, simultaneously, newcomers continued to arrive. Moreover, in any state or city, each ethnic group displayed a somewhat different balance between its generations. The 1890 census showed Massachusetts to possess 657,000 foreign-born inhabitants: it had half a million others, born in the United States but with one or both of their parents born abroad. The oldest group, the Irish, already had slightly more members of the second generation than survivors of the first. By 1910, the census showed more inhabitants of Massachusetts with foreign parentage than had been born abroad. The Irish had a ratio of almost two to one, the Canadians had a small preponderance of the second generation, the British generations were approaching equality. New York State's Germans, like its Irish, had a larger second generation, while, as might be expected, Italians, and peoples from Austria-Hungary and Russia, were dominated by recent arrivals. The overall foreign-ness of certain states and cities was therefore great, enough to impress all observers and horrify some old-stock Americans: as early as 1890, only 300,000 of New York City's one-and-a-half million inhabitants had both parents born in America. But it is the variety of stages of development, as between one group and another, that impresses the modern scholar even more. Variety, of course, was further extended by differences in personal attitudes as between members of any group. American Yiddish developed several words to denote such shades of difference: *deitschuks* (assimilated like German Jews), *machers* (men of affairs), *alrightniks* (smart climbers), *lodgeniks* (joiners), *radikalke* (emancipated women), and *ototots* (half-assimilated men who compromised by wearing only a very small beard).[1] Only when reinforcements from the old country ceased, and the immigrants died in large numbers, was assimilation likely to accelerate markedly and the group's institutional life fall into decline. Even then, the second generation was likely to have mixed attitudes, and the third, unrecognized in the censuses and swallowed up in the category 'native', might still display traces of its ethnic heritage in the way members chose their marriage partners or cast their votes.

Ethnic groups were not all the same, even though it is easy to identify

[1] Alfred Kazin, *A Walker in the City*, 27.

many common needs. An Englishman's situation, on arrival at Fall River from a Lancashire mill town to do an identical job, was very different from that of a French-Canadian farm worker arrived in the same town, and from that of a Slovak peasant just arrived in the steel mills of Homestead, Pennsylvania. A Russian Jew, who despaired of prosperity, dignity, and even safety in the Pale, and who in crossing the Atlantic knew that he was making an irrevocable fresh start, was very different from a Sicilian labourer who hoped in a few years to save enough from his American wages to buy land back home. Skills, ambitions, attitudes to education and to success, all differed greatly from group to group; and immigrants' opportunities and problems also varied according to the American environment in which they lived, and the stage at which they arrived in America's rapid growth.

For all these reasons there could be nothing simple about assimilation. It should not be viewed as a steady fading of memories, as a smooth transition from one set of relationships, one dominant immigrant world, to another. Rather, against a background of most complex change, it was a series of conflicts between competing influences, one environment pressing upon another, influences from the wider American society battling with the entrenched leadership of heads of families or of ethnic institutions. Some parents deplored the loss of their authority over their children's behaviour and over their earnings, and bitterly contrasted the American situation with that of the stable world of the old village. Although Poles and other Slav peoples felt this very acutely, Jews too were sometimes aware of it. 'Once you used to get respect and honour at least,' one of them complained. 'Here they throw you away. You become a back number.'[1] Jewish parents, however, might react very differently. Mary Antin put it thus: 'They had no standards to go by, seeing America was not Polotzk.' Handing over his children, as did Mary's father, to the public school 'as if it were an act of consecration', a parent might defer excessively to his children's ways, or he might expect too much success to follow from their new advantages.[2] For their part, children might dislike their parents' language, resent their religious orthodoxy, rebel against the attempt to limit their dating and arrange their marriages. Yet they could not wholly break away: they felt the pull of affection, and they knew that their acceptance by older Americans was far from complete.[3] The change that occurred, whatever might be

[1] Robert E. Park, *The Immigrant Press and its Control*, 167; William C. Smith, *Americans in the Making*, 250–1, quotes a querulous article from a Milwaukee Polish newspaper: and see also Phyllis H. Williams, *South Italian Folkways in Europe and America*, chapter vi.
[2] Mary Antin, *The Promised Land*, 204–5, 244–8, 271.
[3] Kazin, *op. cit.*, 58–60, 66–7; S. N. Behrman, *The Worcester Account*, 60, 147, 154, 164–8; Theodore Saloutos, *The Greeks in the United States*, chapter xv; Irvin Child, *Italian or American: the Second Generation in Conflict*.

individual attitudes, can be seen in two Polish examples. Quite early in the Polish migration, a Pole in America accepted a bride from the old country, sight unseen, on the basis of a recommendation from a family whose reputation in his home village was beyond question. Half a century later, a third-generation Polish woman explained that she could speak English but scarcely write it, so completely had her parochial school been run in the old language. Yet she could point the contrast between her own generation and her mother's, which wore shawls over their heads as in Poland, and knew no English at all. Even more significant, 'the boys and girls marry for love. The parents don't select the persons they are to marry.'[1]

Ways of life outside the family were equally in dispute. After the Great War, French-Canadian organizations in New England were issuing statements defending the old language. In the 1930s, two generations of Jews in a small Massachusetts town were disputing bitterly the seating arrangements in their synagogue, and the style of its service. Roman Catholic parochial schools were being used, not only to inculcate religious and ethnic values in children, but, through those children, to influence parents. Rural Lutherans in the Middle West in the 1940s were arguing furiously about the character of social activities to be permitted in their high school.[2] Ethnic institutions, however, might themselves help prepare their members for assimilation. Some were designed, from the start, to encourage people to take out first papers for citizenship. Others, social in their emphasis, gave symbolic expression to their respect for the United States by putting up, as in the Slovenes' hall at Waukegan, Illinois, a portrait of Lincoln, and by planning to add similar pictures of Washington and Wilson.[3]

From a reality of such infinite complexity, one can do no more than single out a few areas of life, and examine the processes of assimilation that appear in each. Work, politics, language, and marriage will be discussed in turn, and the scattered evidence reviewed.

II

Initially, many immigrants worked entirely with members of their own ethnic group, in sweatshop or in pick-and-shovel gang. Only through foreman and manager was there an indirect contact with American society.

---

[1] William I. Thomas and Florian Znaniecki, *The Polish Peasant in Europe and America*, I 408; Arthur E. Wood, *Hamtranck Then and Now*, 221.
[2] Frank V. Thompson, *Schooling of the Immigrant*, 135–42; W. Lloyd Warner and Leo Srole, *Social Systems of American Ethnic Groups*, 115–17, 205–17; Joseph H. Fichter, *Social Relations in the Urban Parish*, esp. 169–77; W. Lloyd Warner *et al.*, *Democracy in Jonesville*, 169–91, 252–7.
[3] John Daniels, *America via the Neighborhood*, 142–6.

The contact became much more solid as soon as immigrants qualified for more varied jobs; but for the nineteenth century it is far from clear how many of them did so. The latest study of the subject, dealing with a small Massachusetts mill town between 1850 and 1880, concludes that unskilled labourers found it exceedingly hard to rise, almost impossible to leave the working class, and far from easy to help their children advance themselves. On the other hand, as far as they were willing to raise mortgages, and pay them off through extreme thrift and sending children to work at the earliest lawful age or a little before, they could acquire property and the security that went with it.[1] Such a study is valuable, in that, unlike the published censuses, it traces individuals through time; but the approach has its limitations. The period is very short. The method cannot readily be applied to larger towns, which, with a more varied economy and a quite different scale of activity, may have offered greater opportunities to workers. Nor is any proof brought forward to show that people who started a little higher up the economic ladder found it equally hard to rise further. The census figures themselves, for example those of 1910, seem to show that immigrants' children, overall, were rising significantly beyond their parents – but unfortunately, by that time, the figures about occupations were no longer related to the several ethnic groups.

Although their success was limited, for the most part, to winning advances for skilled workers, and although their leadership was largely British and almost wholly north-west European, labour unions could play some part in immigrants' lives. Even recently-arrived workers can be found organizing unions of their own, especially when, in a city, most members of a trade came from one ethnic group. There were German craft-unions even before the Civil War, trades assemblies linking them in the later 1860s, and more unions in the next decade. Czechs in New York had unions, linked by a council. In the 1880s, in the same city, was organized the group known as the Hebrew Trades. There were unions of Jewish bakers, carpenters, paper-hangers, and waiters in Boston early in the twentieth century, of Italian construction workers in Boston and Lawrence, of French carpenters at Lowell and Fall River. The cigar-makers' union was composed mainly of immigrants; and this was even more true of the garment-workers, whose leaders were overwhelmingly Jews from Russia, Hungary, Austria or Roumania (direct or via England) and whose rank-and-file were pretty certainly the same.[2] Early in the twentieth century, too, examples can be

---

[1] Stephan Thernstrom, *Poverty and Progress,* esp. chapter vi.
[2] Clifton K. Yearley, *Britons in American Labor*; John R. Commons *et al., History of Labor in the United States,* II 223, 313, 518-19; Daniels, *op. cit.,* 324-5; *Reports on Statistics of Labor,*

found of spontaneous strikes among recent immigrants, against bad conditions from the New York subway to the copper mines of Utah.[1] Immigrant workers played a significant part in the efforts to unionize coal and steel. Their activity, in fact, depended not on some innate attitude towards unions, not on some inborn resistance to enlightened common action, but simply on the quality of the leadership offered them. Most foreign-born workers in the Illinois coalfields were in unions, and most of those in Pennsylvania anthracite. The Pennsylvania bituminous field showed much lower figures, but the hardest area to organize proved to be West Virginia, with much the highest proportion of native white workers.[2] For immigrants, their children, and older Americans alike, all these opportunities improved greatly in the 1930s. As this occurred, immigrants were more and more able to develop their talents, and the new conditions encouraged them to view themselves in rather different terms, as members, along with other Americans, of an economic group.

By the 1930s, too, significant numbers of Irish, some Italians and others, but above all a high proportion of Jews, were moving into better areas of big cities, or into suburbs, as they rose to white-collar employment or acquired their own businesses. Some degree of separation was then likely to emerge between the older members of the immigrant generation, who were likely to stay in their early homes, and later generations, not only more affluent but much more American in their style of life.[3] In smaller places, rather fixed residential zones were likely to persist, and opportunities were restricted by the fact that very old-established Americans retained control over business and the professions. In such towns, where the working-class might be largely Italian or French-Canadian, the earlier-arrived and somewhat more successful Irish might stay, using their political skills to assume the role of leaders of an opposition to the American Protestant establishment, on behalf of all ethnic groups.[4]

Massachusetts, 1904, 1905, 1906; Louis Levine, *The Women's Garment Workers*, esp. 553–4, 581–95. For a somewhat later period of the twentieth century, see Works Progress Administration, *The Italians of New York*, 65–7.

[1] Commons, *op. cit.*, II 367, III ix-xi; Graham Adams, *The Age of Industrial Violence*, chapter iv; Donald B. Cole, *Immigrant City*, 177–94; Daniels, *op. cit.*, 331–6; David Brody, *The Steelworkers in America*, 214–25; Vernon H. Jensen, *Heritage of Conflict*, 247–8, 262; William M. Leiserson, *Adjusting Immigrants and Industry*, 187, 199–201, 234–45.

[2] *61 Congress 2 Session, Senate Doc. 633*, Immigration Commission Reports, Immigrants in Industries, Part I, Bituminous Coal Mining, I 101; Part 19, Anthracite, 620.

[3] Louis Wirth, *The Ghetto*, chapter xii; Nathan Glazer and Daniel P. Moynihan, *Beyond the Melting Pot*, 256–62. The subject is pursued further in my Epilogue.

[4] Elin L. Anderson, *We Americans*, 24–6, gives an example.

III

Most immigrants entered the United States when the techniques of two-party democracy were already well established. Although there was much tightening-up of requirements early in the present century, and naturalization rules were elaborately codified in 1906, at earlier times many states permitted aliens to vote, subject only to mild residence provisions. In 1890, it was found that more than half the foreign-born had become citizens and that many more had taken out first papers. Thirty years later, after the greatest wave of immigration in American history, the situation was not very different, and by 1930 the combined figure was over seventy per cent. Such figures, of course, take no account of how long immigrants had been in the United States, and some of the groups whose figures appear very low had in fact been in the United States no more than a few years. Early in the 1920s, a leading authority believed that few immigrants thought seriously about naturalization until they had spent ten years in getting established in a job and in starting a family, as well as learning English. Many who began the process failed to complete it, some through apathy, others because the legal system imposed more complications than they could endure. He concluded that, if all this were taken into account, the figures should be regarded as creditable. He thought, further, that the best record was achieved by those who had risen fairly quickly above poverty in America, but who could contrast their success with earlier life under an oppressive regime. The British, on the other hand, with all their advantages of literacy and skill, tended to feel that American liberty was not greatly preferable to what they had left behind, and showed themselves rather indifferent towards citizenship.[1]

Much more was involved than the mere right to vote. In the nineteenth century, money or favours might be the reward for going to the polls; and employment on the city payroll might also be a consideration of value, at a time when Boston paid its labourers $2 a day, against the fifty cent lower rate in the private sector. Since their votes were of value to party leaders, in certain circumstances immigrants might aspire to minor elective office. In the 1870s, for example, certain townships in western Wisconsin were so heavily Norwegian that members of that group were employed as census-takers, soon came to provide most of the township officers, and between 1875 and 1885 held rather more than half the seats on the county board.[2] Elsewhere in the Middle West, Scandinavians rose even higher. Sam Burnquist,

[1] John P. Gavit, *Americans by Choice*, esp. 206-8, 214-17. See also *Compendium of the Eleventh Census*, II 683; Niles Carpenter, *Immigrants and their Children*, 262; Maurice R. Davie, *World Immigration*, 256, 542; V. O. Key, *Politics, Parties and Pressure Groups* (3rd edn), 626-7.
[2] Merle Curti, *The Making of an American Community*, 295-6, 316-19, 340, 418-26.

first labourer and then businessman in Iowa, became mayor and assembly-man. Testen Johnson, farmer, became county commissioner, assemblyman and state senator. Louis Foss, a farmer with no more than an elementary education, became a probate judge. Jon Lind, teacher and lawyer, was in turn superintendent of schools, receiver in a U.S. Land Office, congressman, and, thirty years after landing in America, the first Swedish state governor.[1]

The second generation was likely to win more widespread success. The lives of a substantial proportion of city bosses – 'Big Tim' Sullivan, 'Com-missioner' Murphy, 'Senator' William Flynn, for example – show Irish immigrant parentage, a youth spent in such humble occupations as newsboy, bootblack, horsecar-driver, or bartender, then a reputation as a gang leader, then a minor party office. Step by step, as he rose within the party, the boss was likely to make money as a contractor or in some other business, and place his relations in positions of influence. Apart from the Irish, Cermak of Chicago rose to be precinct captain, state assemblyman, and ultimately mayor, by building influence within his own Czech community and becom-ing leader of a great anti-Prohibition organization, the United Societies for Local Self-government. La Guardia, of more mixed ethnic origin as well as more adventurous ideas, spent much of his public life working from an Italian base in Manhattan, while also making an appeal to Jewish voters; but he found it necessary to make an even wider appeal before he could dominate a constituency bigger than a congressional district.[2]

Ethnic considerations, too, determined party slates in great cities. In Chicago in 1932, when Cermak was already mayor, state offices were sought by four men with Irish names and by one Czech, while a German was seeking the United States Senate. Congressional candidates had the names of Kelly and O'Brien, Schuetz, Weber and Schlaeger, Sabath (a Bohemian Jew), and Kocialkowski. For the state assembly, half the candidates were Irish, the remainder Poles, Germans, Italians, and Czechs. County and city offices were sought by a similar mixture of people, though newer ethnic groups were rather more fully represented at this lower level.[3]

---

[1] O. M. Nelson, *History of the Scandinavians and Successful Scandinavians in the United States,* I 400–401, 423–4, 430–34, II 159–61.

[2] Harold Zink, *City Bosses in the United States,* esp. 85–95, 147–63, 245–56; Alex Gottfried, *Boss Cermak of Chicago,* 49–54, 95–7, 120–21; Arthur Mann, *La Guardia: a Fighter against his Times,* 67–71, 113–14, 144, 150–58, 173–80, 232–46, 268–80; while Robert A. Woods, *The City Wilderness,* chapter vi, has an interesting view of Boston ward politics. For remarks on later Irish bosses, e.g. Daley of Chicago, with their rather studied working-class style, see Edward M. Levine, *The Irish and Irish Politicians,* 120–25, 147, and chapter vi.

[3] Gottfried, *op. cit.,* 294 and notes on 417–18. Wellington G. Fordyce, 'Nationality Groups in Cleveland Politics', *Ohio State Archeological and Historical Quarterly,* XLVI (1937), 118, shows Slavs, Magyars, Italians, and Jews on the city council in the 1920s, though with rather few spokes-men in proportion to their numbers.

IV

A knowledge of English was a consequence of some of these advances, a prerequisite for others. Although a few attempts were made in factory classes and settlement houses, or as part of a national campaign of americanization during the Great War, most of the teaching had to be done in the public schools, and this affected the second generation, not immigrant adults.[1] Along with their new language, children picked up a simple, standardized set of values, though constant reference to American history and performance of American patriotic ritual; and despite the greater emphasis on the European language and tradition, even the parochial schools exposed their pupils to some of these American influences. Teachers were usually American-born, people at least one stage more deeply rooted than those they taught. 'First grade, Miss O'Rourke,' complained one Italian youth, 'Second grade, Miss Casey. Third grade, Miss Chalmers. Fourth grade, Miss Mooney.' He was not far wrong.[2] To be sure, the educational system was very different from that of today. For working-class children, it occupied fewer years, and in many places fewer months of each year. One-room schools in country districts were taught by girls who themselves had had imperfect schooling, or by young men, professionally untrained, working for enough money to start college or law school. Men as celebrated as George Norris and Charles Evans Hughes engaged in such work.[3]

Schools had a powerful opposition to contend with, though in two generations they triumphed. Immigrants continued to use the old language at home and their children used it there if nowhere else. About 1930, at Milligan, Nebraska, a rather isolated and almost wholly Czech village, nearly all second-generation inhabitants spoke Czech and about half of them spoke it regularly at home. More than one-third could read it, though only one-quarter could write it. On the other hand, few of them still subscribed to Czech-language newspapers, and, although speaking Czech continued into the third generation, the other skills almost wholly disappeared.[4]

[1] Thompson, *op. cit.*, is a leading authority: he is very critical of the methods employed. See also *Hull House Maps and Papers*, 207–30, for an earlier period; and Edward G. Hartmann, *The Movement to Americanize the Immigrant*, esp. 24–36, 75–6, 124–33, 237–52.

[2] William F. Whyte, *Street-Corner Society*, 276. The census reports confirm the impression.

[3] Thompson, *op. cit.*, 283, shows that only Massachusetts and New York had compulsory school-attendance laws before the Civil War. Several industrial states, and others in the Middle West, enacted such laws only after 1890. For first-hand accounts of conditions, see Hamlin Garland, *A Son of the Middle Border*, 80–81; Edward E. Dale, *Frontier Ways: Sketches of Life in the Old West*, 156–61; Herbert Quick, *One Man's Life*, 249–51. See also Richard Lowitt, *George Norris: the Making of a Progressive*, 6–7, 9–10; Robert F. Wesser, *Charles Evans Hughes: Politics and Reform in New York*, 26.

[4] Robert I. Kutak, *The Story of a Bohemian-American Village*, 63–5, 113–16.

A rather similar persistence was possible, in working-class districts of big cities, when these were inhabited by a single group, strongly influenced by nationalist ideology and by Roman Catholic parochial schools. At Hamtranck, Michigan, in the 1940s, half the Poles were using only their old language at home, and many others sometimes did so. Polish was commonly used at public meetings for adults, but it was already noticeable that few high-school pupils were electing to study it.[1] Similarly, as late as 1930, a small pocket of Sicilian settlement could be found in Manhattan, in which the immigrant generation were largely illiterate, and in which many knew no English at all. Thirty years later, Italians of Boston's West End preserved the dialect of their home district for conversation involving the first and second generations, though the third generation were found to have discarded it almost completely.[2] At Burlington, Vermont, a small town with several ethnic groups, linguistic survival might be expected to have been more difficult. In fact, Italians were still using the old language at home, and so were a majority of French-Canadians, though only a minority even of first-generation Jews regularly employed Yiddish. Numbers evidently were not the only factor involved, for Italians and Jews in Burlington were both small groups.[3]

Survival of traditional practices proved easy in the home. In more public areas of life, the need to mix with other ethnic groups, and with older Americans, would necessarily be greater.

Given the central position of the church in the immigrant community, the fate of the European language, in its services and in the education of its clergy, serves as a significant index of wider trends. Of the ethnic groups arriving well before the end of the nineteenth century, the Welsh saw the decline of their language in church after about 1900: first one service in English each Sunday, then Welsh every other week, then Welsh once a month, until by the 1960s only a handful of churches had anything more than a St David's Day service in the old tongue.[4] By the 1920s, the French-Canadians of Burlington were finding their young people attending services at the cathedral, designed primarily for Irish Catholics, because they were easier to understand.[5] About 1920, in a Dutch community on Long Island, the Reformed Church was holding a Sunday afternoon service in Dutch for old people, though the more evangelical Christian Reformed Church

[1] Wood, *op. cit.*, 36–9, 174, 205.

[2] Harry M. Shulman, *Slums of New York*, 21–32, 174–201; Herbert Gans, *The Urban Villagers*, 33–4.

[3] Anderson, *op. cit.*, 140–55.

[4] Edward G. Hartmann, *Americans from Wales*, 123–31, 146–54. English became the dominant language in the modern *Eisteddfod*.

[5] Anderson, *op. cit.*, 85–6.

was still using the old language for most of its services. Thirty years later, in the United States as a whole, even the latter Church had almost dropped Dutch.[1] As for the larger ethnic groups, Germans in St Louis, in 1914, were still holding no more than thirty per cent of their services in English. By 1929 the proportion was seventy-five per cent, and smaller and far more purely German towns were experiencing the same trend. Between the same years, there occurred an almost complete change to English as the language of teaching at Eden Seminary of the Missouri Synod Lutherans.[2] Scandinavians, of course, were being reinforced with new immigrants considerably later than the Germans, and many of them, especially the Norwegians, lived in rural conditions whose isolation and ethnic concentration should both have been highly favourable to the persistence of the old language. In the 1920s, indeed, the very isolated Danish community of Askov, Minnesota, was still using much Danish in its schools. Over a wider area, however, it was found as early as 1900 that the old language was beginning to decline in Swedish colleges, both for lecturing and religious services, though pastors were still required to know it when appointed. In Kansas, Swedish dominated the church scene until the end of the nineteenth century, English was used in the public schools, and Lutherans organized summer schools in Swedish. Early in the present century, one church was organized expressly for English-speaking people. By the 1920s, the two languages were rather evenly balanced. By 1940, English had triumphed. In Norwegian communities, higher education was already being conducted mainly in English in the 1890s. Preaching, however, was mainly in the old language, though a few church publications were being printed in English. By the 1920s, English took the lead in services, and in 1941 no fewer than eighty-eight per cent of all services were being held in it.[3]

While a very few hundred people sufficed for the organization of a church, newspapers, certainly dailies, needed thousands of readers, and the effect of the dying-out of the immigrant generation was disastrous. In 1904, more than 600 publications appeared in German, and this number included 78 daily newspapers. Ten years later, the figures were still 537 and 53. By the end of the Great War they were 278 and 26.[4] The Welsh press vanished

[1] Daniels, op. cit., 42–3; Henry S. Lucas, Netherlanders in America, 597.
[2] John A. Hawgood, The Tragedy of German-America, 124, 128, 300–301.
[3] Edmund de S. Brunner, Immigrant Farmers and their Children, 155–82; J. Iverne Dowie and Ernest M. Espelie, The Swedish Immigrant Community in Transition, 82–5, 121–46 (the latter an essay on the emotional associations of language); Emory K. Lindquist, Smoky Valley People: a History of Lindsborg, Kansas, 96, 128, 182–7; George M. Stephenson, Religious Aspects of Swedish Immigration, 431, 473–5; E. Clifford Nelson and Eugene L. Fevold, The Lutheran Church among Norwegian-Americans, II 242–53.
[4] Carl Wittke, The German-Language Press in America, 208–9.

during the present century, and the decline of the Swedish press was rapid.[1] As late as 1920, as might be expected from their numbers and the time of their arrival, southern and eastern European groups were holding their own in publication, or even expanding. Twenty years later, observers felt them to be in the same danger that had already gone so far towards overwhelming the newspapers of their predecessors.[2] By 1965, no great European group had more than five dailies. Most of the 61 German papers, 46 Italian, 38 Czech, 34 Polish, 29 Hungarian, 19 Yiddish, and so on, were local, religious or trade publications, and some were printed partly in English. The only flourishing foreign-language press was the Spanish, that is to say the Mexican and Puerto Rican, though several of their publications were no more than foreign editions of magazines essentially English-American.[3]

V

A Protestant minister on Long Island who, about 1920, was accustomed to perform marriages for Czech Freethinkers, commented as follows on their changing customs: 'Their weddings used to last three days, the most wonderful meals were served and there was an abundance of everything. But the last time I married a couple we had lemonade, ice cream, and cake.'[4] The question to be asked is, was it only the style of ceremony that changed, or was the choice of partner becoming, not only freer from parental control, but more American, less limited within the ethnic group.

Immigrants might live so completely segregated a life that possible marriage-partners would simply not be met. Three-fifths of Burlington's male Jews in the 1930s, and four-fifths of the women, seem to have had no social life outside their group, and Italians and French-Canadians were even more exclusive.[5] A group might, of course, be so small as to be unable to sustain any independent social life, and a big group might consist so largely of single men that marriage across ethnic lines would be inevitable. Often, however, tens of thousands of an ethnic group would live together, and

---

[1] Hartmann, *Americans from Wales*, 128–31; Finis H. Capps, *From Isolationism to Involvement: the Swedish Immigrant Press in America 1914–1945*, 26–8, 105–6, 149, 153, 163–6. The Scandinavian press as a whole reached its peak in 1909.

[2] Park, *op. cit.*, table facing 318; Edward Corsi, 'Italian Immigrants and their Children', *Annals*, 223 (1942), 103–4; but Wood, *op. cit.*, 36, found that half his Hamtranck households in 1950 were reading Polish newspapers.

[3] *N. W. Ayer and Sons' Directory: Newspapers and Periodicals 1965*, 1392–1405. Even such figures may be out of date: while I was in Rochester, N.Y., in the summer of 1967, the *Abendpost* ended after more than a century.

[4] Daniels, *op. cit.*, 37.

[5] Anderson, *op. cit.*, 127, 140–62.

could sustain a complete pattern of social institutions and relationships. Although ethnic lines might become blurred when the second generation left the original district, preferences could survive, and even if a man chose his wife outside his own group, he might rank other groups according to a scale of values derived from opinions in his own. Such investigations as have been made must now be studied. It is important, however, to stress one fact. All such studies must overstate the incidence of marriage outside the group, simply because members of the third generation are officially recorded as 'native American'.

A very early view of the situation can be derived from the 1880 census returns for Boston's twenty-five wards. For our present purpose, there is no need to look at each ward separately, nor even to distinguish between fathers and mothers of the native-born of mixed origin. It is enough to record that, of the native-born inhabitants with any Irish parentage, more than 66,000 had both parents Irish, somewhat over 8,000 had one parent Irish and one American (which could easily mean Irish in some real ethnic sense), about 3,000 each were mixed Irish-British and Irish-Canadian (about whom the same qualification might be in order), while no other mixed parentage was represented by as many as a thousand examples.[1] Some thirty years later, a much more massive investigation was made into more than a hundred thousand marriage-licences in New York City, and in some ways Drachsler's study remains the best. One of his findings, that second-generation men and women marry outside their group two or three times as often as those of the first generation, will surprise no one. Nor will it seem strange that most people chose partners of the same generation as themselves, sharing, it may be assumed, similar cultural characteristics and a similar degree of americanization. The difference, however, between the habits of one group and another is striking. Among the second generation, Drachsler found that European Jews never exceeded a rate of eight per cent of marriage outside their group, and no eastern European Jews exceeded 3·4 per cent. South Italians showed a rate of 3·51 per cent. North Italians, along with Irish, Slovaks, Czechs and Poles had rates ranging from thirty to fifty per cent, while Scandinavians, Hungarians, British, and Canadians had rates even higher. Such figures are still rather general in character: even more interesting are the groups from which each type of European chose its partners. Combining for this purpose members of the first and second generations, it is found that, of the newer groups, the 1,040 Russian Polish men chose 756 Russian Polish women, 194 Austrian Polish, 33 Slovak, and very small

[1] Carroll D. Wright, *The Social, Commercial and Manufacturing Statistics of the City of Boston*, 30–43.

numbers of German, Irish and Finnish. The 19,411 Russian Jewish men chose 16,070 Russian Jewish women, 1,801 Austrian Jewish, 433 Roumanian Jewish, 410 Hungarian Jewish, 368 German Jewish, 130 'American' Jewish, 67 English Jewish, and fewer than 30 of any Gentile ethnic group. The 4,364 South Italian men chose 3,960 South Italian women, 187 North Italian, 44 German, 41 Irish, and 21 Austrian Poles. The 8,812 Irish men in this very large sample chose 7,271 women who were clearly of their own group, 578 German, 292 English, 140 Scottish, as well as some Canadians and Americans. The effect of cultural similarity, and probably of religion, seems clear.[1]

Studies made of New Haven, Connecticut, for the period 1870 to 1940 show a rising rate of intermarriage, from under one-tenth to more than one-third if members of all ethnic groups are combined. Jews and Italians had much the lowest rates, Germans and Scandinavians (both very small groups) the highest. Perhaps the figures reflect some deep cultural preference, but it is also true that most Jews and Italians lived in large numbers in defined zones, within which most of their social life naturally occurred. It was found, too, that Roman Catholics married non-Catholics more often than Jews married non-Jews, while Protestants married outside their religious world more often than either; but even in 1940 such rates were low, respectively under six, under sixteen, and under twenty-one per cent.[2] At Burlington, Vermont, investigation of 3,677 marriages showed almost no intermarriages by Jews, about one-third among French-Canadians (though in such a community the third-generation factor could be important), about two-thirds among the Irish (with the same reservation). Most members of the very small Italian and German communities were marrying outside their group.[3] At Darby, Connecticut, little change in intermarriage rates was recorded between 1930 and 1940. As elsewhere, Jews intermarried least; about one-fifth of Roman Catholics married outside their ethnic group but inside their faith, but nearly three-quarters married inside in both the ethnic and religious sense. The equivalent rate for Pro-

[1] Julius Drachsler, *Intermarriage in New York City*: he summarizes his findings on 66–70. The reader may be interested to see figures for those men counted as 'Americans'. Of 16,007, 9,542 chose native American wives, 2,356 first- or second-generation Irish, 1,682 German, 681 English, and small numbers of Scots, Canadians, French, Swedish, and Italian. Similar results emerge from Bessie L. Wessel, *An Ethnic Survey of Woonsocket, Rhode Island,* esp. 38–9, 46–53.
[2] Ruby J. Kennedy, 'Premarital Propinquity and Ethnic Endogamy', *American Journal of Sociology,* XLVIII (1942–3), 580–84; 'Single or Triple Melting Pot? Intermarriage Trends in New Haven 1870–1940', *ibid.,* XLIX (1943–4), 331–9; and her article of the same title, extended one decade, *ibid.,* LVIII (1952–3), 56–9, which shows the same ranking, though most ethnic and religious intermarriage, other than Jewish, has increased slightly.
[3] Anderson, *op. cit.,* 187–201. Intermarriage increased with successive generations; but a very high proportion of the people questioned disapproved of *religious* intermarriage.

testants was a little over one-half – but 'Protestant' is a vague term, and some of the groups concerned were very small. Patterns such as these may have been formed by propinquity, or by principle or preference, or by resistance from certain other groups. Certainly Jews and Catholics faced strong disapproval of intermarriage on the part of their religious leaders, while Protestants were likely to be wary of intermarriage with Catholics because of the restrictive conditions imposed by such partners' Church.[1]

These are all urban communities, but a study of the so-called 'U.S. Registration Area', a mixed group of rural and urban states, does little more than confirm the other findings set forth in these pages. British and Canadians apart, members of ethnic groups married their own kind, those of recently-arrived groups conspicuously so. The factor of cultural similarity seems to appear, with Irish marrying British or Canadians when they failed to find Irish or American partners, and Russian-born marrying Americans or Austrian-born as a second choice, probably Jews of the third generation.[2] A large rural sample of Nebraska, Wisconsin and New York, for 1908–12 and 1921–25 showed, as might be expected, a wider range of choice in polyglot New York than in the other states. Intermarriage, not surprisingly, was more common in the later period. An immigrant was most likely to marry one of his own group, then a native American, then a member of another ethnic group. Northern Europeans, especially British, married Americans rather than southern Europeans. Since the communities had a surplus of men, they were more likely than women to marry outside their group.[3] Finally, a sample from Minnesota, combining two generations, confirms the impressions that members of the largest groups find least need to marry outside them; that people who intermarry choose partners from a similar ethnic group, so that Swedes marry Germans or Norwegians when they do not marry Swedes; and that religious intermarriage is less common than ethnic.[4]

An element never seriously studied in these inquiries, and one that can perhaps never be studied on any large scale, is one that logic suggests as highly important. It is impossible to say whether immigrants or the second generation took account of class considerations in choosing partners. Most of the first generation remained within the working class, though that is far from a solid unit in its cultural standards. Many of the second generation

---

[1] Milton L. Barron, *People Who Intermarry*, esp. 128–9, 163–5 (the facts), 31, 40–41 (official attitudes).

[2] Carpenter, *op. cit.*, 234.

[3] Brunner, *op. cit.*, esp. 76–9.

[4] Lowry Nelson, 'Intermarriage among Nationality Groups in a Rural Area of Minnesota', *American Journal of Sociology*, XLVIII (1942–3), 585–92.

rose to the lower-middle class. Propinquity and concern for values alike would surely make it likely that people would marry inside their own class, but whether they did so, or how many exceptions there were to the rule, we cannot tell.

Epilogue

The ones she had borne into the world . . . would from the beginning of their lives say what her own tongue was unable to say, *at home* here in America, *back there* in Sweden.

Vilhelm Moberg, *Unto a Good Land*, 370.

Immigration has often reached 300,000 a year since 1945, though much of it has come from areas other than Europe. Because of the gap occasioned by economic depression and the Second World War, however, and because America's population has almost doubled since 1920, the foreign-born have come to play a smaller part in American society than they did through much of the century of our study. In 1860, the foreign-born numbered somewhat over four millions, about thirteen per cent of the population; in 1900 the number was $10\frac{1}{3}$ millions and the percentage about the same; in 1930, fourteen millions and more than 11 per cent; but in 1960 they were under ten millions and 5·4 per cent.[1]

Even apart from the effect of being statistically swallowed up in the United States, that country's pace of change might itself lead one to expect a rapid assimilation of the foreign-born. The surface phenomena are clear enough: transcontinental highways, universal car-ownership, jet flights within the country and across oceans, widespread higher education, the rush to suburban homes. Behind these facts lie some statistics even more impressive. In the thirty years down to 1950, the proportion of white-collar workers nearly doubled, that of farmers and farmworkers was almost halved, and that of unskilled workers fell sharply – indeed there were a million fewer labourers in 1950 than in 1900. In the fifteen years after 1950, the number of blue-collar jobs rose some three per cent, that of white-collar jobs fifty per cent, and that of farmers was cut in half. Women were more widely employed than ever before, but in clerical, sales or service jobs in commercial establishments, rather than in factories and domestic service. Extreme mobility, rising standards of living for a majority, are other ingredients of a social change from which no ethnic group could be immune.

The foreign-born and their children have indeed shared in America's

---

[1] The figures, as usual, are based on *Historical Statistics of the United States,* 1945, and *Statistical Abstract of the United States,* 196. See also Hutchinson, *Immigrants and their Children 1850–1950.* The German- and Irish-born reached their peak in 1890, Scandinavians in 1910, Russian-born (i.e. mainly Jews) in 1920, Italians in 1930. Since 1945 Europeans have seldom made up half the total immigration, and have often been nearer one-third.

change. The 1950 census figures for surviving immigrants show striking advances over their predecessors of 1910, or their very early selves, in the direction of more highly skilled work, service jobs, or white-collar status. As for the second generation, even in 1910 they were doing better than their parents. By 1950, they had gone far towards assimilation in the common pattern of American work. Using Hutchinson's index of relative concentration once more, in few occupations do the second-generation of 1950 show scores higher than 110 or lower than 90: only in agriculture is their figure really low. Far fewer of the women, too, are in factory work than in their parents' generation. Differences between ethnic groups, on the other hand, can still be seen. Foreign-born Irish, Italians and Poles, and even their children, were still somewhat concentrated in labouring and semi-skilled jobs; the British second generation, though also many Irish, were moving even further into clerical and managerial work; and second-generation Jews came to be heavily represented in the categories of sales, technical, management, and the professions.

Since Europe itself changed vastly as the result of a world war, it would seem at first glance that all the factors upon which the survival of ethnic groups depended must have been weakened, and the historian's first expectation might well be that all groups were moving rapidly towards eclipse. The facts are different. Patterns of ethnic separation have been no more than modified, certainly not obliterated.

The Jewish community of Providence, Rhode Island, and its suburbs will serve as a starting-point. Middle-aged and elderly members are likely to be of the immigrant generation; a second generation has already made marked progress in education, occupation and standard of living; and a third generation, mostly white-collar workers with a good proportion of executives and professional people, has moved to the suburbs. To that extent, as well as in size of family, type of home, and so on, there is little to distinguish such Jews from other Americans of the same status. Yet something far short of assimilation has taken place. Exceedingly few Jewish men, and almost no Jewish women, marry outside their group. Gentile wives are likely to convert to Judaism. Most of the third generation are found to be members of a religious congregation, and to provide their children with a Jewish education to supplement that obtained in the public schools. A high proportion are members of Jewish organizations only. The character of their Judaism, however, has become very different from the Orthodoxy brought in by the immigrants. Yiddish, still spoken at home by most of the old people, is used by little more than one-tenth of young third-generation adults. Whereas half of the old people are still avowedly Orthodox, and another one-third Conservative, half the young third-generation adults are Conservative, and nearly two-fifths Reform. Exceedingly few of these modern Jews attend services every week, few light Sabbath candles, and very few confine themselves to kosher food. Such observances as remain, however, represent something solid. The new pattern of Judaism involves going to services distinctly more often than on High Holidays, holding Passover and Chanukka ceremonies at home, sending boys to combined programmes of part-time classes and Sunday School, and sending girls at any rate to the latter.[1]

In both of the more modern forms of Judaism, the English language is much used. In Reform temples, Sunday services, church music, exchange of pulpits with Unitarian ministers, all show, as it were, americanization.[2] Even more important, the congregation has become the centre of a cluster of activities not too far removed from those to be found in a Catholic parish. When questioned, suburban Jews are likely to speak of identity in the face of the gentile world, of social solidarity, of family unity, and, above all, of the interests of their children, whom they wish to see grow up conscious of their heritage and determined to marry within the group.[3] Rabbis, who in the modern congregations have a standard academic training as well as religious education, are likely to approach their faith in more humane and less legal terms than did their predecessors. They are viewed as counsellors, preachers, and spokesmen for the group. Often, indeed, they are worried at the loss of the more traditional role, based on learning in the Law.[4]

Such vigour and separateness are displayed by a Jewish community no more completely united than other ethnic groups. Sociologists who, a decade ago, studied Jewish life in Minneapolis emphasized the contrasts between the rich, the country-club set, and the craftsmen and small business-men who had stayed in the older residential zone. The former were nearly all of the Reform persuasion, gave their children Christian names, gave few of them a Jewish education, had many gentile friends, and belonged to many gentile organizations. Yet they were still Jews. They took a considerable part in community fund-raising; their gentile associations were not their most intimate; and they had found it necessary to establish a *Jewish* country

---

[1] Sidney Goldstein and Calvin Goldscheider, *Jewish Americans: Three Generations in a Jewish Community*. See also Herbert J. Gans, 'The Origin and Growth of a Jewish Community in the Suburbs: a Study of the Jews of Park Forest', in Marshall Sklare, *The Jews: Social Patterns of an American Group*, 205–48.
[2] Albert I. Gordon, *Jews in Suburbia*, esp. 97–104. See also Marshall Sklare, *Conservative Judaism*; and contrast Howard W. Polsky's essay on Milwaukee's Orthodox Jews in Sklare, *The Jews*, 325–35.
[3] Gordon, *op. cit.*, 83–4, 116–18, 149–51; Gans, 'Park Forest', 214–21.
[4] Gordon, *op. cit.*, 154–8; Jerome E. Carlin and Saul H. Mendlovitz, 'The American Rabbi: a Religious Specialist Responds to Loss of Authority', in Sklare, *The Jews*, 377–414.

club. Suburban Jews as a whole retained, as in Providence, a solid minimum of Jewish consciousness and practice. Commentators, of course, often doubt the reality of such a religion; but modern Jews do not view the matter in that light. They feel their community to be real; and when they have the choice, they prefer their largely 'American' life to be lived in a Jewish or largely Jewish suburb.[1]

It would be misleading to confine our attention to Jews, whose religious and ethnic identity cannot easily be separated. Other groups must be studied, groups most of which are as old-established as the Russian Jews in the United States, and which, therefore, include elderly people born abroad, a second generation brought up in America, and a third generation, already adult, whose ties with the old world must be exceedingly slight. The question must be asked, how far have the later generations, and especially the third, become assimilated, and in what directions.

There has recently developed among scholars a tendency to argue that ethnic differences are becoming less significant in Americans' view of life, and are becoming replaced by classification along religious lines. Will Herberg has argued that after a second generation, filled with doubts and tensions, the third generation wishes to conform to many American patterns, wishes at the same time to preserve an identity, and finds that American society accepts religious differentiations more easily than ethnic. He points out, too, that most Americans feel themselves to be affiliated with broad religious groups, though in the minds of most of them doctrine is exceedingly vague. Herberg suspects, in fact, that older Americans and ethnic third generation alike feel religion to be 'a way of sociability or "belonging"'... without real inner conviction, without genuine existential decision'; and that each main faith regards itself 'as an alternative and variant form of being religious in the American way.'[2] An even more recent study of New York's Italians provides supporting evidence. As members of this group advance into the middle class and move to suburbs, their support for the Roman Catholic Church, and especially for parochial schools and Catholic colleges, grows, even though Italians are rare among priests and bishops.[3] The New Haven marriage investigations could be interpreted in the same way, to suggest that it is the Protestant-Catholic-Jewish grouping that now determines preferences.[4]

To substitute a 'triple melting-pot' for a single one, however, still fails to

---

[1] Judith R. Kramer and Seymour Leventman, *Children of the Gilded Ghetto: Conflict Resolutions of Three Generations of American Jews.*
[2] Will Herberg, *Protestant, Catholic, Jew*; quotations are on 276, 278.
[3] Nathan Glazer and Daniel P. Moynihan, *Beyond the Melting Pot*, esp. 202–5.
[4] See the Kennedy articles cited on p. 270, n. 2.

do justice to the complexity of social fact. Both ethnic and class factors are still important. No group has been able entirely to discard its past.

A group little affected by the drift to suburban life, like the Poles of Hamtranck, may retain into the middle of the twentieth century a few ceremonies and customs of a distinctively ethnic type.[1] It may be argued, too, that the Italians of Boston's West End kept, down to the 1960s, certain attitudes that were southern Italian, not just working-class. They abandoned most of their specifically ethnic institutions, and the third generation showed signs of dropping the old language; but they continued to display lack of educational ambition, assigned very separate roles to the sexes, viewed public authority and even doctors with distrust and cynicism, and saw in the family the proper, the sole, area of loyalty.[2]

Despite the tendency towards occupational uniformity noted earlier, a few instances may be found in the 1950 census of the persistence of ethnic specialization. Using Hutchinson's index for the last time, it is found that, even in the middle of the century, foreign-born Greeks, as proprietors of restaurants and coffee-shops, had an index of relative concentration as high as 2,297 and, as cooks, 3,021. The Russian-born (i.e. chiefly Jews) had an index of 1,690 as tailors and furriers; immigrants (again mostly Jewish) from Poland, Lithuania and Roumania all scored over 1,000 in this occupation, though so also did Italians. The Irish index as porters and cleaners was 1,197, the Germans as bakers was 874, the Italian as masons was 557. With the second generation, of course, all except the Greek extremes are smoothed out, but what remain are index figures among these groups as high as 200 or 250.[3]

Differences remain visible, too, in political life. A recent study of Swedish-American newspapers demonstrates that opinions formed during or before the Great War affected attitudes even after 1945. Early respect for Germany as a leader of civilization in general and Lutheranism in particular, hatred of Russia, distrust of imperialism, pessimism about the chances of introducing any moral order into international affairs, a feeling that self-interest is the only proper basis for American policy, and dislike of centralized authority in American government, combine to produce considerable attachment to isolationism as a governing principle. Germany lost its early position in Swedish thinking in the 1940s, and both Wilson and Franklin Roosevelt, though strong presidents, aroused respect; but suspicion of too much involvement in world affairs, and especially in world organizations, has

[1] Arthur E. Wood, *Hamtranck Then and Now*, 40–42, 197–8.
[2] Herbert J. Gans, *The Urban Villagers*, esp. 36–41, 130–41, 163.
[3] Hutchinson, *op. cit.*, 220–21, 224–39, 335–64.

persisted.[1] Jews tend to remain Democrats even when they rise to affluence; they are likely to be found towards the left of that party; and they will split their ticket in the most sophisticated way, so as to prefer liberal and independent Republicans to machine Democrats. The Irish have been recognizable, within the Democratic party, for their interest in organization and techniques rather than adventurous issues, and as they rise in the social scale they are quite likely to become Republicans, and very conservative ones at that.[2]

Ethnic groups today, as in the past, contain their differences, as when prosperous Catholics choose parochial schools and denominational colleges for their children in such a way as to keep them apart from Catholics of lower status.[3] Nor, when they continue to display ethnic characteristics of the sort outlined above, do groups act as exponents of a European or a half-European culture. Having become largely American in economic affairs, they retain preferences in the more personal areas of life; but they have few ties with the old country. Very largely they have forgotten the old language. They do different work from their European ancestors. Their families have different patterns of authority. Retaining some distinct identity, in short, they act as a special type of American. What may now be coming to act as a force solidifying their group-feelings is not European concerns, but the awareness among the second or third generation, newly arrived at positions of skill and security, of challenges from above and from below. Skilled workers demonstrating their patriotism, policemen using their clubs, families voting for George Wallace, may all be expressing their suspicions of students and middle-class 'doves' in the higher ranks of society, and their violent hostility to the claims of blacks below.

All this is very far from total assimilation, very far, even, from a peaceful equilibrium in the relationship between cultures. Yet although in 1970 the processes of ethnic history in America are not yet at an end, the historian is bound to attempt a summing-up of what has so far occurred, of what contribution immigrants have made to the United States.

Beyond reasonable doubt, their contribution to American economic growth has been massive. Given a democratic political order and the

[1] Finis H. Capps, *From Isolationism to Involvement*.
[2] Edward M. Levine, *The Irish and Irish Politicians*, 35, 109–10, 134–5, 191–202; Glazer and Moynihan, *op. cit.*, 209–15, 222–9, 262–74; Lawrence H. Fuchs, *Political Behaviour of American Jews*.
[3] Joseph H. Fichter, *Social Relations in the Urban Parish*, 46–51; Milton M. Gordon, *Assimilation in American Life*, 187–90, 209–20 (and the entire book is illuminating). With the Roman Catholic Church once more under discussion, it is worth recalling that, in 1948, 1,500 parishes survived that were recognizably related to ethnic groups – C. J. Nuesse and Thomas J. Harte, *The Sociology of the Parish*, 162–4.

accessibility of land, the United States could not have pulled people off the farms fast enough to build industry and cities at anything like the speed that was in fact achieved after the Civil War. The triumph, needless to say, was achieved at considerable cost, in tensions and dislocations, but these were largely at the expense of a foreign working-class.

Ethnic influences on political institutions and social values have surely been far less. To an extent that any European historian must find surprising, the United States, in these respects, is recognizably similar in 1970 and in 1840, despite the many changes in technology and style. The principles and institutions designed at the Revolution, modified by the needs of the early republic, were well established by the time of Jackson. The Civil War failed to break them; and the Confederacy would certainly have denied any intention of doing so. These principles and institutions were accepted as superior by the articulate members of those ethnic groups that were the first to arrive in the nineteenth century, and it is here, and only here, that lies the truth of Marcus Hansen's famous dictum, 'they were Americans before they landed'.

To end on such a note, however, with a discussion of forces and trends, would be to conceal my own bias as an historian. It is to the thirty-five million emigrants, or the few of them that can be identified, that I insist on returning.

As to what their experience had meant to them, immigrants remained divided. A Magyar intellectual might complain of the absence of literary cafés, of the high cost of theatre seats and books. An educated Austrian might talk of the need to learn a new code of behaviour, a new set of re-actions, which left him and his fellows slow and confused. A Norwegian clergyman could remark: 'Ours is the riches of two cultures and often the poverty of the desert wanderer. We live between memory and reality.' A successful Bulgarian insisted: 'I shall always be the adopted child, not the real son'; yet when he visited his old country he felt no more at home, and could not cut himself off from his new country, 'though I am but half American.'[1] Lower down the social scale, who can doubt that immigrants often remembered with longing fjord or farm, church or tavern, or the women gossiping round the village well?[2]

[1] Robert E. Park and Herbert A. Miller, *Old World Traits Transplanted,* 54-6, 113-18; P. M. Glasoe, quoted in E. Clifford Nelson and Eugene L. Fevold, *The Lutheran Church among Norwegian-Americans,* II 240; Stoyan Christowe, *This Is My Country,* 231-2.
[2] Theodore C. Blegen, *Land of their Choice,* 117, 264, 379, 393, 403, 418; William Howett, *The Rural and Domestic Life of Germany,* 18-21. Often the immigrant simply desired a flow of news. His nostalgia was often expressed in the language of religious resignation – see Henry S. Lucas, *Dutch Immigrant Memoirs and Related Writings,* I 498-9 (Engbertus van der Veen's dream of Amsterdam).

Other immigrants, achieving a modest success, felt nothing but satisfaction. At the age of eighty-two, looking back upon his forty-six years of farming in Michigan, Kasper Lahnis recalled that the region had developed from 'dark forest' to 'many fine farms'. From his comfortable retirement he commented on his own place in these changes: 'One more step yet awaits us. We shall be laid aside along with so many of the pioneers who have gone beyond and with whom we have shared one and the same portion in life . . . Dominie Christiaan van der Veen once remarked "I am happy to have lived during this time," and we repeat the sentiment after him.'[1] Mary Antin, musing on the steps of the Boston Public Library, felt able to take a less prosaic view. Like Henry Adams on his more famous Roman steps, she reflected upon the meaning of history, but in terms of liberation rather than doubt. 'The past,' she wrote, 'was only my cradle, and now it cannot contain me.' The home at Polotzk, which she had left as a child, was now no more to her than 'a toy of memory'. She felt that the past belonged to her, 'the youngest of America's children', just as America itself, newest of nations, inherited everything that had gone before.[2]

Most immigrants said nothing that we can hear, though from time to time, in a letter or a fragment of a diary, in the record of a speech or a riot, they impress themselves on our minds. Their descendants, of course, cannot interpret them: they are merely surprised at their parents' or grandparents' preoccupation with worlds that are not their own. It is for the historian to employ such skill as he possesses to uncover individual stories and to detect patterns in the imperfect evidence. If he judges the effort worth making, it will be because he can feel respect and fascination when confronted by the hardships, the disillusion, the modest achievements of the millions who crossed the Atlantic. Fascination above all: for now and again, from the faceless crowd, there emerge, in Lewis Hine's photographs or the sketches of Jacob Epstein and Joseph Stella,[3] features more striking, more noble even, than those of the generals and prelates, the politicians and magnates, of whom most history is told.

[1] Lucas, *op. cit.*, I 117; and see, II 188–9, Cornelius van der Meulen's speech of 1872.
[2] Mary Antin, *The Promised Land*, 364.
[3] Sketches by the young Jacob Epstein illustrate Hutchins Hapgood's *The Spirit of the Ghetto*. Joseph Stella's sketches appear in Margaret Byington's *Homestead* and John Fitch's *The Steel Workers*.

29   Italian family on the ferry near Ellis Island, 1905
Photograph by Lewis Hine, George Eastman House Collection.

30   Pittsburgh steelworker, early twentieth century
Photograph by Lewis Hine, George Eastman House Collection.

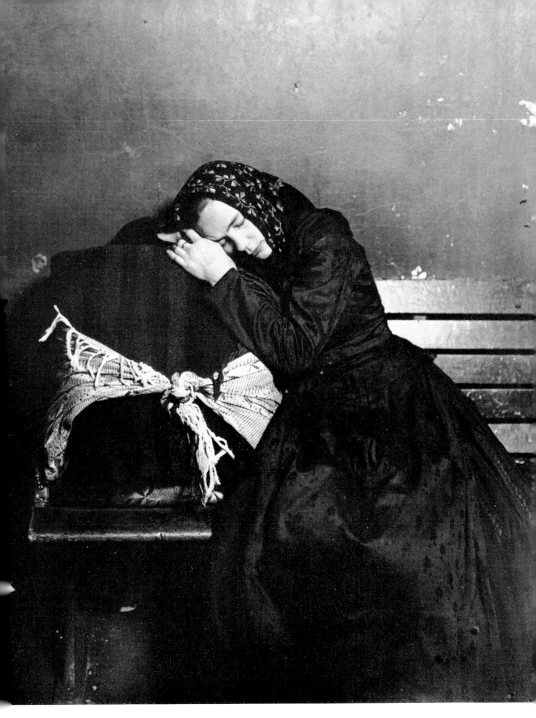

31   Slovak woman at Ellis Island, 1905
Photograph by Lewis Hine, George Eastman House Collection.

32　Jewish garment worker, early twentieth century
Photograph by Lewis Hine, George Eastman House Collection.

Bibliography

Bibliography

Since my book is a work of synthesis rather than, in more than a few directions, one of original research, several sources have not been used at all. Such are the American consular reports before 1880, papers in the National Archives, Washington, derived from the administration of Castle Garden and Ellis Island, the British Colonial Office records, and, above all, the foreign-language press in the United States. I have confined myself to printed sources, most of which can be found in one department or another of the British Museum.

Certain reference books must be used by students of emigration again and again: Walter F. Willcox and Imre Ferenczi, *International Migrations* (2 vols., New York, 1929–31); *Historical Statistics of the United States* (Washington, D.C., my own edition is that of 1945); N. H. Carrier and J. R. Jeffery, *External Migration: a study of the available statistics* [i.e. migration from Britain] (London, 1953).

Four general books on immigration must be cited, though my own approach has differed greatly from all of them: Maurice R. Davie, *World Immigration* (New York, 1936); Carl Wittke, *We Who Built America* (New York, 1939); Oscar Handlin, *The Uprooted* (Boston, Mass., 1951); Maldwyn A. Jones, *American Immigration* (Chicago, 1957).

The bibliography that follows is divided by chapters or groups of chapters. My aim is to suggest useful further reading to people who do not regard themselves as specialists; then to mention, and when necessary discuss, the monographs and primary sources to which the professional student must turn. There is a degree of overlap, but this I have accepted in the interests of coherent connection with the text. Many books used only once or twice are not listed, though they appear in my footnotes. For these, no publication details have been given. The general reader will not be interested: the professional student can easily find them for himself.

I end with a section on books which have not yet been written, but which, in my judgment, ought to be written soon.

Many of the books listed have been reprinted, sometimes in paperback, but I have not expanded my bibliography to take full account of this. I must call attention, however, to the Irish Universities Press series of British Parliamentary Papers, which includes several volumes on emigration; and to the Arno Press Immigration Collection, which already runs to several score volumes.

Chapters 1 to 3

Although the subject of chapter 1 is the unification of the nineteenth-century world and its effect on emigration, while chapters 2 and 3 deal in more detail with conditions in particular countries, the sources used are essentially the same.

The general reader who desires to take the subject further should begin with a few studies of Europe and the wider world in the period 1830–1930, and then select a few outstanding monographs and accessible travellers' accounts, disregarding the fact that some regions of Europe may remain untouched. Perhaps the best introduction to the broad theme is Charles Morazé, *Les bourgeois conquérants: XIXe siècle* (Paris, 1957, translated under the weaker title *The Triumph of the Middle Classes,* London, 1966); while Michael Robbins, *The Railway Age* (London, 1962) and Desmond Young, *Member for Mexico: a Biography of Weetman Pearson, First Viscount Cowdray* (London, 1966) are useful supplements. On population growth, one of the century's key phenomena, there are useful essays in David V. Glass and D. C. Eversley, *Population in History* (London, 1965), though some deal with earlier periods. An excellent general history of Europe, not exclusively political, is David Thomson, *Europe since Napoleon* (London, 1957, 1962); while a shorter period is described and analysed, with great power, in Eric J. Hobsbawm, *The Age of Revolution* (London, 1962). On the machinery of government, Abbot L. Lowell, *Governments and Parties in Continental Europe* (2 vols., London, 1916, 1st edn 1896) gives very full description, though John A. Hawgood, *Modern Constitutions* (London, 1939), much less detailed, may be more easily available.

On single countries or regions, the following are outstanding: Cecil Woodham-Smith, *The Great Hunger: Ireland 1845–9* (London, 1962); Theodore C. Blegen, *Norwegian Migration to America 1825–1860* (North-field, Minn., 1931); [Carl Artur] Vilhelm Moberg, *The Emigrants* (English translation, London, 1956 – a novel but based on much research) and the same author's *When I Was a Child* (English translation, London, 1957, a novel in form, but in fact heavily autobiographical); Marcus L. Hansen, *The Atlantic Migration 1607–1860* (Cambridge, Mass., 1940, 1951, especially solid on the German states); Robert F. Foerster, *The Italian Emigration of our Time* (Cambridge, Mass., 1919, with a good summary of background conditions, as well as an account of migration to Latin America and Mediterranean and European countries as well as to the United States); Norman Douglas, *Old Calabria* (London, 1915, 1962); Emily G. Balch, *Our Slavic Fellow-Citizens* (New York, 1910, a work of travel in Europe and America as well as of documentary scholarship); Doreen Warriner, ed., *Contrasts in Emerging Societies* (London, 1965, a collection of readings from travellers and scholars on conditions in eastern Europe in the nineteenth century, with useful introductions to each country); Mark Zborowski and Elizabeth Herzog, *Life is with People: the Culture of the Shtetl* (New York, 1962, 1st edn 1952, nostalgic because based on reminiscences, but immensely interesting on eastern European Jewish institutions and attitudes); Wayne Vucinic, ed., *The Peasant in Nineteenth-Century Russia* (Stanford, Calif., 1968, important not because many Russians emigrated to the United States but because it will set the reader thinking about the lost world of nineteenth-century peasant Europe). As to the overseas world, the general reader will probably be satisfied to confine himself to the United States. Beyond the familiar economic history texts of Harold U. Faulkner or Edward C. Kirkland, he should read Jared Van Wagenen, *The Golden Age of Homespun* (New York, 1953, 1963, a classic account of early nineteenth-century farming by a man whose family tradition reached back into it); Allan G. Bogue, *From Prairie to Cornbelt* (Chicago, 1963) and Gilbert C. Fite, *The Farmers' Frontier 1865–1900* (New York, 1966), expert but readable accounts of two later phases of American agricultural growth. The textbooks may suffice for the much more familiar subjects of cities and industry.

The more specialized student, wishing to deepen his knowledge of particular regions, can choose from a wide range of monographs, which are listed below, first under the heading of world unification, then region by region.

Important general books are Michael M. Postan and Hrothgar J. Habakkuk, eds., *Cambridge Economic History of Europe: Part VI, The Industrial Revolutions and After* (2 vols., Cambridge, 1965); William A. Ashworth, *A Short History of the International Economy 1850–1950* (London, 1952); Herbert Feis, *Europe, the World's Banker 1870–1914* (New Haven, Conn., 1930); Brinley Thomas, *Migration and Economic Growth: a Study of Great Britain and the Atlantic Economy* (Cambridge, 1954); William O. Henderson, *Britain and the Industrial Revolution in Europe 1750–1870* (Liverpool, 1954); Rondo E. Cameron, *France and the Economic Development of Europe 1800–1914* (Princeton, N. J., 1961); while Gerald S. Graham's article, 'The Ascendancy of the Sailing Ship 1850–85', *Economic History Review*, Second Series, IX (1956), 74–88, is most illuminating.

Further understanding of British economic problems can be gained from William Ashworth, *An Economic History of England 1870–1939* (London,

1960); John H. Clapham, *Economic History of Modern Britain* (3 vols., Cambridge, 1926–38); and Sidney Pollard, *The Genesis of Modern Management* (London, 1965). Special aspects of interest are treated in John Saville, *Rural Depopulation in England 1850–1950* (London, 1957), Theodore C. Barker and Michael Robbins, *London Transport: Volume I The Nineteenth Century* (London, 1963) and Rowland T. Berthoff, *British Immigrants in Industrial America* (Cambridge, Mass., 1952); but even the last-named cannot be called an adequate treatment of the background of British emigration. Perhaps no such book can be written. Stanley C. Johnson, *A History of Emigration from the United Kingdom to North America 1763–1912* (London, 1913) is a dull compilation of public projects; and William A. Carrothers, *Emigration from the British Isles* (London, 1929) is also superficial.

On the special problems of Ireland, several books and articles of very high quality now exist. Robert Dudley Edwards and T. D. Williams, *The Great Famine* (Dublin, 1956) which includes a long chapter on emigration by Oliver MacDonagh; Thomas W. Freeman, *Pre-Famine Ireland* (Manchester, 1957); William F. Adams, *Ireland and the Irish Emigration to the New World from 1815 to the Famine* (New Haven, Conn., 1932); Arnold Schrier, *Ireland and the American Emigration 1850–1900* (Minneapolis, 1958); Barbara Kerr 'Irish Seasonal Migration to Great Britain 1800–1838', *Irish Historical Studies*, III (1942–3), 365–80; S. H. Cousens, 'The Regional Variations in Emigration from Ireland between 1821 and 1841', *Transactions of the Institute of British Geographers*, XXXVII (1965), 15–29; 'The Regional Pattern of Emigration during the Great Famine 1846–51', *Transactions of the Institute of British Geographers*, XXVIII (1960), 119–34; 'Emigration and Demographic Change in Ireland 1851–1861', *Economic History Review*, Second Series, XIV (1961), 275–88. To these may be added the reports of three parliamentary inquiries: *Parliamentary Papers 1845*, XIX, Evidence... Commission of Inquiry into the State of the Law and Practice ... Occupation of Land in Ireland, Part I (the 'Devon Commission'); *1847* VI, 1847–8 XVII, *1849* XI, Report of the Select Committee of the House of Lords on Colonization from Ireland; *1852* XIV, Report from the Select Committee on Outrages (Ireland).

North-west Europe as a whole is treated in a pioneer work of statistics and commentary, Emile Legoyt, *L'émigration européenne, son importance, ses causes, ses effets* (Paris, 1861). On Norway, much may be learned from Michael Drake, *Population and Society in Norway 1735–1865* (Cambridge, 1969); Einar Molland, *Church Life in Norway 1800–1950* (trans. Harris Kaasa, Minneapolis, 1957); Rigmor Frimmenshend, 'Farm Community and Neighbourhood Community', *Scandinavian Economic History Review*, IV

(1956), 62–81; Ingrid Semmingsen 'The Dissolution of Estate Society in Norway', *ibid.* II (1954), 166–203, and the same author's 'Norwegian Emigration in the Nineteenth Century', *ibid.*, VIII (1960), 150–60. On Sweden, the most valuable authority is the very closely argued Dorothy S. Thomas, *Social and Economic Aspects of Swedish Population Movements 1750–1933* (New York, 1941). Easier to read, and almost equally logical in arrangement, is John S. Lindberg, *The Background of Swedish Emigration to the United States* (Minneapolis, 1930); while far more local detail is presented in Florence E. Janson, *The Background of Swedish Immigration* (Chicago, 1931). George M. Stephenson, *Religious Aspects of Swedish Immigration* (Minneapolis, 1932) is equally valuable for developments on both sides of the Atlantic. A much older book may provide factual rein-forcement in some areas: Gustav Sundbarg, *Sweden: Its People and its Industry* (Stockholm, 1904). Henry S. Lucas, *Netherlanders in America* (Ann Arbor, Mich., 1955) deals sufficiently with the background of the small Dutch emigration. On the German states, the nearest to a standard work is now Mack Walker, *Germany and the Emigration 1816–1885* (Cambridge, Mass., 1964), though it is thinner than might be expected on the social background. Aspects of this are shown in fascinating detail in Theodore C. Hamerow, *Restoration, Revolution, Reaction* (Princeton, N.J., 1958). Later economic growth is briefly but conveniently dealt with in William H. Dawson, *Industrial Germany* (London, 1912), and religious developments in Andrew L. Drummond, *German Protestantism since Luther* (London, 1951). Many rural problems emerge clearly from *Parl. Papers 1870* LXVII, Reports from H.M. Representatives . . . Tenure of Land in the several countries of Europe, the best sections of which are the German.

It cannot be said that it is equally easy to study the even less familiar problems of southern and eastern Europe; but a few eye-witness accounts exist, and several modern monographs and articles. Population movements can be seen in outline (though detailed sources are not clearly stated) in Gustav Sundbarg, *Aperçus statistiques internationaux* (Stockholm, 1908). On Austria-Hungary, Geoffrey Drage, *Austria-Hungary* (London, 1908) is useful, as is Guillaume Vautier, *La Hongrie économique* (Paris, 1893). On special problems, see Ignatius Daranyi, *The State and Agriculture in Hungary* (trans. Andrew György, London, 1905), Robert W. Seton-Watson, *Absolutism in Croatia* (London, 1912), and the same author's much larger, and brilliant, *Racial Problems in Hungary* (London, 1908). Seton-Watson was a defender of the subject peoples, and a vigorous critic of the Hungarian government's claim to liberalism. Jozo Tomasevich, *Peasants, Politics and Economic Change in Yugoslavia* (Stanford, 1955) is excellent on rural questions, though two-thirds of the book deal with the period after the First World War. A recent article throws much light on concentration of land-holding: Scott M. Eddie, 'The Changing Pattern of Landownership in Hungary 1867–1914', *Economic History Review*, Second Series, XX (1967), 293–309. Theodore Saloutos, *The Greeks in the United States* (Cambridge, Mass., 1964) has a brief but interesting early section on background. Very valuable, though all too brief, is Jerze Zubrzycki, 'Emigration from Poland in the Nineteenth and Twentieth Centuries', *Population Studies*, VI (1952–3), 248–72; while William I. Thomas and Florian Znaniecki, *The Polish Peasant in Europe and America* (2 vols, New York, 1958, 1st edn 5 vols, Boston, 1918–20) combines extended introduction and a wealth of source-material. Markus Wischnitzer, *To Dwell in Safety: the story of Jewish migration since 1800* (Philadelphia, 1948) deals with eastern Europe as a whole, and is something like a standard work; but Samuel Joseph, *Jewish Immigration to the United States* (New York, 1914) is still worth reading. For background, the most exhaustive treatment is in Semen Dubnow, *History of the Jews in Russia and Poland* (English translation, I. Friedlander, 3 vols, Philadelphia, 1916–20). Two government investigations are of value: *Parl. Papers 1903*, IX, Royal Commission on Alien Immigration, especially Major Evans-Gordon's long report on eastern Europe following Q. 13,349; and in *61 Congress 3 Session, Senate Doc. 748*, Immigration Commission Reports, a study of Russian Jewish economic problems by I. M. Rubinow. Not directly relevant, but interesting for background, is Donald W. Treadgold, *The Great Siberian Migration* (Princeton, N.J., 1957). Very different approaches to Italy may be found in Phyllis H. Williams, *South Italian Folkways in Europe and America* (Chicago, 1938) and in J. S. Macdonald, 'Agricultural Organization, Migration, and Labour Militancy', *Economic History Review*, Second Series, XVI (1963), 61–75. Mainly on Italy and Spain, and illuminating on one aspect of social and political life, is Eric J. Hobsbawm, *Primitive Rebels* (Manchester, 1959).

Few students will wish to go into as much detail about the overseas world other than the United States; and this is fortunate, since several important areas have been very imperfectly treated by scholars. A useful survey is Edward Shann, *Economic History of Australia* (Cambridge, 1930). Sufficiently comprehensive on the background are Pierre Denis, *Le Brésil au XXe siècle* (Paris, 1909) and Celso Furtado, *The Economic Growth of Brazil* (English trans., R. W. de Aguier and E. C. Drysdale, Berkeley, Calif., 1963). Similar in scope for Argentina are Aldo Ferrer, *The Argentine Economy* (trans. Marjory M. Urquidi, Berkeley, Calif., 1967) and Pierre Denis, *La république argentine: la mise en valeur du pays* (Paris, 1920). Informative, but nearer to a guide-book in arrangement, is Albert B. Martinez and Maurice Lewandowski, *The Argentine in the Twentieth Century* (London, 1911), while an earlier example of the same form is Michael G. and E. T. Mulhall, *Handbook of the River Plate* (Buenos Aires, 1869). Very valuable is the specialized Mark Jefferson, *Peopling the Argentine Pampa* (New York, 1926). On Canada, it is probably sufficient to read W. T. Easterbrook and H. G. J. Aitken, *Canadian Economic History* (Toronto, 1958) and Marcus L. Hansen, *The Mingling of the Canadian and American Peoples* (New Haven, Conn., 1940).

On the United States, the serious student will need to master some substantial proportion of the economic history series published by Holt, Rinehart and Winston: Paul W. Gates, *The Farmer's Age* (New York, 1960); George R. Taylor, *The Transportation Revolution* (New York, 1951); Fred A. Shannon, *The Farmer's Last Frontier* (New York, 1945); Edward C. Kirkland, *Industry Comes of Age* (New York, 1961); Harold U. Faulkner, *The Decline of Laissez-faire* (New York, 1951). Interesting on their more limited topics are Richard C. Wade, *The Urban Frontier: the Rise of Western Cities 1790–1830* (Cambridge, Mass., 1959); Louis C. Hunter, *Steamboats on the Western Rivers* (Cambridge, Mass., 1949); R. Carlyle Buley, *The Old Northwest* (2 vols, Bloomington, Ind., 1964, 1st edn 1951); Chilton Williamson, *American Suffrage, from Property to Democracy* (Princeton, N.J., 1960); Stanley Elkins and Eric C. McKitrick, 'A Meaning for Turner's Frontier', *Political Science Quarterly*, LXIX (1954); John F. Stover, *American Railroads* (Chicago, 1961); George R. Taylor and Irene D. Neu, *The American Railroad Network 1861* (Cambridge, Mass., 1956); Blake McKelvey, *The Urbanization of America* (New Brunswick, N.J., 1963); Sam B. Warner, *Streetcar Suburbs* (Cambridge, Mass., 1962).

Monographs are not enough. For vivid description, and a sense of closeness to the subject, nothing can rival the writings of British and French travellers. They exist in abundance; and those which were widely used are listed region by region, and within each region in chronological order. For Ireland, see Henry D. Inglis, *A Journey through Ireland during the spring, summer and autumn of 1834* (2 vols, London, 1835), the best of the group; Johann G. Kohl, *Ireland* (London, 1843); James Hack Tuke, *A Visit to Connaught in the autumn of 1847* (London, 1848), a vivid account of the Famine in Ireland's poorest region. On Scandinavia, see two books by Samuel Laing, the difference in depth between them emerging clearly from the two words 'residence' and 'tour'. They are *Journal of a Residence in Norway during the years 1834, 1835 and 1836* (London, 1836) and *A Tour of Sweden in 1838* (London, 1839). On western Europe and the German states, it is sufficient

20

to refer to Samuel Laing, *Notes of a Traveller on the Social and Political State of France, Prussia . . . and other parts of Europe* (London, 1842); Thomas C. Banfield, *Industry of the Rhine* (2 vols, London, 1846–8); and Laing's *Observations on the Social and Political State of the European People in 1848 and 1849* (London, 1850). Banfield's book is much the best. On Italy, one book on the South deserves mention, Crauford T. Ramage, *The Nooks and Byways of Italy* (Liverpool, 1868, though it records a journey in 1828 – a reprint is London, 1965). On eastern Europe, see William Jacob, *Report on the Trade in Foreign Corn and on the Agriculture of the North of Europe* (London, 1826); Michael J. Quin, *A Steam Voyage down the Danube* (2 vols, London, 1835); C. B. Elliott, *Travels in the Three Great Empires of Austria, Russia and Turkey* (2 vols, London, 1838, but vol 2 does not concern us); G. R. Gleig, *Germany, Bohemia and Hungary visited in 1837* (3 vols, London, 1839), the Hungarian section is especially interesting; John Paget, *Hungary and Transylvania* (2 vols, London, 1839), outstanding; Johann G. Kohl, *Austria: Vienna, Prague, Hungary . . . .* (London, 1843), particularly valuable for Galicia; Charles Boner, *Transylvania: its Products and its People* (London, 1865), penetrating on many topics, especially ethnic differences and conflicts; Emile de Laveleye, *The Balkan Peninsula* (trans. Mary Thorpe, London, 1887); Edward Dicey, *The Peasant State: an account of Bulgaria in 1894* (London, 1894); Harold Frederic, *The New Exodus* (London, 1892), on the treatment of Russia's Jews, especially the expulsion from Moscow in 1891; William Miller, *Travel and Politics in the Near East* (London, 1898), chiefly on Dalmatia, Bosnia and Greece, and, like Dicey, showing both first-hand observation and considerable study; Michael Davitt, *Within the Pale* (London, 1903), principally on the Kishinev *pogrom*; William Miller, *Greek Life in Town and Country* (London, 1905); Louis de Launay, *La Bulgarie d'hier et de demain* (Paris, 1907); Henry C. Woods, *Washed by Four Seas: an English Officer's Travels in the Near East* (London, 1908), largely on Turkey in Europe; Will S. Monroe, *Bohemia and the Czechs* (Boston, Mass., 1910); his *Bulgaria and her People* (Boston, 1914); Lucy Garnett, *Balkan Home Life* (London, 1917); Louis Adamic, *The Native's Return* (New York, 1934), on Carniola and other parts of what was by then Yugoslavia.

Travellers explored the overseas lands too, but I have used them only to describe conditions in rather early years. On the Australian colonies, see P. Cunningham, *Two Years in New South Wales* (2 vols, London, 1827), excellent also on the convict ships in which the author sailed as surgeon-superintendent; and Charles Griffith, *The Present State and Prospects of the Port Phillip District of New South Wales* (Dublin, 1845), informative on what was later called Victoria. Thomas Walsh, *Notices of Brazil in 1828 and 1829* (London, 1830) and Thomas Ewbank, *Life in Brazil* (New York, 1856) are of interest. On Argentina, Woodbine Parish, *Buenos Ayres and the Provinces of the Rio de la Plata* (London, 1838), is excellent. For later years, see Wilfrid Latham, *The States of the River Plate* (London, 1866) and John A. Hammerton, *The Real Argentine* (New York, 1915). For the eastern parts of Canada in the early nineteenth century, see Adam Fergusson, *Practical Notes made during a Tour of Canada and a portion of the United States in MDCCCXXXI* (Edinburgh, 1833) and James Silk Buckingham, *Canada, Nova Scotia, New Brunswick, and the other British Provinces in North America* (London, 1843); and for primitive days in the West, see William Newton's vivid *Twenty Years in the Saskatchewan* (London, 1897). Since monographs are so much more numerous, I have selected only a handful of travel books about the United States: Harriet Martineau, *Society in America* (3 vols, London, 1837); Patrick Shirreff, *A Tour through North America . . . .* (Edinburgh, 1835); James Silk Buckingham, *Eastern and Western States of America* (3 vols, London, 1842); J. Richard Beste, *The Wabash: or Adventures of an English Gentleman's Family in the Interior of North America* (2 vols, London, 1855). See also the excerpts from journals in George W. Pierson, *Tocqueville and Beaumont in America* (New Haven, Conn., 1938). Illustrations of great interest may be found in the volumes edited by Ralph H. Gabriel, *Pageant of America* (15 vols, New Haven, Conn., 1925-9); James T. Adams, ed., *Album of American History* (5 vols, New York, 1944-9); and John A. Hammerton, ed., *Countries of the World* (6 vols, London, 1924-5), whose travellers' impressions, and above all, photographs enable the student to move back nearly half a century towards his subject.

Chapter 4

Most general readers, seeking further insight into the news which Europeans received from America, will be content with the information provided by the standard books on ethnic groups – Berthoff, Schrier, Blegen, Janson, Walker, Hansen, Lucas, Foerster, Balch, Saloutos – and by Stephenson's *Religious Aspects of Swedish Immigration*, Douglas' *Old Calabria*, and Moberg's *When I Was a Child*. An admirable article, with extensive references, is Merle Curti and Kendall Burr, 'The Immigrant and the American Image in Europe 1860-1914', *Mississippi Valley Historical Review*, XXXVII (1950-51), 203-30. Additional information on several aspects of the subject may be found in Allan Nevins, *American Social History as recorded by British Travellers* (London, 1924); Wilbur S. Shepperson, *The Promotion of British Emigration by Agents of American Lands 1840–1860* (Reno, Nev., 1954) and his *British Emigration to North America: Projects and Opinions in the Early Victorian Period* (Oxford, 1957); Charlotte Erickson, *American Industry and the European Immigrant 1860–1885* (Cambridge, Mass., 1957); Bertus Wabeke, *Dutch Emigration to North America 1624–1940* (New York, 1944); James B. Hedges, *Henry Villard and the Railways of the Northwest* (New Haven, Conn., 1930); Paul W. Gates, *The Illinois Central and its Colonization Work* (Cambridge, Mass., 1934); Richard C. Overton, *Burlington West* (Cambridge, Mass., 1941). Glimpses of the propaganda organized from other emigration fields may be caught from Robert B. Madgwick, *Immigration into Eastern Australia 1788–1851* (London, 1937); John S. Marais, *The Colonization of New Zealand* (London, 1927); Helen I. Cowan, *British Emigration to British North America: the First Hundred Years* (Toronto, 1961); Norman Macdonald, *Canada 1763–1841: Immigration and Settlement* (London, 1939) and *Canada: Immigration and Colonization 1841–1903* (Aberdeen, 1966), which unfortunately stops on the eve of the most remarkable developments.

   Much of the important information, however, is to be found only in the historical journals of states and ethnic groups. The most important articles are: Rowland T. Berthoff, 'Southern Attitudes towards Immigration 1865–1914', *Journal of Southern History*, XVII (1951), 328–60; William L. Jenks, 'Michigan Immigration', *Michigan History Magazine*, XXVIII (1944), 69–100; Maurice G. Baxter, 'Encouragement of Immigration to the Middle West during the Era of the Civil War', *Indiana Magazine of History*, XLVI (1950), esp. 31–8; Marcus L. Hansen, 'Official Encouragement of Immigration to Iowa', *Iowa Journal of History and Politics*, XIX (1921), 165–92; Karl E. Erickson, 'The Emigrant Journey of the Fifties', Norwegian-American Historical Association, *Studies and Records*, VIII (1934); Theodore C. Blegen, 'The Competition of the Northwestern States for Immigrants', *Wisconsin Magazine of History*, III (1919), 3–28, and 'Minnesota's Campaign for Immigrants: Illustrative Documents', *Yearbook* of Swedish Historical Society of America, XI (1926), esp. 60–73; George M. Stephenson, 'When America was the Land of Canaan', *Minnesota History*, X (1929), esp. 239–47; Albert O. Barton, 'Norwegian-American Emigration Societies in the Forties and Fifties', Norwegian-American Historical Association, *Studies and Records*, III (1928), 23–42; Harold E. Briggs, 'The Settlement and Development of the Territory of Dakota 1860–70', *North Dakota Historical Quarterly*, VII (1932–3), and, in the same number, 5–24, Herbert E. Schell, 'Official Immigration Activities of Dakota Territory'; Arthur J. Brown, 'The Promotion of Emigration to Washington 1854–1909', *Pacific*

Northwest Quarterly, XXXVI (1945), 3–17; Edna Parker, 'The Southern Pacific Railroad and Settlement in Southern California', *Pacific Historical Review*, VI (1937), 103–19; and, more on immigrants' attitudes than the machinery of propaganda, Charlotte Erickson, 'Agrarian Myths of English Immigrants', in Oscar Fritiof Ander, *In the Trek of the Immigrants* (Rock Island, Ill., 1964), 23–42. It should be pointed out, once more, that American communities aimed their propaganda at least as much to native Americans as to foreigners. Franklin D. Scott, 'Sweden's Constructive Opposition to Emigration', *Journal of Modern History*, XXXVII (1965), 307–35, is the fullest treatment of this theme for any country.

Behind these articles lie extensive primary sources, and a significant proportion of these may be found in Britain.

Much of this material may broadly be described as guide-books and propaganda pamphlets, their objectivity varying widely. Gottfried Duden's *Bericht über eine Reise nach den westlichen Staaten Nordamerikas* (1829) is translated by G. Bek and published in instalments in *Missouri Historical Review*, XII and XIII (1917–19). Ole Rynning's *True Account of America* (1838) is translated by Professor Blegen in *Minnesota History Bulletin*, II (1917); while Reierson's *Pathfinder for Norwegian Emigrants* (1844) is summarized in Blegen's *Norwegian Migration to the United States*, 243–7. Other early guide-books include *British Mechanic's and Labourer's Handbook and True Guide to the United States* (London, 1842); *Wiley and Putnam's Emigrant's Guide* (London, 1845); Traugott Bromme, *Rathgeber für Auswanderungslustige* (Stuttgart, 1846); Francis Wyse, *America, its Realities and Resources* (3 vols, London, 1846); John Regan, *The Emigrant's Guide to the Western States of America* (Edinburgh, 1852). Examples from a generation later are Evan Jones, *The Emigrants' Friend . . .* (London and Newcastle, 1880); Walter Hazel and Howard Hodgson, *The Australian Colonies: Emigration and Colonization* (London, 1887); Canadian Pacific Railway Company, *Free Farms* (1890); *The Canadian Settler's Handbook* (London, 1911); Liévin Coppin, *L'empire du Brésil au point de vue de l'émigration* (Charleroi, 1888); Casimiro Marro, *Manuale pratico dell' emigrante all' Argentina, Uruguay, e Brasile* (Genoa, 1889); *Lo Stato di Rio de Janeiro nel Brasile* (Genoa, 1897); Argentina Department of Agriculture, *Sketch of the Argentine Republic as a Country for Immigration* (Buenos Aires, 1904). Pamphlets issued by American communities include: *Georgia, from the Immigrant Settler's Stand-point* (Atlanta, Ga., 1879); *North, or Cherokee Georgia. Advantages to Emigrants and Families with Small Capital* (Rome, Ga., 1876); *The Commonwealth of Missouri, or the Empire State of the American Union* (London, 1880); *Colorado, a Statement of Facts, prepared and published by authority of the Territorial Board of Immigration* (Denver, 1872); *Iowa: the Home for Immigrants, being a Treatise on the Resources of Iowa* (Des Moines, Iowa, 1870); *Wisconsin, What It Offers to the Immigrant* (Milwaukee, Wis., 1879); *Minnesota, the Empire State of the New North-West, the Commercial, Manufacturing and Geographical Centre of the American Continent* (St Paul, Minn., 1878); *The Resources and Attractions of Idaho* (St Louis, Mo. 1893) was issued by the Union Pacific railroad. Periodicals specializing in emigration include: *Colonial Gazette* (1838–47), *Colonial Magazine and East India Review* (1851–2), *Emigrants' Penny Magazine* (1850–1), *Emigration Record and Colonial Journal* (1856–8), *Sidney's Emigrants' Journal* (1848–50) and *Simmonds' Colonial Magazine and Foreign Miscellany* (1844–8): all except the third were published in London, the *Penny Magazine* at Plymouth. *Land and Emigration* (London, 1871–3) was issued by the Northern Pacific railroad. The *Colonization Circulars*, which appeared at irregular intervals from 1843 to 1873, were published by the Colonial Land and Emigration Commissioners. Further light on propaganda is thrown by the memoirs of three men who acted as agents: A. A. Stomberg, 'Letters of an Early Emigration Agent in the Scandinavian Countries', *Swedish-American Historical Bulletin*, III (1930), 7–52; Carl B. Schmidt, 'Reminiscences of Foreign Immigration Work for Kansas', *Kansas Historical Collections*, IX (1905–6), 485–97; and Hans Mattson, *Reminiscences: the Story of an Emigrant* (St Paul, Minn., 2nd edn, 1892).

Advertisements appear in all newspapers of the period. I have used especially *Birmingham Journal, Liverpool Mercury* (useful for emigration news too), and *Sherborne, Dorchester and Taunton Journal*.

Collections of emigrants' letters may be found in William I. Thomas and Florian Znaniecki, *The Polish Peasant in Europe and America* (2 vols, New York, 1958: a 5-vol edn appeared in Boston, 1918–20 – but most of the letters printed were written not in America but in Poland); Theodore C. Blegen, *Land of their Choice* (Minneapolis, Minn., 1955); Alan Conway, *The Welsh in America* (Cardiff, 1961).

Finally, many references to emigration propaganda may be found in British and American government documents. Particularly valuable are the *Annual Reports* of the Colonial Land and Emigration Commissioners, which appeared regularly in *Parliamentary Papers* from 1840 to 1873; *Parl. Papers 1907*, LXVII, Memorandum on the History and Functions of the Emigrants' Information Office; the *Commercial Relations of the United States, Reports from Consuls* (printed from 1880, and to be found in the B.M. State Paper Room); *49 Congress 2 Session, House Exec. Doc. 157*, Emigration and Immigration: Reports of the Consular Officers of the United States (1887);

50 Congress 1 Session, House Misc. Doc. 572 (1888), the Ford Committee on Contract Labour; *52 Congress 1 Session, House Exec. Doc. 235* (2 parts, 1892), Reports of the Commissioners of Immigration upon the Causes which incite Immigration to the United States; *52 Congress 1 Session, House Misc. Docs. 19 and 20*, Special Consular Reports; *61 Congress 3 Session, Senate Doc. 761*, Immigration Commission Reports, The Immigration Situation in Other Countries.

Chapter 5

All the standard works on single ethnic groups contain some relevant material, as do Edwards and Williams, *The Great Famine* and Thomas and Znaniecki, *The Polish Peasant in Europe and America.* Also useful are the following monographs: Harry Jerome, *Migration and Business Cycles* (New York, 1926); Willard L. Thorp, *Business Annals* (New York, 1926); Hunter, *Steamboats on the Western Rivers*; Lamar Cecil, *Albert Ballin: Business and Politics in Imperial Germany* (Princeton, N.J., 1967); John F. Maguire, *The Irish in America* (London, 1868); Erickson, *American Industry and the European Immigrant*, and her 'Encouragement of Emigration by British Trade Unions', *Population Studies*, III (1949), 248–73; Harold Owen, *The Staffordshire Potter* (London, 1901); Ray Ginger, 'Labor in a Massachusetts Cotton Mill 1853–60', *Business History Review*, XXVIII (1954), 67–91; Samuel Joseph, *History of the Baron de Hirsch Fund* (Philadelphia, 1935). To these may be added Moberg's novel *The Emigrants*, and Johan Bojer's novel of the same title (trans., New York, 1925).

Most of what we need, however, is scattered through many primary sources. A few of these are personal accounts: Frederic's *New Exodus*, Mary Antin's *Promised Land*, Stoyan Christowe's *This Is My Country*, 'The Early Life of Eric Norelius', *Augustana Historical Society Publications*, IV Part I (1934), and Lucas, *Dutch Immigrant Memoirs*. Far more consist of guidebooks, newspapers, and government documents of various kinds.

Wiley and Putnam's Guide has already been mentioned, and it is one of the best. Others include: John M. Peck, *A New Guide for Emigrants to the West* (Boston, 1837); J. Calvin Smith, *The Emigrants' Hand-Book and New Guide for Travellers through the United States of America* (London, 1850); John Disturnell, *Disturnell's American and European Railway and Steamship Guide* (New York, 1851); [John Cassel] *The Emigrants' Handbook* (London, 1852); *Appleton's Railway and Steam Navigation Guide* (5 vols, New York, 1856–7); 'Americus', *Where to Emigrate and Why* (London, 1869); and Evan Jones' *The Emigrant's Friend* (1880).

In addition to newspapers already mentioned, *De Bow's Review* (1846–64, under various titles; a reprint now exists, New York, 1967), *New York World*, *Aris' Birmingham Gazette*, *Hull News* and *Grimsby News*, have been used for a few years each.

Of the *British Parliamentary Papers*, the most useful are the Annual Reports of the Colonial Land and Emigration Commissioners; but *1826–7*, V, Report of Emigration Committee and *1851*, XIX, Select Committee on the Passengers' Acts, have items of value. The American *Consular Reports*, The Treasury Department's *Annual Reports . . . Foreign Commerce and Navigation of the United States, Industrial Commission Reports*, XV, *52 Congress 1 Session, House Exec. Doc. 235* and *House Misc. Docs. 19 and 20*, and *61 Congress 3 Session, Senate Docs. 748, 753 and 756*, Immigration Commission Reports, have all been used.

Chapter 6

Although every book about emigration is likely to contain scraps of information, very few monographs exist which focus on the subject of laws and their enforcement, and of these most are concerned with Britain. A pioneer work is Kathleen A. Walpole, 'Emigration to British North America under the Early Passenger Acts', an unpublished London M.A. thesis, 1929. Much information on a later period is contained in Fred H. Hitchins, *The Colonial Land and Emigration Commission* (Philadelphia, 1931). Best of all is Oliver MacDonagh, *A Pattern of Government Growth: The Passenger Acts and their Enforcement 1800–1860* (London, 1961). Useful on various aspects of the subject are: Friedrich Kapp, *Immigration and the Commissioners of Emigration of the State of New York* (New York, 1870); Kate H. Claghorn, *The Immigrant's Day in Court* (New York, 1923); Alan Conway, 'New Orleans as a Port of Immigration 1820–1860', unpublished London M.A. thesis, 1949; John F. Nau, *The German People of New Orleans 1850–1900* (Leiden, 1958).

Many of the travellers' reports mentioned in connection with chapters 7 and 8 refer to Castle Garden or Ellis Island, or to embarkation arrangements in Europe. First-hand accounts with substantial detail include: Broughton Brandenburg, *Imported Americans* (New York, 1904); Philip Cowen, *Memories of an American Jew* (New York, 1932); Edward Corsi, *In the Shadow of Liberty* (New York, 1937); Stoyan Christowe, *This Is My Country*. The guide-books already cited are sometimes helpful. Overwhelmingly, however, the subject has to be studied from governmental sources, though they do not always describe the situation which existed in practice.

Of British sources, the Reports of the Colonial Land and Emigration Commissioners are of great value. So are the reports of special inquiries, and the evidence given to them: *Parliamentary Papers 1826* V, Select Committee on Emigration; *1851* XIX, Select Committee on Passengers' Acts; *1854* XIII, Select Committee on Emigrant Ships; *1893-4* LXXI, Reports to the Board of Trade on Alien Immigration (some fifty pages by Mr Schloss, who examined European and American regulations in practice); *1903* IX, Royal Commission on Alien Immigration (includes reports on British and continental seaports). American sources are almost equally important: *50 Congress 1 Session, House Misc. Doc. 572*, Select Committee . . . Contract Labor (especially valuable for the last days of Castle Garden); *51 Congress 2 Session, House Report 3472*, Select Committee on Immigration and Naturalization (on the same topic); *52 Congress 1 Session, House Exec. Doc. 235*, Reports of Commissioners of Immigration upon the Causes which incite Immigration to the United States (many details about European ports); *52 Congress 1 Session, House Misc. Docs. 19 and 20*, Special Consular Reports (the main series of Reports also contains, from time to time, translations of European laws and other relevant material); *52 Congress 1 Session, House Report 2090*, the report of a Joint Committee which investigated the first depot on Ellis Island; *Reports of the Industrial Commission*, XV, on the inspection system at Ellis Island, as well as on European laws and practice; *61 Congress 3 Session, Senate Docs. 748, 753, 758*, Reports of Immigration Commission, Emigration Conditions in Europe, Steerage Conditions etc., and Immigration Legislation. Early European laws are to be found also in A. Legoyt, *L'émigration européenne, son importance, ses causes, ses effets* (Paris, 1861); early American laws in William J. Bromwell, *History of Immigration* (New York, 1855); while many documents on regulations and their enforcement in America may be found in Edith Abbott, *Immigration: Select Documents and Case Records* (Chicago, 1924) – especially important on the work of private agencies.

Miscellaneous sources include the newspapers, especially the reports of the stipendiary magistrate's court in *Liverpool Mercury; Liverpool Customs Bills of Entry*, for details of the ships to which British regulations were meant to apply; Cunard and White Star Line material in Liverpool City Museum, especially the pocket-book on Cunard's Adriatic emigration traffic; the photographs of Ellis Island in Allon Schoener, *Portal to America: the Lower East Side 1870–1925* (New York, 1967); and the series of photographs taken by Lewis Hine in 1905 and 1926, at Ellis Island, some of which are reproduced in Schoener and elsewhere, but many of which can be seen only at George Eastman House, Rochester, N.Y.

Chapters 7 and 8

Except for descriptions of pioneer elements, the subject has been neglected in the monographs on ethnic groups. Scraps of information may be found in newspapers and guide-books; in George Dow, *Great Central* (2 vols, London, 1959, 1962); in Hunter, *Steamboats on the Western Rivers;* while the first part of Mark Twain's *Life on the Mississippi* is relevant, and so are Vilhelm Moberg's novels *The Emigrants* and *Unto a Good Land.*

Apart from those already cited in the section on chapter 6, the following government documents are important: *Parliamentary Papers 1847–8*, Select Committee of House of Lords, Colonization from Ireland, especially the letter from Stephen de Vere on pp. 49–52; *1847–8* XLVII and *1849* XXXVIII, reports from A. C. Buchanan at Quebec; *1849* LI, 397–431, Captain Denham's Report on Passenger Accommodation in Steamers between Ireland and Liverpool; *1851* XL, 434–9, letter from Vere Foster; *1881* LXXXII, Report of Board of Trade on Accommodation and Treatment of Emigrants on board Atlantic Steamships; *1882* LXII, Reports received by Board of Trade and Local Government Board relating to the Transit of Scandinavian Emigrants through the Port of Hull. *The Report on Emigrant Ships by the Sanitary Commission of the 'Lancet'* (London, 1873) should also be mentioned. Of American government documents, several have already been cited in connection with chapter 6, but others of importance are the series *Commerce and Navigation of the United States,* with mortality figures; *43 Congress 1 Session, Senate Doc. 23* (1873–4), though the investigation into steamship conditions was very imperfect; and *61 Congress 3 Session, Senate Doc. 753,* the Immigration Commission's reports on steerage conditions, must be singled out, because they comprise first-hand accounts by investigators disguised as immigrants, rather than remarks by armchair investigators or officials travelling short distances as passengers.

It is still true, however, that governmental inquiries were most reliable when they dealt with conditions at the ports, rather than at sea; and for the latter one must rely on accounts by emigrants themselves. Inevitably, they are not very numerous, for most emigrants did not belong to the more articulate classes. The following are important collections, worth citing again: Blegen, *Land of their Choice* (Norwegian letters); Conway, *The Welsh in America*; and Lucas, *Dutch Immigrant Memoirs.* The following are accounts by individual emigrants, or occasionally middle-class observers close to them; and they are listed in chronological order: Robert H. Billigmeier and Fred A. Picard, *The Old Land and the New: the Journals of Two Swiss Families* [Schweizer and Rütlinger] *in America in the 1820s* (Minneapolis, 1965); Rebecca Burlend, *A True Picture of Emigration* (Milo M. Quaife, ed., Chicago, 1936; but the first edn was London, 1848, and the journey took place in 1831); Gustav Koerner, *Memoirs* (2 vols, Cedar Rapids, Iowa, 1909, a voyage of 1833); Patrick Shirreff, *A Tour through North America* (Edinburgh, 1835); James F. Logan, *Notes of a Journey through Canada, the U.S.A. and the West Indies* (Edinburgh, 1838). For the 1840s: *A Pioneer in Northwest America: the Memoirs of Gustaf Unonius* (trans. Jonas O. Backlund, ed. Nils W. Olsson, 2 vols, Minneapolis, 1950); 'An English Settler [Edwin Bottomley] in Pioneer Wisconsin . . . 1842–50', ed. Milo M. Quaife, *Wisconsin Historical Society Collections*, XXV (1918); George Lewis, *Impressions of America and the American Churches* (Edinburgh, 1845). For the 1850s: J. Richard Beste, *The Wabash: or Adventures of an English Gentleman's Family in the Interior of America* (2 vols, London, 1855); Hans Mattson, *Reminiscences: the story of an Immigrant* (St Paul, Minn., 1892 – a journey of 1852); William Hancock, *An Emigrant's Five Years in the Free States of America* (London, 1860); Franz J. Ennemoser, *Eine Reise vom Mittelrhein . . . nach den nordamerikanischen freistaaten* (Kaiserslauten, 1857); T. L. Nichols, *Forty Years of American Life* (2 vols, London, 1864); 'Diary of Heinrich Egge, a German Immigrant', trans. Esther Bienhoff, *Mississippi Valley Historical Review*, XVII (1930–1), 123–34; William Ferguson, *America by River and Rail* (London, 1856); Erastus F. Beadle, *To Nebraska in '57* (New York, 1923).

The 1860s saw the change from sail to steam. Apart from letters in the Blegen and Conway collections already cited, few records of journeys exist. Edward A. Hall, *The Great West: guide and hand-book for travellers, miners, and emigrants* (London, 1867) has some useful information, while P. P. Quist, 'Recollections of an Immigrant of 1865', *Swedish–American Historical Bulletin*, IV (1931), is a personal account. For the 1870s, see 'An Emigrant's Letter from Iowa, 1871', ed. Charlotte Erickson, *Bulletin* of British Association for American Studies, New Series, XII and XIII (1966), especially 11–16; and Robert Louis Stevenson, *The Amateur Emigrant* (Works, Tusitala Edition, XVIII, London, 1924). For the 1890s, see William Smith, *A Yorkshireman's Trip to the United States and Canada* (London, 1892); Adolph B. Benson, *Farm, Forge and Philosophy* (Chicago, 1961); A. G. Carlson, Guide Book, 1894, in Roy W. Swanson, ed., 'Some Swedish Emigrant Guide Books of the Second Half of the Nineteenth Century', *Year Book of the Swedish Historical Society of America*, XI (1926), 121–4; 'An Excerpt from the Diary of Jacob Dolwig', trans. Richard J. Dolwig, *North Dakota Historical Quarterly*, III (1929), especially 204–8; Mary Antin, *The Promised Land* (Boston, 1912 – unfortunately only the journey through Europe); Samuel Chotzinoff, *A Lost Paradise* (London, 1956). The years between 1900 and the Great War are particularly well represented by Broughton Brandenburg, *Imported Americans* (New York, 1904 – perhaps the best of all descriptions); Edward A. Steiner, *On the Trail of the Immigrant* (New York, 1906) and *From Alien to Citizen* (New York, 1914); Philip Cowen, *Memories of an American Jew* (New York, 1932, with some interesting details on eastern Europe); Edward Corsi, *In the Shadow of Liberty* (New York, 1937); Stoyan Christowe, *This Is My Country* (London, 1938); Stephen Graham, *With Poor Immigrants to America* (London, 1914); Louis Adamic, *Laughing in the Jungle: the autobiography of an immigrant in America* (New York, 1932).

The rather scanty records of the steamship period can be supplemented by visual evidence, in the shape of photographs and plans of ships. For everything connected with ships, including dimensions, number of passengers carried, type of Atlantic service, etc., the essential reference work is Noel R. P. Bonsor, *North Atlantic Seaway* (Prescot, Lancs., 1955 edn and 1960 supplement). The ship plans used, in chronological order, were: *Gallia* (1879), *Official Guide and Album of the Cunard Steamship Service*, 1878–9, Cunard Building, Liverpool (and a model in the same building); *Servia* (1882), in a booklet entitled *Cabin Plans*, Box File 1880–90, Cunard Building (and model in Science Museum, South Kensington); *Aller* (1886), *Dresden* (1888), and *Normannia* (1890), all at National Maritime Museum; *Campania* (1893), Naval Architect's Department, Cunard Building (see also *Cunard Passengers' Log-Book*, Glasgow, 1893, and model in Science Museum, South Kensington); *Oceanic* (1899), an imperfect plan in Department of Shipping, Liverpool City Museum; *Southwark* (1899), National Maritime Museum, Greenwich; *Ultonia* (1899), Naval Architect's Department, Cunard Building; *Celtic* (1901), Harland and Wolff, Belfast; *Caronia* (1904), Science Museum, South Kensington (a cut-away side view rather than a deck plan); *Amerika* (1905), Harland and Wolff; *Nieuw Amsterdam* (1906), Harland and Wolff; *Adriatic* (1907), Harland and Wolff; *President Grant* and *President Lincoln* (1907), Harland and Wolff; *Mauretania* (1907), National Maritime Museum; *Tomaso di Savoia* (1908), National Maritime Museum; *Olympic* (1911), Harland and Wolff; *Aquitania* (1914), small-scale plans in *Marine Engineer and Naval Architect*, August 1914. Exterior photographs in great numbers are to be found in the National Maritime Museum and Liverpool City Library. Interior photographs are rarer; but the National Maritime Museum has an important collection, including a few of third-class accommodation. The several boxes of the Bedford Lemere Collection are outstanding (including the whole of Box 3 on *Aquitania*); while the collection entitled 'Travellers by Sea' includes photographs of *Mauretania*. The Department of Shipping, Liverpool City Museum, has a large set of interior views of *Oceanic*.

Chapters 9, 10 and 12, and Epilogue

Despite their differences of approach, these three chapters are based on similar sources. The largest single source, especially for chapter 9, is the United States Censuses, especially the five from 1870 to 1910. The first three are of particular value, in that they relate ethnic with occupational groupings; 1880 has two important volumes on 'Social Statistics of Cities'; and 1890 has a volume on 'Religious Denominations'. Valuable Compilations based on the censuses are Niles Carpenter, *Immigrants and their Children* (Washington, D.C., 1927) and Edward P. Hutchinson, *Immigrants and their Children 1850–1950* (New York, 1956).

Apart from the monographs on ethnic groups, already frequently cited, and the general works on American economic history, it is to be feared that few of the sources used for the three chapters will be accessible to the general reader. It is for that reason that I have grouped the material in this section of my bibliography rather differently. Beginning with a review of rural conditions and life in small towns and cities in nineteenth-century America, I go on to studies of those ethnic groups that were especially prominent in those environments. I then turn to industry and the modern city, then treat those groups which overwhelmingly lived in those conditions. The advantage of this method, I hope, is that the specialized student will be able to grasp both the features common to several ethnic groups and those unique to each.

On working and living conditions in the older America, see especially Paul W. Gates, *The Farmer's Age* (New York, 1960); Roscoe Carlyle Buley, *The Old Northwest* (2 vols, Bloomington, Ind., 1964, 1st edn 1951); Joseph Schafer, *A History of Agriculture in Wisconsin* (Madison, Wis., 1922); Allan Bogue, *From Prairie to Cornbelt* (Chicago, 1963); Merle Curti, *The Making of an American Community* (Stanford, 1959); Gilbert C. Fite, *The Farmers' Frontier* (New York, 1966); Everett Dick, *The Sod House Frontier 1854–1890* (Lincoln, Neb., 1954); Everett Dale, *Frontier Ways: Sketches of Life in the Old West* (Austin, Tex., 1959); Lewis Atherton, *Main Street on the Middle Border* (Bloomington, Ind., 1954). Valuable supplements are the following novels: Vilhelm Moberg, *Unto a Good Land* (trans., London, 1957); Hamlin Garland, *Son of the Middle Border* and *Boy Life on the Prairie*; Willa Cather, *O Pioneers* and *My Antonia*; Ole E. Rolvaag, *Giants in the*

Earth; together with Hans Mattson, *Reminiscences* and *The Autobiography of William Allen White* (New York, 1946). On early cities, Oscar Handlin, *Boston's Immigrants: a study in acculturation* (Cambridge, Mass., 1959, 1st edn 1941) and Robert Ernst, *Immigrant Life in New York City* (New York, 1949) are excellent. An interesting view of New York City is Charles Loring Brace, *The Dangerous Classes of New York, and Twenty Years' Work among them* (New York, 1872). A wide-ranging study, based on literary sources as well as statistics, is Edgar W. Martin, *The Standard of Living in 1860* (Chicago, 1942).

On British immigrants (though of course these and the groups referred to in subsequent paragraphs contributed also to America's later development), see: Rowland T. Berthoff, *British Immigrants in Industrial America* (Cambridge, Mass., 1952); Clifton K. Yearley, *Britons in American Labor 1820–1914* (Baltimore, Md., 1957); A. L. Rowse, *The Cornish in America* (London, 1969); Edward G. Hartmann, *Americans from Wales* (Boston, Mass., 1967); Alan Conway, *The Welsh in America* (Cardiff, 1961).

On the Irish, the only book to cover their American activities in an even half-satisfactory way is Carl Wittke, *The Irish in America* (Baton Rouge, La., 1956). Handlin's Boston immigrants were of course largely Irish, and the same group were prominent in Ernst's New York. See also Earl F. Niehaus, *The Irish in New Orleans 1800–1860* (Baton Rouge, La., 1965). John Gilmary Shea, *A History of the Catholic Church within the limits of the United States* (4 vols, New York, 1886–92) is exceedingly old-fashioned in its arrangement, but it contains a great deal of valuable information. That Church's activities may also be seen in John T. Ellis, *Documents of American Catholic History* (2nd edn, Milwaukee, Wis., 1962); Frederick J. Zwierlein, *The Life and Letters of Bishop McQuaid* (3 vols, Louvain, 1925–7); Robert H. Lord, J. E. Sexton, E. T. Harrington, *History of the Archdiocese of Boston* (3 vols, New York, 1944); Joseph B. Code, *Dictionary of the American Hierarchy* (New York, 1940); Peter Guilday, *History of the Councils of Baltimore* (New York, 1932); James H. Moynihan, *The Life of Archbishop John Ireland* (New York, 1953); James A. Burns, *Catholic Education: a study of conditions* (New York, 1917); and some of its problems can be seen in Anson P. Stokes, *Church and State in the United States* (3 vols, New York, 1950).

The Germans have been written about as imperfectly as the Irish, despite their great numbers and the numerous institutions of their communities in America. The following are of value: John A. Hawgood, *The Tragedy of German-America* (London, 1940); John F. Nau, *The German People of New Orleans 1850–1900* (Leiden, 1958); Albert J. Townsend, 'The Germans of Chicago', *Deutsch-Amerikanische Geschichtsbtlätter*, XXXII (1932); Adolf E.

Zucker, ed., *The Forty-Eighters: Political Refugees of the German Revolution of 1848* (New York, 1950); Carl Wittke, *Refugees of Revolution: the German Forty-Eighters in America* (Philadelphia, 1952) and *The German-Language Press in America* (Lexington, Ky., 1957); Terry G. Jordan, *German Seed in Texas Soil: immigrant farmers in nineteenth-century Texas* (Austin, Tex., 1966); Carl E. Schneider, *The German Church on the American Frontier* (St Louis, Mo., 1939); Emmett H. Rothan, *The German Catholic Immigrant in the United States 1830-1860* (Washington, D.C., 1946); Colman J. Barry, *The Catholic Church and German Americans* (Washington, D.C., 1953); Benjamin J. Blied, *Austrian Aid to American Catholics 1830-1860* (Milwaukee, Wis., 1944); and Germans made up many of the Catholics ably discussed in John H. Lamott, *History of the Archdiocese of Cincinnati 1821-1921* (New York, 1921) and John Rothensteiner, *History of the Archdiocese of St Louis* (2 vols, St Louis, 1928).

On the Dutch, see Henry S. Lucas, *Netherlanders in America* (Ann Arbor, Mich., 1955) and his edition of *Dutch Immigrant Memoirs and Related Writings* (2 vols, Assen, Netherlands, 1955).

On Scandinavians, Blegen's three volumes – *Norwegian Migration to America, The American Transition*, and *Land of their Choice* – are all valuable, as is Carlton C. Qualey, *Norwegian Settlement in the United States* (Northfield, Minn., 1938). Also of interest are O. M. Nelson, *History of the Scandinavians and Successful Scandinavians in the United States* (2 vols, Minneapolis, 1900); Lawrence M. Larson, *The Changing West* (Northfield, Minn., 1937); Emory K. Lindquist, *Smoky Valley People: a History of Lindsborg, Kansas* (Lindsborg, Kan., 1953). There are two outstanding works on Lutheranism in all its aspects: E. Clifford Nelson and Eugene L. Fevold, *The Lutheran Church among Norwegian-Americans* (2 vols, Minneapolis, 1960) and George M. Stephenson, *The Religious Aspects of Swedish Immigration* (Minneapolis, 1932). On the press, Finis H. Capps, *From Isolationism to Involvement: the Swedish Immigrant Press in America 1914-1945* (Chicago, 1966) is overwhelmingly concerned with foreign-policy questions. There is one useful, though all too brief, volume on a smaller and later Scandinavian group, A. William Hoglund, *Finnish Immigrants in America 1880-1920* (Madison, Wis., 1960).

On working conditions and living standards in the period of modern industry, the following are useful: Clifton K. Yearley, *Enterprise and Anthracite: Economics and Democracy in Schuylkill County 1820-1875* (Baltimore, Md., 1961); Peter Roberts, *Anthracite Coal Communities* (New York, 1904); John Brophy, *A Miner's Life* (Madison, Wis., 1964); John A. Fitch, *The Steel Workers* (New York, 1910); Margaret F. Byington, *Home-*

stead: Households of a Mill Town (New York, 1910); David Brody, *Steelworkers in America: the non-union era* (Cambridge, Mass., 1960); Graham Adams, *The Age of Industrial Violence 1910–1915* (New York, 1966); Vernon H. Jensen, *Heritage of Conflict: Labor relations in the non-ferrous metals industry up to 1930* (Ithaca, N.Y., 1950); Charlotte Erickson, *American Industry and the European Immigrant* (Cambridge, Mass., 1957); Gerd Korman, *Industrialization, Immigrants and Americanizers: the view from Milwaukee* (Madison, Wis., 1967); Stephan Thernstrom, *Poverty and Progress: social mobility in a nineteenth-century city* (Cambridge, Mass., 1964); Clarence D. Long, *Wages and Earnings in the United States 1860–1890* (Princeton, 1960); Albert Rees, *Real Wages in Manufacturing 1880–1914* (Princeton, 1961); to which may be added the annual reports of the Commissioner of Labor for the years around 1890, and the fifteen volumes of the Immigration Commission's Reports on immigrants in industries, *61 Congress 2 Session, Senate Doc. 633*, of which the detailed sections on specimen communities are the most interesting. Jeremiah W. Jenks and W. J. Lauck, *The Immigration Problem* (New York, 1926, 1st edn 1911) provides a semi-official summary of the Commission's evidence and conclusions, while Isaac A. Hourwich, *Immigration and Labor* (New York, 1922, 1st edn 1912) launches vigorous criticism of its methods and presuppositions. Life in cities may be viewed through Jacob Riis, *How the Other Half Lives* (New York, 1957, 1st edn, 1890); *Hull-House Maps and Papers* (New York, 1895); Robert W. DeForest and Lawrence Veiller, *The Tenement House Problem* (2 vols, New York, 1903); Thomas J. Jones, *The Sociology of a New York City Block* (New York, 1904); Robert C. Chapin, *The Standard of Living among Workingmen's Families in New York City* (New York, 1909); Harry M. Shulman, *Slums of New York* (New York, 1938). Industrial scenes are prominent among the great Lewis Hine photographic collection at George Eastman House, Rochester, N.Y.

Ethnic groups can be seen at rather closer quarters, living together but at different stages of development as American communities, in the histories of single cities and districts, and in certain monographs on immigrants' problems. Among the best are: Robert A. Woods, *The City Wilderness* (Boston, 1898) and Albert B. Wolfe, *The Lodging House Problem in Boston* (Boston, 1906) on Boston's South End; Robert A. Woods, *Americans in Process* (Boston, 1902), on the North and West Ends; Robert A. Woods and Albert J. Kennedy, *The Zone of Emergence* (ed. Sam B. Warner, Cambridge, Mass., 1969, abridged from a manuscript prepared 1905–14); Frederick A. Bushee, *Ethnic Factors in the Population of Boston* (New York, 1903); Constance M. Green, *Holyoke, Massachusetts: a Case History of the*

Industrial Revolution in America (New Haven, Conn., 1939) and *A History of Naugatuck, Connecticut* (New Haven, 1948); Rollin G. Osterweis, *Three Centuries of New Haven 1638–1938* (New Haven, 1953); Kate H. Claghorn, 'The Immigrant in New York City', *Industrial Commission Reports*, XV; Blake McKelvey, *Rochester* (4 vols, Cambridge, Mass., 1945–1961); Bessie L. Pierce, *A History of Chicago* (3 vols, New York, 1937–57), which unfortunately reaches no further than 1893; Walter B. Stevens, *St Louis: the Fourth City 1764–1909* (3 vols, St Louis, Mo., 1909); Bayrd Still, *Milwaukee: the History of a City* (Madison, Wis., 1948); Timothy L. Smith, 'New Approaches to the History of Immigration in Twentieth-Century America', *American Historical Review*, LXXI (1965–6), 1256–79, on the Lake Superior mining communities; the two volumes of the Immigration Commission's Reports on cities, *61 Congress 2 Session, Senate Doc. 338*; Robert E. Park, *The Immigrant Press and its Control* (New York, 1922); Robert E. Park and Herbert A. Miller, *Old World Traits Transplanted* (New York, 1921); Sophonisba P. Breckinridge, *New Homes for Old* (New York, 1921); John Daniels, *America via the Neighborhood* (New York, 1920); W. Lloyd Warner and Leo Srole, *Social Systems of American Ethnic Groups* (New Haven, Conn., 1945).

Further information on single ethnic groups may be found in a large number of modern monographs, while a few first-hand accounts also exist.

On the Jews, see: Oscar Handlin, *Adventure in Freedom: three hundred years of Jewish life in America* (New York, 1954); Hutchins Hapgood, *The Spirit of the Ghetto* (Cambridge, Mass., 1967, 1st edn 1902); Jesse E. Pope, *The Clothing Industry in New York City* (Columbia, Mo., 1905); Louis Levine, *The Women's Garment Workers* (New York, 1924); Philip Cowen, *Memories of an American Jew* (New York, 1932); Moses Rischin, *The Promised City: New York's Jews 1870–1914* (Cambridge, Mass., 1962); Allon Schoener, *Portal to America: the Lower East Side 1870–1925* (New York, 1967); Alfred Kazin, *A Walker in the City* (London, 1953); Samuel Chotzinoff, *A Lost Paradise* (London, 1956); Samuel N. Behrman, *The Worcester Account* (London, 1954); Louis Wirth, *The Ghetto* (Chicago, 1956, 1st edn 1928).

Much less has been written on Italians. The Works Progress Administration, Federal Writers' project, volume, *Italians of New York* (New York, 1938), is slight but interesting. William F. Whyte, *Street-Corner Society* (Chicago, 1955, 1st edn 1938) and Herbert Gans, *The Urban Villagers* (New York, 1962) are admirable studies of Italians in Boston by participating sociologists. Rudolph Vecoli, '*Contadini* in Chicago: a critique of *The Uprooted*', *Journal of American History*, LI (1964–5), 404–17, is based on a

Ph.D. dissertation, and the same writer's 'Prelates and Peasants: Italian Immigrants and the Catholic Church', *Journal of Social History*, II (1969), is a fascinating study of attitudes. Andrew Rolle, *The Immigrant Upraised* (Norman, Okla., 1968) deals with Italians west of the Mississippi.

On Greeks, much the most thorough study is Theodore Saloutos, *The Greeks in the United States* (Cambridge, Mass., 1964), though his *They Remember America: the story of the repatriated Greek-Americans* (Berkeley, Calif., 1956) is also interesting.

On the peoples of eastern Europe the most interesting study is still Emily G. Balch, *Our Slavic Fellow Citizens* (New York, 1910), the second half of which deals with the American communities. Also useful are: Francis J. Swehla, 'Bohemians in Central Kansas', *Kansas Historical Collections*, XIII (1913–14), 469–512; Robert I. Kutak, *The Story of a Bohemian-American Village* (Louisville, Ky., 1933); Alex Gottfried, *Boss Cermak of Chicago* (Seattle, Wash., 1962); Stoyan Christowe, *This Is My Country* (London, 1939); Joseph A. Wytrwal, *America: Polish Heritage: a social history of the Poles in America* (Detroit, 1961) and *Poles in American History and Tradition* (Detroit, 1969), the first being more valuable; William I. Thomas and Florian Znaniecki, *The Polish Peasant in Europe and America* (2 vols, New York, 1958, 1st edn 1918–20); Arthur E. Wood, *Hamtranck Then and Now* (New York, 1955); Jerome Davis, *The Russian Immigrant* (New York, 1922).

Centred particularly on assimilation problems are the following: Milton M. Gordon, *Assimilation in American Life* (New York, 1964); Elin L. Anderson, *We Americans: a study of cleavage in an American city* (Cambridge, Mass., 1937); Emil de S. Brunner, *Immigrant Farmers and their Children* (New York, 1929); Frank V. Thompson, *Schooling of the Immigrant* (New York, 1920); Edward G. Hartmann, *The Movement to Americanize the Immigrant* (New York, 1948); John P. Gavit, *Americans by Choice* (New York, 1922); Will Herberg, *Protestant, Catholic, Jew* (Garden City, N.Y., 1956); Julius Drachsler, *Intermarriage in New York City* (New York, 1921); Bessie B. Wessel, *An Ethnic Survey of Woonsocket, Rhode Island* (Chicago, 1931); Milton L. Barron, *People Who Intermarry: intermarriage in a New England industrial Community* (Syracuse, N.Y., 1946), a study of Derby, Conn., but also a summary of many other people's work elsewhere; Ruby J. R. Kennedy, 'Premarital Residential Propinquity and Ethnic Endogamy', *American Journal of Sociology*, XLVIII (1942–3), 580–4, 'Single or Triple Melting Pot? Intermarriage Trends in New Haven 1870–1940', *ibid.*, XLIX (1943–4), 331–9, and 'Single or Triple Melting Pot? Intermarriage in New Haven 1870–1950', *ibid.*, LVIII (1952–3), 56–9; Lowry Nelson, 'Intermarriage among Nationality Groups in a Rural Area of Minnesota', *ibid.*, XLVIII (1942–3), 585–92; Thomas N. Brown, *Irish-American Nationalism* (Philadelphia, 1966); William D'Arcy, *The Fenian Movement in the United States* (Washington, D.C., 1947); Henry J. Browne, *The Catholic Church and the Knights of Labor* (Washington, D.C., 1949); John J. Meng, 'Cahenslyism: the First Stage 1883–1891', *Catholic Historical Review*, XXXI (1945–6) and 'Cahenslyism: the Second Chapter 1891–1910', *ibid.*, XXXII (1946–7); William V. Shannon, *The American Irish* (New York, 1963); Harold Zink, *City Bosses in the United States* (Durham, N.C., 1930); Edward M. Levine, *The Irish and Irish Politicians* (Notre Dame, Ind., 1966); Nathan Glazer and Daniel P. Moynihan, *Beyond the Melting Pot: the Negroes, Puerto Ricans, Jews, Italians, and Irish in New York City* (Cambridge, Mass., 1964, 1st edn 1964); W. Lloyd Warner *et al*, *Democracy in Jonesville* (New York, 1949); Irvin L. Child, *Italian or American? The Second Generation in Conflict* (New Haven, Conn., 1943); Christine A. Galitzi, *A Study of Assimilation among Roumanians in the United States* (New York, 1929); Mary Antin, *The Promised Land* (New York, 1914); Marshall Sklare, ed., *The Jews: Social Patterns of an American Ethnic Group* (New York, 1958), mixed in quality, but at its best, as in Herbert Gans' account of Park Forest, outstanding; Albert I. Gordon, *Jews in Suburbia* (Boston, 1959); Judith R. Kramer and Seymour Leventman, *Children of the Gilded Ghetto: conflict resolutions of three generations of American Jews* (New Haven, Conn., 1961); Sidney Goldstein and Calvin Goldscheider, *Jewish Americans: three generations in a Jewish community* (Englewood Cliffs, N.J., 1968); Lawrence H. Fuchs, *The Political Behaviour of American Jews* (Glencoe, Ill., 1956).

Chapter 11

The central book on anti-immigrant prejudice and campaigns to restrict immigration is John Higham, *Strangers in the Land* (New Brunswick, N.J., 1955). Few general readers will feel the need to go further, but Higham has an interesting article, stressing tensions connected with rivalries over social status, 'Another Look at Nativism', *Catholic Historical Review*, XLIV (1958–9), 147–58. Supplementing it in various directions, however, are several other studies: Ray A. Billington, *The Protestant Crusade* (New York, 1938), on agitations of the second quarter of the nineteenth century; Barbara Solomon, *Ancestors and Immigrants: a changing New England tradition* (Cambridge, Mass., 1956), on the upper-class racialism of the 1890s and after; Roy L. Garis, *Immigration Restriction* (New York, 1927), particularly on the background of the Quota laws; Morrell Heald, 'Business Attitudes towards European Immigration 1880–1900', *Journal of Economic History*, XIII (1953), 291–304; Edward N. Saveth, *American Historians and European Immigrants 1875–1925* (New York, 1948); Robert A. Divine, *American Immigration Policy 1924–1952* (New Haven, Conn., 1957), a clear discussion of the background of laws; Marion T. Bennett, *American Immigration Policies: a History* (Washington, D.C., 1963), encyclopoedic on legislation, but interesting also for its quotations from, or summaries of, reports of congressional committees.

A few of the most interesting books attacking immigration are the following: Samuel F. B. Morse, *Imminent Dangers to the Free Institutions of the United States through Foreign Immigration* (New York, 1969, 1st edn 1835); Samuel C. Busey, *Immigration: its evils and consequences* (New York, 1969, 1st edn 1856); Prescott F. Hall, *Immigration, and its Effects upon the United States* (New York, 1906); John R. Commons, *Races and Immigrants in America* (New York, 1930, 1st edn 1907); Edward A. Ross, *The Old World and the New* (London, 1914); Madison Grant, *The Passing of the Great Race* (New York, 1918, 1st edn 1916); Henry P. Fairchild, *The Melting-Pot Mistake* (Boston, 1926). Other documents may be found in Edith Abbott, *Historical Aspects of the Immigration Problem* (Chicago, 1926). Political pronouncements can be seen in Kirk H. Porter and Donald B. Johnson, *National Party Platforms 1840–1960* (Urbana, Ill., 1961). Congressional debates can be followed in the *Congressional Record,* though only the 1896–7 literacy-test bill debates have been analysed in my chapter.

Books that still need to be written, and in English

1. The Steamboat Age in Europe.
2. The Construction and Operation of Railways in Central and Eastern Europe.
3. European Agriculture in the Nineteenth Century, with a clear picture of village life in central and eastern regions, as well as of land tenure and farming techniques.
4. Migration from the European Countryside to Cities, both close-up monographs and a general study.
5. British Emigration in the half-century before 1914, and Irish too.
6. German Emigration probably needs to be done again, with emphasis on people and places rather than on government policy.
7. Almost everything remains to be done on Brazilian and Argentine Immigration, and very much on Canadian and Australian, especially after the middle of the nineteenth century.

8. Much more is still needed on the growth of the Roman Catholic Church in America, and especially its organization and finance.

9. Studies are needed of Ethnic Newspapers, not so much the opinions in editorials as advertisements and small news items as providing a close-up view of the life of communities.

10. Very little, indeed, is known about community life and leadership among ethnic groups, despite a few valuable pioneer studies by Handlin, Nau, Niehaus and others. Germans in Middle Western cities, the urban Scandinavians, the Irish after the Civil War,[1] the French-Canadians of New England, *all* Slav groups, the mixed districts in mining and heavy industry – all urgently need study. Only rural Norwegians and the Jews have been at all adequately treated; and I sometimes feel that the greatest service to the subject would be rendered if Jewish scholars would cease from studying their own people and turn their brilliant talents to *any* other group.

[1] I myself hope to spend several years in studying the Irish community of Greater Boston in the half-century following the Civil War; but there is room for several scholars in this field.

Index

Index

22